THE THEATRE ROYAL
BRISTOL

THE THEATRE ROYAL
BRISTOL

1766-1966

Two Centuries of Stage History

KATHLEEN BARKER

1974
The Society for Theatre Research
London

First published 1974
by The Society for Theatre Research
© Kathleen Barker 1974

ISBN 0 85430 022 8

Designed and printed at
The Compton Press,
Compton Chamberlayne, Salisbury,
Wiltshire

IN MEMORIAM
WILFRID LEIGHTON
Chairman of the Trustees of the Theatre Royal
1942-1965

Foreword

There have been many theatres with a distinguished history in the provincial towns of England, and during the second half of the eighteenth century a small number of them were granted the honour of a Royal Patent and permission officially to entitle themselves Theatres Royal. Among this select group, the Theatre Royal at Bristol is the only building to survive as a working theatre, and indeed its recent history has been no less distinguished than its earlier one. This gives its story a particular interest, and The Society for Theatre Research is proud to have been granted the opportunity of publishing Kathleen Barker's account, which is the result of long and detailed study.

The Theatres Royal at Manchester and Norwich have already been treated in works published by the Society. We hope that this further volume will contribute still more to the understanding and appreciation of the rich heritage of the English provincial theatre.

The Society would like to express its gratitude to Professor Arthur Sprague, to the Trustees of the Theatre Royal, and to the University of Bristol for assistance towards the publication of this book.

GEORGE SPEAIGHT
General Editor of Publications,
The Society for Theatre Research.

Contents

Acknowledgements xi

Prologue 1

Notes 15

PART I. THE GENTLEMEN FROM LONDON

Chapter One 1766-1769 19

Chapter Two 1770-1773 26

Chapter Three 1774-1778 32

Notes 41

PART II. THE HEYDAY OF THE STOCK COMPANY

Chapter One 1778-1791 45

Chapter Two 1791-1801 57

Chapter Three 1801-1817 67

Notes 79

PART III. THE SUPREMACY OF THE STAR

Chapter One 1817-1819 85

Chapter Two 1819-1829 89

Chapter Three 1829-1834 102

Chapter Four 1834-1845 109

Chapter Five   1845-1853   121

Notes   128

PART IV. INDIAN SUMMER

Chapter One   1853-1862   135

Chapter Two   1862-1867   149

Notes   157

PART V. STRUGGLE FOR SURVIVAL

Chapter One   1867-1881   163

Chapter Two   1881-1894   168

Chapter Three   1894-1909   176

Chapter Four   1910-1924   184

Chapter Five   1924-1943   196

Notes   205

PART VI. RENAISSANCE

Chapter One   1943-1954   213

Chapter Two   1954-1966   221

Notes   227

Bibliography   231

Appendix   235

Index   268

List of Subscribers   275

Acknowledgements

The collection of material for this book has employed much of my free time since 1948, when Mr. Joseph Macleod drew my attention to the collection of M'Cready Promptbooks then kept at the City Art Gallery in Bristol. When, or even whether, the task would have been completed, is doubtful, had I not been fortunate enough to be awarded a Leverhulme Fellowship in 1968-9, the taking up of which was much facilitated by the generous co-operation of the University of London Institute of Education; I was also greatly helped by grants from the *Bristol Evening Post* and the Society of Merchant Venturers.

In twenty-five years I have owed so much to so many people, that it is impossible to mention all; among those to whom I am most deeply indebted for encouragement and practical help over many years are, pre-eminently, my mother and late father; the late Mr. Wilfrid Leighton, Chairman of the Trustees of the Theatre Royal from 1942 to 1965; and Mr. John Coe of the *Bristol Evening Post*. To Mr. George Rowell of Bristol University Drama Department I have owed in turn the delight of being a junior collaborator in *Sixty Thousand Nights*, support and advice as a temporary post-graduate student under his guidance, and invaluable assistance in reading and commenting on the draft of this book. Among the many fellow-members of the Society for Theatre Research who have helped me I should like specially to mention Dr. Arnold Hare, Miss Monica Murray, Mr. Jack Reading, Miss Sybil Rosenfeld, Mr. George Speaight and Professor Arthur Sprague.

I am also particularly indebted to Miss E. Ralph, former Bristol City Archivist, and to Mr. Geoffrey Langley of Bristol Reference Library; and to Mrs. Anne Merriman for typing the first draft of the manuscript.

I gratefully acknowledge permission to reproduce copyright matter from

Bristol Old Vic Trust Ltd. (*Sixty Thousand Nights*)

Bristol Playgoers' Club (Minutes; *Bristol Playgoer*)

British Theatre Museum (Letters of Tom Taylor)

Mrs. Joan Farjeon (Extract from the late Herbert Farjeon's Prologue for the 1943 re-opening)

Harvard Theatre Collection (William Powell's letter of 6.9.1766 and W. C. Macready's letter of 17.11.1820)

Estate of C. V. Hassall deceased (Prologue for the first night of the Bristol Old Vic)

Henry Huntington Library (Three letters written by Dora Jordan)

Executors of the late Wilfrid Leighton (*The Preservation of the Theatre Royal, Bristol*)

Martin Secker & Warburg (Extract from John Fernald's *Sense of Direction*)

Office of the Lord Chamberlain (Correspondence)

* * *

The process of selection among a truly embarrassing wealth of fascinating material has been not only difficult but sometimes painful. The problem has been especially acute in respect of the most recent period, and it may well be felt that scant justice has been done to the artistic achievements of the Bristol Old Vic, and particularly to the great number of leading contemporary actors whom they have nurtured. However, many of these have received detailed attention in published biographies, or in Williamson and Landstone's *The Bristol Old Vic: the First Ten Years*. Taking the long view, and given the necessity of selection imposed by limitations of space, it seemed better to concentrate on the evolution of policy in repertory and organisation, which do more than is often recognised to shape those performances which make the immediate popular impact.

Prologue

MR. POWELL desires to assure the Public, that he entertains a most grateful Sense of their repeated Favours to him . . . 'Tis with great concern he thinks of the ill Accommodation they had at Jacob's-Wells, but hopes to see a Satisfaction accrue to them in future, by the Elegance of a new Theatre in King-street.

Sarah Farley's Bristol Journal, 24.8.1765

Prologue

No social institution, least of all a theatre, can be treated as an independent static phenomenon, parthenogenetically created. Like the human beings who shape its destiny, it is the product both of its heredity and of its environment; it is influenced by changes in aesthetic taste, in education, in economics, in politics : in short, by every contemporary social movement. So with the Theatre Royal, Bristol.

The history of post-Restoration dramatic activity in the provinces has been only fragmentarily charted. Several licences to raise companies to tour outside London were granted by King Charles II, e.g. to John Rhodes (the Duchess of Portsmouth's Servants) in January 1663-4; to George Jolly in January 1667-8; and to Edward Bedford (the Duke of Monmouth's Company) in November 1669. Sybil Rosenfeld has extracted from the Norwich records mention of a steady stream of visiting companies during the fifty years following the Restoration;[1] it would be strange if Bristol, then rising to be a major city and within easy reach of fashionable Bath, went playless.

However, no records have yet been discovered of dramatic activity (other than Fair booths) before a visit by John Power's Company (the Duke of Grafton's Servants) in 1704. By this time theatricals were being reborn on a national scale – but so was Puritan opposition. It is not surprising that in a city which had on balance been Roundhead in sympathies in the Civil War, which had been a nursery of Quakerism and was to be that of Methodism, Power met with intermittent attack over the three seasons during which he acted in Bristol – each year on a different site. For his 1706 season he built, or at least materially adapted, his own theatre in the very heart of the city, only to find himself once more threatened with "presentation" to the magistrates.[2]

Of dramatic activity during the following twenty years there is virtually no remaining trace, but visits must have continued. Charles Macklin is said by his biographer Kirkman to have started his acting career in and around Bristol about this period;[3] in 1726 a strolling company headed by Charles Williams, a supporting actor at Drury Lane, played a summer season at "the Bristol Theatre on St. Augustine's Back," and another such company, with Thomas Lewis at its head, was there two years later, unfortunately falling foul of the Bristol magistrates again.

Lewis's performances however were overshadowed by the enormous success of the Bath Company, who brought their production of *The Beggar's Opera* (directed by Gay himself) to the Long Room at Hotwells and "their Great Booth in Bridewell-Lane." They were joined in mid-July by John Hippisley,[4] the original Peachum, who was himself a Somerset man from Wookey, twenty miles away across the Mendip Hills. Peachum had provided him with his first great opportunity on the London stage, and his first major success. Summer theatres where metropolitan actors could find provincial employment during the London closure were beginning to spring up; it is not illogical that, with Bath pre-empted and with Lewis's fate in mind, Hippisley should hit on the idea of investing his first savings in building a theatre which would serve Bristol and the increasingly popular summer spa of the Hotwells from just outside the boundaries of the Bristol magistrates' jurisdiction.

Hippisley's theatre, known as the Jacob's Wells Theatre, which opened on 23 July 1729, was built on the west side of Woodwell (now Jacob's Wells) Road; its position is shown clearly on a map of Clifton made for the Merchant Venturers in 1746.[5] Chatterton's slighting reference, written after the Jacob's Wells Theatre had been closed some years,

And PLEASURE had a *hut* at Jacob's Well

and the gossipy reminiscences of the early local theatre historian, Richard Jenkins, have helped to build up a popular picture of a primitive affair, not much better than a strollers' barn, which is quite unjust. It was one of the earliest purpose-built theatres in the provinces; its prices (from 3s. to 1s. in 1743) were little below London levels; and its company, repertoire and production resources were drawn likewise from the London patent theatres. By its success it established a theatrical pattern for Bristol : a summer season of plays, given by established London and Bath actors, for the benefit of Society visiting the Hot Wells and Clifton, for those citizens of Bristol who believed in culture as well as *"Virtute et Industria,"* and those Bath devotees whose theatre closed in the summer but whose addiction to plays would bring them over the country roads (Bristol actors advertised their benefit performances in the Bath papers also, an expense in which they would certainly not have indulged had they not expected a return).

4

Jacob's Wells does not seem to have been affected by the passing of the 1737 Licensing Act, which outlawed all theatrical performances held without "Authority by Letters Patent from His Majesty . . . or without Licence from the Lord Chamberlain". In the first place, it was technically in the County of Gloucestershire, whose county town was 35 miles away; it would be an enthusiastic informer indeed who would travel that distance. In the second place, it is now becoming recognised that, so far as respectable established provincial companies were concerned, this notorious Act had derisorily little effect, though for a few years it checked the expansion of new theatres.

Hippisley's theatre was successful from the beginning; after his death his widow seems to have sold the lease of the theatre to a consortium in return for an annuity, but till she herself died she retained a connection with it, acting as Box-Book Keeper, while her daughter Jane (Mrs. Green, a popular Drury Lane comedienne) was a regular member of the summer company. Charles Macklin followed his historic appearance as Shylock by a summer season in Bristol in 1741; Henry Woodward, renowned Harlequin and Mercutio to Garrick's Romeo, and Mrs. Hannah Pritchard, the finest Lady Macbeth of the period, were also members of the company for some years. Bristol came to be regarded as one of the plums among summer engagements.

The city partook to the full of the upsurge of national prosperity in the mid-eighteenth century; new public buildings were undertaken, port facilities increased, new housing schemes extended her effective boundaries. And, although culture still took a very poor second place to trade, the tremendous expansion all over England of the provincial theatre and its growing respectability could hardly leave so important a centre untouched. Civic pride was involved; a theatre built in 1729 at a distance from the main residential area was no longer worthy of the second city in the kingdom; moreover, as Bath had shown since the erection of the Orchard Street theatre in 1750, a new theatre was a viable business investment.

John Latimer in his *Annals of Bristol in the Eighteenth Century* states, without quoting his evidence, that the movement for the erection of a new Bristol Theatre started early in 1764. It was undoubtedly given impetus by the events of that summer's season, chief among them the addition to the company, probably as one of its managers, of the newest star of the London theatres, William Powell. Powell was a Hereford boy who came to work in London in the office of Sir Robert Ladbroke, but devoted most of his energies to amateur theatricals in "spouting clubs." Impressed by his talent, however immature, Garrick coached Powell to take over the leading roles at Drury Lane while he himself went on a tour of the Continent with his wife. Powell made his debut, as Philaster in Beaumont and Fletcher's tragedy of that name (adapted by George Colman), on 8 October 1763, and was greeted with wild enthusiasm and displays of emotion.

Bristol responded as enthusiastically as London. If we are to believe Richard Jenkins, "Powell was the chief subject of conversation at our coffee-houses, taverns, and tea-tables, and anyone who had not seen and applauded his performances, must (like Lady Teazle) never have pretended to any taste again."[6]

Immediately after the close of the summer season the new plans were leaked to the press, the *Bath Chronicle* of 13 September 1764 reporting: "We hear a new Theatre is intended to be erected in Baldwin-street, and that the Leases are now preparing." Four days later, forty citizens "Mutually Agreed to Erect and Build a Theatre or Playhouse in the City of Bristol on a piece of Ground lying behind a Messuage or Tenement known by the Name or Sign of the Bull's Head situate in Baldwin Street and extending to the Back part of the Cooper's Hall in King Street."

Among these forty were City Councillors, leading merchants, two future M.P.'s (George Daubeny and Henry Cruger), and, rather startlingly, at least three Quakers, Joseph Harford and William and Richard Champion. Richard Champion is thought to have been the author of a gloomy letter on "The Consequences of a New Theatre" published in *Felix Farley's Bristol Journal* of 8 December 1764, and a later lengthy rhymed diatribe, *Bristol Theatre*. Clearly the left hand had decided to remain in obstinate ignorance of what the right hand was doing. Business, after all, was business.

The Proprietors set up an Executive Committee of five; John Vaughan, Alexander Edgar, Roger Watts, William Jones and Thomas Symons. The last-named, an attorney, played a prominent part in all the initial negotiations. This Committee of Proprietors, as it became known, was empowered to complete the legal agreements for the site, to enter into contracts for the building of the theatre, and "to let the intended Theatre or Playhouse to William Powell John Arthur John Palmer and Nathaniel [*sic*] Clark".

It is a significant list. Arthur, although he had also been concerned with the Jacob's Wells theatre for some years, was one of the Managers of the Bath Theatre, another indication of the enduring nature of the theatrical link between the two cities. Palmer and Matthew (not Nathaniel) Clarke had been steady, dependable actors of the second rank at Drury Lane and Covent Garden respectively for many years, and had acted at Jacob's Wells since 1754. But it is the name of the 29-year-old William Powell which heads the list, and Powell who was regarded as the leader and the man with whom to negotiate.

The Proprietors agreed to pay £10 on the execution of the Proposal and the remainder of their £50 share as required. Were more than £2,000 needed "and the said Subscribers and Proprietors shall be unwilling to advance any future Sum for that purpose that [*sic*] then a still further Number of Subscribers over and above those for the Forty Shares before mentioned shall and may be admitted" – a provision whose wisdom was justified by events. In return they hoped for an annual rent equivalent to 5 per cent of expenditure over and above the cost of rates and taxes, and each subscriber was to be allotted a "silver ticket" which admitted him to the Theatre "every Night the said Lessees or any other Person or Persons shall Exhibit any Play or other Entertainment in the said intended Theatre to any part or place therein (the Stage only Excepted)." These tickets however were transferrable, and so often became separated from the shares, leading to considerable confusion and argument in years to come.

The first recorded meeting of the Committee of Proprietors was on 25 October 1764 and was concerned with the conveying of the site of the theatre and adjacent properties needed for the creation of entrances to the building. The owners of the site were the family of one Richard Parker; his daughter Bethia had a two-thirds interest and her widowed sister-in-law Ann Parker a life interest in the remaining third. This was to pass after her death to her late husband's children by an earlier marriage, Mrs. Ann Crump and Joseph Parker, a Portsmouth shipwright. Mrs. Crump's husband Edward seems to have played a not inconsiderable part in the proceedings : in consideration of the "great Trouble and Expense" to which he had put himself to persuade the various parties to make over the land for a yearly rent of £22, he and his wife were granted Admission Tickets similar to those of the Proprietors. Additionally, Crump was chosen as carpenter for the new theatre.

From the plan attached to the Conveyance [Plate 2], it will be appreciated how hemmed in by properties was the space needed for the stage and auditorium of the new theatre. But, then as now, vacant lots in central and highly fashionable city areas were hard to come by, and no doubt the location of the site in the very heart of Bristol, within minutes of Queen Square where some of its most moneyed families had their residences, was felt to compensate for any disadvantages.[7] The houses between the vacant site and King Street were purchased and audience entrances constructed through them; the Winston drawing of c. 1804 [see Plate 1] shows the resultant frontage. Two tenements at the foot of the Rackhay backing on the site were also bought up. One of these, with a ground area cited as 23 feet 6 inches by 13 feet, was demolished to provide a side passage to the theatre (apparently for goods only; the stage door for more than a century was in King Street), and a fresh building erected, abutting on the second tenement, which probably provided the original green-room and offices of the Theatre.

Thomas Paty, a prominent Bristol builder-architect, was selected to supervise the erection and fitting up of the building. For the actual design of the theatre, however, the Committee looked farther afield. Their representatives, after settling the matter of the lease with Joseph Parker at Portsmouth (with the help of a two-guinea tip to his attorney), went on to London, settled the contracts with the intended managers and

surveyed and have taken the Measurements of both the playhouses [presumably Covent Garden and Drury Lane] in London, and have also engaged a draft of Drury-lane hº and consulting a very ingenious Carpenter Mr. Saunderson the carpenter of the hº they have collected such Prints as they flatter themselves will be a means of saving some hundreds in Building yᵉ intended hoº in Bristol.[8]

Saunderson was indeed a "very ingenious Carpenter" and one with a considerable practical interest in theatre architecture. At the time of the Proprietors' visit, he had been engaged by James Love to design and build the theatre at Richmond, Surrey, upon which Garrick commented approvingly : "You cannot have a better Man for yr Business than Saunderson clear-brain'd to ye skull of him."[9]

Saunderson's ingenuity was soon called upon. As a result of what was tactfully described as "a Mistake . . . in the Calculation" the foundations were dug for a building "8 Feet larger in the Clear, than the Theatre Royal in Drury-Lane".[10] Hastily the Proprietors sent off to Saunderson, and at their meeting on 3 December

were produced an Elevation Ground Plan and Section of a Theatre Drawn by Mr. Saunders [sic] Carpenter of Drury Lane Play House. Resolved to Execute the Playhouse agreeable to the Above mentioned Plan as nearly as the circumstances of the Ground will admitt.

Meanwhile on 30 November the foundation stone had been laid, the accounts duly recording a payment to the workmen of £1 7s., but not without comment. *Felix Farley's Bristol Journal* for 1 December 1764 recorded :

Yesterday Afternoon was laid the Foundation Stone of the new intended Theatre in King-street, which will be opened the Beginning of next Summer, with a Play for the Benefit of the BRISTOL INFIRMARY.

What a melancholy Prospect must it afford to every considerate Mind, to observe with what Facility Buildings of this Kind are erected, and at the same Time the Difficulty with which those set apart for religious Services are carried on.

8

The final jibe was often repeated, and with some truth. St. Nicholas Church, begun before the Theatre, was finished considerably later. There was, however, a severe shortage of carpenters and joiners in the city as a result of the general expansion earlier alluded to, and it may be suspected that the merchants were in a better position to bid for scarce labour than the church.

Despite the proprietors' hopes, the summer of 1765 found the King Street theatre still unfinished, very possibly because of site difficulties. The area was little better than marshland, and the 1970 demolitions revealed that to combat this a "raft" of rushes was laid down as foundation for the building.

Whatever the reason, the company had to return to Jacob's Wells for a further season. Powell concluded his Card of Thanks sent to the press after his Benefit :

'Tis with great concern he thinks of the ill Accommodation they [the audience] had at Jacob's Wells, but hopes to see a Satisfaction accrue to them in future, by the Elegance of a new Theatre in King-street. – Where he will always think it an incumbent Duty on him to assist, so far as in his Power, to their Theatrical Entertainments.

Disregarding the sniping of the Puritanical opposition, the Proprietors pressed forward with the building of the new theatre, and on 10 April 1766 David Garrick himself, paying a short visit to Bath, was prevailed upon to visit the nearly-completed building, "with which," according to *Felix Farley's Bristol Journal*, "he was very much pleased". (Tradition later rephrased this as a pronouncement that the theatre was "the most complete in Europe of its dimensions.") Garrick also provided John Arthur, the joint manager and low comedian of the company, with a first-night Epilogue; in sending it, he appended various instructions on its delivery :

Mr. Garrick's compliments to Mr. Arthur – he desires him not to give a Copy of it upon any account – that is ye first condition – the next is that he takes pains to give the full Effect of it in ye speaking – Mr. G. has vary'd ye Matter on purpose – Mr. A. must mimic the *Prude** drawing up herself and speaking affectedly – and he must pronounce ye french *Madame* not like our *Madam* – but broad

---

* The lines referred to run :
> Hold, cries a Prude, (thus rising from her stays)
> "I hate a Playhouse, and their wicked Plays!
> "O 'tis a Shame to suffer such an Evil!
> "For seeing Plays is dealing with the Devil !"
> I beg your Pardon, Madam, 'tis not true;
> We Play'rs are moral Folk – I'll prove it too

9

& long *Mawdawme* – The Epilogue will have a good Effect if Mr. Arthur will think it worth his trouble – remember no Copy.[11]

Independently, Powell successfully petitioned Garrick for a Prologue on the same occasion.[12]

Because no bills were paid until after the theatre was opened, it is not possible to chart precisely the course of the building operations; what is clear is that it was very soon necessary to take up the option provided in the articles of agreement to increase the number of subscribers. The addition of ten further shareholders was not regularised till 30 May 1766, but as early as November 1764 the accounts show payment of £50 shares by fifty subscribers, and a further £30 by 47 of the fifty. (These entries were in fact slightly erroneous, for it was discovered many years later that Samuel Sedgeley had not even paid on the original call; and, yet more surprisingly, Thomas Symons, the attorney who did so much of the preliminary work for the Committee of Proprietors, consistently repudiated in later years any claim to a share.)

The craftsmen responsible for building the theatre are itemised in the Minutes and Accounts, the operation as a whole being superintended by Thomas Paty. Michael Edkins is said to have been responsible for the original painting and decoration of the house, but unfortunately the pages dealing with these years are missing from his Account Book.

It is less easy to allocate responsibility for the design. Obviously the original intention was closely to copy Drury Lane; but the Minute of 3 December 1764 alluding to the designs sent by Saunderson does not say specifically that they related to that theatre. Comparison is extremely difficult because of uncertainty about the appearance of Drury Lane in the early 1760s. Most authorities have referred back to the 1674 Drawing of a Theatre attributed to Wren, and Richard Southern points out that the proportions of the theatre shown in the Wren drawing and those of the Bristol theatre are very similar, though it is quite possible that the likenesses are generic rather than due to deliberate copying.[13] On the other hand, the main features of the Richmond (Surrey) Theatre which Saunderson designed for Love, as revealed in drawings made just before its demolition in 1884 [see Plate 3], so closely resemble what we know about the original appearance of the King Street house that I am convinced we should attribute to Saunderson the design of the Theatre Royal, Bristol. That he should base his plans on the theatre he knew best is hardly surprising; but, though Drury Lane of 1764 may have been the Bristol theatre's cousin, Richmond Theatre of 1765 was surely its blood brother.

The Bristol Theatre was built within a rectangular shape, the greenroom, &c., forming an added projection on the Rackhay side (P.S.) of the stage. At basement level, at the very back there were two dressing rooms, later used as the Band Room and the Oil Room; below the stage, the standard traps and other machinery (not those surviving in the 1960s, however, which were Victorian). Beyond lay the flat, benched pit, reached by playgoers through underground pit passages debouching into the courtyards behind the King Street houses. (One passage was stopped up in Victorian times, and destroyed in ignorance of its identity by the contractors constructing additional emergency exits in 1949.)

In each back corner of the stage were two more dressing rooms, one above the other, each pair surmounted by a penthouse which, in the early 19th Century at least, was used for the wardrobe. These sets of rooms were separated by an almost square recess reaching to the back wall of the theatre, which was used to give additional depth to scenic effects [see Plate 5.] The raked stage itself stretched to the Pit side of the Stage Boxes. Scenery was constructed and painted in the attic space above the ceiling of the auditorium, manhandled into the fly-gallery P.S. and so to the stage, where it was shifted, as was customary, by the groove system – one set of upper grooves is still preserved.[14]

In 1766, as we know from newspapers and memoirs, the auditorium possessed only two Circles. At stage level the Dress Boxes numbered nine; over the doors which led from the foyer were inscribed the names of leading dramatists – from O.P. to P.S., Cibber, Otway, Congreve, Fletcher, Shakespeare, Jonson, Vanbrugh, Rowe and Steele. Most of the partitions have now been removed but the reeded pillars still mark the divisions, to the annoyance of a 20th Century audience. There has been considerable argument about whether these pillars are original, or whether, as Summerson believed,[15] the heavier ornamented square columns of the stage boxes were once typical of the whole [see Plate 6]. Bryan Little has, however, brought evidence that reeded pillars do occur as early as 1766,[16] and the drawings of the Richmond (Surrey) and other Georgian theatres are also in their favour.

In the upper tier, the central portion was occupied by the theatre's Gallery, and only at the sides were boxes constructed. The booking plan [see Plate 4] shows two groups of three flanking a central space, and a further detached box at the extremity of each side; these were named after Garrick, Wycherley, Addison, Farquhar, Dryden, Lee, Shadwell and Colman. If we follow the lay-out on the plan literally, the Gallery would have covered only the central Dress Box, an intrinsically improbable and quite uncharacteristically narrow area for a theatre gallery of the period. It is much more likely that the spacing shown is attributable to the restrictions imposed by the size and shape of the booking-sheet, and that the Gallery, as at Richmond, extended over the three central Dress Boxes. Each set of three would then extend down the side of the theatre, and the remaining boxes would be accounted for by assuming a box over the proscenium door on each side of the stage, as was certainly the case at Jacob's Wells. The proscenium area has been so much altered that it is impossible to make any accurate reconstruction of its original appearance.

Since the present Gallery did not then exist, the proscenium arch was probably, and the ceiling certainly, lower than now, and the ceiling was probably flat. The space above it not only provided scene-dock facilities but also contained the thunder-run, a sloping vee-shaped wooden trough, down which balls about the size of those used at bowls were allowed to run, the resulting vibration producing a fine rumble of thunder from over the very heads of the audience.

There is little contemporary evidence of the interior decoration, save that Richard Jenkins, who was old enough to remember it, says that "the front pannels of the boxes were painted in green and gold" and "the whole decorated with carving, painting, and gilding, executed with much taste." (One would have more faith in this if the wording were not almost identical with that of the various *Bristol Guides* about the end of the 18th Century, and of at least one of the ms. contributions to Winston's *Theatric Tourist*, dating presumably from about 1804.) Stripping off the plaster heads over the pillars flanking what was the central (Shakespeare) box, Richard Southern discovered part of the original classically designed frieze of triglyphs, which has now been gilded and restored. No such good fortune attended an attempt to discover the original design on the panelling, and indeed in view of the multiplicity of redecorations undergone by the theatre over two centuries this is hardly surprising. Jenkins tells us that the boxes were lined with flock paper, and that there were "crimson curtains over the balconies," which would accord with the traditional colour scheme for Georgian theatres.

The present plasterwork ornamenting the cornices of the pillars, and that on the fronts of the boxes, is certainly late Victorian, as is most of the ornament on the ceiling, which consists of independent panels of gilded plasterwork or carved wood mounted onto the ceiling itself. Mr. Gordon Priest, of the University of Bristol Department of Architecture, has pointed out that there are four strips of acanthus wreath decorations which match the decorations of the shafts of the stage box pilasters and the soffit of the proscenium arch, and which appear to be somewhat arbitrarily placed around the central ventilator rose. The design on these features is very different in character from the rest of the Victorian "fretwork" and the bold coarse gilded work of the ventilator; Mr. Priest thinks they certainly date from an earlier period and could possibly be original.

In most respects the Bristol theatre was typical of its period, but one important novelty was introduced into the design; the shaping of the five central boxes into a semi-circle. The traditional construction of the boxes followed three sides of a rectangle, though the Richmond Theatre shows a slight curve across the front boxes (as indeed Wren's 1674 drawing seems to do). But the precisely-measured semi-circle, the lines of the box partitions radiating from a central point, was, so far as is known, a new feature in an English playhouse (as distinct from opera house), and, with the slanting inwards of the frontage of the Stage Boxes, it helped to make the stage the real architectural as well as artistic focus of the theatre. The overall effect made a nation-wide impression : when alterations were made to the Bath Theatre in 1767 there were grumbles that the managers had failed to copy the features of Bristol, while a prospectus for a theatre in Margate in 1770 (not, however, the one finally built) advertised that it would be an exact model of the much admired new theatre in Bristol.

The capacity of the house can be fairly exactly calculated. The booking plan gives figures for each box which represent the number of places bookable in each row; these amount to 267 for the Dress Circle and 148 for the upper tier. In 1826 the capacity of the Pit, whose size had not altered in the meantime, was quoted as c. 320. The difficulty lies in estimating the seating capacity of the 18th Century Gallery; perhaps it would be fair to suggest a little more than half the 1826 figure of 530, which refers to a Gallery extending over a complete tier. If we accept a figure of around 300, this would give a total of something over 1,000.

The question of seat prices appears to have caused a slight disagreement between managers and proprietors. On the preliminary bill for the opening night, Friday 30 May 1766, the charges were announced as Boxes, 4s.; Pit, 2s. 6d.; Gallery, 1s.; and a note was added :

The Managers hope the Ladies and Gentlemen will not think the Prices fix'd for Admittance exorbitant, when they will please to consider their very great Expences; particularly the high Charge of Rent, that the House will be illuminated with Wax, That the Clothes, Scenes, and all Decorations are entirely new, and, That they will spare no Pain or Expence to make the Entertainments as Elegant and Pleasing as in the most Established Theatre.

However, on 29 May the Proprietors held a General Meeting, at which "It was the Unanimous Opinion that the Prices of Admission into the Boxes ought to be Three Shillings and Six pence." The lessees seem to have fought successfully for a compensatory increase in the Gallery prices, for a fresh playbill (also conveying a change in the afterpiece from

The King and the Miller of Mansfield to *The Citizen*), quoted prices as Boxes, 4s.; Pit, 2s. 6d.; Gallery, 1s. 6d.; adding :

At a meeting of the Proprietors of the Theatre yesterday, it was by them determined, That the Prices of Admittance in future should be for the Boxes 3s. 6d. the Pit 2s. 6d. and the Gallery 1s. 6d. – The Managers think it their duty to comply with their determination, and after this night the Prices will be fixed agreeable to the foregoing resolution.

This second bill has not survived, but fortunately it was transcribed in the second (1800) edition of Edwards' *New Bristol Guide*.

So open was all this activity – the conveyances, the building, the newspaper puffs and the advertisement of performances (bills were even distributed in Bath) – that it is easy to forget the whole affair was entirely illegal. In 1766 no provincial theatre held the necessary indemnifying Royal Patent, though two (Bath and Norwich) were to obtain it in 1768, proof if any were needed of the increasing social acceptance of the theatre. And while Puritan attacks on the morality of the playhouse were not wanting, there is rarely any accusation that it was actually contravening the law, nor apparently was there any organised attempt to bring the law into force by laying an information with the Magistrates. Undoubtedly the King Street company were safeguarded to a great extent by the influential positions held by the Proprietors; however, the managers did initially take the precaution of reviving an old device for circumventing the letter of the law, and advertising "a Concert of Musick" between the parts of which would be presented "Specimens of Rhetorick". This device had long since been proved in the London law-courts no more valid than the "Club Theatre" designation was as a 20th Century escape from the Lord Chamberlain's censorship, but in both cases it provided a front which might by gentleman's agreement be accepted as an excuse for no action.

The opening night of the New Theatre in King Street arrived. Ladies and gentlemen could send their servants at 5 p.m. to keep seats until at 6.30 William Powell appeared to speak Garrick's Prologue, and the curtain rose on Steele's sentimental comedy, *The Conscious Lovers*, followed by an entr'acte dance and the rattling farce of *The Citizen*. Fortunately for posterity, one of the audience thought to send to the press a copy of his letter to a London friend, describing the occasion, and his vivid evocation of the atmosphere on that first night makes a fitting opening to the theatre's two hundred years of stage history.

Last Night Curiosity and the Fashion, led me to see the Comedy of the Conscious Lovers, at the New Theatre in King-street; upon entering, it appeared rather gloomy and disagreeable, owing to not having proper Lights placed in the Passages leading to the Pit; however, with feeling my Way, I arrived at the Pit; after I was seated I was most agreeably surprized with the elegant and neat Construction of the House; but, when the whole was illuminated, there then appeared one of the finest Scenes Imagination can conceive; the rich Paintings, together with the Brilliancy of the Ladies, formed so complete a View, that Malice herself, had she been there, must (for that Night at least) have put on a Smile of Approbation.[17]

NOTES

[1] S. Rosenfeld: *Strolling Players and Drama in the Provinces* 1660-1765, Cambridge, 1939, pp. 35-47.

[2] See A. Bedford: *The Evil and Danger of Stage-Plays*, Bristol/London, 1706. G. T. Watts: *Theatrical Bristol*, Bristol, 1915, pp. 15-36, devotes considerable space to this period.

[3] J. T. Kirkman: *Memoirs of the Life of Charles Macklin*, London, 1799, I, pp. 57 ff.

[4] *Farley's Bristol News*, May-July 1728; *Gloucester Journal*, 18.6.1728.

[5] Reproduced in P. K. Stembridge: *Goldney, a House and a Family*, Bristol, 1969. Richard Jenkins' description of Jacob's Wells will be found in his *Memoirs of the Bristol Stage*, Bristol, 1826, pp. 8-9.

[6] Jenkins, *op. cit.*, p. 49.

[7] At the beginning of November 1764 the Proprietors had the offer of a slightly cheaper site in Limekiln Lane, which ran from the bottom of Park Street along the foot of Brandon Hill. However, the conveyance for the King Street site was then too far forward for the offer to be considered. See Minutes of Proprietors, 12.11.1764.

[8] Minutes, 6.11.1764.

[9] D. M. Little & G. M. Kahrl (eds.): *Letters of David Garrick*, London, 1965, No. 351.

[10] *Felix Farley's Bristol Journal*, 24.11.1764.

[11] Little & Kahrl, *op. cit.*, No. 404.

[12] Both Prologue and Epilogue were printed in local and national papers at the time, and have been reprinted in previous histories of the Bristol stage, e.g. Jenkins, *op. cit.*, pp. 78-80; Watts, *op. cit.*, pp. 73-5.

[13] See R. Southern: *The Georgian Playhouse*, London, 1948, pp. 37-40; E. Langhans: Wren's Restoration playhouses, *Theatre Notebook*, XVIII, 3, 91-100, and D. Mullin and B. Koenig: Christopher Wren's Theatre Royal, *Theatre Notebook*, XXI, 4, 180-7.

[14] For a full description of Georgian stage machinery and methods, see R. Southern: *Changeable Scenery, its Origin and Development in the English Theatre*, London, 1952.

[15] J. Summerson: The Theatre Royal, Bristol, *Architectural Review*, 94, 167-8 (December 1943).

[16] B. Little: *The Theatre Royal: the Beginning of a Bicentenary*, Bristol, 1964, pp. 8-9.

[17] *Sarah Farley's Bristol Journal*, 21.6.1766.

Part One

The Gentlemen from London

Resolved to Have the Lott of Players now agreed upon, and to Refuse several Others now objected to . . .
Theatre Proprietors' Committee Minutes, 6.11.1764

. . . the said Lease and every future Lease to be granted only to Persons that are Performers . . . in order to prevent the possibility of such Lease or Leases falling by Sale or otherwise into the hands of persons who are not possessed of Theatrical Talents for the Entertainment of the Town. . .
do., 6.9.1774

One

1766–1769

In many respects the King Street theatre in its early years merely continued, in roomier surroundings and with more lavish resources, the practices of Jacob's Wells. Performances were given on Mondays, Wednesdays and Fridays only, except during the period of St. James's Fair, when the influx of country visitors made it worth while to open the theatre every night. The season, of course, was still restricted to the period during which the London theatres were closed, i.e. from the beginning of June to mid-September, so that there were only between forty and fifty playing nights in all.

It is a considerable tribute to the drawing-power of the new theatre – and more particularly of William Powell – that at the end of the first season Powell could report to Garrick total receipts of £3,607 (a Puritan pamphlet put them at over £4,000). The first night alone, advertised for the Benefit of the Bristol Infirmary, produced a profit of sixty guineas which Powell duly presented to the Committee of that institution; they, ignoring a suggestion that such a donation should be treated as tainted money, "politely accepted" the sum.

In personnel, in repertoire, indeed in virtually all respects, an evening in King Street continued to represent the translation of the London theatre to the Bristol stage. Naturally enough the choice of main pieces was very considerably influenced by Powell's own predilections; as manager he was able to play in Bristol a much wider range of parts than the established casts in London allowed him to do, and it is significant that of 42 identifiable performances in the first season, Shakespeare provided 19 of the main pieces, and 15 of the remainder were drawn from Restoration and 18th Century tragedies. It is also noteworthy that the afterpieces were almost entirely derived from the stock farces of the day, varied with an occasional musical piece, but excluding pantomime.

19

There is no doubt that Powell "carried" the initial season, and generally speaking the response to his acting was so adulatory as almost to
justify the mock-S.O.S. put out for the lost Mrs. Prose, who "went off in
a Phrenzy Fever, and has been thought delirious ever since Mr. POWELL
first perform'd the part of LEAR."[1] Even for the age of sentimental comedy
and tragedy, the near-hysteria he engendered was exceptional; it became
an apparently boundless love affair between actor and spectator, to which
each gave himself too easily. Powell seemed to his audiences to identify
with his part; he surrendered to its passions unrestrainedly, and it is clear
from both London and Bristol notices that he lacked the technique which
might have enabled him to produce such effects without the immense
strain they imposed on him both emotionally and physically. Cape
Everard, a child-actor and dancer with the Company in 1766, describes
how Powell watched from the wings the incident in *King John* where
Prince Arthur is threatened with blinding, and was so moved by Everard's
acting as the young Prince that "he could not recover himself in the 5th
act, and never in future came near the stage all that scene."[2]

Although the Palmers, who had been among the principal actors at
Jacob's Wells, seem to have withdrawn their connection before the season
started, Powell had sound support from Matthew Clarke, and his new
leading lady, Mrs. Jane Barry (wife of Spranger Barry's brother), though
outshone in London by her sister-in-law Ann, became much admired in
Bristol. The anonymous playgoer who penned so sympathetic a description of the theatre on its first night said of her Indiana in *The Conscious
Lovers*:

It is no forced compliment to *Mrs. Barry* to say, that she appeared the very
Person Sir Richard Steel [*sic*] intended, exemplifying by her whole Behaviour
that her Soul felt all the Force of Strong Imagination.

The company also included Richard Winstone, a former Bristol merchant,
and Mrs. Jane Green, John Hippisley's daughter, both established local
favourites of long standing. James Dodd was engaged for the more
foppish comedy parts, while Arthur was principal low comedian.

Arthur, unfortunately, proved as unpopular and incompetent a manager in Bristol as, apparently, he was to do in Bath the following year.[3] By
the end of the first season Powell was writing to Garrick that

from repeated ill treatment Myself & Clark have had from Arthur, his very
great inattention to our Business in his Department and the very disgustful Light
He stood in with the Public oblig'd me to call the Proprietors together – they
have mutually agreed to Cancel all our Agreements – & they have permitted me
to take Holland [his great friend and Drury Lane colleague, Charles Holland,
who had originally introduced him to Garrick] with me into the management.[4]

Accordingly on 28 February 1767 a fresh agreement to lease was made out, but was not executed, possibly because the lessees jibbed at being asked to pay a rent of "ffive pounds for every One Hundred Pounds that the said Proprietors have expended and paid or shall expend and here-after pay" in purchasing the ground, building and decorating the theatre, completing the approaches, in legal expenses "& for all Charges & Expenses that have or shall be incident to the said Theatre" – that is, they were to bind themselves to pay five per cent on expenditure still largely undetermined and completely outside their control, as well as all rents, rates, taxes and insurance on the property. It was not until 28 August 1767 that a seven-year retrospective lease was signed, Powell, Holland and Clarke agreeing to pay £450 for the first two years' rent and £300 a year thereafter – though it was 1769 before the Account Books recorded payment of rent to the extent of £750. Meanwhile, of course, the bills were coming in for the erection of the theatre; early in 1767 the Proprietors paid out £1,358 10s. to Gilbert Davies, £613 4s. to Evans & Co. for timber and £930 to Samuel Foot, the mason. By April 1767 the balance in hand was only £16 5s. 1½d.

The acquisition of Charles Holland as manager undoubtedly strength-ened the company considerably, he and Powell often sharing a bill as Pierre and Jaffier in *Venice Preserv'd*, the Bastard Faulconbridge and King John, or Hamlet and the Ghost. Their performances drew forth a balanced and objective series of criticisms in *Felix Farley's Bristol Journal* during the 1767 season, the contributor being particularly struck by Holland's voice, "the most manly, and at the same Time the most har-monious . . . that ever pleased the public ear."* Neither were Clarke's sterling if less spectacular qualities overlooked :

His just Comportment demonstrates, that he is wholly taken up with the Part he personates; Of this Truth we have a clear Demonstration, in his playing *Bellamy* [in *The Suspicious Husband*], (tho' not a first Rate Character) as he seems to be the very Person intended.

Such restrained praise is leavened with occasional dry wit : "Mr. *Bates* in *Essex* said little, but stood like a Colossus."[5]

The comic parts were shared by Dodd and Robert Baddeley, of whose performance in *Love Makes a Man* it was said :

there was such a Fund of techy, testy, merry Humour in Don Lewis, that had

---

* There is a marked absence in the Bristol notices of the complaints of rant and exaggerated vocal effects often made against Holland in London. Doubtless a pro-vincial audience was less sensitive to such faults, but perhaps too Holland was able to relax more in the less competitive atmosphere of the Bristol season.

not Mr. *Baddeley* before distinguished himself in Comedy, he had proved sufficient in *that Character alone* to deserve the Name of a *great Actor*.[6]

Pantomime enlivened the repertoire in this season, which was however
still dominated by tragic main pieces (28 out of 36 known performances,
twelve being Shakespearian plays). The acquisition the following season
of the low comedian Ned Shuter, coupled with an illness which kept
Powell away from the theatre for part of July, brought a marked swing
towards comedy, *As You Like It* and *The Merry Wives* entering the King
Street repertory for the first time. Perhaps audiences had become conditioned to tragedy; perhaps they were put off by a rumour that the advertisement of a Benefit for Shuter was merely a managerial device to raise
the takings that night; in any event, if we are to believe John Bernard,
the "Bristol Hogs" (as the materialistic citizens were unkindly nicknamed
by visitors) responded but poorly, and

on his [Shuter's] benefit-night the receipts barely covered the charges. The next
day he took a handful of his neglected night's bills, and walking in the midst of
a principal street, strewed them about, crying "Chuck, chuck, chuck!" (the
term used in feeding their swine).[7]

Such newspaper reviews and biographical reminiscences give us a fairly
clear picture of the standard of performance at this time : in marked
contrast with later periods, they mention little or nothing about the
staging. This does not imply any poverty of provision : the managers
claimed to have supplied a complete new wardrobe and new scenery on
the opening of the theatre, and the playbills on various occasions advertised "The Characters dress'd in the Habits of the Times, with new
Scenes and Decorations." John French of Drury Lane was responsible for
the original stock of scenery, day to day renovations of which, as well as
the provision of properties and "decorations", were in the hands of
Michael Edkins, Bristol painter and singer, who had been responsible for
the internal decoration of the theatre. The entries in Edkins' account
book make it clear that a high standard of smartness in stage decor was
maintained.[8] One has nevertheless an overwhelming impression that while
Powell was manager, the appeal of the theatre was primarily that of
serious drama acted with intense emotional rapport between actor and
audience.

It would appear that the very marked success of the first season was
not entirely maintained. John Henderson, offered a share in the Bristol
management while he was leading man at Bath in 1772, heard that the
Bristol theatre "was rather a losing scheme to Powell and Holland," and
summed up :

The people of Bristol, I suppose, are like other people, capricious, inconstant.
The theatre was supported, it seems, by them for one season, but after that it
flagged even when *Powell* was there.[9]

Nevertheless, it was becoming unshakably established as part of the
city's life. It would have been too much to hope that Puritan opposition
would die down entirely, but the theatre's supporters were now ready
with their retorts, pointing out, for example, the moral influence of plays
like *The Conscious Lovers* and *George Barnwell*. That legally the theatre
had no right to be open did not prevent the Duke of York, on a visit to
the Hotwells, attending it on 27 June 1766 to see *The Clandestine
Marriage*, in which Powell played his original part of Lovewell; "and we
hear," reported next day's edition of *Felix Farley's Bristol Journal*, "his
Royal Highness expressed an high approbation of that Structure, and of
the Performance." The following year the Duke of Cumberland saw two
performances, of *The Clandestine Marriage* and *Hamlet*, on 5 and 7
August, though his comments are not on record.

If further proof were needed of the increasingly secure position of the
theatre, it could be found in the fact that after the first night of the 1768
season the face-saving advertisement of "A Concert of Musick" was
permanently discontinued. It is unlikely to be a coincidence that the
Bath Theatre obtained a legalising Patent at the end of January 1768.

By the opening of the 1769 season it seemed that the only real remaining worries would be financial. A final call on the subscribers had to be
made to meet the heavy bills still coming in : "To Cash Reced of Subscribers to make up the Sum of £5,000 – £1,090 – Less by Saml. Sedgley
not paid £50 – £1,040." In all, Bryan Little has calculated that at least
£4,831 9s. 8d. was spent directly on the theatre building.[10]

But the summer brought tragedy. Hardly had the season opened when
Powell was taken ill – according to Richard Jenkins, he overheated himself playing cricket and lying naked in damp grass to cool himself caught
a chill. Exhaustion after a gruelling London season, and the unrestrained
social indulgence which had so worried Garrick, took their toll; the chill
turned to pneumonia. Throughout June Powell lay desperately ill, frequently delirious, in his house next to the theatre; on Friday 30 June the
managers cancelled the performance to avoid the disturbing bustle and
noise in the street outside, and the invalid seemed to take a turn for the
better.

The events of the following Monday are unemotionally summarised in
two ms. notes written by John Harris, later of the Lord Chamberlain's
Office, on contemporary playbills :

Mr. Powell died on Monday the 3ᵈ of July 1769 at Seven O Clock in the

Evening just before the Play begun 'twas K Richard 3d, The Padlock that Evening.

Mr. Powell Died at 7 oclock on Monday July 3d 1769 the Padlock whas putt of on account Mr. Dodd being at London.

The occasion itself was anything but unemotional. The varying accounts all more or less confirm that given by the contemporary *St. James's Gazette* and later by Richard Jenkins, who say that the actors heard the news just as the curtain drew up, and tried to get through the play –

> But what an affecting instance was it of the true regard they bore for their lost brother, and what humanity of the spectators! – scarce an actor appeared, without streaming eyes, and a broken voice. The fictitious lamentations, in the second act, for the loss of *King Edward,* were converted into real anguish for their *own* loss, and aggravated their sensations so much, that the Manager (Mr. HOLLAND) was compelled to apologise for their incapacity to acquit themselves as usual.

Even had Dodd not gone to London, it is doubtful whether actors or audience could have contemplated a farcical entertainment to follow.

The funeral service was held in Bristol Cathedral in an almost equally emotional atmosphere;[11] the monument to Powell, erected by his widow and renovated later by his daughter Ann, still forms an impressive feature in the north wall of the Cathedral [see Plate 7].

A Benefit for Powell's family on 14 July was an overflow, and shortly afterwards it was announced that Mrs. Powell had sold the management share she had inherited to Thomas King of Drury Lane, who was addicted to dabbling in provincial theatricals, and was already known to Bristolians as a ripe character comedian from seasons at Jacob's Wells.

Perhaps it was ominous that the most publicised feature in the remainder of the season was not the new tragedy of *Zingis* but an exhibition dance, an Allemande, given by the ballet-master Aldridge and the beautiful actress and former dancer, Mrs. Mary Bulkley, mistress of James Dodd. Mrs. Bulkley, trading on the letter of her engagement as an actress only, made difficulties about the number of repetitions demanded; Aldridge took umbrage on his own account; and there was a public rumpus of a type hitherto carefully avoided, though all was finally smoothed over. At the same time Dodd's affair with Mrs. Bulkley was also attracting publicity, local sympathy being very much with the wronged Mrs. Dodd.

Nor was this the only dispute which marked the end of the season. A group of Proprietors, led by the prominent sugar-merchant and future M.P. George Daubeny, exasperated at receiving no detailed accounts – still less any dividends – called a special General Meeting. At this Edgar was deposed from the post of Treasurer, Daubeny being elected in his place, and his fellow-Committee Men were Roger Watts, William Jones and John Vaughan of the old Committee, with Jeremy Baker. All but Vaughan had been members of the rebel group.[12]

Hardly was the new Committee of Proprietors installed than they heard of the death from smallpox of Charles Holland on 7 December 1769. Within six months the two outstanding managers and most attractive actors of the company had gone. It was not an encouraging prospect.

Two

1770-1773

NATURE receiv'd a wound when Powell dy'd;
Which bled afresh o'er Holland's hapless tomb:
Such a repeated stroke affected all,
Delighted with the Muse's fav'rite haunt;
Who heat receiv'd from Shakespeare's tragic fire:
The brightest eyes their hapless loss deplor'd,
And the big sigh burst from each manly breast. —
Now dry your tears, ye fair! – ye generous sigh no more:
Reddish and *King* behold! – see! – hand in hand
Walk the same path – with the same laurel crown –
By the same Muses crown'd![13]

This decidedly blank verse heralded the new managers of the King Street theatre when they opened the 1770 season on 11 June in association with Matthew Clarke. Certain changes became almost immediately noticeable, one being the increase in the comic strength of the company, which, headed by King, also included Lee Lewes, John Moody and the elder Bannister. (James Dodd tactfully absented himself for two years.)

This change of emphasis of course was reflected in the composition of the programme. In the 46-nights' season Shakespeare was still fairly well represented by eleven performances, including, for the first time at King Street, *Measure for Measure*; but while there was still a fair amount of ranting tragedy for Reddish, Clarke and Thomas Hull, comedy accounted for nineteen nights against tragedy's sixteen. The following year, thanks principally to the popularity of *The West Indian*, Shakespeare's share shrank to eight out of 48 evenings, while comedy claimed 24.

The second most noticeable new feature was the vigorous exploitation of editorial advertisement in most of the forms prescribed by the eminent Mr. Puff. Particular attempt was made in 1770 to build up Samuel Reddish, who must have bought Holland's share after his death. Much was made of his being a Westcountry lad (he was born and educated at Frome in Somerset). His "wife", probably Polly Hart, was kept in the background.

Most of the resources of puffing, however, were devoted to the repertoire. For the first time, the afterpieces attract as much attention as the main pieces, if not more. A spice of scandal is neatly insinuated : Foote's *The Author* "was on Account of some Strokes of personal Satire, withdrawn for some Seasons"; *The Minor* "originally contain'd an Imitation of a very popular Preacher, which we hear has been the Reason of its never being perform'd here, the Managers of our Theatre being cautious of giving Offence."

At times the puffs, even for the period, savour of the ludicrous : to ornament the burletta introduced into *A Peep Behind the Curtain* Bristolians were promised :

The Music by Mr. Barthelemon; the Sheep and other necessary Decorations made by Mr. Johnston, mechanist of the Theatre Royal, in Drury-lane, and procured at a very considerable expense.[14]

Again,

We have Authority to assure the Public, that the much admired Scene of Harlequin's jumping through a Tub on a Man's Head, in the Entertainment of *Mother Shipton* . . . [is] now preparing to be introduced in the Entertainment of *Harlequin's Invasion*.[15]

Puff Reddish as they would, he was no Powell; nor was his more dignified successor, Richard Bensley. Something other than the magic of a star would have to draw in the crowds, and the choice fell upon mechanical sheep, and Harlequin jumping through a tub on a man's head. However, at least the rent was promptly paid, and the proprietors voted themselves their first dividend, of six pounds per share, on 27 September 1770.

King continued his share in the management in 1771, though the start to the season was personally inauspicious. On their way to Bristol the post-chaise in which he and his wife were travelling overturned near Marlborough; King himself escaped with bruises, but his wife, a principal danseuse and Columbine, broke her left arm.[16] Mrs. Barry had left the company, and Elizabeth Younge shared the leading parts with Mrs. Bulkley. An unremarkable and largely unremarked season concluded on a sad note, with the serious illness of Lee Lewes at the beginning of September. The lamentable tale was told in an advertisement in *Felix Farley's Bristol Journal* on 12 October :

Mr. LEWIS [*sic*], of Covent-Garden Theatre, hath long languished upon a Bed of Sickness (surrounded by a Family of little ones!) whose Endeavours to please, to the utmost of his Abilities, the Public are well acquainted with. A MUSICAL ENTERTAINMENT is therefore proposed for his Benefit, in order to enable him to satisfy certain Demands, which are the natural Consequence of so long and painful an Illness, before his Return to London.

Thomas Linley of Bath, father of the famous musical family, was prominent in making arrangements for the entertainment, which was so successful as to spark off a demand for a series of twelve subscription concerts in Bristol – also organised, of course, by Linley, who never missed a financial opportunity.

King gave up his share at the end of the 1771 season, having, according to Henderson, lost over £80 on his investment. His place was taken by James Dodd, who rapidly became the dominant partner. But Bristolians had long memories for scandal and Dodd was subjected to perpetual sniping, especially for his somewhat cavalier attitude towards published programmes and castings. Theatricus in the *Bristol Gazette* of 23 July 1772 further complained that the main pieces too often consisted of "insipid Comedy" and the farces "those worn-out pieces of *Midas, Mayor of Garrat, Guardian*, &c."

The Bath papers were just as free in stirring up personal scandal. The *Bath Chronicle* of 20 August reported that "A celebrated actress at Bristol has been detected in bed with the sing-song insignificant Mr. D—." A hot denial of this paragraph as "intirely malicious, false, and groundless" was followed by a letter from a Friend to Injured Merit in the next week's *Chronicle*, which vigorously defended the lady's irreproachable conduct and purity of character, "the truth of which incontestably appears from the remarkably numerous, and very genteel appearance of company at the lady's late benefit". The dating of actresses' Benefits makes it clear that the lady, as might be surmised, was Mrs. Bulkley,[17] but it is rather more probable that the unlikely sight of James Dodd, expert in fops and coxcombs, playing the doomed gambler Beverley in *The Gamester*, rather than the lady's already shop-soiled reputation, drew the crowds. (Dodd followed up this managerial indulgence by playing Mark Antony in *Julius Caesar* for his own benefit.)

The season closed on 17 September, and Henderson heard that "each partner lost between one and two hundred pounds". Invited in November to buy a share (probably Bensley's) in the management for £400, "the most that ever was given for any share", Henderson deemed it prudent on all counts to decline. By this time, he pointed out, "the whole property belonging to the partners, of clothes, scenes, etc., is supposed to be worth under a thousand pounds, and there are only two years to come of the lease".[18]

In addition there was more trouble among the company. Only two days after the season closed, *Felix Farley's Bristol Journal* bore a long and indignant letter from Mrs. Elizabeth Hartley, who had taken Miss Younge's place this season, defending herself against accusations that she had refused to study new parts. On only one occasion, she claimed, had she so refused, and then with good reason; but *"From that Day, viz. the 9th of July to the End of the Season, he* [Dodd] *never offer'd her a single Part* (excepting that of one of the Women in the *Beggar's Opera* by way of Insult)". This she attributed to a deliberate attempt by Dodd to keep her back "lest *she* should be *mistaken* for the *principal* Actress" (i.e. Mrs. Bulkley). Mrs. Hartley was not strictly accurate in her facts; for example, she had played Indiana in *The Conscious Lovers* on 17 July, Louisa Dudley in *The West Indian* on 27 July and Euphrasia in *The Grecian Daughter* on 3 August, and in all of these Mrs. Bulkley played a secondary role or was not cast at all. Moreover, a member of "THE PUBLIC" wrote to retort that Dodd "might very safely have ventured her playing *every* Night in the Season without the least Danger of her having been ever taken – or (as she herself expresses it) *mistaken* for the *principal* Actress."[19]

The excitement of such scandals was eclipsed by the outcome of an apparently innocent advertisement in *Felix Farley* on 14 November 1772 :

We hear that a Subscription Book will be opened on Monday next for the Concert in the Coopers-Hall, during the present Winter Season: – And that such Ladies and Gentlemen who shall chuse to become Subscribers, may by applying at the Proprietors Office, at Miss Lambe's in King-street, be informed upon what Terms the Tickets will be issued.

"Miss Lambe's in King Street" housed, however, not musicians, but two actors, Kennedy and Booth, who managed a sizeable and reputable company, and who designed to provide Bristolians with entertainment in the winter months under the tactful description of a Concert of Music with "divers Specimens of ELOCUTION". They fitted up the Coopers' Hall, next door to the Theatre, charging 3s., 2s. and 1s. for seats, and commissioned Michael Edkins to paint the interior stone colour and provide "6 Cloths with Pannells and Festoones". An Eskimo Chief and his lady, who were among their regular visitors, eventually bespoke *Macbeth* and *The National Lovers* (an unauthorised version of Macklin's *Love à la Mode*) for Kennedy's Benefit.

The presence of these theatrical interlopers caused alarm not only to the puritanical element, but to the Proprietors of the King Street Theatre, who were only too conscious of dangerous rivalry which could hardly be crushed without exposing their own vulnerability to the law. Accordingly at a General Meeting on 29 December 1772 it was "Agreed unanimously that Application be forthwith made to Parliament for a Patent or Licence under the direction of the Committee." Dodd was seen in Bristol, and apparently made no bones about his intention "to raise the storm, and to horsewhip (as he termed it in derision) the present Company out of town". Kennedy had a good deal of public encouragement and indeed was urged to solicit a Patent on his own account.[20]

However, an information was laid against the Coopers' Hall company, and on 20 January 1773 the Magistrates "levied a Fine of 50 l. each on four of the Performers, for acting some Part or Parts of Plays".[21] A fine of £200 was penal by contemporary standards – yet the Company continued acting as before, advertising freely in the local press and playing without further interruption till the end of their season on 3 April, after which they went on to Richmond. It is impossible not to suspect that the fine was paid by local sympathisers.

The action of the Theatre Proprietors in seeking a Patent soon became known, and counterpetitions to the Bishop of Bristol and the two local M.P.s, Lord Clare and Matthew Brickdale, were rapidly organised by Edward Garlick. They met, however, with but a tepid reception. The Bishop evaded any action whatever in masterly fashion :

> The Petition to the House of Lords is this moment given to my Hands; and I am sorry that my Health will not permit me to present it for you and the other Gentlemen. I have not been once at the House of Lords these two last Sessions: and at this Season of the Year, in the cold North and East Winds, I am under a Necessity of Keeping Close at Home, or my tender Lungs might be inflamed, and my Life endangered. The Citizens of Bristol have always my best Wishes, and I should be glad if it was in my Power to contribute more to their Welfare and Happiness. Would you commission any one to call for the Petition, it shall be delivered to him, by Sir, your faithful humble Servant
>
> THOMAS, BRISTOL.[22]

From the two M.P.s they had little more satisfaction except expressions of sadness that Bristolians should be at variance with each other – and a sharp reminder from Lord Clare that they had let the theatre continue without protest for six years already.

The bill "for licensing a playhouse within the city of Bristol" was introduced at the beginning of March, but no more was heard of it, and when the summer season of 1773 was due the Proprietors had spent £57 18s. 6d. and still owned an unlicensed theatre. Moreover, the *Bristol Gazette* had it "from very good authority, that our summer's company of comedians, who are shortly expected here, will meet with an unfavour-

able reception; as there are some persons determined to oppose their acting, or subject them to the penalty of the law".[23]

The 1773 Company was still led by Dodd, with Clarke as his passive
partner, and, in place of Bensley, William Parsons (a broad comedian
from Drury Lane) and the musician George Bulkley, complaisant husband
of Dodd's inamorata, who had jointly purchased Bensley's share. Miss
Younge displaced Mrs. Hartley. One familiar figure was missing, however : Mrs. Jane Green. To the local press she sent a copy of her letter to
Dodd, which plainly revealed her bitterness :

I am sorry to declare to you that your *Ill-treatment* of me *last* Summer, has
obliged me to decline going *this*. You did not keep your *Word,* which was greatly
to my *Disadvantage,* and at the same Time made my whole Summer disagreeable by your rude Behaviour. It is with the utmost Regret I quit my native
Place, which is so dear to me : Nor did I think Mr. Dodd would have had it in
his Power or Inclination to tell Mrs. Green that she should never belong to
the Company *if he could help it.*[24]

Dodd's attempts at self-exculpation were unimpressive, as were the protestations in his opening prologue of innocence in the matter of the
attempt to suppress Kennedy and Booth's company :

> Could I to Informations give Consent?
> To stop your Pleasure have the least Intent?
> No – 'tis a Forgery, a base Design,
> Contriv'd our wish'd Success to undermine.[24]

Nor was this the end of complaints : some visitors applying to see the
theatre one Saturday were met by a porter who told them he had Dodd's
instructions to turn them out. By the end of that summer Dodd had
endured (or provoked) enough of the trials of management : he sold his
share to Samuel Reddish. He may have had some belated satisfaction,
just before doing so, in hearing that a second attempted season by
Kennedy and Booth had petered out in apparent disaster.[25]

Three

1774-1778

> The Lovers of Theatrical Entertainments have great
> Reason to expect the ensuing Summer, much more Regu-
> larity at the Theatre, and the Plays infinitely better acted
> than they have been, since the Direction of *Messrs. Powell*
> and *Holland*. The sole Management of the Theatre is vested
> in the Hands of Mr. Reddish, a principal Actor of Drury-
> Lane Theatre . . .[26]

Samuel Reddish, so carefully puffed, thus assumed the manager's role for
the second time, but on this occasion he was the dominant partner and
continued so until violent disputes within the company led to his abrupt
withdrawal in August 1777.

It has to be granted to him that he brought to his task not only skill as
a puff-master, but ability as an actor and energy as an organiser. One of
his first actions was to invite ladies and gentlemen not regularly receiving
advance bills of the play to leave their addresses at the Theatre. He took
particular pains to bring forward the latest London productions, frequently, as he stressed, with the original performers in principal roles, and
was willing to postpone a production "to give due Time to the Performers
to be digested in their Characters, and the proper dresses to be prepared".
He provided a fresh wardrobe for the tragedy of *Zara*, but took equal
trouble over the staging of a pantomime, *Love's Magic*,

> in which will be introduced several new Scenes, and Pieces of Machinery
> collected at great Expence – particularly a *Boat* will sail down the *Stage*, which
> will be converted into a Sea.[27]

The producer of this most popular piece, played ten times in thirty nights,
was Signor Giuseppe Grimaldi, father of the immortal Clown Joseph
Grimaldi.

In view of all these efforts, it seems hardly justice that, returning from a country walk one Saturday evening in July, Reddish was "stopt in the New Road, leading to Durdham Down, by three Fellows, and robbed of nine Guineas." Nor was he free of other troubles. Having given out that he had obtained special permission from Hannah More to bring out her latest tragedy, *The Inflexible Captive*, he had to defer the production, first because of alleged illness among the company and then, according to persistent rumour, because of the intransigence of Elizabeth Younge, who insisted she should have the first night for her Benefit. Though Miss Younge was sharing the leading parts with Reddish's current mistress, Mrs. Mary Ann Canning, it was "an unprecedented thing in a performer to claim a new piece, which the Managers proposed for their own emolument."[28]

For whatever reason, *The Inflexible Captive* was not played that season, Miss Younge contenting herself at her Benefit with the second night of Dow's *Sethona*. Reddish himself had a splendid Benefit – almost too successful, for some who could not get seats pushed in behind the scenes, and Reddish had to publish an apology for "so great an Interruption to the Representation of the Play with consistent Propriety".[29]

The current lease of the theatre expiring that summer, the Proprietors approached the problem with caution. They decided to grant the new lease for three years only; in order to avoid the possibility, which the frequent changes of manager must have suggested to them, that the lease might fall "by Sale or otherwise into the hands of persons who are not possessed of Theatrical Talents for the Entertainment of the Town", it was agreed to insert a clause providing that the lease should be forfeit if any such sale took place without the Proprietors' consent. In this form the lease was made out to Clarke and Reddish at a rent of £250 per year for the summer seasons. The lessees were to "lay out and expend in painting, Papering and other Improvements to the part of the Theatre before the Curtain . . . a Sum not less than One Hundred and fifty pounds."[30]

Michael Edkins was engaged to undertake this redecoration, though it is exceedingly doubtful whether anything like £150 was ever expended. On 10 June Edkins charged the managers £12 12s. for "Painting the Theatre Pea Green two Coats in Oil Silvering, Lacqering [sic] and Painting in Dead White all the Ornamental work", and an extra guinea for "Painting twice in Oil all the Ballustrades Cornish &c. over the Boxes which was by agreement to have been done once in Water Colour". Seven and sixpence accounted for "Paint^g green and Gilding the Mouldings of the Stage Door which was before done Mahogany Colour without Gilding". In addition, even before the season started Edkins was working with French, priming flats and set pieces for Dryden's *King Arthur*, which was planned to be the *pièce de résistance* of the season.

Reddish had also taken some care about selecting his company. He persuaded the Bath favourite, John Henderson, who had already rejected several overtures from London, to share the leads with him (Reddish was beginning to fancy himself in romantic rather than tragic parts). It was during this season, according to Ireland, that "from the accidental indisposition of a performer, he [Henderson] on the seventeenth of August played Falstaff",[31] a character which, after Shylock, became Henderson's most famous impersonation. There is, however, some inaccuracy here, for 17 August 1775 was a Thursday, not then a playing day at Bristol. Henderson did play Falstaff (in *The Merry Wives*) for his Benefit on Monday, 11 September, but this could hardly have been the result of another actor's illness. There is no record of how Henderson was received in this or any other part in Bristol, though at the beginning of the season a critic described his general style with modified rapture :

This prince of country performers, though avowedly inferior to the deceased tragedian [Powell], in expressing the finer sensations of humanity, is very happy in the expression of other passions, and though a little awkward in his manner, and disagreeable in his voice, may be considered as a very valuable acquisition to the Bristol theatre.[32]

In addition to Henderson, Reddish still had the faithful Clarke; he added Garrick's pupil and protégé, Samuel Cautherley, and for comedy he had Parsons and John Quick. Quick had played small parts in Bristol in 1768 and 1769, but since then had made his name in characters such as Tony Lumpkin and Bob Acres, and he became a tremendous favourite in Bristol.

Besides *King Arthur*, frankly a spectacular with "Variety of new Scenes, Decorations, Dresses and Machinery", there was in prospect Sheridan's *Rivals* (which met with great success, according to Mary Linley), a new pantomime, and, belatedly, *The Inflexible Captive*. All these considerations led Clarke and Reddish to raise the Box price from 3s. 6d. to 4s. – "A Measure long since adopted at a neighbouring City [Bath] of much less Consequence upon a similar Occasion". To offset this they offered a Subscription Ticket for the first twenty-four nights (i.e. up to the start of the Benefits) for two guineas – less than half price, even at the old rates.

Such an action was bound to arouse criticism, and Theatricus set about Reddish roundly. He agreed that some of the arguments for raising the Box price were valid, including the "expensive engagements . . . [of] good performers" "as, in your choice of pieces, the Hero not the Heroine, seems to be the object". But, he complained, the actors were still forced to provide new dresses for themselves or spoil the effect of a play by inappropriate costume, while many of the scenes advertised as painted by French did him little credit.[34]

The inferred weakness of the company's female acting strength was certainly demonstrable. Elizabeth Younge, the best of the group, left at the end of June, possibly in pique at the preference given to Mrs. Canning. Reddish was also accused of keeping back Mrs. Lamon, who took a similar range of parts, and it was a preference which caused a major crisis the following season. Nor were jealousies restricted to the women in the company, for Reddish himself fell out with John Quick – according to the latter, out of annoyance at "the *extraordinary* favours Mr. Quick was honoured with" during the season. Whatever the cause, when Reddish heard a rumour that Clarke had sold part of his share to Quick he wrote to Clarke :

> Mr. Reddish never intending to play where Mr. Quick is concerned, requests to know if the report is *true*; as Mr. Reddish shall drop all thoughts of playing any more at Bristol, when Mr. Clarke confirms the intelligence which Mr. Reddish has so unexpectedly received.[35]

Despite this difference, both actors returned for the 1776 season, the unhappiest to date. For over a year Reddish had shown signs of mental instability – "mad as a March hare" was the Drury Lane prompter's blunt description of him. It was probably because of this that the 1776 Company included fewer London actors than ever before, the numbers being made up by some of the more prominent members of the Bath Company : Francis Blissett, a character comedian of ability; Abraham Didier (fops and coxcombs) and his wife Margaret (light comedy); and Samuel Rowbotham, a sound "walking gentleman". Clarke and Cautherley, as well as Quick, returned; and John and Hester Jackson joined the company, Mrs. Jackson as principal tragic actress with a cast overlapping that of Mrs. Canning, who now emerged under the title of Mrs. Reddish. (Even the straitlaced Hannah More commented to Garrick that this was the second or third wife Reddish had produced at Bristol.[36]) And here lay the root of the trouble, for in his amorous obsession Reddish cast his "wife" for parts she was incapable of adequately sustaining.

The couple joined the company a week after the season began, playing Richard III and Queen Elizabeth, to be met with a rowdy demonstration at Mrs. Reddish's first appearance. Reddish had had prior warning, and had tried to pack the house, but, whatever the extent of the uproar and whoever its principal object, it was sufficient to ensure that Mrs. Reddish, billed for Belvidera in *Venice Preserv'd*, played no more; she was officially, perhaps genuinely, "indisposed". An otherwise sympathetic bystander warned Reddish that where we find private affection operating against public satisfaction, and connubial love against the desire of pleasing, we cannot but lament the misfortune of a person who, blinded by tenderness, can suffer the dictates of judgment to be superceded by the calls of ambition . . . I would remind Mr. Reddish that an *Heroine* is full as necessary on the stage as a *Hero*.[37]

This attitude was widely held, even among those who appreciated the acting abilities of Reddish himself.

Despite numerous well-puffed novelties, the houses were but moderate. This may have been partly due to there not being a sufficiently large potential audience to justify the increase of playing nights this season from three to four – Monday, Wednesday, Thursday and Friday; it was probably also influenced by the general malaise about the outcome of the war in America which had not only affected commerce but, less definably though quite as effectively, public morale. Reddish attempted to boost receipts (at least, that was his ostensible motive) by announcing himself as Romeo, a part promised to Samuel Cautherley. Cautherley stood on the letter of his agreement; Reddish was forced to yield; and the house amounted to twelve guineas, though this was at least partly due to the last-minute alteration of the night to Saturday, when the theatre was not normally open.

It was Cautherley and Mrs. Jackson whom Mrs. Reddish suspected of having instigated the hissing which greeted her first appearance, and it was over Cautherley's Benefit that the storm broke. He had selected *King John* and Reddish had promised to play the title role. The part of Constance was in Mrs. Reddish's cast, but she had not played since her unlucky debut; Cautherley said brutally that he

thought it would have been an Indignity offer'd to the Public to intrude Mrs. Reddish upon them in so principal a Character, so soon after she had been expelled from the Stage on her first appearance by the united Voice of the Audience.[38]

Instead he asked Hester Jackson to play Constance, and when Wrighten, who had the next Benefit, also ignored Mrs. Reddish's claims to the heroine's part (this time in *Alfred the Great*) and offered it likewise to Mrs. Jackson, Redding was immediately sure of a conspiracy, and refused to play for Cautherley.

Feeling was undoubtedly exacerbated by a very funny and quite scandalous newspaper feature in the form of a mock-quarrel between "R——h" and "Mrs. C——g", depicting Reddish as coarse-tongued, greedy, insanely jealous and caring only for his twelve pounds a week; a boaster whose puffs were composed by a vulgar innkeeper. He and his consort were depicted as united only in cursing their colleagues Quick and Clarke, whom "Mrs. C——g" described as

the one a *Pygmy Paymaster*, whose punctual honesty we long have scorn'd – and joyous MATT, with bird and bottle at the *Bush*, quaffing nectareous wine! 'while all around, like *Falstaff*'s crew, drink health and happiness to him alone! – Ev'n *they*, regardfull of the *chandeliers* [which might be broken by missiles], oppose my matchless acting on the stage![39]

The Bristol press carried long and acrimonious correspondence between Cautherley, Reddish and, finally, Mrs. Reddish; three days after the date of the lady's apologia, another communication was sent for publication :

MESSRS. CLARKE and QUICK, beg Leave to Inform the Public, Frequenters of the Theatre, that in Consequence of Mr. REDDISH's withdrawing himself from the Management and his Duty as an Actor; they are under the Necessity of altering the Plan of Business intended to have been pursued; and assure them they will exert their utmost Endeavours to render the remaining Performances as worthy of their Approbation as their Situation will now permit; and hope by *their* Indulgence to extricate themselves from the Difficulties they are under by the Absence of their Colleague.[40]

The season limped to its end, closing with the play which had started the whole unhappy affair : *King Richard III*. This time Quick "attempted" the title part; Jenkins, who saw it, says that "he began *seriously*; but, finding his audience inclined to mirth, he gave them a complete burlesque, and met with general laughter and applause." One cannot help wondering whether the burlesque was not of the ex-manager who never intended to play where Mr. Quick was concerned.[41]

For the summer of 1777 Clarke seems to have shared the management with Quick and, once more, Bensley. The company reverted to being a London one, with the Jacksons and Cautherley, as well as John Moody, the Hopkins family from Drury Lane (including Priscilla Hopkins, the future wife of John Philip Kemble), and Kennedy – that same Kennedy whose venture at the Coopers' Hall had had such unplanned consequences. In this season the managers seem to have made a genuine effort to introduce more serious plays, most notably several Shakespeare histories (*King Henry IV Part I, King Henry V* and *King Henry VIII*) and Richard Savage's tragedy of *Sir Thomas Overbury*, said to have been planned while Savage was in gaol in Bristol – a local link well publicised in the press, and the subject of a somewhat apologetic Prologue.

One visitor to Bristol early in the season was John Bernard, a stage-struck youth seeking an engagement with Bensley. He was duly accorded an audition, for which, he recorded,

I was shown into the manager's room, lumbered with books, banners, helmets, playbills, and pictures, and in a few minutes more Bensley stalked in, with all the solemn ponderosity for which, in Wolsey, he had so often drawn down the Olympian thunders of Covent Garden.[42]

Bernard started to render "To be or not to be," but unfortunately dried up; Bensley, unimpressed, recommended an immediate return home, but offered the lad a free seat to see that night's play. Seven years later, Bernard was playing on the Bristol stage himself.

Bensley earned a good deal of polite approval for his tragic acting, in parts as varied as Hamlet and Evander, the old father in *The Grecian Daughter*. However, when 61-year-old lawyer and statesman Samuel Curwen, "an American Refugee in England", visited the Bristol theatre it was the comic actors whose ability struck him most. In *The West Indian* "Major O'Flaherty [was] well taken off by Mr. Moody, the best imitation of an Irishman I ever saw."[43]

Altogether, though there is a good deal more puffing than genuine critical comment, one has the impression of a reasonably successful season – the last, of course, before the three-year lease expired. What went on behind the scenes during the winter is unrecorded : the Proprietors left no minutes of meetings which must certainly have taken place, for they had resolved on another attempt at a Patent before offering any further lease. In February 1778 a bill was introduced into Parliament and, with surprisingly little fuss, the act for licensing a play-house in Bristol went through both houses, the grant (made out to George Daubeny) passing the great seal on 27 April. The Letters Patent dated from 10 April and were to be valid for twenty-one years from that date.[44] At a cost of £275 3s., the Bristol Theatre was now the Theatre Royal.

It was generally believed, and with some likelihood, that the Proprietors had had the discreet assistance of John Palmer of the Bath Theatre Royal, who already had considerable political contacts. Nor was this entirely a disinterested action; Palmer undoubtedly had his eye on the possibility of running the Bath and Bristol theatres in circuit, which would enable him more fully to utilise his resources. Neither city would support more than three performances a week, save in exceptional circumstances, and social pressures were causing the Bath season to begin later and later, so cutting down further the theatrically profitable part of the year.[45] Moreover, the growth of theatre circuits in the West was steadily diminishing the opportunities of touring hitherto enjoyed by the Bath Company.

Curiously, two Bristol papers mention a Bath news paragraph "purporting an opposition to the Bristol patent now being made by the managers of [the Bath] theatre", though they mention it only to stigmatise it as "an infamous falsehood". A rather different rumour reached the London *Morning Post* of 21 April from its Bristol correspondent :

Notwithstanding the solemn promise of the proprietors of our theatre to Mr. Palmer, the Bath manager, who was principally instrumental in procuring them the late Royal patent, they have, in defiance of all decency, signed an agreement with Messrs. Quick and Moody, for the said property, at 400 l. per ann.

Quick and Moody were indeed granted a lease on 17 April, against general expectation. It is possible that in any case Palmer would have been reluctant to open his campaign in May or June when many of his best actors would already have accepted summer engagements elsewhere; likely, too, that Quick and Moody had their own plans well advanced and that the Proprietors felt under some obligation to them also.

Whatever the motives, the London company returned, and started with a gesture bound to bring them popularity – they lowered the Gallery price from 1s. 6d. to 1s., though abolishing the Half Price there (it had previously been possible to enter late and see the last two acts of the main piece and all the "entertainments" for 1s.). The managers also whetted their audience's appetites by an advance puff of a new actress, Charlotte Walpole :

She is a good Singer, an excellent Actress, and it is a matter of dispute with the young Londoners in which characters she appears to most advantage, *male* or *female*.[46]

She was quite as popular in Bristol, though Hilario was shocked to see an audience of "matrons and their children" when she played Sir Harry Wildair in *The Constant Couple* for her Benefit :

and when he expected an effusion of blushes, he observed nothing but laughing, winking, and an indecorum of behaviour that disgusted men of delicacy.[47]

Such performances represented a deliberate appeal to the more popular element rather than to the Box audience, and, though quite a number of pseudo-historical tragedies were brought forward, they were more praised than supported. The reasons undoubtedly were as much economic as aesthetic : even in Bath there were complaints of "the want of money, particularly amongst the nobility and gentry".[48] Perhaps a falling-off in quality, as well as in quantity, among the Box occupants may have led to the complaint inserted in *Felix Farley's Bristol Journal* of 29 August 1778:

SEVERAL Ladies who frequent the Theatre, beg leave to remark, that any Gentleman who wears his Hat in the Boxes, or talks louder than the performers, gives no proof of his good sense or good breeding, and they hope that all those who have any politeness will in future desist from such improper behaviour.

The retort came the following week :

SEVERAL Gentlemen, who frequent the Theatre, beg leave to remark, That the present preposterous size of the Ladies Head-Dresses is extremely incommodious to, and obstructs the View of all, who *unfortunately* are seated behind them, at the Representation of a Play . . .

But squabbles were forgotten in the excitement generated by a visit at the beginning of September from Mrs. Crawford – formerly Mrs. Ann Barry, wife of Spranger Barry, and sister-in-law to that Mrs. Jane Barry who had played opposite Powell in the first King Street seasons. She had just completed triumphant engagements in Ireland, and compared with the tragic actresses Bristol had recently seen she seemed to bring back the glamour of "the good old days".

Mrs. Crawford's Belvidera [in *Venice Preserv'd*] was receiv'd with wonder and applause, which by degrees work'd so powerfully upon the passions, that in the last scene several ladies were so overcome as to be oblig'd to retire from a *general scene* of extreme sensibility – tears and astonishment.

When Hannah More's *Percy* was announced

The Avenues of the Playhouse were . . . crouded soon after four o'clock, so great was the expectation of the public . . . and the house overflowed in a few minutes.[49]

A Bristol audience was unlikely to consider that by now 44-year-old Mrs. Crawford was well past her prime as an actress; indeed, proverbially the provinces were old-fashioned in their acting tastes. The Gentlemen from London departed for the last time in a blaze of glory, and few, if any, noticed that it was provided by a setting sun.

NOTES

[1] *Sarah Farley's Bristol Journal*, 8.12.1764.

[2] E. C. Everard: *Memoirs of an Unfortunate Son of Thespis*, Edinburgh, 1818, Ch. 1.

[3] See B. S. Penley: *The Bath Stage*, London/Bath, 1892, p. 39, and *Bath Chronicle* for October 1767.

[4] Letter of 6.9.1766 in Harvard Theatre Collection; see also Minutes of General Meeting of Proprietors, 13.9.1766.

[5] *Felix Farley's Bristol Journal*, 20.6., 4 & 11.7.1767.

[6] *ibid.*, 5.9.1767.

[7] J. Bernard: *Retrospections of the Stage*, London, 1830, Vol. 2, Ch. 1. I have made little use of Bernard's anecdotes of the earlier years of the Bristol theatre, which were necessarily acquired second-hand and tend to be either quite unverifiable or demonstrably untrue. In this case, there is some circumstantial evidence to support the story, though Bernard also says that Shuter took a second Benefit, which is certainly incorrect.

[8] A transcript of the entries from Edkins' account book which relate to Bristol theatres is included in K. M. D. Barker: Michael Edkins, painter; *Theatre Notebook*, XVI, 2, 39-55.

[9] J. Ireland: *Letters and Poems by the Late Mr. John Henderson*, London, 1786, pp. 96, 99-100.

[10] Little, *op. cit.*, p. 11.

[11] See K. M. D. Barker: William Powell – a Forgotten Star; in K. Richards and P. Thomson (eds.): *The Eighteenth Century English Stage*, London, 1972, pp. 73-83.

[12] Minutes of General Meeting, 12.9.1769.

[13] *Bristol and Bath Chronicle*, 14.6.1770.

[14] *Felix Farley's Bristol Journal*, 4.8.1770.

[15] *ibid.*, 31.8.1771.

[16] *ibid.*, 8.6.1771. It is almost certainly this misadventure to which Garrick alludes in his worried P.S. to a letter to John Moody at Bristol: "I have this moment been shock'd with an account of Mr. King's accident . . ." (Little & Kahrl, *op. cit.*, Letter 635 of 6 June 1771.)

[17] Bath references supplied by Dr. Arnold Hare; Professor P. J. Highfill sent an abundance of ancillary material amply confirming the identification of the "celebrated actress" with Mrs. Bulkley.

[18] Ireland, *op. cit.*, p. 97.

[19] *Felix Farley's Bristol Journal*, 19. & 26.9.1772.

[20] *Sarah Farley's Bristol Journal*, 16.1.1773.

[21] *Felix Farley's Bristol Journal*, 23.1.1773.

[22] *Bristol Gazette*, 18.2.1773.

[23] *ibid.*, 27.5.1773.

[24] *Felix Farley's Bristol Journal*, 12.6.1773.

[25] They seem to have had to organise their Benefits from prison. Fate had not done with poor Kennedy, who subsequently lost his wife and all his possessions, and nearly his own life, in a London fire in May 1775.

[26] *Felix Farley's Bristol Journal*, 21.5.1774.

[27] *ibid.*, 2.7.1774.

[28] *Sarah Farley's Bristol Journal*, 6.8.1774.

[29] *Bristol Gazette*, 18.8.1774. The practice of admitting paying spectators on to the stage was common in Georgian theatres, especially at Benefits. It had been accepted at Jacob's Wells, at least until the last few years, but at the King Street theatre it seems to have been simply "not done".

[30] Minutes of General Meeting, 6.9.1774.

[31] Ireland, *op. cit.*, p. 179.

[32] *Bristol Gazette*, 15.6.1775.

[33] *Felix Farley's Bristol Journal*, 27.5.1775.

[34] *Bonner & Middleton's Bristol Journal*, 29.7.1775.

[35] *Bristol Gazette*, 23.11.1775.

[36] F. E. Wood: Canning's mother and the stage; *Notes & Queries*, 157, 11, 183.

[37] *Bristol Gazette*, 20.6.1776; *Bonner & Middleton's Bristol Journal*, 22.6.1776; *Sarah Farley's Bristol Journal*, 22.6.1776, &c.

[38] *Felix Farley's Bristol Journal*, 24.8.1776.

[39] *Sarah Farley's Bristol Journal*, 24.8.1776.

[40] *Felix Farley's Bristol Journal*, 31.8.1776.

[41] See Jenkins, *op. cit.*, p. 91. Back in London, Reddish's mental instability gradually increased until he had to be committed to York Asylum where he died in 1785. Mary Ann, with whom one can have nothing but sympathy, remarried in 1783. Her son by her first marriage, George Canning, who eventually became Prime Minister, secured her a pension which she enjoyed till her death in 1827.

[42] Bernard, *op. cit.*, p. 32, dates this " 'Hegira' of a country Comedian" as the summer of 1775, but Bensley was not in Bristol that year. Bernard also mentions going to see the Bath Company en route for Bristol, and if his recollection of the members of the Company can be relied on 1777 seems the only possible date. In any case, in 1771 or 1772, the other years in which Bensley acted in Bristol, Bernard would have been a mere schoolboy.

[43] S. Curwen: *Journals and Letters*, ed. G. A. Ward, London, 1842, Journal entry for 11.7.1777.

[44] Watts, *op. cit.*, pp. 123-8, reprints the text of both Act and Letters Patent.

[45] See *Bath Chronicle*, 17.9.1778 and *Bath Journal*, 21.1.1782.

[46] *Sarah Farley's Bristol Journal*, 23.5.1778.

[47] *Bonner & Middleton's Bristol Journal*, 1.8.1778.

[48] *Bath Chronicle*, 11.6.1778.

[49] *Felix Farley's Bristol Journal*, 5. & 12.9.1778.

Part Two
The Heyday of the Stock Company

The Theatres of the Metropolis have not raised a single recruit for many years past, but what has been train'd at the drill *dramatique* of the Bath and Bristol Company, which not only reflects the highest credit on the management thereof, but it also secures for us a certain succession of professional excellence, from the acknowledged advantages this Company has over every other in the Kingdom, as the nearest *Stage* to the grand termination of the Theatrical Traveller's Journey.

Felix Farley's Bristol Journal, 17.5.1783

One

1778–1791

It might have been expected that when the summer company had returned to London the Proprietors of the Theatre Royal would have offered the lease forthwith to the Bath managers. Instead, for reasons which remain obscure, they leased the theatre for a winter season to a minor provincial company, normally based on Exeter and Plymouth, but which had been playing at Richmond during the summer. The company was headed by Thomas Jefferson of Drury Lane and two actors from the Exeter Theatre, Wolfe and Josiah Foote.[1] (The presence of the latter, an ex-butcher and a colourful character in his own right, has led to a long-standing legend that Samuel Foote – who died in 1777 – acted at the Bristol Theatre.)

The new managers paid £300 rent for the season, acting on Monday, Wednesday and Friday and opening at the former prices of 4s. for the Boxes, 2s. 6d. for the Pit and 1s. (with no half price) for the Gallery. Just before Christmas they brought out *The School for Scandal* in excellent style, and promptly made high production costs an excuse to raise the Gallery price to 1s. 6d. (1s. after the end of the third act). This was evidently taken ill, for a fortnight later they not only restored the Gallery price to 1s. but reduced that of the Pit to 2s. until the start of the Benefits; "but no Half Price will be taken for any Part of the House except the Boxes".

This, taken with the almost total lack of comment in the local press, strongly suggests that, despite the appeal of *The School for Scandal* and *The Duenna*, the season as a whole did not go too well. William Douglas gleaned from Jefferson that the managers covered their expenses, but "the high rent made them resign it"; one of James Winston's informants was told that the Bath managers paid Foote and Jefferson £100 to take over the last part of the lease.[2] What is certain is that on Monday, 8

March, Foote took his Benefit and announced "the LAST NIGHT of the Company's performing this Season", and on Wednesday, 10 March, the Bath Company took over the Theatre Royal, Bristol, for a fortnight's season, acting three times a week. Then, after a gap of just over three weeks, they returned to play on Mondays only from 19 April to 31 May (including a Benefit for Matt Clarke). Thereafter they were established in Bristol without opposition till 1817.

How much the Proprietors knew about the negotiations it is impossible to say. It was not till 3 April that they met "to receive Proposals to determine about letting the Theatre", and they put no minutes on record. However, there is no doubt that the Bath Company, having taken possession of the Bristol Theatre, were determined to hold it, and at the summer season prices of 4s., 2s. 6d. and 1s.

Those who still hankered after a London company comforted themselves by asserting that "no receipts can possibly repay the enormous expense of bringing [the Bath] company, musicians, scenes, etc., over here."[3] Palmer and his acting manager, William Keasberry, were not deterred. They obtained a 20-year lease at £200 a year plus ground-rent and taxes amounting to over £80; on Palmer's promising "to make an entire alteration in the theatre, enlarge the lobby, to build an elegant tea room and other accommodations" the Proprietors gave up three years' rent towards the expenses.[4]

On Monday, 31 May, the theatre closed for the summer, to reopen on 4 October with Mrs. Siddons as Portia in *The Merchant of Venice*. The theatre was reported "greatly altered and improved" and there were many compliments on its elegance, but the nature of the "improvements" is not reported. Latimer says, without quoting any evidence, that "the chief feature of the alterations was the erection over the centre of the dress circle of a second tier of boxes". However, this cannot be correct, for not only have we a record of this particular alteration being made in 1800, but surviving Box Booking Plans for 1792-3 show precisely the same number and arrangement of Boxes as in 1773-4. It is possible that, if square pilasters were general in the original building, the present reeded columns were substituted at this date.

Probably the building was redecorated and reseated, though Edkins had done a considerable amount of touching up and regilding for Quick the previous year; a fragmentary undated bill, rebound into the front of his Account Book, records his charging Palmer a modest three guineas for "4 Corinthian Capitals 90 Rosels 9 Braggats for the Chandeliers and the Kings Arms on the front of the Gallery sized, Silverd, and Laquer'd"; there must almost certainly have been further items now lost. Neither the enlargement of the lobby nor the establishment of a tea room is anywhere mentioned. In November 1780 it was announced "that the upper part of the Theatre over the stage is entirely closing in, so that the House will be made extremely warm, and comfortable for the winter" which implies that there was previously only partial roofing above the grid. In December 1786 the Managers installed "A NEW-INVENTED STOVE on each side of the Pit."

From the opening of the Autumn Season (usually the beginning of September) until Bath began to fill up early in November, the Company played Monday, Wednesday and Friday in Bristol and Saturday in Bath; thereafter they played Monday only in Bristol, and Tuesday, Thursday and Saturday in Bath until the beginning of June. By this time company was gathering at the Hotwells, and Bath began to be thin, so the Company returned to Bristol for three nights a week and took their annual Benefits. This pattern remained unchanged for nearly forty years.

While certainly far less demanding than the programme of many a country company, it was still tiring enough. Mrs. Siddons recalled :

Hard labour indeed it was; for after the rehearsal at Bath on a Monday morning, I had to go and act at Bristol in the evening of the same day, and reaching Bath again after a drive of twelve miles, long after midnight, I was obliged to represent some fatigueing [sic] part there on the Tuesday evening.[6]

John Bernard too recollected that, while the trip was pleasant enough on fine summer evenings, "when the season advanced, returning nine [actually thirteen] miles at one o'clock in the morning, after a long night's performance, was anything but desirable" – especially as the cast were put down in the centre of the city and then had to walk to their own lodgings. Palmer solved the transport problem by ordering the construction by Morton and Speakman of two special coaches, each providing room for twelve actors and their luggage, which from their exceptional length were referred to as "The Caterpillars".[7] It is said that Palmer's success with these coaches was the basis of his later reform of the mail-carrying system. It is certainly no small tribute that only three times in 38 years did the Bristol theatre have to be closed because road conditions prevented the coaches getting through.

The acting standards of the company were high. The limitation in number of the London Patent Theatres severely restricted the opportunities of promising newcomers to the acting profession; a talented actor might be better off as leading man in a good provincial circuit like that of Bath and Bristol. William Wyatt Dimond (Plate 8), for example, had been recommended to Bath by Garrick, who approved his London debut but warned him of the limited chances of advancement, and Dimond in

47

the end preferred to stay all his life in Bath, where he became leading man, and, after 1786, acting manager.

It was a very popular appointment, for, unlike many actor-managers, Dimond was scrupulous about the parts for which he cast himself, and consistent in encouraging young talent. In Bristol he was particularly admired for his carefully-studied Hamlet, in which he was not afraid to introduce his own stage business.

In the closet scene, instead of the threadbare trick of starting from his chair on entrance of the Ghost, he sank fainting into it, and on recovery drop'd on his knee, in an attitude finely expressive of filial reverence; his soliloquies were also feelingly delivered, and the pauses, being well kept, had their due effect.[8]

Somewhat formal in his delivery, restrained and intellectual rather than emotional in general acting style, he may have lacked Powell's ability to arouse excitement, but he had nonetheless sterling merits. According to Genest, Sheridan told Dimond "that he played Joseph Surface in a manner more consonant with his own ideas, when he wrote the part, than any body else."

Not only Dimond, but a number of supporting actors, including Abraham and Margaret Didier and Francis Blissett, all of whom appeared with success in London, preferred the certainty of a provincial stock company salary and a succession of good parts in their particular cast. Charles Murray, the "heavy man" of the Company, stayed for eleven years, and Thomas and Margaret Knight for eight, before finally accepting contracts with the Patent Theatres.

At the same time an ambitious actor could be sure of remaining under observation, for the London managers and their agents were frequent visitors to Bath, on pleasure or business. There was a continuing loss of leading players to London, a fact which aroused mixed feelings in the local managers, who complained that

after the fostering kindness and generosity of a judicious public have drawn forth and improv'd the merit of Performers, they have generally had the disappointment and the Proprietor the mortification of losing them.

Nevertheless they were also able to claim that "the scheme has . . . grown of so much more value and attraction to Performers of merit, that it is prefer'd by them to any other situation out of London."[9] And when a provincial stock company was judged (as indeed it still is) by the number of actors it contributed to the London theatres, local regret was outweighed by pride.

The most famous of stars to graduate from the Bath and Bristol Company of the period was of course Sarah Siddons, who had already established herself at Bath prior to the addition of Bristol to the circuit. Her salary, £3 a week, was generous by provincial standards (and compared favourably with a skilled artisan's wage of under £1). Her first recorded Bristol performance was as the Countess of Salisbury on Monday 15 March 1779,* and it so impressed an anonymous Young Lady living at the Hotwells that she contributed some lines to the *Bath Journal* which pay glowing tribute to the sympathetic emotion which the young tragic actress evoked :

> In thee, no cold, dull passion mars the line;
> The fiction ceases – real sorrows shine;
> From eyes expressive starts th'unbidden tear,
> The soft effusions of a soul sincere;
> And the fair face to the fine heart allied;
> Speaks all the griefs – the joys which there abide.[10]

Mrs. Siddons was perhaps more admired than popular – it was commented about one of her Benefits that "We often remember to have had a more numerous, but never a more elegant appearance" – but there was ample appreciation of her "interesting countenance and pathetic manner". Her Countess of Salisbury called forth a further versified tribute to her dignity, grace and natural depiction of the passions,[11] while in Jephson's *Count of Narbonne* she was "throughout the part of the Countess, admirably just, spirited, and pathetic, as her different situations required". For her husband's Benefit in 1781 she played Hamlet, for the sixth time in her career to date, but her first and only attempt at a breeches part in Bristol, "and went thro' the character to the entire approbation of a numerous and polite audience."

Miss Summers, a minor actress in the Company, told Genest that, thanks partly to the tuition of her husband, Mrs. Siddons greatly improved during this engagement. Her farewell Benefit in Bristol on 17 June 1782 came immediately after a severe influenza epidemic, which had shut the house for a week and reduced the proceeds of many Benefits to the point of actual loss. It is the more noteworthy that hers realised £106 13s., though the patronage of the Duchess of Devonshire no doubt counted for a good deal. The secret of her Three Reasons for Quitting the Theatre (her three children), which she promised to produce as part of a Poetical Address of her own writing, was probably fairly widely known, since she had gone through a similar programme at Bath on 21 May, but no doubt

---

* She may have played on 10 or 12 March but the main pieces for those dates are not on record.

it was still effective. It certainly made an impression within the company. At the joint Benefit of Miss Wewitzer and Mrs. Didier :

Miss WEWITZER will produce THREE REASONS For Her CONTINUANCE on the BRISTOL Stage, and Mrs. DIDIER will attempt their INVESTIGATION.[12]

As late as 1807, when Mrs. Didier retired, she recited a farewell address specifically recalling that of Mrs. Siddons, but claiming that *she* had sixty-six reasons for quitting the stage : the years of her life. Coupled with the resentful tone in which Mrs. Siddons speaks in her *Reminiscences* of "the mortification of being obliged to Personate many subordinate characters in Comedy, the first being in the possession of another Lady" (Mrs. Didier), this strongly suggests a certain amount of friction between the two.

After her Benefit Sarah Siddons played one more night in Bristol, acting Mrs. Belville in *The School for Wives* on the following Wednesday for the Benefit of Mrs. Brett. It was bound to be an anticlimax, and in the event the proceeds amounted to a derisory £24 13s. Mrs. Brett's husband William, a highly popular singer, seems to have created some kind of drunken disturbance – possibly he told the audience what he thought of their patronage ! – and on 21 June the Managers issued a notice :

The Public are respectfully informed, from Mr. Brett's exceeding ill behaviour on Wednesday night, and that they may not experience a second insult from him, he is discharged from the theatre.[13]

In the autumn of 1783 Brett obtained an engagement at Covent Garden, but the following January, illness having sadly depleted the Bristol Company's singing strength, the managers had to overlook the past and ask for the loan of his services. Brett, nervous about his reception, took the precaution of adding to the advertisements of his reappearance :

Conscious of the Impropriety of his Behaviour when last in this City, and deeply sensible of the many Favours he has received here, Mr. Brett hoped that his present Endeavours to prevent any Disappointment in its Amusements, will be considered as some Apology for past Faults, and a Mark of the real Respect he entertains for so generous and indulgent a Public.[14]

The Bristol public was feeling neither generous nor indulgent, and booed him off the stage, whereupon he threw up his engagement and returned to Covent Garden forthwith. Such disturbances, however, were rare, for, though relations were not invariably harmonious, there was a degree of trust in the management, and a benevolent paternalism by that management, which at any period would be remarkable in the theatre.

The close links forged with London were particularly useful to the managers in obtaining the newest entertainments almost immediately after their first production. *The Critic,* which came out at Drury Lane on 30 October 1779, reached Bristol at the beginning of the following February; Hannah Cowley's *Belle's Stratagem* and Sophia Lee's *Chapter of Accidents* took only two months to make the journey in 1780. One of Mrs. Cowley's most popular afterpieces, *Who's the Dupe?* was given in Bristol only seven weeks after its Drury Lane production. The repertoire in Bath and Bristol closely imitated that of the London Theatres; any idea of creating "regional drama" would have been unimaginable to the London-centred 18th Century provincial theatre.

Nonetheless this period saw some attempts by the managers to foster local talent. One of the most successful was a pantomime, *Brystowe, or Harlequin Mariner,* its book put together by Floor the prompter, with lyrics by William Meyler, a local litterateur, and music by Brooks, one of the company's musicians. This was given in Bristol on 1 October 1788, played nine times that month, and revived in Bath and Bristol at intervals over the next three years. Richard Jenkins, author of *Memoirs of the Bristol Stage* and for many years dramatic critic of the *Bristol Gazette,* wrote a two-act afterpiece, *One Rake in a Thousand,* on 9 July 1783 for the Benefit of Browne, who played second leads in the company.[15] The piece, a mildly satirical comedy, was so well received that John Brunton asked to be allowed to repeat it at his Benefit the following week, and it was revived again the next year. Its success encouraged Jenkins to a more ambitious effort, a four-act comedy called *The Married Man,* produced for Mrs. Keasberry's Benefit on 17 July 1786.

> The dialogue was easy and sprightly, and the scenes appeared like close copies from nature. – With the addition of another act and some trifling alterations, we think this piece might be rendered as entertaining as almost any of our modern comedies.[16]

This play seems never to have been revived in Bristol, but Jenkins' efforts brought him a permanent free pass to the theatre, renewed by successive managements.

More important as examples of patronage were the productions of Frederick Reynolds' *Werter* in December 1785 and of Ann Yearsley the Bristol Milkmaid's *Earl Goodwin* in November 1789. Reynolds became one of the most successful playwrights of the late 18th and early 19th Centuries; *Werter* was his first play, and it dealt with "the too prevalent crime of this kingdom – Suicide." To counteract any fears that Reynolds had treated over-sympathetically the already notorious tale of Werter and Charlotte, much advance propaganda was put out. An epilogue by

William Meyler, reminding the audiences of their fostering sponsorship of budding actors (with verses discreetly varied in Bath and in Bristol), begged their patronage for a new author. After two performances in Bristol, some alterations were made, and it was re-introduced in the new year. In March 1786 the tragedy was put on at Covent Garden and Bristol had the satisfaction of finding in its success "a flattering confirmation of the propriety with which judgment was originally passed in its favour here".[17]

Ann Yearsley's tragedy was in rather a different category. Originally befriended when in wretched circumstances by Hannah More, who spent many months improving her education and raising a subscription for her benefit, she had by now turned against her erstwhile patroness, and *Earl Goodwin* was something of a gesture of independence.

> As the first dramatic effort of the *"unlettered muse"* it was admitted to be a very extraordinary one, the language in general being highly poetic, and many of the images new and beautiful, so that it was received with the loudest plaudits.[18]

First produced in Bristol on 2 November 1789 and repeated at Bath the next night, *Earl Goodwin* had four performances in Bristol in five playing nights, the last being for Mrs. Yearsley's Benefit; it then disappeared from the repertory.

It must be stressed that these examples of local initiative were the exception, not the rule, but they are indicative of a swing in public taste away from the classics and towards novelty which may also be seen in the selection of stock pieces generally. Not that every new piece was received uncritically: the satiric afterpiece of *Tony Lumpkin in Town*, staged in November 1780, was stigmatised by the indignant Theatricus as "one of the most blackguard and indelicate Farces that my ears were ever shocked with." He considered its selection an insult to the taste of the city, and his apologia for the Bristol audiences is testimony to a growing conscious pride in culture among the "Bristol Hogs" :

> Every merchant, and every tradesman now of any property, gives his children a liberal education, this, with the constant communication they have with London, and their contiguousness to Bath . . . places them in point of taste and judgment with the first audiences in the country.[19]

It is a common mistake to write off 18th Century provincial audiences as if all their members were naive, ignorant bumpkins; comments from the Bristol press show they were at least as ready as their London counterparts to notice clumsy handling of scenery or inconsistencies in historical costume. The production of Holcroft's *The Follies of a Day, or, The Marriage of Figaro* (an adaptation of Beaumarchais' famous play, staged in Bristol barely six weeks after its Covent Garden premiere) met with applause, but, Dramaticus pertinently enquired, "Why are soldiers dress'd in the French uniform introduced in a piece the scene of which evidently lies in Spain?"[20] Objection was similarly expressed to the Roman ambassador in *Cymbeline* appearing with powdered head and white kid gloves.[21]

On the other hand, a regular contributor to *Felix Farley's Bristol Journal* during 1786, who signed himself "Z", praised the attention to historical costume:

> I have been much pleas'd to observe, that in the plays lately represented, particularly in Richard the 3d. the characters were all dress'd in the habits of the times – this has been shamefully neglected even in the Capital, and I notice this instance of attention in the manager as deserving the approbation of the public; for certainly when such subjects of antiquity are represented, nothing in the picture ought to remind us of modern times; the mind is thrown back as it were into past ages, and everything should be avoided which may tend to awaken it from its illusion.[22]

Almost a paraphrase of this argument was being put forward eighty years later by Edward Godwin.

It must certainly be said to the credit of the Bath managers that some, at least, of the savings in production costs brought about by the union of the two theatres, were ploughed back into better scenery, richer costumes, and more lavish stage effects, and this was fully appreciated. Pantomime of course provided the most obvious outlet; in *The Necromancer*, another home-made pantomime, produced in October 1782,

> Mr. [Thomas] French's scene of Mount Vesuvius, is universally spoken of as the best exhibition of painting that has ever been produced here; it is, we understand, an exact copy from the Moonlight View of the eruption that was taken on the spot by the celebrated Mr. Wright, of Derby.[23]

French's excellence as a scenic artist was not confined to pantomimes, however. *Mahomet*, revived late in 1783, drew three or four good houses, less through the merits of the play than because it was "enriched with every decoration in point of dress and scenery that can possibly be bestowed upon it," and in *The Castle of Andalusia* French was praised for "the best exhibition of a cavern we ever remember."[24] Spectacular patriotic effects were always well received; to celebrate the Proclamation of the Peace of Versailles in 1783, the brother of Charles Bonnor (the Company's low comedian) produced a most complicated allegorical transparency in which Cupid, Apollo, Tragedy, Comedy, a Satyr and a Hydra (*inter alia*) served to represent Peace bringing forward Commerce and Plenty.[25]

All in all, when Palmer and Keasberry claimed that they had been "enabled . . . to get up many pieces equal in exhibition to the London Theatres",[26] the evidence is that they were not going beyond allowable managerial exaggeration. Nor were their efforts restricted to the drama, for the scale of the Bath Concerts gave scope for singers and instrumentalists of quality to combine two careers, and both theatre and concert hall benefited by the dual opportunities offered to the performers. The musical resources available enabled the theatre managers in 1779 to mount not only the standard ballad operas but such pieces as the recently revised version of Milton's *Comus*, in which "the singing parts were excellently supported, the Choruses particularly were superior to any thing we ever remember here."[27] Tragedies like Mason's *Caractacus*, decked out with semi-operatic set pieces, drew similar praise, the critic taking particular satisfaction in the fact that the chorus singers were Bristolians.

The Company was therefore able to attract good singers as well as actors, the most noteworthy acquisition in this department being that of Charles Incledon, who became one of the greatest lyric tenors of the day. He joined the Bath and Bristol Company in 1785 after a period with Collins, the Wessex manager, but as an early biographer noted :

> It was his musical powers alone that obtained him this engagement, for his abilities as an actor were not much valued . . . He was regarded as little better than a chorus singer.[28]

However, as a concert and glee club performer he was appreciated at his full value, and it was on the strength of his concert rather than his stage reputation that he was engaged at Covent Garden in 1790.

Singers from the theatre company were also employed in the Oratorios which were for several years successfully performed at the Theatre Royal during Lent; while this was very largely a Bath enterprise, Bristol doubtless contributed towards the chorus and orchestra. Most performances went smoothly enough, but near-disaster followed the failure of the famous castrato Tenducci to arrive for *Messiah* on 28 March 1782. Handbills of apology were not distributed, it was alleged, until the company had actually assembled, and then only in the Boxes. Rauzzini, standing in for the sick singer, rendered only one solo in the whole work, and the conductor appeared merely anxious to finish and get home !

> Songs – duets – choruses, were omitted – the audience disgusted – and the band thrown into confusion. – The first violin led off *one* air, while the violoncello had begun the accompaniment of *another*.

The chorus singers were repeatedly at a loss whether to stand up or keep their seats; and Mr. Rauzzini had almost trampled Miss Storer to death, in endeavouring to sing from Mr. Corfe's paper, instead of his own, which neither himself or the conductor of the band knew anything of.[29]

After this debacle it is not perhaps surprising that no more Lenten Oratorios were brought out at Bristol for many years.

Besides the attractions of the Stock Company, a few stars visited the theatre in this period, but they mainly presented speciality acts. It is easily forgotten just how inclusive an entertainment the theatre provided at this time – and indeed right up to the latter part of the 19th Century. A hundred years later most of these visitors would have been seen on the music halls : Moses Kean with his impersonations of London actors; Signor Rossignol and his bird-imitations; The Little Devil and his troupe of acrobats. Even in 1783 the managers were somewhat anxious about the public's reaction to tumblers appearing on the stage of a Theatre Royal, but they need not have worried : The Little Devil's visit drew such enormous houses that the managers were forced by public demand to renew the engagement and grant the performers an extra Benefit. Parties came from as far as Exeter to the Bristol theatre to see them, and they were engaged again in 1785-6.

Signor Rossignol was probably even longer remembered by the Company. As they were all returning from Bristol one fine May night he stopped the coach a few miles outside Bath,

got out, and began his imitations of the nightingale, which was presently answer'd by one of those enchanting songsters from the opposite side of the river.[30]

Gradually more and more birds joined in, Rossignol imitating their calls and encouraging them to come closer, while the Company sat breathless, listening to this lovely night chorus all about them. It is one of the most charming pictures we have of this period and must have remained a long-cherished memory in the minds of all who were present.

The enormous popularity of The Little Devil and his companions, Messieurs Dupuis and Meunie, is perhaps a straw in the wind of change which is discernible in studying the composition and behaviour of audiences. The theatre was considered a social rather than an artistic institution by all but a devoted minority, and the fashionable company probably had always gone there as much to be seen as to see; but a slackening of manners does become detectible in the 1780's. There are complaints of lady spectators who blocked the sight of those behind them with their enormous hats, and the gentlemen who arrived late and drowned the play with their conversation.[31] "Z" found himself quite unable to concentrate on the first two acts of the play as a result :

The continual passing and repassing, slamming of doors and contention about places, effectually prevent our hearing anything; the monstrous hats, and extended head-dresses of the ladies form a testudinated phalanx as impervious to sight, as the most solid screen that can be interposed. – The ladies are no sooner seated than the young men begin their rounds and from the vanity of shewing themselves in a variety of attitudes, skip from box to box to the perpetual disquiet of those who, like myself, come there to hear and attend to the business of the drama.[32]

The emotional response once evoked by a Powell, a Crawford or a Siddons now took a new form. Outbursts of patriotic enthusiasm were a natural reaction to the threat to established order represented abroad by the first rumblings of the French Revolution, and at home by King George's collapse in 1788. There was a mania for patriotic spectacles, and Loyal and Constitutional Songs, particularly "God Save the King". On its rendering in November 1788

Scarcely an eye appeared without the tears of loyalty gently stealing from it, and not a tongue that did not heartily join in the chorus.

An additional verse praying for the King's recovery was sung by Charles Incledon with "animated warmth and fervency." When recovery was pronounced, William Meyler produced "A New LOYAL ODE on the joyful recovery of his MAJESTY", set by Rauzzini and sung by Incledon.

To political uncertainty was added local economic stagnation. The Port of Bristol was losing trade, the city itself was no longer the second in the kingdom; but the initiative to regain leadership was lacking. The cumulative effect on the theatre began to be felt about 1790; the death of the Duke of Cumberland delayed the opening of the season and this had a generally depressing effect. A contributor to *Felix Farley's Bristol Journal,* signing himself "The Wanderer", sadly recorded :

Some of the most meritorious plays are frequently represented at our Theatre, almost to empty benches; and, excepting two or three instances, the players are generally *losers* by their benefits.[33]

The end of the 1790-1 season was marked by the death, on 20 August, of Mrs. Jane Green, John Hippisley's daughter, who had played for twenty years at her father's Bristol theatre and seven more at the King Street house. In retrospect this breaking of the last link with the Jacob's Wells Theatre can be seen as to some extent symbolic; the summer of 1791 proved a turning point in the fortunes of the Bath and Bristol Company.

Two

1791–1801

The managers' answer to the relatively poor success of the 1790-1 season did them credit; it was to invest a good deal of money in improving the theatre and making it more attractive. The ceiling was raised, which gave better aesthetic proportions; the boxes were newly lined, and the whole theatre redecorated and regilded by Thomas French and William and Michael Edkins. "A lover of Theatrical Entertainment" was, however, a little puzzled by the fact that the sky and clouds on the ceiling seemed unfinished :

There is also something intended in the ventilator over the pit, which I cannot by any means discover. And with respect to the boys on the sound-board, they certainly are in an imperfect, unfinished state, nor can I explain the design, but only by supposing that *they are carrying a cheese as a present to Jupiter.*[34]

The managers remained, too, fortunate in many of their engagements. Perhaps the most significant, though almost unnoticed at the time, had been made in April 1791 when

A Young Gentleman . . . made his first essay in the character of Tressel in Richard the Third,* whose modesty in the choice of that character was no less admired than the capital specimen he gave of great theatrical talents.[35]

Nine years later a critic remembered :

He delivered the narrative of the gallant Prince Edward's fall, by the bloody hand of Glo'ster, after the fatal battle near Tewkesbury, with a sensibility and pathos which charmed the audience.[36]

There being no suitable vacancy for the beginner at that stage of the

* It was, of course, Cibber's version of *King Richard III* which was being played.

57

season, he obtained an engagement at York, but came back to Bath and Bristol in 1793. His name was Robert William Elliston, and on his return *Sarah Farley's Bristol Journal* commented prophetically :

His voice has force and melody, regulated by a sound and well-cultivated understanding. In such characters as Mr. Dimond may think proper to relinquish, he has found in Mr. Elliston, a respectable successor.[37]

Dimond recognised this. Like Garrick, he became more selective in his parts, wisely leaving to the volatile and lively Elliston such roles as Prince Hal in *King Henry IV i,* Young Rapid in *A Cure for the Heartache* and the heroes of the dramatic afterpieces.[38] In the summer of 1796 Elliston accepted his first engagement in London at the Haymarket, with a Benefit grossing over £244, and on 1 October, *Sarah Farley's Bristol Journal* reported :

We hear the London Managers, not being able to keep this admirable Actor wholly to themselves, have succeeded so far with our Manager, that Mr. Elliston will probably play once a fortnight at Covent-Garden during the Winter. An arduous task! but the professional zeal of this young man never tires.

In the light comedies of the end of the century Elliston particularly shone; his face was expressive, his eye bright and sparkling. Wherever unaffected, natural acting was called for in romantic parts, or dash and bustle in comedy, Elliston was irresistible, and in serious parts an attention to realistic detail would often carry him through. He even essayed Macbeth, and was "much beyond what might have been expected"; and if further proof of his versatility were needed, in the absence of established singers in the company he occasionally took leading parts in ballad opera with some success.

Though failing to produce another Siddons, the Company fostered a number of the leading actresses of the decades to come, several of them either children of Stock Company members or natives of Bath or Bristol. One of the first was Anne Brunton (later Mrs. Merry, a prominent actress on the American stage), whose father had been a member of the company since 1780. She made her first appearance (as Euphrasia, the dedicated Grecian Daughter of Arthur Murphy's tragedy) in April 1785 when still only fifteen, and at the end of her first season she was snapped up by Covent Garden, who offered her father and herself a joint engagement at £12 a week.

One of the best-known of the locally-born actresses was Tryphosa Wallis, later Mrs. Campbell (Plate 8), who was only fifteen when she made her debut as Rosalind in Bristol in 1789. The support of a large family, whose mother had died giving birth to the youngest, Miss Wallis was always generous in her tributes to the care with which Keasberry and Dimond developed her talents. From 1791 she was leading lady of the Company, occasionally attempting such roles as Lady Macbeth, though most popular in romantic and pathetic parts until her departure for Covent Garden in the autumn of 1794. At her final Benefit in Bristol the receipts were £163, "and the overflow would have half filled another house."

Another "child of the company" was Julia Betterton, known best to posterity under her married name of Mrs. Glover, who with her father joined the company in the autumn of 1795. Miss Betterton opened as Edwina in Hannah More's *Percy* and "deservedly received the warmest approbation from a brilliant though not crowded audience."[39] At the age of sixteen she plunged into a gruelling succession of leading parts from Lady Teazle to Cordelia. In Holcroft's *Deserted Daughter* she played Joanna and was accounted "a charming breeches figure." After two seasons she also was engaged by Covent Garden, but she did not forget Bristol. Generations of Glovers to come were to have experience in its stock companies.

Another local actress was Julia Grimani; her father, a teacher of languages in Bath, was in poor health, and she went on the stage in May 1800 in order to support him and her younger brother and sisters at the age of sixteen; her father died barely a year later.[40] She left for the Haymarket in 1803, and the following year married Charles Mayne Young. In 1805 she died in childbirth; a brief life of successes crowned with tragedy.

Among the well-known comic actors of the late 18th Century for whom Bath and Bristol were stepping stones to London were the sharp, friendly, eccentric Andrew Cherry; Thomas Knight, a clever character comedian, and his wife Peggy, one of the Farren sisters; and John Edwin jun. and his wife. Edwin, like his father, was at his best in broad comedy; though he was often careless about his lines and prone to play to the gallery, even Thespis, the somewhat carping critic of *Felix Farley's Bristol Journal,* had to compliment him on his Tipple in *The Flitch of Bacon* : "it was true, genuine humour, unadulterated by that vile buffoonery, so frequently the stumbling block of low comedians."[41] Elizabeth Edwin made herself popular at once; playing on the same evening Amanthis, the Child of Nature, and the pert Roxalana in *The Sultan,*

she sustained both these parts with such spirit, vivacity and correctness, as we have rarely witnessed . . . Her person is small, but her figure is elegant, and her countenance uncommonly animated, interesting and expressive.[42]

Intermixed with the stock company performances, however, and becoming markedly more frequent and important, were star engagements. Bristol, as a packet station for Ireland, had occasionally been visited by a star passing through – Mrs. Crawford in 1778, Moss in 1786. As we have seen, strolling entertainers, musicians, acrobats and the like, were quite often incorporated in the bill. But from 1796 onwards we can date the rise of the London star, whose attractions in the end helped to undermine the provincial stock company system. Ironically, the very success of the local circuits encouraged the emergence of the touring star, for, as in Bristol, locally based companies had almost everywhere superseded the summer companies which had hitherto been the hunting-ground of the London actor between seasons. Cities like Bath and Bristol, which had given so many players to the London stage, might naturally be expected to welcome back their erstwhile protégés, and the great majority of stars visiting Bristol in the last years of the 18th Century fell into this category: Miss Wallis, John Quick, Charles Incledon, Mrs. Siddons herself.

The first intended re-engagement of the last-named, in September 1798, was overtaken by tragedy : the death of her daughter Sally at the Hotwells. Mrs. Siddons finally visited the following February, playing Euphrasia in *The Grecian Daughter,* Jane Shore, Isabella and Lady Macbeth. As Euphrasia

those superior powers she possesses, and which had attracted a most brilliant and crowded audience, were exerted with such wonderful effect, as to astonish and delight in the highest degree. A more finished piece of acting, perhaps, was never exhibited.[43]

She returned for three weeks in April 1801, opening as Jane Shore

to a crowded and brilliant audience, who testified the strong impression she made on their feelings, by a copious tribute of sighs and tears.[44]

Miss Wallis came back to Bath and Bristol twice in 1796; on her first visit on 28 March,

For some moments, on her entrance, so great were her feelings, that she could scarcely articulate. – The improvement, that we perceive, is, a better acquaintance with stage effect; a greater volume of voice; superior elegance of figure, and much stronger expression of features.[45]

She continued, however, to play romantic and high comedy parts rather than the more deeply tragic ones.

"Little Quick," who came for three years running in the early Autumn, combined his performances with visits to the Hotwells for his health; he had married a Bristol girl, owned a house in College Green, and was a shareholder in the theatre. These local links ensured him the special proprietary affection of Bristolians; his Benefit at the end of his first visit at the beginning of the 1797-8 season brought in £149. Noting these receipts, however, a contributor to *Felix Farley's Bristol Journal* could not but lament

that several of the Performers of our Theatre, who *constantly* and effectually exert themselves to afford amusement to the public, and whose merits, even in the scale of comparison, are very generally acknowledged, should so frequently feel the want of similar support, on which they are surely entitled to place some reliance.[46]

This was the first murmur of what was to become a growing chorus of grievance.

A considerable change in the nature and behaviour of the audiences also marked the last decade of the 18th Century. Mobilisation of the militia for the Napoleonic Wars meant a considerable swelling of the military population of Bristol, whose Downs provided an ideal encampment ground, and, while traditionally soldiers and sailors were keen theatre patrons, their behaviour, even that of the officers, was not always ideal. The first complaints of a rougher element in the audience come in the early years of the 1790's. The *Bristol Gazette* of 4 October 1792 noted:

The frequenters of our Theatre as well as the Performers, are greatly indebted to the spirited exertions of several Gentlemen on Friday last, who severely chastised those miscreants who make a practice of throwing apples, stones, &c. at the Performers whilst on the stage.

Young bloods in the Gallery and Upper Boxes took to beating their sticks on the balustrades to express their applause (incidentally knocking off the new gilding). On one occasion a galleryite fired off a pistol during the performance, though he was let off with a warning by the Magistrates. On another, a dispute between two army officers in the theatre led to a duel on Kingsdown. There were recurrent reports of pickpockets being active in and about the theatre. Sometimes of course the uproar merely indicated an over-zealous patriotism; Allan Ramsay's *Gentle Shepherd* was interrupted by "the honest English tars aloft" shouting for "Rule Britannia" ("God Save the King" having already been rendered twice).[47]

The presence of an encampment of ever-changing regiments near the city led not only to increased audiences but to direct patronage of Benefits, and even to active participation. Elliston produced a Grand Pantomime Ballet, *The Siege of Quebec and Death of General Wolfe,* for his Benefit on 11 July 1796, when "to give the Spectacle its full effect, Mr. E. has engaged a Detachment of the Northampton Militia". The soldiers were chiefly used in Scene IV, The British Camp and Review of the Troops, in which they "perform various Military Evolutions; after which General Wolfe exhorts his Soldiers to conquer or to die, and they march off in full Chorus to Purcell's popular Air of 'Britons, Strike Home'."[48] Mr. and Mrs. Taylor chose the afterpiece of *The Deserter* for their Benefit on 20 June 1798, and borrowed the Military Band, Grenadiers and Light Infantry of the Royal Cheshire Militia, in full uniform, to add realism to the scene in which the Deserter was due to meet his fate. One could indeed trace military movements in the West by the playbills of the theatres.

The Duke of York visited Bristol on 27 November 1795 to review the troops encamped on the Downs, and expressed his intention to visit the Theatre, which was specially opened on the occasion. Dimond naturally enough wanted to "erect a State-Box for his reception, which his Highness politely declin'd, saying he wish'd no distinction to be made but to sit with the Company and be considered as a private Gentleman".[49] The Duke was greeted with enormous enthusiasm both when he arrived (one and a half hours late) and when he left (at the end of the main piece, the comedy of *The Rage*).

Inevitably, too, the repertory was modified to suit the mood of the times. *King Henry V* was revived on 29 July 1793 for Mrs. Keasberry's Benefit, for the first time since 1781, and continued to be played occasionally till 1815. New patriotic afterpieces were produced: *Sprigs of Laurel, Bantry Bay* (only a month after its Covent Garden production), *The Mouth of the Nile,* and a topical sketch, *Voluntary Contributions,* by Walsh Porter, which was produced in Bath and Bristol in February/ March 1798 before being taken up by Covent Garden. The royal procession to St. Paul's following the naval victory of Cape St. Vincent was reproduced on the stage: "a Gentleman present, who was also a spectator of the original Procession in London, assures us that he was upon the whole better entertained with the mimic display of it by the Theatre."[50]

It is a not unnatural reaction to wartime stresses that theatre audiences demand lighter fare, and this was reflected in the popularity of spectacular pieces. Serious pantomimes – stories in mime, not harlequinades – and versions of romantic fairy tales and legends were prominent, especially in the latter years of the 1790's. The playbills tempted the spectator with elaborate synopses. *Don Juan* ended with a transformation scene to the Infernal Regions:

in vain [Don Juan] attempts to escape, the Furies meet him at every turn – at

length he is borne away, amidst a shower of REAL FIRE, and thrown into the burning ABYSS ! ! !
₊*₊ Thus concludes one of the finest Morals and most Awful Spectacles ever presented on the Stage.[51]

Blue Beard was even more remarkable :

The scenery does so much credit to the abilities of Mr. FRENCH and his SON, that it must engage our first attention as it deserves our best praise. – The Hall of Abomelique's Castle is such a composition, that for design, execution and effect, places the YOUNGER FRENCH amongst the most rising Artists of the present day. The other scenes and transparencies, machinery, mechanisms, and expensive and elegantly appropriate dresses do infinite credit to the several persons by whom they were executed.[52]

This was also the period of some of the most enduring 18th Century comedies : of *The Poor Gentleman, A Cure for the Heartache* and *Speed the Plough,* all of which remained in the repertory while stock companies lasted, even though forgotten now. The emergence of German romanticism on the English stage also dates from these years, *Lovers' Vows* being produced in Bristol on 10 December 1798, two months after its Covent Garden premiere, and played four of the next six acting nights, maintaining its place in the repertory up to 1828. *The Stranger,* also a translation from Kotzebue, rapidly succeeded it, and Dimond's performance in the name-part, dignified, manly and impressive, was greatly admired. "We never saw tears shed so abundantly on any similar occasion, as at the last scene between the *Stranger* and *Mrs. Haller.*"[53] From then on it was never out of the programme for more than a season or two until the very end of the Stock Company's existence at the Theatre Royal in 1867, being preserved, long after the play had ceased to command any respect, by the showiness of its two leading roles.

Both these plays, however, were surpassed in impact by Sheridan's adaptation of *Pizarro.* First brought out in Bristol on 28 October 1799, it ran for eight successive playing nights – easily a record for any main piece under contemporary repertory conditions – and was acted seven times more before the summer Benefits. As a stock piece it lasted as long as *The Stranger* and its revivals were even more frequent. The management brought it forward decked out with the richest trappings they could devise; Thespis of *Felix Farley's Bristol Journal admitted* :

No expence has been spared to render it magnificent, and it must be confessed that the decorations do much credit to the liberality of the Manager. In the dresses, the *costume* of the times and countries is not badly preserved; and the scenery is very splendid, but in some respects not well executed; the chastity and colouring which painters call keeping, is too frequently sacrificed to a gaudy glare of tints, calculated only *"ad captandum vulgus"*; and it would puzzle Linnaeus himself to gloss some of the trees – so much does the foliage resemble mushrooms and ram's horns.[54]

"Q" of *Bonnor & Middleton's Bristol Journal*, on the contrary, resented any criticism (it was hinted by the ill-disposed that he was a close friend of one of the company), and the pair fell into a wordy inter-critical dispute, fruitless in itself, but including a mass of valuable description of productions during the first half of 1800.

It is clear from such notices that the costumes, scenery and effects played no small part in making even the most "legitimate" dramas attractive. French was frequently praised for his romantic and "Gothic" scenes; in *Speed the Plough* "the burning castle forms a beautiful coup d'oeil, which will never fail in attracting a peal of applause." Just how naturalistic it originally was, however, the reader begins to wonder on finding a week later that

We were pleased to see so great an improvement made in the burning castle – the addition of smoke and flames renders it more natural and interesting.[55]

Audiences demanded verisimilitude as well as spectacle; the inevitable occasional lapses were commented on unfavourably. Sometimes it was more than a mere lapse: in *Raymond and Agnes* the scenery and machinery were "so wretchedly conducted, that were it not for the able manner in which the respective performers carried off the piece, to stifle the hisses and groans of the audience, it might, perhaps, have incurred high displeasure."[56]

Lighting, too, was expected to be realistic; in the "burning castle" scene mentioned above, Thespis recommended :

The person who attends the lamps, should sink them lower, and keep them under the stage, during the fire-scene, as the effect would be much heightened by a dark fore-ground.

The candle-snuffer, however, with a proper professional contempt for newspaper critics, so far from taking the hint about the footlights at the next representation, "did not chuse to sink them at all."[57] Most of these and other similar complaints clearly arose from the pressure under which the stage staff worked as a result of the continual introduction of novelties, and do not essentially detract from the impression of a high standard of decor.

There is no indication that the management saw below the surface of the apparent prosperity which the visits of the stars and the wartime inflation of audiences brought with them. After Keasberry retired in 1795, Charles Charlton, who had joined the company as a character actor in 1791, was promptly appointed assistant manager to Dimond, thus ensuring the succession; Palmer still maintained his oversight of administration, and both he and Dimond bought shares in the Bristol Theatre.

The confidence which the Proprietors still maintained in the managers was amply demonstrated when the lease came up for renewal in 1799. Tucked into the Proprietors' Minute Book is a loose sheet representing the first draft of the Minutes of the Annual General Meeting on 1 August 1799, which gives a good deal of information not included in the official record. It notes, for example, receipt of an anonymous letter "requesting to know if the Meeting was an open meeting that he had a liberal proposal to make, but did not wish to interfere with the Intr or well doing of Mr. Dimond". (This almost certainly came from Elliston, whose biographer, Raymond, lays stress on Elliston's anxiety to obtain the management of one or other of the theatres in the circuit.) Then the meeting heard of a proposal from William M'Cready the elder, manager of the Birmingham Theatre, "offering £300 for the use of the House for 4 mos commencing in Jany Yearly for a term of 3, 5, 7, 9, or 14 Years". It is tempting to speculate what might have happened to the career of William Charles Macready if his father's offer had been accepted.

By an overwhelming majority, however, the Proprietors agreed to Dimond's proposals for a new Lease for a term of eighteen years at 250 guineas a year plus taxes, ground rents and insurance,

the said Lessees also undertaking to build at their own Expence a large Commodious Scene Room, and also to make the Enlargement and Alterations in the House by them proposed, agreeable to the Model now produced . . . in which Alterations and Improvements the said Lessees shall expend a Sum not less than One Thousand Pounds.

The appropriate lease was duly made out, though Richard Smith, who saw the document (which has now disappeared) says it was not executed until 16 February 1810 – proof in itself of the mutual trust of both parties.[58]

Of the plans for a "Commodious Scene Room" nothing more is heard, but the alterations were considerable, and gave us the auditorium substantially in its present form. The centre portion of the Upper Circle, hitherto the Gallery, was converted into Boxes, and an extra gallery tier was built above it, which of course necessitated raising the ceiling further.

The form was always admired by the best judges of that species of architecture – this form is still preserved, but the additional boxes all round the front, and the altitude given to the ceiling, which was entirely new and considerably raised, has so greatly improved the general appearance, that it has all the effect of the London Theatres without the inconvenience of their too great magnitude. The decorations and ornaments are in the best style of elegant simplicity – the house is a stone colour, and the pannels a tender green, with gold mouldings and cornices; the columns that support the two rows of boxes are cabled with stone-colour and gold alternately, and have a light and beautiful effect.

The raising of the ceiling was said to have "wonderfully improved the sound of the music and voices, which may be clearly and distinctly heard to the back of the gallery".[59]

Several times during the previous four years the lighting of both stage and auditorium had been improved,[60] and on this occasion new lustres were introduced to light the lower Boxes while the former ones were removed to the upper tier.

Two advantages in particular accrued to the Managers : primarily, of course, the change resulted in a great increase in the seating and money capacity of the house, which according to figures given by Richard Jenkins in 1826 now held a potential maximum of £229 15s. (750 people in the boxes, 320 in the pit and 550 in the new gallery). The re-siting of the Gallery also separated its inhabitants from the rest of the theatre, to the relief of the more respectable tradesmen and minor professional men who traditionally frequented the Upper Boxes. That the galleryites did not take too kindly to their enforced exile is suggested by a note to an advertisement less than two months after the alterations :

Complaints having been made to the Manager, by the Frequenters of the GALLERY, that from the Seats not being sufficiently *elevated,* their Sight of the Front of the Stage was much impeded, – as it is his most earnest Desire that *every Part* of the Theatre should be rendered as complete and commodious as possible, The Public are respectfully acquainted, that he has at a considerable *additional* Expence, had the Whole of the Gallery altered, which he presumes to hope will now meet with Approbation.[61]

So the new century opened with a newly improved and popular play-house, and an established company. The security which the managers still felt is attested by the setting up of a Benevolent Fund for the Bath and Bristol Companies, the first Bristol Benefit for which was given in June 1801. But that very summer the concern received a considerable blow by Dimond's retirement from the stage (though he retained a share in the general management). His last appearance on the stage was in Bristol on 1 July 1801 when, for the Benefit of Charles Taylor, singer and comedian, and Smith, the Treasurer, he played a favourite role: Edgar in *King Lear* (in, of course, Nahum Tate's version). Perhaps symbolically, the actor playing King Lear, attempting the part for the first time, was Elliston.

Three

1801-1817

For some years after Dimond's retirement from acting the company contined with apparent success. It was, however, running largely on its old momentum, and on the prestige of a single actor, Elliston. With Murray's departure and Dimond's retirement, there was no one but he competent to essay leading roles, and Elliston's name was consequently at the head of the bill virtually every night, whether the play were *King Lear* or *Speed the Plough*. Add to this his concurrent engagements in London and Windsor, and it is not surprising that his energy and versatility were the amazement of all theatre-goers.

But Elliston was not a manager and had no direct stake in the circuit's fortunes, much as he would have liked to have one. Charlton, the acting manager, was a very creditable supporting actor with an engaging manner in his addresses to the public, but he never became a personality to be reckoned with. The power – and everyone knew it – lay with Dimond and Palmer in Bath, where they had a new and bigger theatre built for them in Beaufort Square in 1805; Bristol, sensitive generally about its prestige, began to be aware that it was very much second fiddle in the theatrical duo, and to resent the fact.

In the earlier years of the century the presence of large numbers of troops still helped to swell audiences and mask any appearance of decline in popularity. In particular, military patronage continued to be important at Benefits; Lovegrove changed his date from Monday, 8 July 1805, to the following day, "in consequence of the Absence of the Military, who were ordered to Bath Yesterday". Patriotic pieces and ebullitions of patriotism continued to mark the programmes; Robert Dyer, a spectator at Edmund Kean's second night in Bristol on 11 July 1815, recounts how on the arrival of the news of the surrender of the French capital, the audience shouted for the orchestra to play "The Downfall of Paris" and refused to let the afterpiece proceed till they had satisfaction.[62]

Politics were mixed with patriotism. At a performance of *Measure for Measure* in April 1813 (the period of the "Delicate Investigation" into the conduct of Princess Caroline),

When *Lucio* complained of the harshness of his sentence, being no less than "whipping and hanging", the Duke rejoins –
"Sland'ring a *Prince* deserves it":
the audience seconded the assertion by a peal of applause; upon the cessation of which some person from the gallery exclaimed – "More so a *Princess*!" which drew forth a volley of approbation, three times repeated.[63]

Such episodes indicate that the separation of the Gallery from the Upper Boxes tempered, rather than abolished, the more violent forms of horse-play among its inhabitants. Spectators were still quite ready to demonstrate their opinions of plays and performers, hissing a minor actor prematurely promoted to a part too much for his singing abilities, insisting on the reinstatement of the Witches' Dance in *Macbeth*, and making a noisy holiday of the appearance on 16 December 1816 of the notorious "Romeo" Coates, who delivered "An Address to Britannia upon her Nelson's fall", wearing "his ROMEO's DRESS and JEWELS". The address was almost drowned by ironic cries of "Bravo!" and counter-cries of "Silence!"

The skirt of his coat, or by what ever name you call it, was (*accidentally on purpose*) pushed under the waistband of the small-clothes – and at the words (or some such) of "nature cast away", the Amateur of Fashion suddenly laid hold of it, disentangled it with such a jerk, and *cast it away* so gracefully, and so pathetically, that the whole House was electrified.[64]

Disregarded cries of "encore" at the close led to a quarter of an hour's uproar, drowning the orchestra, and when the curtain rose on the play the spectators pelted the actors with nuts, apples and oranges till they fled the stage. With difficulty Charlton appeased an audience whose high spirits had verged on riot.

The Box audience was quite as much to blame as the Gallery in this rowdy episode, and the complaints about their casual social manners, and their fashionable chatter which drowned the performance, continue. Even more unhelpful to the reputation of the theatre was the growing number of prostitutes patronising the theatre, a clientele which became in some provincial theatres quite influential in this period.[65] "Between the acts, the lobby is a perfect Bagnio", thundered a contributor to the *Bristol Mirror*.[66] In the Upper Boxes, where the "Cyprians" chiefly gathered, their behaviour much upset more respectable ladies, who found themselves driven into the side boxes.

It is easy to overestimate the importance of these complaints: it is noticeable that they originate almost entirely in two papers, the *Bristol Mirror* and the *Bristol Mercury*. The theatre continued to receive the patronage of senior army officers from the militia regiments, once of two members of Blucher's staff, and occasionally of members of the Royal Family. The Duke of Cumberland, following a review of the military units under his command, attended on 14 October 1803. In 1807 there were strong rumours that the Prince Regent would visit the Bristol theatre following a municipal dinner given in his honour.

Mr. Dimond gave an extra play in honor of his Royal Highness and by way of a *hit*, we presume, fixed upon the Heir at Law, and Catch him who can. His Royal Highness, however, was not to be caught,[67]

and instead set off straight away for Berkeley Castle. His brother-in-law, the Duke of Gloucester, was more amenable. After the customary military review in October 1808 he dined with Richard Hart Davis, the local M.P.,

and in the evening visited the Theatre, accompanied by his liberal and munificent host and his party. He was ushered into the stage-box on the King's side, which was canopied with scarlet and ornamented with lustres, by Mr. Dimond, dressed in full court dress, and bearing a pair of candlesticks before the Duke, the audience standing and the performers singing God Save the King.[68]

We should be equally cautious in evaluating the expressions of dissatisfaction with the acting standards which are noticeable in this period. Winston in the *Theatric Tourist* wrote that "the present company" (presumably that of 1804-5, the date of publication) "in point of merit, is far inferior to what has been repeatedly witnessed", and in Bristol itself a correspondent of the *Mirror* wrote in July 1804:

I understand some new performers, possessed of merit, are to be engaged for the ensuing season; and I believe the public think it is highly necessary.

Criticism was more particularly aimed at the minor characters. Rhadamanthus wrote acidly:

If our Manager would take a hint, he might fix a label on the breast of some of our actors to this effect:—This is a Queen, this a Waiting-woman, this a Lord, this a Barber, &c. By this method he would prevent any mistakes, and save all the money.[69]

As early as 1802 George Frederick Cooke had cursed "a whiffling monkey-looking thing" (Tebay) who "shamefully mangled" Mordecai in

Love à la Mode, while Mrs. Jordan in 1811 wrote to the Duke of Clarence "The company is in general *bad*" – though perhaps these were no more than examples of the London stars' proverbial scorn for their provincial support.

That there was a falling-off of standards seems undeniable, but it was less a local phenomenon than a reflection of the lack of outstanding personalities in the theatre generally. This is attested by the fact that the recruitment of local performers to the London theatres continued – Miss Smith, Montague Talbot, William Abbott, Egerton, Chatterly, Harriet Cooke (better known as Mrs. Waylett) and the notorious Mrs. Charlotte Mardyn, who claimed to have made a conquest of the poet Byron. John Vandenhoff was leading tragedian for the 1813-4 season; he was unfortunate in having to make his debut while the polished Charles Mayne Young was "starring", which showed up a certain inflexibility of voice and expression, but he rapidly improved and his King Henry IV was described as "natural and dignified, with a discrimination of emphasis, and a knowledge of metrical propriety which bespoke the scholar".[70]

Vandenhoff was succeeded by no less able an actor than William Charles Macready, but the managers confined his performances almost exclusively to Bath. Although he joined the company at the end of December 1814 he played in Bristol only three nights in February; and, thanks to a contemporary newspaper boycott, it is only from Macready himself we know that he "was very warmly received in the characters of Orestes and Alexander in Bristol".[71] The following season he acted six more times in Bristol before being engaged at Covent Garden.

Increasingly during these years, however, star engagements began to dominate the calendar. The periods just before and just after the London patent theatres' season naturally offered most scope, but it soon became the accepted thing that London actors might take engagements in the provinces whenever not needed for a period in London. The dislocation caused by the burning down of Covent Garden in 1808 and Drury Lane in 1809 also contributed its share.

What *amateur* could have foreseen, only a few months since, that the Bristol boards could have been favoured with the presence of a Catalani, and the inimitable Jordan, in the very depths of the winter season in London? . . . Such, however, is the miracle wrought by the destruction of Drury-Lane.[72]

It was not long before the puffs at the beginning of the season were itemising, as of far more importance than the new acquisitions to the company, the forthcoming list of star engagements; which some were unkind enough to consider a realistic assessment.[73]

Even more than the declining standard of the stock company, however, the poverty of the repertoire attracted criticism. This was something to a large extent out of the managers' control; of all the main pieces brought out in the first fifteen years of the 19th Century, almost the only one to outlast its initial run was John Tobin's *The Honeymoon,* which had the additional local interest that the author had spent many years in Bristol and been educated at its Grammar School. Critical feeling was further exasperated by the understandable but unwise persistence of the management in puffing every novelty as if it were a masterpiece, and by the rarity of worthwhile revivals, as stock pieces, of the older plays. The neglect was not total : there were, for example, productions of Goldsmith's *The Good Natur'd Man* in January 1805 and May 1814, and of Shakespeare's *Twelfth Night* in 1806, both of which drew critical applause but failed to re-establish the plays in the repertory.

Attempts to reintroduce the comedies of Congreve, Wycherley and Vanbrugh were defeated by one of Bristol's recurrent attacks of moral prudery,[74] and a similar reaction met a production in October 1813 of Mrs. Hannah Cowley's 1786 comedy, *The School for Greybeards,* which drew only an £18 house – "thirty-seven persons only appearing, during the whole evening, in the lower boxes!"[75]

The real attractions of the period, following the trend of the previous decade, were the melodramas, the pantomimes and the spectacles; pieces which came almost to dominate the repertoire of the early 19th Century theatre as the basis of its popularity broadened. *Blue Beard, Cinderella, Aladdin* and *Mother Goose, The Castle Spectre* and *The Miller and his Men* had full-scale revivals till almost mid-century, and in some cases later.

Scenery and effects therefore gained even more in importance, and here again the trend was away from locally-based talent. After Thomas French died on 6 September 1803, his son continued for a year or so as scene-painter, but after 1805, the date of the opening of the new Bath Theatre Royal, his name appears only as collaborator with various London designers, and disappears altogether after 1806. The most regular contributor henceforth was John Henderson Grieve of Covent Garden, who designed and often painted the bulk of the new scenery brought forward in the next decade. Other designers occasionally mentioned are Marchbanks "from London", Lupino of the King's Theatre,[76] and William Capon, who had contributed so much to Kemble's historical productions.

There were times when the appeal to spectacle verged on the ridiculous. *Othello* was repeated in October 1801 to introduce "THE MAGNIFICENT STATE-BED lately purchased at Mr. BECKFORD's at *Fonthill,* allowed to be the most Superb in the Kingdom; with the Costly FURNITURE of

Crimson Velvet and Burnished Gold, belonging to the Room in which it stood" – which must have been a comfort to Desdemona. The bills for a revival of *Blue Beard* in 1812 announced :

In Act 1st, the Procession over the Mountains, preparatory to the Nuptials of ABOMELIQUE and FATIMA; in which he makes his entry mounted on a Stupendous ELEPHANT, Richly Caparisoned; the same originally used at the Theatre-Royal, Covent-Garden.

Genest, however, reveals that the original Elephant had in the meantime died, and it was his stuffed carcase that was lent to Bath and Bristol.

The "grand serious pantomime" of *Perouse* in 1810 drew particular praise for its scenery, which was painted by Grieve :

Those who have a taste for the picturesque and beautiful representations of wild romantic nature, in the frozen regions of the frigid zone, must be highly gratified with the sublime specimens here exhibited.*[77]

But the glories of *Mother Goose* only drew the mournful comment : "To see our best Tragedies and Comedies deserted, while all the world is running after a Goose, is lamentable !"[79]

The popularity of new genres of entertainment had also an effect on the composition of the company. The conventional figures of pantomime, Harlequin, Columbine, Pantaloon and more recently Clown, had always been represented by members of the regular company, and now these specialities became ever more skilled and more important (and so more highly paid). They were still primarily mime and movement roles, the spoken opening scenes being but brief, and the distinctions between panto-mime, acrobatics and theatrical dancing were still very vague indeed. To make the most of these performers, there was a greater use of short narra-tive or character dances between main piece and afterpiece.

Our Manager, I think, does well in introducing short *ballets* between the Play and Farce: it agreeably fills up a space, which is otherwise too often rendered unpleasant by the discords of *the Gods.*[80]

Ballet was certainly not yet an art in its own right in provincial theatres, but it was taking the first steps towards becoming one. The Giroux family of Bath, who had very well-established Dancing Academies in both Bath and Bristol, kept a close connection with the theatre from 1802 to 1824,

---

* To represent these frozen regions, we learn from a report of William Edkins (son of Michael), almost all the old Box Booking Plans of the theatre were torn up and pulped for *papier mâché*, only a couple of books being saved by Edkins' intervention.[78]

and so did Benjamin Webster, father of Ben Webster of the Haymarket and of the English ballerina Clara Webster. These resources also enabled reasonable backing to be given to stars of the dance, such as Vestris and Mme. Didelot in November 1812.

Critics of the current repertoire were usually ready to concede that its deficiencies were the fault as much of popular pressures as of poor managerial taste. After the sudden death of William Wyatt Dimond at the beginning of 1812, however, the managers' own standards were by no means the same, for Dimond's successor, his son William, was a successful writer of melodramas and his tastes rose little above his own productions. Moreover, he spent most of his time in London, and his main consideration was simply what would pay. This is perhaps all that can excuse the introduction of performing dogs (managed by Elliston) and troupes of horses in the equestrian spectacles of *Lodoiska* and *Timour the Tartar*. As in London, the purists lamented, while the populace flocked to applaud.

Other factors also affected the choice of play. Some at least of the swing away from classical productions by the stock company was undoubtedly due to the prominence these held in the repertoire of the stars. Charles Mayne Young, Master Betty, George Frederick Cooke, John, Stephen and Charles Kemble, Mrs. Siddons, and, towards the end of the period, Conway and Edmund Kean, were regular visitors, and all included a high proportion of plays by Shakespeare, Rowe and Otway. There could be only a limited audience for such dramas, and it was likely to be pre-empted by the stars' performances.

Another effect of these visits was to reduce the opportunities of the leading stock company actors to develop in classical parts, then as now the touchstone for all serious and many comedy actors. Strict adherence to an agreed cast of parts prevented the displaced provincial from taking over a secondary role; thus not only was he deprived of his opportunity but the supporting cast was less good than it might have been. Nor of course under the conditions of the time was there any possibility of that interplay of dramatic effect possible between actors who know each others' performances and capabilities, which had, for example, distinguished the Jaffier and Pierre of Dimond and Murray.

So strongly did Miss Marriott, leading actress from 1805 to 1810, feel on this topic that she resigned from the company and advertised on the occasion of her farewell Benefit:

Having had so few opportunities of appearing before them [i.e. the public], from the constant succession of Auxiliaries, she has little claim to their attention, yet still trusts a liberal Bristol audience will not abandon the interests of one who has been honoured by their approbation; and had occasion offered, would have exerted her utmost abilities to have contributed to their amusement.[81]

Her frustrations were real enough. Miss Smith had returned as a star in most of Miss Marriott's best roles for the whole of October, and thereafter the engagements of Elliston, Bannister, Mrs. Dickons and Braham had concentrated attention on comedy and ballad-opera. Miss Marriott was no doubt recompensed by being engaged at Covent Garden in September 1812, but at least she was consistent enough not to reappear at Bath or Bristol as a star.

Against all this, it must be admitted that it is doubtful whether *The Man of the World, Coriolanus* or *King John,* for example, would have been seen at all at this period had it not been for Cooke, Younge and J. P. Kemble (Master Betty's revivals of *Mahomet, Barbarossa* and similar fustian could perhaps have been spared). Again, it was through star engagements that *opera seria* first came to be staged in Bristol. While British-born and trained singers confined themselves almost entirely to ballad-opera, Catalani in February 1809 produced *Semiramide* and *Il Fanatico per la Musica* in Italian – and charged 10s. 6d. for the Boxes, 7s. for the Pit and 4s. for the Gallery. (A skilled workman's wage was still little more than £1 a week.) On her first night "the boxes and gallery were nearly full, but in the language of the house, the *pit was shy";* on her second night (*La Didone* and *Il Furbo contra Il Furbo*) the house was full.[82]

We should not underestimate what it meant to drama and music lovers to be able to hear the foremost performers in the country, nor was their reception always one of uncritical adulation. An extremely perceptive essay on the stage presentation of *King Henry IV i* in *Felix Farley's Bristol Journal* of 22 January 1803 was acid about Stephen Kemble's Falstaff :

> Laying aside his bulk, this man has not a single ability to represent *Falstaff,* with a smooth unmeaning lady-face, an eye of no penetration, a tone of voice without humour or vivacity, and action without energy or spirit.

Mrs. Jordan's pretensions, at the age of 54 and with fourteen children to her credit, to play teen-age romps and naive young Misses, were also assessed with a realistic eye :

> To see a woman of her age, and (heaven save the mark!) figure and appearance, hopping and trotting about the stage (for it is not walking) on a pair of stilts, in the shape of shoes, to see her flirting a fan, and to hear her simpering out a *nimine-pimine* DOUBLE ENTENDRE, in a tone of voice which grates upon the ear like the turning of a rusty hinge, are perfectly ridiculous.[83]

Grimaldi, though greatly followed, was thought not so much better than the stock company Clown, Gomery. Even Master Betty had a decidedly mixed reception, though during his first two visits in April and December 1806 enthusiasm predominated. Less to the credit of Bristol audiences, they stayed away from the performances of William Dowton in January 1816 – clever actor though he was, he never appealed to Bristolians, who liked their comedians of broader style.

Charles Mayne Young, on the other hand, became very warmly esteemed; and as he almost invariably came early in the season, Bristol saw much more of him than Bath. Bristol also had a partiality for Junius Brutus Booth, and he had serious support locally in his rivalry with Kean. There is abundant evidence of the popularity of many other stars. Robert Dyer, attending Kean's first performances in Bristol, "went with a party, and paid box admission, but box places could not be obtained – we tried the pit, and were equally unsuccessful – and only by determination we at last obtained seats in the gallery, at box prices."[84] When Incledon played Don Carlos in *The Duenna* in March 1805, nearly fifty pounds was turned away from the box office. In 1809 the Bristol populace almost mobbed Mrs. Jordan; she reported to the Duke of Clarence : "The Town of Bristol was in an uproar last night, there never was such a concourse of people collected together on any occasion." During her 1811 engagement she grossed £800 from Bath and Bristol, though her later visits were much less successful.[85] Grimaldi realised £287 from his first engagement in November/December 1814 and £294 from his return visit in 1815.[86]

Of all these actors, valuable detailed criticisms remain : the first fifteen years of the 19th Century represent one of the best periods of local theatrical journalism, for the reviews are perceptive, well-argued, and full of minute descriptions of business and interpretation of lines.[87] Nevertheless, despite the amount of critical attention, there is a perceptible hardening of editorial attitude towards the theatre after 1810, and it seems probable that at least as regards the Box public this reflects a hardening in public attitude; for otherwise the press would hardly have sustained the virtual boycott of the theatre conducted by some of them over considerable periods, a boycott only lifted to print some denigratory letter or anecdote, or alternatively a too obviously prepaid puff, which was in its way nearly as damaging.[88]

Probably the most foolish action of the managers, in retrospect, was their joint action with the Proprietors to close the Regency Theatre, as the Assembly Rooms in Prince's Street became known after being adapted for dramatic use in 1811 by the owner, Walter Jenkins. In August 1812 Lawler from the Surrey Theatre, and later Clarke from Exeter, ran it as a burletta theatre throughout the rest of the year, specifically avoiding as far as possible nights on which the Theatre Royal was open. Despite this, Charlton complained to the Proprietors "that the Performances at the Regency Theatre are extremely injurious to their [the managers'] Interests (consequently eventually to those of the Proprietors) and in their opinion were acting Contrary to Law as well as in defiance of the Patent." One Robert Jeffery, who was "well acquainted with the persons of some of the performers at that Theatre", was persuaded to turn informer on the occasion of the Benefit of John Betterton, junior, brother of Julia Betterton (now Mrs. Glover).

The evidence went to prove that the informer paid his pit admission money and saw Mr. Betterton in the character of *Timour the Tartar*. Upon this fact being proved, he was sentenced to *seven days imprisonment*.[89]

The performances still continuing, it was proposed to lay an information against the Manager himself, pressing for the maximum penalty of £50, but this proved unnecessary, as Clarke had had enough and retired from the field.

This action aroused all the Englishman's proverbial sympathy for the "little man" crushed by the "establishment", and the feeling was intense and long-lasting. The Proprietors were indeed beginning to approach their responsibilities rather differently from the past. Their business organisation had sometimes bordered on the haphazard, typified by the fact that, though the Treasurer, George Daubeny the elder, died in 1806, a successor (his son, also George) was not elected till May 1810. Nevertheless the early Proprietors had in most cases been men who actively wanted a theatre, and, having helped to create one, were wise enough to co-operate with their chosen managers and not to harry them. By 1815, however, almost every share had changed hands, some many times; the majority of shareholders had no particular interest in the theatre, merely in drawing dividends, and the dominating outlook was a strictly commercial one.

This was not without its good effects; a good deal was attempted and something done in the way of regularising the tenure of various parts of the site; the King Street house through which the main entrances were made was acquired on a 75-year lease and made available as a residence for the manager, and an additional freehold house in the Rackhay was bought for £230 in 1815. Moreover, a serious endeavour to keep check on the ownership of shares was made and after 1815 maintained regularly.

Since the reconstruction of 1800 little had been done for the theatre building, the lessees' attention having been concentrated on their new theatre in Bath. The most important development – it was quite possibly carried out in 1800 but the first reference is in 1803 – was the substitution of Argand (oil) lamps for candles in at least part of the stage lighting. When an early type of gas lighting was demonstrated in Bristol 1805 Thespis pointed out the possible saving to the theatre managers. He listed their current lighting equipment as 36 spermaceti candles in the "first range of chandeliers", 40 in the second; "there are also 7 mutton lights in the orchestra; and the Argand's [sic] lamps, in front of the stage, amount to 41".[91] The Managers were not enticed into experiment.

In the autumn of 1807 the theatre was redecorated, the panels of the Boxes being painted French green "with a simple, uniform white ornament relieved . . . the styles are salmon and stone colour, with gilt cornices".[92] On several occasions the house was reported cleaned and its paintwork touched up,[93] but no structural alterations were made.

The lease to the Bath managers was due to expire on 25 March 1817 and the preceding November the Proprietors approached Palmer, the surviving lessee, through Charlton. They offered a renewal of the lease for 21 years at the same rent,

Lessee to erect and compleatly fit up a new Stage and thoroughly repair and paint all other parts of the Theatre premises both inside and outside at his own expense.
To make all the additions alterations Improvements and decorations, both interior and exterior, of the body of the Theatre which are set out in the Plans prepared by Mr. Pinch, architect, Bath under Mr. Palmer's direction . . .
No alterations to be made in the price of admission to the Boxes Pit and Gallery excepting to the Lower or Dress Boxes and Private Boxes to which 5/- per ticket or Sitting and no more may be taken.[94]

Palmer for his part wanted additional permission to raise seat prices for star visits, but surprisingly the crucial difficulty arose over his wish to make more structural improvements than the Proprietors felt necessary – all they stipulated for, apparently, was to have separate entrances made to the Upper and Lower Boxes. Finally the Bath managers decided against seeking a renewal of their lease and Palmer called on Daubeny to tell him so. They were then infuriated by a rumour that the Proprietors intended to take advantage of the fact that to complete the 1816-7 season meant playing after the expiry of the lease, to insist on the lessees paying a full year's rent. Palmer thereupon wrote to the Committee :

I have now only to observe that if it be possible for such an advantage even to be attempted to be taken, we shall not only resist it to the utmost, but neither now or at any further Period, on any consideration enter into any agreement for the use of that property.

In the face of this indignant protest, the Proprietors decided to make no attempt to coerce Palmer; to accept possession of the theatre on 29 September, and to undertake the new entrance themselves according to plans submitted by Mr. Henwood.[95]

The news soon leaked out: the *Bristol Mirror* of 18 May 1817 reported, "The Bristol Theatre, we understand, has turned but a losing concern, and is to be sold to the highest bidder." In a later number, Malvolio attacked the Bath managers, claiming that they had exaggerated their losses in dealing with the Proprietors, and warning them that the splitting up of the circuit would lead to financial disaster, since Bath could not support a respectable Company on its own. The virulent attack on Dimond and Charlton contained in this letter was strongly resented by Benvolio in the *Bristol Mercury,* and his arguments echo Palmer's letter to the Proprietors so closely as to arouse a strong suspicion that either Charlton or he wrote it.

The whole affair left an unpleasant taste in the mouth at the time, and still does. It seems certain that the Proprietors behaved, if not with actual duplicity, at best according to the same sort of legal but inequitable sharp practice they had shown over the suppression of the Regency Theatre. On the other hand, the Bath management was certainly not of its former calibre; indeed, with the death of William Wyatt Dimond the heart seems to have gone out of the concern. Once the end of the Napoleonic Wars brought about the demobilisation of troops, the inadequacy of the true local following for the theatre was revealed; only the stimulus of a major star would bring a good audience. Bristol, too, increasingly felt it no longer had a real stake in its stock company, and the long-established ambivalence of its attitude towards Bath, the city of *ton* and culture, as opposed to Bristol, the city of practical tradesmen, certainly increased the bad feeling.

The Proprietors inserted an advertisement in the local press towards the end of June, offering to "treat with any Persons who may be disposed to take a LEASE" of the Theatre Royal. The irrepressible Elliston offered "to undertake the management of the Theatre for one Year and to divide any profits with the Proprietors,"[96] a suggestion unsympathetically received. Instead the Committee of Proprietors entered into negotiations with John Boles Watson, owner of the Cheltenham and Gloucester Theatres, for a lease at a considerably increased rent (400 guineas a year plus parish, parliamentary and land taxes), Watson with apparent enthusiasm putting forward amended plans for the alterations and improvements within the overall limit of £500. On 26 July the Agreement to Lease was signed.

NOTES

[1] That this was the Exeter Theatre company is supported by the fact that for the first time in many years Exeter had no winter theatrical season in 1778-9. I owe the identification of the company to information supplied by Mrs. M. Toms.

[2] Wm. Douglas Ms. in Johannesburg Library, Winston Mss. at Harvard.

[3] *Felix Farley's Bristol Journal*, 20.3.1779.

[4] *Bristol Gazette*, 15.4.1779, &c.

[5] J. Latimer: *Annals of Bristol in the Eighteenth Century*, Bristol, 1893, p. 439.

[6] *Reminiscences of Sarah Kemble Siddons*, Harvard, 1942.

[7] See *Bristol Gazette*, 7.10.1779; *Bath Journal*, 11.101779; and *The Theatric Tourist*, London, 1805, section on Bath.

[8] *Felix Farley's Bristol Journal*, 26.4.1788.

[9] *Bath Journal*, 21.1.1782.

[10] *ibid.*, 5.4.1779.

[11] *Felix Farley's Bristol Journal*, 20.10.1781.

[12] Advertisement in *Felix Farley's Bristol Journal*, 6.7.1782.

[13] J. Genest: *Some Account of the English Stage*, Bath, 1832, Vol. VI, pp. 233ff.

[14] Advertisement in *Felix Farley's Bristol Journal*, 10.1.1784.

[15] Browne was one of the many British refugees from America consequent upon the War of Independence, a fact which was well blazoned on Benefit occasions to encourage sympathetic support – see *Felix Farley's Bristol Journal*, 21.7.1781.

[16] *Bonnor & Middleton's Bristol Journal*, 22.7.1786.

[17] *Felix Farley's Bristol Journal*, 1.4.1786. There is no suggestion in Bristol, however, of the hyper-emotional reaction which greeted *Werter* in Bath. See *The Life and Times of Frederick Reynolds, Written by Himself*, London, 1826, Vol. II, p. 306.

[18] *Felix Farley's Bristol Journal*, 7.11.1789. Most biographies of Hannah More give some account of Ann Yearsley. See particularly W. Roberts: *Memoirs of the Life and Correspondence of Hannah More*, London, 1834.

[19] *Bristol Gazette*, 30.11.1780.

[20] *Sarah Farley's Bristol Journal*, 29.1.1785.

[21] *Felix Farley's Bristol Journal*, 14.4.1787.

[22] *ibid.*, 15.7.1786.

[23] *ibid.*, 26.10.1782.

[24] *ibid.*, 7.2.1784.

[25] *Bath Chronicle*, 9.10.1783.

[26] *Bath Journal*, 21.1.1782.

[27] *Felix Farley's Bristol Journal*, 6.11.1779.

[28] *Sarah Farley's Bristol Journal*, 9.8.1794, quoting an article in the *York Herald*.

[29] *Bonnor & Middleton's Bristol Journal*, 30.3.1782.

[30] *ibid.*, 17.5.1783.

[31] See, e.g., *Bristol Gazette*, 24.2.1780; *Sarah Farley's Bristol Journal*, 17.2.1785; *Felix Farley's Bristol Journal*, 7.1.1786.

[32] *Felix Farley's Bristol Journal*, 15.7.1786.

[33] *ibid.*, 2.10.1790.

[34] *Sarah Farley's Bristol Journal*, 8.10.1791.

[35] *Felix Farley's Bristol Journal*, 23.4.1791.

[36] *ibid.*, 12.7.1800.

[37] *Sarah Farley's Bristol Journal*, 28.9.1793.

[38] A most interesting series of articles, comparing Dimond and Elliston, was published in *Felix Farley's Bristol Journal*, 28.6, 5., 12., 19. and 26.7.1800.

[39] *Felix Farley's Bristol Journal*. 26.9.1795.

[40] J. C. Young, in his *Memoir of Charles Mayne Young* (London/New York, 1871, Vol. I, p. 30), says Miss Grimani took to the stage only after the death of her

father. This is incorrect. (See *Felix Farley's Bristol Journal*, 7.6.1800, and *Bonnor & Middleton's Bristol Journal*, 25.7.1801.)

[41] *Felix Farley's Bristol Journal.* 1.3.1800.
[42] *ibid.*, 14.10.1797.
[43] *ibid.*, 2.2.1799.
[44] *ibid.*, 11.4.1801.
[45] *Sarah Farley's Bristol Journal*, 2.4.1796.
[46] *Felix Farley's Bristol Journal*, 14.10.1797.
[47] *ibid.*, 8.12.1792.
[48] Playbill, 11.7.1798.
[49] *Bristol Gazette*, 26.11.1795.
[50] *Felix Farley's Bristol Journal*, 6.1.1798.
[51] Advertisement, *Felix Farley's Bristol Journal*, 14.2.1795.
[52] *Sarah Farley's Bristol Journal*, 11.5.1799.
[53] *Felix Farley's Bristol Journal*, 26.1.1799.
[54] *ibid.*, 8.2.1800.
[55] *ibid.*, 3.5.1800, and *Bonnor & Middleton's Bristol Journal*, 10.5.1800.
[56] *Bonnor & Middleton's Bristol Journal*, 26.4.1800; the extent of the chaos is amply confirmed by the account in *Felix Farley* of the same date.
[57] *Felix Farley's Bristol Journal*, 10. and 17.5.1800.
[58] Note in Richard Smith Collection; Smith says the lease was at the time of writing in the hands of James Harris.
[59] *Felix Farley's Bristol Journal*, 4.10.1800.
[60] See, e.g., *Felix Farley's Bristol Journal*, 1.10.1796 and 30.9.1797.
[61] *Felix Farley's* and *Bonnor & Middleton's Bristol Journals*, 29.11.1800.
[62] R. Dyer: *Nine Years of an Actor's Life*, London, 1833.
[63] *Bristol Gazette*, 29.4.1813.
[64] *Bristol Mirror*, 21.12.1816.
[65] Crisp is said to have had to close the Chester theatre because of lack of support after his efforts to exclude "women of the town". See *Bristol Mirror*, 6.1.1816.
[66] *Bristol Mirror*, 3.2.1816.
[67] *Mirror*, 10.10.1807.
[68] *Bristol Gazette*, 3.11.1808.
[69] *ibid.*, 10.1.1805.
[70] *ibid.*, 24.2.1812.
[71] W. C. Macready: *Reminiscences*, London, 1876, p. 70.
[72] *Felix Farley's Bristol Journal*, 8.4.1809.
[73] *Mirror*, 7.10.1809.
[74] *Bristol Mirror*, 6.2.1813.
[75] *ibid.*, 30.10.1813.
[76] Either Thomas Frederick Lupino or his son, Samuel George.
[77] *Felix Farley's Bristol Journal*, 3.11.1810.
[78] Note in Richard Smith Collection.
[79] *Mirror*, 31.10.1807.
[80] *Felix Farley's Bristol Journal*, 15.12.1804.
[81] Advertisement in *Felix Farley's Bristol Journal*, 16.6.1810.
[82] *Bristol Gazette*, 23.2. and 2.3.1809.
[83] *Bristol Mirror*, 15.1.1814.
[84] Dyer, *op. cit.*
[85] See Letters of 2.5.1809 and 14.2.1811 in Henry Huntington Library.
[86] C. Dickens: *Memoirs of Joseph Grimaldi* (ed. Findlater), London, 1968, pp. 217 and 224. Dickens mistakenly places Grimaldi's first visit in October/November 1812, instead of November/December 1814, to which engagement also the story of the practical joke played on Billy Coombes belongs.
[87] Notices particularly valuable for their detail include the following: Master Betty, *Felix Farley's Bristol Journal* and *Mirror*, 26.4.1806, *Bristol Gazette*,

1.5.1806; Francis Blissett, *Felix Farley's Bristol Journal*, 23.6.1804; Junius Brutus Booth, *Bristol Gazette*, 15.5.1817; G. F. Cooke, *Mirror*, 29.3. and 19.4.1806, *Bristol Gazette*, 24.2.1814; R. W. Elliston, *Felix Farley's Bristol Journal*, 25.11.1809, *Bristol Gazette*, 21.2.1811; Joseph Holman, *Bristol Gazette*, 22.11.1804; Edmund Kean, *Felix Farley's Bristol Journal*, 15.7.1815; John Philip Kemble, *Bristol Gazette*, 26.11. and 3.12.1812, *Felix Farley's Bristol Journal*, 5.12.1812, *Bristol Gazette*, 5.5.1814; Sarah Siddons, *Bristol Gazette*, 14. and 21.1.1808; Charles Mayne Young, *Mirror*, 24.10.1807, *Bristol Gazette*, 13.10.1808 and 14.10.1813.

[88] The *Bristol Mercury* maintained incessant attacks on the company throughout 1809, and both *Mercury* and *Mirror* continued to ventilate strong criticisms throughout the period. All papers except the *Bristol Gazette* almost completely ignored the theatre during 1815.

[89] Committee Minutes of 7.1.1813 and *Bristol Mercury*, 25.1.1813. For a fuller account, see K. M. D. Barker: The Assembly Rooms; *Bristol Evening Post*, 5.9.1956.

[90] See General Meeting Minutes of 2.8.1803, 13.7. and 19.10.1815, and Committee Minutes of 9.11. and 14.12.1815.

[91] *Mirror*, 16.2.1805.

[92] *Felix Farley's Bristol Journal*, 3.10.1807.

[93] See, e.g., *Bristol Gazette*, 2.10.1806 and 3.10.1811, and *Bristol Mirror*, 3.10.1816.

[94] Committee Minutes, 13.3.1817.

[95] *ibid.*, 29.4.1817.

[96] *ibid.*, 10.7.1817.

Part Three
The Supremacy of the Star

But it is yet problematical, whether in Bristol the Stage shall preserve its legitimate appropriation to the representation of the divine Shakespeare's works, and to the exercise of our first Actors' talents, – or whether it shall be converted into an arena for the display of Pugilistic Contests, and the low senseless mummeries, by which (falling into the hands of inexperienced and grasping adventurers) it must eventually be disgraced and polluted.

William M'Cready's *Prospectus,* 6.3.1819

The lessee must . . . have learned . . . that a regular company will not attract, and that the only plan to remedy this is to keep up a succession of stars.

Bristol Journal, 20.1.1849

One

1817-1819

John Boles Watson's brief period of management was a disastrous farce for all concerned. Looking back in 1820, the editor of *Felix Farley's Bristol Journal* recalled him as "a man, whom it would be a misnomer to call Manager. A man who disgusted us as much by his bad management as by his miserable attempts to conceal it".

It must be owned that Watson faced difficulties enough to daunt any lessee. The post-Napoleonic War depression cast an economic blight which had already affected the theatre's prosperity, and which in Bristol was unalleviated by new industrial growth. By 1817, too, the residential centre of Bristol had moved westwards towards Clifton, which was rapidly expanding; but the first permanent bridge over the River Frome to the old city area was nearly at St. John's Gate, though there was a drawbridge at Broad Quay. The environs of the Theatre Royal more and more took on the character of the docks at either end of King Street, and sailors and dockyard workers, rather than merchants and aldermen, walked the pavements. The great houses in Queen Square now mainly provided lodgings for city clerks. Then, too, there was still a strong party among theatregoers which regretted the break with Bath and went to the Bristol theatre, when they went at all, like Goldsmith's fine lady, with an intention to be displeased. It soon became apparent that neither Bristol nor Bath really had a large enough drama-loving public to support a separate theatre company.

The provincial theatre generally was facing internal upheavals as well as external disadvantages. The insidious effects of continual star engagements on the standard of the stock company and on its power to draw an audience have already been mentioned. These effects were magnified as, during the first forty years of the 19th Century, a growing number of non-patent theatres were established in London, producing their own stars and their own essentially popular entertainments in competition with more legitimate attractions, and increasing the restlessness of provincial actors with their eyes on metropolitan fame.

All these difficulties faced Boles Watson; he speedily provided other and crucial ones himself. One may disregard such unfortunate moments as the forty-three foot fall, in mid-performance, of the theatre's hairdresser, who was taking a short cut over the stage via one of the bridges. The audience remembered longer the fact that, while grandiloquently announcing substantial improvements in the theatre, Watson achieved only a partial cleaning and redecoration. His defenders made the best of these :

Instead of the old paltry imitations of railings and loopholes, the boxes are painted in neat square pannels of green upon pink. The old knocker-heads on the stage pedestals, which were meant to pass for the tragic and comic masks, have disappeared. The stage chandeliers are improved by handsome bell-glasses.

But even this writer had to admit

The scenery is incomplete; and the drop-scene, it may confidently be prophesied, will be disposed of to some booth in St. James's Fair.[1]

The less well-disposed pointed out that the "improved" chandeliers held only tallow candles, whose "intolerable stench" Richard Smith still remembered twenty-five years later.

Watson's company when he opened on 25 August was a respectable one, and he was initially lavish in his engagement of stars – Dowton, Maria Foote, and, triumphantly, Eliza O'Neil, to meet the cost of whose engagement the box price was raised by a shilling. Her Juliet, her Isabella, her Belvidera, were emotional experiences of a kind Bristol had almost forgotten :

She forgets the actress; the spectators disappear before her eyes; she sees nothing, remembers nothing, but the scenic situation in which she is placed; she is lost, self-abandoned, utterly devoted to the feelings of the moment; and her cries and sobs, uttered from overwhelming and uncontroulable [sic] emotion strike deep to the heart and maintain their mastery in the memory, when the cache of tears which they forcibly elicited has been dried away.[2]

Cozens, the box-book keeper, was well occupied reserving places in the Boxes; advertisements warned : "The exact number of Tickets must be taken at the time, which will be duly registered, to avoid mistake, at the office, purposely opened in the box entrance." He was given an extra Benefit for his exertions.

After a brief closure in November the house re-opened with a much-needed new drop-scene and some allegedly new scenery painted by Seyward, but without major stars; and within a matter of a month or two the whole concern was obviously on the point of collapse. Attendances dropped to a miserable level; there was a tell-tale turnover of stock actors and a suspicious degree of reliance upon the attraction of amateurs. The Bath actor, H. W. Grosette, was awarded a Benefit (for reasons which are not clear, since he was not a member of Watson's company), but when his friends arrived at the theatre they found it shut :

Their astonishment at the disappointment can only be equalled by his own, that the Theatre doors should have been closed at a moment's notice, because, for the FIRST time, it was discovered to be *Friday in Lent*! ! ![3]

As early as January 1818 the Proprietors, suspicious at Watson's failure to produce rent, suspended the preparation of the lease, and in March began to press for overdue payment. It was particularly aggravating, since the Proprietors had the chance of buying for £600 the two leasehold houses "adjoining the front Entrance to the Theatre on the Eastward side, one behind the other, the whole premises extending from King Street to the Court", but they had to lose their opportunity through lack of funds.

A brief return visit of Eliza O'Neil and William Conway enlivened the Easter period, but the theatre then shut till mid-May, when it was opened for a fortnight to display the talents of Mrs. Charles Kemble and "Jerry Sneak" Russell,* after which it was closed again, with little prospect of re-opening. The Proprietors' Minutes are filled with their fruitless endeavours to obtain the rent arrears, and Watson's various excuses. In May they decided to distrain on the theatre's contents and the house occupied by Watson, whereupon he sent them two notes of hand, encashable at Cheltenham. Penny, one of the Committee Members, made the journey and presented the notes, but "after repeated Interviews with Mr. Watson and his Sol^r and Messrs. Fisher and Ashmore, Bankers, Cheltenham, he co^d not succeed in obtaining payment of the Note for £100 payable on demand or any security or promise of Security for the Rent in arrear or any part of it". Watson was in fact on the verge of bankruptcy.

The distress was postponed to allow Stansbury, the leader of the band, to hold a concert for his Benefit with Braham as star, but 23 June was finally fixed on. At this, quite unabashed, Watson wrote in "stating his inability to pay any rent before Christmas but requesting indulgence until that time."[4] Unmoved, the Committee sought a magistrates' order to regain possession of the premises, and the distress went forward.

* So nicknamed after his impersonation of that character in Foote's farce, *The Mayor of Garratt*.

The resultant sale of effects was a flop. The Account Books show that the total income from the sale was £48 16s. 9d., of which auction and legal fees swallowed up £43 5s. 3d.; to save face the Proprietors themselves had to buy in scenery and decorations to the value of £250. "X.Y.", in the *Bristol Mercury* of 12 October, wickedly reported on the fate of the various lots :

Imprimis. – Nine chandeliers, with sundry ends of tallow-candle.
  Bought for a Chapel in reversion . . .
One Looking-Glass. Bought in by a Proprietor, who has, since looking into it, been heard to complain of the unpleasantness of the reflection . . .

The continued closure of the theatre called forth a good deal of adverse comment on the policy of the Proprietors. While Liverpool and Manchester were setting up a Theatrical Fund, "Bristol has not even a Theatre, and the meritorious servants of the drama are actually starving in our streets".[5] The Proprietors were accused of misusing the monopoly granted by their Patent – the closure of the Regency Theatre was not forgotten – and of putting profits before the requirements of "propriety and the accommodation of their Fellow-Citizens".[6] There was debate not only on the question of management, but also about the actual site of the theatre in view of the deterioration of the King Street area.

Watson continuing to prevaricate, Daubeny "opened a Negociation with the Bath Managers, upon his private Interference", but not surprisingly was snubbed. Apart from a two-nights' let to Charles Mathews, producing £35, the theatre remained closed all winter, and at the end of December 1818 the Proprietors advertised for a fresh lessee – or, as "X.Y." put it, "desperate adventurer".

Two

1819–1829

Remarkably, no fewer than four "desperate adventurers" put forward their names to the Proprietors: the unquenchable Grosette and three experienced provincial managers, Henry Lee from Taunton, Robert Hoy from Worcester and William M'Cready (Plate 9), who was nearing his 64th birthday and currently extricating himself from his latest bankruptcy at the Theatre Royal Whitehaven. M'Cready was the first to make specific proposals: a year's lease at £300, to be paid off at the rate of £20 a week; and these were accepted.

The funds to supply M'Cready's removal to Bristol were raised by some of his late wife's relations and by his son, William Charles Macready, now rapidly rising as leading actor at Covent Garden. The announcement of three Covent Garden stars – young Macready, Daniel Terry and Mrs. Yates – for the opening performances of *Othello, The Gamester* and *Hamlet* almost justified the terms of M'Cready's Prospectus, though, as will be seen, M'Cready was equally ready to engage almost any "low senseless mummeries" which would bring money at the door, and even organised the "display of Pugilistic Contests" in Egan's *Tom and Jerry,* during one of which the Bristol champion, Neat, nearly knocked his opponent into the orchestra.

The success of the opening was slightly marred by misadventure *en route.*

The vessel, in which were embarked the Wardrobe and several Performers, was unfortunately encountered by a severe gale of wind, and obliged to put into a port on the Western Coast.[7]

But the Proprietors had at least had the theatre cleaned and the passages whitewashed, and there was a surprising amount of goodwill yet in the city towards a manager who could justify the promise of "restoring to the Theatre its early respectability by rendering it *worthy* the attention and encouragement of a great and commercial city."[8]

M'Cready was hardly helped in his meritorious aim by the behaviour of some of his company during his "season of experiment" from April to July 1819. The leading singer, Huckel, took part in a performance of *Love in a Village* when clearly drunk, and failed to arrive at a Music Festival a few days later, so that his next appearance at the Theatre was greeted with "expressions of disapprobation . . . from all parts of the house". Immediately after this, Junius Brutus Booth, on a starring engagement, involved himself with the wife of a visiting rope-dancer, Il Diavolo Antonio; wounded the latter in a Sunday evening duel; and cut the manager's own Benefit the following Tuesday, necessitating a mollifying speech from M'Cready and subsequent personal apologies.[9] [See Plate 10.] It says something for M'Cready that neither event was taken to reflect upon him as manager.

One of the biggest problems facing M'Cready when his initial season ended was that of the pattern of performances in the future. The factors which had influenced the Bath management no longer obtained. The most vital difference, of course, was the fact that M'Cready's potential audience was confined to Bristol, and it was not yet clear, so confused had Watson's season been, just what size that audience was. By trial and error M'Cready found the most satisfactory compromise to be four nights a week (Wednesday or Thursday being the most usual midweek evening closure), though the run of an attractive novelty, or the demands of a star paid by the night, often extended it to five. Exceptionally, for example at the time of the September Fair, the company might play six nights a week, but it was late in the 19th Century before Saturday became an established play night in Bristol.

Once the Fairtime crowds had dispersed, and with no Bath season to take up the slack, it was nearly Christmas before Bristolians were ready to think of theatre-going in economic numbers. The Bristol Hotwells had declined almost to extinction by 1819, so there was no longer a fashionable summer audience seeking amusement; seaside watering-places, however, were growing in popularity. Hence the pattern which M'Cready adopted, with minor variations, was to open about Christmas for a continuous season till the end of May or early June; to take his company to one of the South Wales resorts for the summer holiday months and return to Bristol for the period of the St. James's Fair. The Company then resumed its touring, in early years to M'Cready's old base at Whitehaven. Later, however, M'Cready kept his South Wales company going continuously through the summer and autumn, Bristol being supplied for the Fair with a company consisting of a nucleus of "old hands" and a larger number of special engagements.

Some idea of the economic basis on which M'Cready was working may be gained from the repeated assertion that, if he could be assured of one "fashionable night" a week (preferably Monday, the traditional play-going evening in Bristol), he could scrape along with any kind of a house for the rest of the week. But with the growth of social activities in Bristol and Clifton, and the virtual disappearance of patronage in the 18th Century sense, even one good house was not always to be obtained. It was almost five years before M'Cready re-established any settled degree of prosperity, and several times in the early years he was perilously behind with his rent. No one, however, could complain that he lacked enthusiasm or energy : very soon he was dubbed "the indefatigable Mr. M'Cready" by the press and the sobriquet was well deserved. Star of any and every kind followed star; Scott adaptations, 18th Century comedies, sensational melodramas, Shakespearean revivals, pantomimes and equestrian pieces succeeded each other. It is hardly surprising to read recurrent complaints of the need for the prompter's services.

So far from boycotting the theatre, the press almost overwhelmed M'Cready with attention, and with good advice and adjurations. They gave extensive coverage to all his productions (there was even a short-lived weekly, *The Thespian*, devoted exclusively to the drama) and some of their notices are genuinely evocative. Daniel Terry's Iago, said the *Bristol Mercury*, "was particularly successful in the pliable hypocrisy of the character; which even appeared to mould his limbs, and give the turn and posture to his movements, as he passed on and about the stage with the quiet and gliding sinuosity of the serpent."[10] The *Bristol Observer* touched off Denning's Bob Acres neatly : "The comic valour of Fighting Bob rose in his speech, and oozed out again at the palms of his hands."[11]

Occasionally press relations were less harmonious: the theatre's musical director, Charles Cummins, precipitated a major dispute when the great Angelica Catalani was engaged in 1825. Cummins had been in the habit of writing anonymous critiques in the *Bristol Mercury* violently attacking Catalani as an "insolent and rapacious foreigner" who had "murdered Handel". However, when, on accepting an engagement at the Bristol theatre, she not only entertained Cummins to dinner but promised to sing at his Benefit, the *Mercury*'s editor, T. J. Manchee, was startled to receive a notice reading :

Madame Catalani's merits are too well known to need particularising now, but the unparalleled beauty and volume of tone, the velocity and rocket-like flights, so admirably contrasted by a pathos and feeling *never surely equalled by human being,* came upon us as freshly as in the first moment of hearing . . .[12]

This was too much for Manchee, who owed Cummins a grudge for involving him in a libel suit some time previously, and he took the greatest pleasure in exposing the whole shabby business, while Cummins volubly defended himself in the *Bristol Gazette.* M'Cready himself quarrelled with the *Bristol Mirror* over the alleged inaccuracy of their notices.

M'Cready was not in any case an easy "Governor", as contemporary theatrical memoirs attest, but even Francis Wemyss, who considered himself unfairly dismissed by M'Cready, admitted "I learned more during my short stay in his company, of the practical part of my profession, than any two years of past experience had afforded me".[13] Standards did fluctuate from season to season, and much of the polish which had distinguished the best of the Bath Company's productions disappeared under the pressures of the demand for incessant novelty and the economic necessity of playing as many nights as possible; but M'Cready succeeded in attracting numerous young actors and singers who, though forgotten now, made some mark in the early and mid-19th Century theatre.

Prominent among these was John Reeve, a low comedian with a gift of mimicry and of racy ad-libbing. This latter once nearly cost him dear, for when in a stage fight he was accidentally shot in the face, "a few moments elapsed before the sufferer attracted the attention of the other personages of the drama, they supposing that he was protracting his share of the performance for his own amusement".[14] His two engagements in Bristol (1820-1 and the summer of 1822) were, however, most notable for being the only period in his life when Reeve essayed classical comedy, and his Falstaff in particular was felt to have added to his reputation, though he was criticised for indulging in occasional vulgarities.[15]

William Charles Macready, himself quite a frequent visitor, also introduced his future wife, Catherine Atkins, and her parents to Bristol. In a lively letter to his father dated 17 November 1820, he enquired tactfully about his father's financial stability, and then introduced Catherine as "a girl of more promise than any thing I have seen through the country" – though he wrote off her father as "a d—d hick . . . and her mother a *female hick* – or hickess : – but she can deliver messages very well and can 'make up a show' – and the Sire can paint very fairly indeed".[16] The salaries Macready suggests as realistic indicate the reduced status of the provincial actor – £2 a week for Catherine in leading ingenue roles, £1.5.0 for her father and 15s. for her mother.

M'Cready took his son's advice, and Miss Atkins, from the Theatre

Royal, Edinburgh, appeared on 10 January 1821. Initially she failed to make any great impression, being accused of a certain whining monotony, but in her second season her great improvement was generally noticed and by the time she left, with an engagement to play leading parts in Dublin in the autumn of 1822, she had won both the professional and personal respect of Bristolians.

Another family link was maintained when Mrs. Glover entrusted her daughter to M'Cready to take over Catherine Atkins' cast of parts for the season 1822-3. Though acceptable in some tragic roles, she was better in characters calling for homespun pathos, such as Cicely in *The Heir at Law*. Other London stars who were glad to place their near relatives with M'Cready, and support them on Benefit nights, were the comedian, Paul Bedford, who himself had been a junior member of the Bath and Bristol Company in 1816-7 and whose brother joined M'Cready in 1824; the Covent Garden soprano, Miss Hammersley, whose sister, later Mrs. Toye, sang in 1824-5; and Sapio, the Drury Lane tenor, whose brother Antonio made his stage debut as principal bass in Bristol in April 1825.

Other actors who achieved more than local fame included the young soprano, Miss George (1822), the comic actor Robert Strickland (1822-3), and several of the leading men: D. W. Osbaldiston (1821-2), Samuel Butler (1824) and J. H. Barton (1824-6). George Stansbury, son of the leader of the theatre band and himself established as an orchestral player of ability, made his first attempt in a singing part on 17 May 1827. He later became a well known buffo bass, joining with Braham in his initial management of the St. James's; since his first Bristol singing role was Hawthorn, the young hero of *Love in a Village,* one can only conclude either that his voice had not yet settled in 1827, or that the songs were drastically transposed.

M'Cready himself was greatly admired in the Irish characters in which he specialised; his Major O'Flaherty in *The West Indian* was "the genuine Irishman, equally disposed to fight or make love, [who] delivered his bills, or fell into blows, with an easy unconscious air and tone".[17] It was felt to be a real loss when age and the weight of management caused him to give up acting, save on very rare occasions, after 1824.

However, the most striking figure in the company throughout M'Cready's ten years of management was undoubtedly his mistress, from 1821 his second wife, Sarah Desmond. A handsome woman of commanding presence, her Emilia in the opening performance of *Othello* was generally singled out for praise, and Charles Mayne Young is said to have considered it one of the best on the stage.[18] Usually wise in her choice of roles (save for an occasional lapse into Juliet and a proclivity for breeches parts), her Helen MacGregor, her Meg Merrilies, Hermione in *A Winter's*

Tale, Lady Macbeth and Mrs. Haller were all highly impressive. Most of all, however, she shone – almost literally – as Queen Elizabeth in *Kenilworth*. "The dress of Mrs. Macready as *Queen Elizabeth* beggars description; it was magnificent in the extreme, and she moved beneath her gorgeous attire with action becoming the descendant of the Henry's."[19] An obituary writer in 1853

sees her now before him, in her gold brocade and bristling ruff, as vividly, and hears her shrill-toned "Gad 'a mercy, girl", as plainly as he did full thirty years ago, when she lived her regal hour upon the stage in King-street.[18]

M'Cready's attention to the standard of his stock company was accompanied by considerable attention to their repertoire. Among "the divine Shakespeare's works" alone, he revived *A Winter's Tale* with splendid new scenery on two occasions; *Julius Caesar, King Henry IV* (both Parts), *Hamlet* and *King Richard III* were all cast entirely from the company; even *King Richard II* had a week's run in 1829. Despite the multitude of stars, no actor could fairly claim insufficient opportunities to impress the Bristol public.

On the musical side the company was, especially in the later years of M'Cready's management, particularly strong. Although the Italian Opera toured as a unit, other singing stars – Catherine Stephens, Mary Paton, Eliza Vestris, Sapio, John Braham – expected reasonable local support in the ballad operas and popularised versions of Rossini, Mozart and Weber now coming into the height of favour. In general this support was forthcoming, though there were a number of complaints about the inadequacy of the orchestral accompaniment. Under Cummins the band seems to have grown deplorably slack, occasionally resulting in a song having to be omitted because no players were in their seats to take up their cue. The most lamentable debacle – and, be it said in fairness to M'Cready, an apparently untypical one – occurred on the second night of a revival of *Der Freischutz* in December 1825, when in the incantation scene nothing went right :

First we had the House so impregnated with sulphur that many were glad to make a hasty retreat into the air to escape suffocation; then we had Mr. Barton's wig on fire and our worthy Manager rushing on the stage to extinguish it

and finally the property reptiles failed to explode. No wonder the *Mercury* critic complained that Barton "seemed to sympathize with the fire-works, and *would not go off*".[20]

It was impossible for a 19th Century manager to do without elaborate stage effect. While one must be cautious in assessing playbill claims, a number of M'Cready's prompt books remain which can be related to this period, and they provide considerable evidence of the care he took over stage grouping, business and physical effects.[21] *Faustus*, for example, was an enormous success largely because of its spectacle :

> The new Scenery, Dresses, and Machinery, reflect the highest credit on all concerned; the change to the "Venetian Carnival", and the spirited manner in which the whole of that scene was kept up, aided by some excellent dancing, drew from a well-filled house shouts of applause; equally so, the appearance and disappearance of Faustus and the Fiend in Act 2nd, and the "Magic Mirror" in Act 3rd; together with the splendid Palace and concluding Scene.[22]

This complicated and expensive production was followed only three weeks later by one of *Malvina*, with "An Extensive Mountain, Torrent and Cascade, Invented, Designed, and Executed by Mr. Donaldson" and after another month by *The Pilot* with its dioramic storm effects – "The OCEAN Dreadfully AGITATED !"

The Cataract of the Ganges, produced during one of Ducrow's engagements, was another impressive show. "The *picturesque* and *stupendous Cataract* of *real water*, with which the piece concludes", and up which Mrs. M'Cready rode her live steed, "was cheered each night with acclamations of applause from all parts of the Theatre".[23] The cataract's water was, apparently, provided by the Sun and Norwich Union Fire Brigades[24] – mains water being a thing of the future.

Nor was M'Cready less generous in providing for more classical drama. His revival of *A Winter's Tale* in 1819 included "a new Library Scene very neatly painted, indeed, too much so, for general effect. The Trial Scene (3rd Act) gallery, and window, in imitation of stained glass, was superior in execution, formation, and regularity to any, we believe, ever witnessed within these walls".[25] (Its historicity was another matter, perhaps, like the introduction of Del Caro's Hornpipe in Act 4.) *King Richard II* in 1829 received as much attention from the scene painter (Henry, of the Theatre Royal, York) as any pantomime or sensation piece. The list of scenery and properties at the theatre compiled after M'Cready's death[26] is witness both to the scenic resources of the period and to the balance between stock scenes and *ad hoc* pieces imposed by the constant change of repertoire.

For understandable economic reasons the standard of costuming was not so uniformly high. Sarah Desmond as leading lady was always praised for her appropriate dress – this had been so even in her touring days with M'Cready on the northern circuit. Mrs. Mara, for several years the company's First Old Woman, was also singled out for her good wardrobe. But these showed up the deficiencies of others, and critics were becoming noticeably more fastidious about realistic effect. An 1822 revival of Cumberland's *The Brothers* opened unpromisingly :

Scene, the coast of Cornwall; enter on shore, lately escaped from the wreck of a privateer, a Portuguese lady who had been taken out of a sinking pacquet . . . a white Spanish transparent [head] dress but not at all concealing the taste and skill of her hairdresser – train of black velvet puffed with snowy white, and white satin shoes . . . Some of the destitute crew, too, exhibited nice lily-white musquito trowsers, quite fresh, not from "the salt-sea ocean", but from the laundress's patent mangle . . .[27]

The Witches in *Macbeth*, too, were more than once heavily criticised for the motley selection of garments in which they appeared, but overall the standard seems to have been reasonable, and certainly it never sank so low as to arouse popular contempt.

However much attention was paid to novelty and the grandeur of its staging, M'Cready needed his stars, and he was as cheerfully catholic in his engagements as in his choice of repertoire. In seven months, between November 1825 and June 1826, the Theatre Royal displayed the talents of entertainers, opera singers, pantomimists, tragedians, dancers, broad comedians, child prodigies and tight-rope artists. Ducrow's stud of horses was always popular, and other and varied animal acts (cats, dogs and bears among them), juggling and acrobatics were frequently introduced – most often, to be just to M'Cready, at the period of the September fair.

There were expostulations, but the more realistic appreciated the overriding value judgment of financial attractiveness. Some of the finest comic players of the contemporary theatre could not command a house : neither Dowton, Fawcett nor Emery succeeded in their engagements. On the other hand, broad comedians such as Liston and Joseph Munden drew packed houses, and so did a succession of those singing comediennes whom the 1820s produced in abundance. The entrancing Kitty Stephens came for three successive Fair-time engagements; Maria Foote maintained her popularity even after the scandal of her breach-of-promise action – indeed, playing one night immediately after the conclusion of the case, she brought about such an overflow that M'Cready found it prudent to open the doors early to prevent an unseemly scramble for places.

Her first appearance was hailed by an enthusiastic burst of applause from every part of the house; and the feeling that evidently prevailed in her favour was greatly increased by the beautiful but agitated creature that bent in grateful acknowledgement for their indulgence. Accustomed as she has all her life been to acting, she could not in the first scene entirely suppress the feeling which shook her frame; but she soon recovered her self-possession, and went through her part [Letitia Hardy, in *The Belle's Stratagem*] with her usual grace and spirit.[28]

But probably the most popular of all was Madame Vestris, who acted at the Theatre Royal for the first time in April 1827, having previously sung in a number of concerts in the city. The impressario Ebers was so rash as to announce a rival Concert which clashed with Madame Vestris' stage performance – and the audience went to the Theatre Royal, to the wrath of Ebers' supporters, who made sneering remarks about the attractive power of Madame's neat ankle. The *Mercury* poured scorn on this allegation:

Her *ancle*! did her ancle attract the crowds of *ladies* that filled the boxes? was it for the sake of her ancle that they applauded and encored her songs?[29]

Such legitimate stars as the contemporary theatre afforded continued to visit Bristol, with varying success. Daniel Terry, whether in classical or Adelphi roles, commanded more respect than popularity, and even Charles Mayne Young's support dropped away during his visit in 1820. On the other hand, Junius Brutus Booth continued to be popular and draw good critical notices, and this despite the repercussions of the Antonio scandal earlier described. Edmund Kean, in Bristol as elsewhere, lost ground markedly with audiences during the 1820s, though there are some fine detailed descriptions of his Richard III, Shylock and Othello as played in 1823.[30] His son, Charles, engaged during the Fair season in 1828, was unanimously recommended to adopt another profession:

We cannot compliment this gentleman on possessing either figure, face, action or judgment for the stage: he has certainly mistaken his *forte,* and in our opinion is losing his time woefully.[31]

Easily the most popular of the legitimate stars was William Charles Macready, in whom the Bristol public took an almost proprietory interest. His generosity in making special journeys to play for his father's Benefit aroused favourable comment, and the Bristol papers followed his career in London and abroad with consistent attention. Whenever he played in Bristol he commanded packed houses, and some of the fullest and most interesting critiques of the period are devoted to his principal roles.[32] Before his visit to America in September 1826 he dashed down from Birmingham to play William Tell at Bristol on 25 August, when at the conclusion "his very elegant and classical farewell address called forth the loudest plaudits, accompanied with showers of tears and a great display of white handkerchiefs."[33] Returning in February 1828 in the same part he "was received with loud and enthusiastic plaudits" from "one of the best and most elegant houses we have witnessed this season".[34]

Such emotional outbursts by the audience were liable to be provoked also in less commendable circumstances. The patriotic fervour which had been a built-in risk with playgoers at the beginning of the century had largely spent itself by the time the older M'Cready entered management, but the political ferment of George IV's reign, and more particularly the popular agitation over his behaviour towards his unfortunate Queen, Caroline of Brunswick (of which agitation Bristol was a centre), caused many an uproar in the theatre. Any man who failed to remove his hat when "God Save the King" was being played was liable to have it knocked off, or be subjected to personal assault – even when he turned out to be "a Foreigner, uninterested in our political affairs, and almost a stranger to our language".[35] Shouts for "The King" were met by counter-shouts of "The Queen", the uproar continuing after the curtain had risen, until "some well-disposed persons . . . interfered, and in consequence of their repeatedly assuring the Queen's *friends* that the orchestra could not play any tune expressive of popular attachment to her Majesty (no such air having been as yet composed) . . . the noise gradually subsided, and the piece was allowed to proceed".[36]

M'Cready himself was as conservative in his attachment to the establishment as any provincial theatre manager was bound to be, and quite properly he did his best to profit thereby. The re-opening performances after the death of George III were marked by a Monody impressively recited by Sarah Desmond, and the subsequent Coronation by an illuminated transparency of figures symbolising the four countries of the Union; England was represented, not altogether happily, by "a figure of an English sailor with a bottle and glass under the title of George". The funeral of the Duke of York in February 1827 gave occasion for another stage spectacle, "to conclude with Beethoven's Unrivalled Requiem".

The personal esteem in which M'Cready was held, as a man of generous enthusiasms ever ready to devote a Benefit night to relieve distress, whether local or national, was nowhere greater than among the local Freemasons, of whom he was a prominent member. At his Lodge he met Richard Smith (later its D.P.G.M.), surgeon, theatre lover and antiquary, and the Masonic bespeaks were not only financially beneficial but helped to re-establish the respectability of the theatre.

In no department was M'Cready's energy and reforming zeal more vigorously employed than in the theatre building itself. For his very first Fair Season in August 1819 he commissioned a local firm, Fothergills of Redcliffe Street, to install "that brilliant mode of illumination, the gaslight". Since this admirable innovation, not long established in the London patent theatres, tended only to expose the lamentable want of paint, during the autumn recess M'Cready put painters to work on interior redecoration and on new scenery, and builders on a saloon for half-price

Box patrons who had long been complaining of having to wait in a chilly courtyard; while the Proprietors set about the long-projected new Box-entrance.

The building, however, was temporarily brought to a halt by difficulties over ancient lights raised by the owners of the King Street houses, two of which the Proprietors proceeded to buy up, while in the meantime a "Boudoir" was provided – and warmly welcomed. Westmacott, engaged on the painting, had a quarrel with M'Cready and left in a huff; Carroll, actor as well as scene-painter, completed a scheme in which the predominant colour was light salmon, with national emblems in gilt on the box and gallery fronts.

The stage-doors are white and gold, and the pilasters on either side the stage appear like Sienna marble. The ceiling represents an open sky, with Cupids in different attitudes.[37]

Amid all this new glory, it was a matter of relatively minor importance to the audience that the hitherto efficient gas lighting failed on the first night of the winter season three times. "The Audience were in extreme good humour, sang 'God Save the King' each time, and when Mr. M'Cready came to apologise for the occurrence, greeted him with rounds of applause."[38] The new leading man, F. C. Wemyss, already nervous at the thought of what comparisons might be made between his Rover (in *Wild Oats*) and that of Elliston and Stanley on the same boards, was even further disconcerted – and the press was by no means so loud in his praise as he infers in his Biography. However, after only a few more lapses, the gas lighting ceased to give trouble, and proved a most appreciated amenity. Nine years later it was commented :

The gas has been introduced without offence to the most delicate sense, and to manifest advantage of the scenic representation, as well as of the personal appearance of the audience.[39]

M'Cready did not attempt to improve on his Boudoir – money did not permit – though in February 1821 he added a "comfortable Saloon with a fire, &c." for the half-price visitors to the Pit. In the autumn of 1820, however, he engaged William Edkins (son of Michael Edkins, who had decorated the theatre for its 1766 opening). The Cupids disappeared in favour of "Apollo's Lyre, supported by appropriate ornaments, and on the verge is a tasteful wreath of flowers" on a background of "a warm drab-colour". Lavish gilt was applied to Box fronts and pilasters; the panels of the Upper Boxes were newly decorated with "emblematical figures of the elements, Fire, Water, Earth, and Air, intermixed with theatrical trophies, descriptive of Tragedy, Comedy and Satire".[40]

The following year Edkins refreshed the ornaments and repainted the Boudoirs and approaches; in November 1822 M'Cready engaged Stanton to paint a new Drop-scene with a view of Bristol "taken from an *eminence* near *Clifton Wood*", and for the 1823-4 season the Box seats were covered and the theatre again redecorated, the allegorical figures on the Upper Boxes being replaced by a more uniform scheme of adornment. Henry, who had joined M'Cready as scenic artist for this season, contributed a "New SPLENDID DROP CURTAIN, & PROSCENIUM" at the beginning of March 1824. That autumn Edkins once again repainted the lobbies and approaches, and there were "boxes newly lined, and handsome cornices, a mirror in each stage-box, with elegant draperies, &c." while more lights were added in the auditorium.[41]

Never content, in the autumn of 1826 M'Cready made a substantial alteration to the stage. He removed the proscenium doors and instead constructed two private boxes, fitted up with chairs, which were thought to "add to the beauty and symmetry of the circle; they must prove very desirable and accommodating to families or select parties, having such complete command of the stage." These remained in place till 1831. To counterbalance this innovation, M'Cready restored the traditional Green Curtain; and Edkins, who had been up to London to inspect theatres there, once more repainted the auditorium, this time with national emblems on the front of the gallery, "a very tasty scroll ornament, in burnished gold" on the upper boxes, and an abundance of gilding everywhere against a predominantly cream background.[42]

This, however, was the last renovation undertaken by M'Cready. During the summer of 1828, while the company was playing Cardiff and Swansea, he was taken seriously ill, making his will on 12 July,

being mindful of the ffrailty and Mortality of Human Nature and that it is appointed for all Men to die but considering the uncertainty thereof.

Deeming his children by his first marriage adequately provided for, he left all his rights in the Bristol, Swansea and Cardiff theatres and all his personal property to be divided equally between Sarah M'Cready, "our daughter Mazarina Emily McCready and the boy known by the name of George William McCready".[43]

Sarah M'Cready very efficiently took over the management of the South Wales season; M'Cready made a partial recovery, but on 11 April 1829 he died.

His loss will be deeply felt and regretted by his family and a wide circle of friends. He was indeed universally esteemed, and the qualities both of his head and heart were such, as would have done honour to any profession.[44]

The funeral (at the Cathedral) was private, political unrest making it inadvisable to encourage any large gathering; the theatre re-opened on the following (Easter) Monday, and by unanimous acclaim the Free-masons decided to bespeak a play for the benefit of Mrs. M'Cready on Thursday, 7 May, an occasion graced by the Lord Mayor, Lady Mayoress and Sheriffs.

The following week, the last of the season, William Charles Macready came down to play four nights, closing the theatre on Friday, 15 May. On the following day he wrote to the Proprietors asking "in behalf of the Widow of my late lamented Father" to be allowed to transfer the remainder of the existing theatre lease to Richard Brunton, with the possibility of a renewal for three years at £300. "I beg to offer at the same time, in evidence of my own opinion of his professional qualifications and gentlemanly character, the tender of my guarantee for the punctual discharge of the rent."[45]

There was only one contender, but that a somewhat surprising one : B. P. Bellamy of the Theatre Royal, Bath. The rivalry between the two theatres had gradually diminished to spiteful bickering and then died away as old M'Cready re-established the standing of the Bristol theatre while the position of the Bath Theatre Royal became more and more insecure. The management shares passed eventually into the hands of Palmer's son, Colonel (later General) Charles Palmer, who knew so little of the theatre that he had to ask a friend "what sort of play 'Hamlet' was,"[46] and when Bellamy, his agent, made his offer to treat for the Bristol lease the Bath concern was on the verge of bankruptcy.

In view of later events it seems unlikely that the Bristol Proprietors realised this; it was almost certainly the prestige of Macready (and his guarantee of rent), coupled with commendable sentiment towards the family generally, which induced them to agree to a joint lease to Brunton and Macready.

Not everyone was happy about their decision : the *Bristol Mercury* in particular recognised the economic and artistic advantages theoretically accruing by the union of the two theatres. Its editor issued a warning :

We hear that Mr. Brunton . . . has acted with great spirit and ability in his management of the Plymouth Theatre; but we fear that he will find that spirit and ability are not all that is requested to ensure success . . . We cordially hope he may succeed; but he will find that he has embarked on an arduous under-taking.[47]

Three

1829–1834

Richard Brunton came to Bristol with a varied experience of management, by no means all of it encouraging. A recent venture at Birmingham had ended in bankruptcy, Brunton being able to offer only 3s. 6d. in the £ to his creditors. He returned to the Exeter-Plymouth circuit in 1828, where he was more successful, but when he came to Bristol, after a summer season at Swansea, he was still crippled by debt.

The Company with whom Brunton opened in the autumn of 1829 was very largely composed of his Birmingham and Plymouth colleagues, supplemented by his father, John Brunton, from Covent Garden (who had played as a boy with the Bath-Bristol Company), and, in the leading serious roles, Sarah M'Cready, who on the first night received so great a welcome as almost to overwhelm her. Leading man was Charles Kemble Mason, son of Jane, a younger sister of John Philip Kemble, and physically extremely like his famous uncle; other members later achieving some fame were Mr. and Mrs. Charles Selby and "Mr. Chew", which according to Rennie Powell was an early pseudonym of James Henry Chute, a future manager of the Theatre Royal.

On the whole Brunton's programme elicited warm praise. Soon after the opening of the winter season William Charles Macready, mindful of his managerial interest (which was, however, kept a complete secret) produced his adaptation of Byron's *Werner* for the first time on 25 January 1830 after a brush with the censorship.[48] Jones, the scene painter, produced an impressive first act set:

The cheerless and melancholy aspect of the baronial hall with its mouldering tapestry dropping from the wall, and its rotting and shattered wainscoat, seemed emblematic of the pride and desolate condition of its inmates; while the stately figure of Werner, as he paced the chamber, appeared to give depth to the gloom that flung its shades about him.[49]

Supporting Macready in the name part were Sarah M'Cready as Werner's wife, Josephine (apparently not the original choice for the part — see Plate 11); Mason as Ulric, his son; and John Brunton as Gabor. All gave creditable performances, but it was necessarily Macready who dominated the production :

In the pinchings of poverty; in the bitterness of remorse; in the fear of detection; in the anguish of grief; and in the abandonment of hope and life, his powers of face, eye, gesture and action, all spoke the complete actor, and the perfect delineator of passion.[50]

Thenceforth Macready included Werner in his repertoire on almost every visit to Bristol, and while he was on the stage no other actor essayed the part there.

Brunton did not rely solely on such attractions, however; *Black-Eyed Susan* and *The Red Rover* satisfied a taste for nautical melodrama, and "the talented and stupendous ELEPHANT" entertained the Easter audiences. The Rackhay entrance proving too low to admit the animal, Brunton had to obtain permission to take down part of the rear wall of the Theatre[51] — probably the central part at the back of the recess. He capitalised on this by using the yard behind as an extension to the stage, a device further exploited by his successors.

After a further summer visit to Swansea, Brunton re-opened for the Fair in Bristol, adding to his company a young actor from Peterborough already specialising in old men's parts — W. H. Chippendale, who was eventually to become doyen of classical comedians at the Haymarket. The brief season closed with what was intended as the farewell visit of Edmund Kean in his most famous roles, Richard III, Shylock, Sir Giles Overreach and Othello :

But alas! for the ravages of time and of dissipation: the pantomime of action (with an excess of which he was always truly and justly chargeable) still remains — but the passions of the mind, the workings of the soul which were wont so often to awe into silent admiration or to agitate into tumultous applause the listening audience, have sunk, deeply sunk.[52]

Kean closed his Benefit with a brief address which still reads movingly :

I am called upon, ladies and gentlemen, to perform a most painful duty which almost agonises my feelings and destroys the little portion of eloquence I am otherwise possessed [of]; it is that of bidding, perhaps, an eternal farewell to that public who have supported me so long and so kindly. The profession of an actor is one of the most difficult in the world — the ladder by which he ascends is so broken and so shattered, that few are able to ascend beyond the second or third step. Envy, malice, and falsehood, are the powerful streams against which he has to contend, and he who can successfully pass these is the only one likely to arrive at the summit of his profession . . . It will always be a source of gratification to me as long as I think and feel that the Bristol Public were among my best – my latest – my most candid supporters. With real wishes for your health and happiness . . . I beg leave, respectfully, to tender you my thanks, and farewell.[53]

The next season seemed equally promising, the musical strength of the company in particular being considerably increased by the engagement of M'Keon, Martyn and Emma Romer, later a leading soprano at Covent Garden. Altogether the auguries were good enough for the Proprietors to determine on consolidating their position. They entered into treaty for compounding the ground rent of the Theatre, which cost them £500, and for the purchase of "the freehold Entrance with Room over . . . situate in the Rackhay", which took a more modest £105. This by the spring of 1831 had involved them in an overdraft of £237, which they hoped to clear by foregoing a year's dividends.

However, in the uncertain political atmosphere, support for the theatre fell away, and even splendid productions of *Masaniello* and Rossini's *Cinderella* (the latter cast entirely from the stock company) failed to arrest the decline. The season petered out in mid-June, but the prospect of engaging Fanny Kemble on her first provincial tour with her father, Charles Kemble, in support, induced Brunton to re-open for a fortnight in July.

Fanny Kemble in her *Record of a Girlhood*[54] has a lively account of her experiences. The version of *Romeo and Juliet* in which she appeared on her first night she describes as "a shocking hash" and on the second night, when *Venice Preserv'd* was on the bill, things were even worse :

> I certainly have seldom seen a more shameful exhibition. In the first place C— [Charles Kemble Mason, her cousin, who was playing Jaffier to her Belvidera] did not even know his words, and that was bad enough; but when he was out, instead of coming to a stop decently, and finishing at least with his cue, he went on extemporising line after line, and speech after speech, of his own, by way of mending matters . . . He quivers and quavers in his speech, and pulls and *wrenches* me so inhumanly, that what with inward laughter and extreme rage and pain, I was really all but dead in earnest at the end of the play. I acted very ill myself till the last scene, when my Jaffier having been done justice to by the Venetian Government, I was able to do justice to myself, and having gone mad, and no wonder, died rather better than I had lived through the piece.

Writing to her friend, Mrs. Jameson, however, she admitted that "the company are by no means bad"; she was shrewd enough to note in the same letter how the poor condition of local trade and the failure of several mercantile houses were affecting the theatre. Unknown to her at that moment, personal difficulties also were gathering again for Brunton. An unnamed creditor, a "Mr. D—" (apparently an intimate friend of Brunton's acting as his agent) demanded additional security for his loans in the shape of the theatre lease. When told this was illegal, he installed himself at the Box Office and pocketed the ticket money – even that for Charles Kemble's Benefit. The actors presented him with a memorial in which "they declined exerting themselves merely to put money into his pocket . . . the reply was, that the money obtained should be held in defiance of all claims."[55]

In an attempt to save his actors, Brunton surrendered himself and was promptly thrown into the debtors' prison, which aroused a public outcry; the completely disoriented company was taken in hand by Charles Kemble, and he and Fanny performed in *Venice Preserv'd* once again, raising £150, which paid the performers 5s. 8d. in the £ on their arrears.

Brunton made over his share in the lease to Macready, who promptly surrendered it to the Proprietors, paying the last quarter's rent himself. Thereupon, without further consultation (their action not being minuted till a year later) the Committee granted a lease to General Palmer of Bath for 21 years at an annual rent of £340, the increase "having been made in consideration of the Proprietors abandoning to the Tenant the old Scenery which had become of trifling value".[56]

Palmer and his manager, Bellamy, put on a brave front, allegedly spending between £800 and £1,000 on improving the theatre. The stage was taken up and relaid six inches lower; the understage machinery was entirely renovated; and according to Richard Smith "at the wings and behind there were alterations which enabled the Managers to use the large Bath scenery". The private boxes on the stage were removed and stage doors reintroduced. "The staircases leading to the upper side boxes are likewise removed to another part of the building, by which means 'a certain class of females' will very properly be excluded from the lobby communicating with the circle of dress boxes." The five front boxes were subdivided, and new cushions supplied in all the boxes. Lighting too was improved. The gas machinery was overhauled; new fittings, giving the impression of shaded wax candles, were installed; "the old 'float' has gone, and in its stead a row of single gas burners adorns the front of the stage." The first steps towards modern lighting distribution were taken : "more light has been thrown upon the stage, and less in the body of the house."[57]

Malvolio of the *Bristol Mirror* dropped in shortly before the re-opening and commented favourably on all the activity :

There, the tide scenes were shooting backwards and forwards on their slides – here, the myrmidons of EDKINS, up to their elbows in size and whiting, ochre and Dutch pink, salmonizing and distempering away, driving all before them at one "fell swoop".

A good deal of money had had to be expended, Malvolio was told, in replacing main timbers which had rotted to danger-point.[58]

A week later than had originally been planned, the "RE-UNION OF THE THEATRES-ROYAL, BATH AND BRISTOL" took place on 24 October, Mrs. M'Cready being conspicuous at Bellamy's right hand when the curtain rose. For the second week Ducrow's Equestrian Troupe was advertised, but that weekend, 29-30 October 1831, the Bristol Riots broke out in adjacent Queen Square. On Monday morning the mob raged up King Street, attacking many of the buildings; the set-back site of the Theatre Royal saved it from almost certain damage, possible destruction.

It was hardly a good omen. The actual farewell visit of Edmund Kean, though almost in the last stages of his decline, did a little to promote enthusiasm; but, to public indignation, when Paganini was engaged for three concerts, the seat prices were raised to 10s., 7s. and 3s. 6d., against the normal prices of 4s., 2s. 6d. and 1s. 6d., and Bellamy appealed (vainly) to silver ticket holders to forego the exercise of their rights. There were threats of a demonstration, which fortunately came to nothing, but it is noticeable that at the last of the three concerts the prices had been reduced to 10s., 5s. and 3s.

During the winter season Bristol was reduced to one performance a week, on Mondays. Opera and comedy were interspersed with occasional stars : Ira Aldridge, Macready, Charles Mayne Young on his farewell visit, and at the other extreme Il Diavolo Antonio and Monsieur Martin with his lions (also a Peruvian llama, two boa-constrictors, a kangaroo and a baboon). Probably the most impressive production was reserved for the close of the season, when Sheridan Knowles' *The Hunchback* was brought out with Miss Jarman as Julia, her acting being so powerful as to cause two ladies in the Dress Circle to faint away. In a close of season speech Bellamy alluded delicately to the "circumstances more unpropitious than ever attended any speculation" which had reduced the length of the season and consequently his receipts. In the meantime he had paid no rent whatsoever.

The season at Bath had been even more disastrous; in September the owners of the Bath Theatre Royal advertised for a new tenant, while Bellamy applied to the Bristol Proprietors for permission to underlet, delaying tactics which failed of effect. In Richard Smith's paraphrase of the Committee Minutes, "The Proprietors . . . seem to have had enough of General Palmer and commence a process for ejectment & into the bargain put an execution upon the Property. – A very angry interchange of Letters takes place between the Attornies on both sides and the Theatre was closed".[59] There was a rumour that Kean (probably Edmund) was in treaty for a lease; Macready certainly contemplated the possibility, but it came to nothing.[60]

Bellamy succeeded in re-opening the Bath theatre in January 1833, and the Bristol house on 4 February, reducing the gallery price to 1s., a very popular move. The rent arrears were supposed to be paid off at £20 per week – the Account Books show payments by Palmer of £60 a month from February to June – during which period there were scattered performances, reasonably well attended, with the emphasis still on musical pieces and comedy, including song-strewn versions of *The Tempest* and *Twelfth Night*. The leading soprano, Miss Turpin, obtained an engagement at the Haymarket and had some success there.

On 29 May the season closed, rather abruptly; in a speech Bellamy told his audience that "there has been no loss upon the season, although the profit has been very small. Whilst almost every theatre in Britain is sinking to ruin, it is gratifying to know that the joint theatres of Bristol and Bath have been, to a certain extent, successful."[61] They were not, however, successful enough to tempt him to continue management; instead the war of words between the Proprietors and Palmer's solicitors continued until in October 1833 agreement was reached. Palmer delivered up his lease, in return for which he was allowed to take back the scenery belonging to the Bath Theatre, while the Proprietors "are to release General Palmer from all Claims for Rent or Taxes in respect of the Theatre."[62]

Towards the end of October they advertised for a new lessee, the *Bristol Mirror* commenting optimistically :

We are informed, by those who are well acquainted with theatricals, that any spirited manager, with a few hundred pounds, may make the Bristol theatre a source of considerable profit.[63]

A Mr. John West, of London, made tentative approaches, but soon faded from the scene. In truth it was not an inviting prospect for any manager, for such scenery as remained was dilapidated; there was little, if anything, in the way of wardrobe; even the curtain and drop-scene were almost unusable. With a courage born no doubt of near-desperation, Sarah M'Cready offered to undertake an experimental opening of the Theatre for three months, which was refused; but in January 1834 the Proprietors, by now deeply worried at their financial position, agreed to allow her to open for three months at a total rent of £100, to be paid back at the rate of £10 a week.

Active and indefatigable as her late husband, Sarah M'Cready went up to London to gather a company. With the theatre cleaned and aired, a new Green Curtain hung, and the prospect of a new act-drop to be painted by Gordon of the Olympic, she embarked on the management of the Bristol Theatre Royal on 3 February 1834.

Four

1834-1845

It is hardly surprising that the Committee of Proprietors were hesitant about accepting Sarah M'Cready as lessee; apart from any prejudice against having a woman as manager, their experiences over the past seventeen years had made them very wary indeed about the financial stability of their tenants – and Mrs. M'Cready could produce no security for her venture. Hence the Proprietors insisted on short-term leases of three years at a time, and the insertion of a clause (privately admitted to be of dubious legality)[64] providing for summary ejectment in case of non-payment of rent.

The age of the Theatre Royal, too, was beginning to bring its disadvantages. It was partly a matter of deterioration of the fabric, which, as Palmer and Bellamy had found, was beginning to be substantial and expensive to put right. In the increasingly unfavourable circumstances of the provincial theatre the Proprietors were reluctant to make costly investment in a building whose continued life was so uncertain. Mrs. M'Cready had repeatedly to bring urgently necessary repairs to the Committee's notice; in October 1843 they commissioned a report, but of the £250 expenditure the architect deemed necessary they would authorise work only on "the Articles of necessary and immediate attention" to the value of £60. By 1845 the roof needed almost complete renewal, which cost them nearly £275. The Proprietors were several times strongly criticised for their apparent unwillingness to help Sarah M'Cready, even after she had proved an honourable and honest tenant. At the Annual General Meeting in 1845

the very extraordinary fact appeared, showing that our highly-esteemed Manageress (who is never daunted, and fulfils all her engagements in every sense of the word) as the spirited lessee since 1834, had paid to the Proprietors £4000, and had been allowed for repairs, &c. about £350 only![65]

Nevertheless, Mrs. M'Cready did achieve some improvements, essential to meet the other disadvantage of age : that the facilities of the theatre would no longer suffice to meet the standard of accommodation, and elaborateness of spectacle, demanded by the public. The Proprietors allowed her £50 off her rent for two successive years towards the cost of redecorating in the autumn of 1835; in addition she removed "an unsightly Beam . . . from the Ceiling of the Proscenium" which by raising the height of the proscenium opening much improved the slightlines of the "Gods", who could now see to the very back of the stage; and she converted the proscenium doors once again into private boxes. The entire auditorium was repainted in the "Arabesque or Raphaelic" style :

The idea of the Ceiling is taken from the ancient Valarium [sic] a tent which used to cover the Greek and Roman Theatres, this is divided into ten parts, the medallions of which contain busts of Shakespeare, Homer, Virgil, Dryden and Milton; the two sitting figures on the red ground are river deities – the Avon and Severn. On the Dress Circle allegorical figures are introduced, representing Poetry, Painting, Sculpture, Navigation, Rhetoric, Music and Astronomy. The Second Tier contains classic emblems; and the pannels of the Gallery, the figures of infants, emblematic of Tragedy, Comedy, Horticulture, Botany, Genius, Dancing, &c. &c.[66]

Two of the Dress Circle panels of this period have been recovered [see Plate 13]; it is probable that the remainder still exist below the present plasterwork.

In May 1838 Mrs. M'Cready wrote to the Proprietors asking them to consider erecting a new Paint Room : "The one which we are now using over the Pit is considered extremely dangerous from the immense weight of scenery and Property's, which we are of necessity compelled to keep there."[67] The Insurance Office also objected, not surprisingly, to the fire risk involved in the use of an oil stove in the current Paint Room, and the Proprietors allowed Mrs. M'Cready seventy guineas towards the total estimated cost of £102 involved in the required alterations. (When she contrived to cut her estimates, they reduced their allowance to £65.) The change she made remained the basis of the scene-dock arrangements until 1970, and is described by Richard Smith :

She curtailed a portion of the old "Green Room" and added it to a new Building over the Rackhay entrance where there are both space and light and by the aid of a little machinery the canvas to be covered is always level with the hand of the Painter as he stands upon the ordinary floor.[68]

Only three years later the Proprietors had to accept responsibility for the repair of the flies, and when the theatre reopened in August 1841

Mrs. M'Cready was able to advertise that "the whole of the internal machinery has been remodelled and constructed on a novel plan, so as to give greater and more certain facilities to the Scenic arrangements".[69] The Proprietors paid J. Watson £38 for "alterations, renewing and Repairs to Stage, Flies, and Machinery".[70] A new act-drop and a refurbishing of the Boxes, which had been re-upholstered only two years previously, were provided for the winter season.

By October 1844, however, Mrs. M'Cready was becoming desperate. The Theatre was so shabby she was almost ashamed to open it; the premises generally were in a "very deteriorated state"; but she herself could not afford a penny towards the expense. Thus appealed to, the Committee had to agree to meet the cost, the lowest estimate of which was £118. The contract was awarded to Hayman, Fowler of Clifton, who replaced the allegorical nymphs of nine years ago with panels of pink and white, with burnished gold mouldings, and ornamental centres with raised heads of *papier mâché*. The Stage Boxes had *bas reliefs* of assorted mythological subjects. The ceiling was "formed into radiating panels, most exquisitely painted" and the old ventilator was replaced by "a superb flower, in the style of Louis Quatorze, modelled for the Duke of Suther-land's mansion in London".[71] Hayman, Fowler also rebuilt the proscenium arch – it may be suspected that Mrs. M'Cready's almost casual removal of the "unsightly beam" had left some structural weakness.

Besides the struggle against the increasing dilapidation of the theatre, Mrs. M'Cready faced a decline in stock company acting standards at least partly consequent on the wretched salaries which were all that could be afforded, and above all audience apathy. "There is no disguising the fact that Bristol is not a play-going place", lamented the *Bristol Standard* in 1840.

The public insisted on stars, but the necessity of engaging them brought some embarrassing results for the supporters of the drama. It was difficult to argue the case for the theatre as a place of rational entertainment when the attraction was Signor Hervio Nano, the "man-fly", Yankee Smith and Piccaninni Coleman, or Miss Heron, "the Infant Power". Not all these so-called popular entertainers justified themselves even financially; with some satisfaction the *Bristol Journal* commented on "the celebrated 'Jim Crow' ", T. D. Rice :

Much as we lament the poor encouragement the legitimate drama experiences at the hands of the Bristol public, yet we cannot regret that empty houses have marked the manner in which such a ridiculous performance as that of Mr. Rice is appreciated by our fellow-citizens.[72]

Again, Bristol's response to the incredible acrobatics of the Morocco

Arabians was to stay away in such numbers that Mrs. M'Cready had to close the theatre after three nights.

But it was no better with the majority of the classical stars. Sheridan Knowles, John Vandenhoff, William Farren, James Anderson, Helen Faucit : all drew excellent notices and disappointing houses. On the other hand, while never entirely winning round the critics, Charles Kean usually received good support from the public. In March 1839 he acted for six nights, his terms being one-third receipts for two nights and one half for the rest, and netted £200; though in October the following year, the weather being, as he noted in his Account Book, "very wet and in-clement", he took as his half-share of all receipts only £141. 19s. 6d. over his six nights.[73] Nonetheless, "as a mark of his gratitude for the support he received from Bristol citizens, he generously sent a very handsome dona-tion to 'The Grateful Society' ".[74] Mrs. M'Cready must almost certainly have been out of pocket, averaging less than £25 a night to meet her house charges. Seat prices had to be raised (to 5s., 2s. 6d. and 1s. 6d.) for Fanny Elssler. The ballerina was said to have charged a hundred guineas for her appearance – which one critic indignantly calculated as five guineas a minute of her performance.

Judged even by the extravagant records of the stage, the recompense is most exorbitant: and one reason why the regular drama does not, and cannot, prosper, is the vast sums thus recklessly thrown at the feet of reigning favourites.[75]

Of more practical help was William Charles Macready, who did not abandon his interest in the Bristol theatre with the collapse of his partner-ship with Brunton. Whatever his personal feelings about his stepmother, his sense of family responsibility was too strong – and so also, it is permis-sible to hope, was his affection for "good old Bristol", whose citizens could be counted on to provide a warm welcome and full houses for him – not to do what he could in the way of new plays and personal visits. His out-standing contribution in this respect, of course, was his two-months' con-nection with the Bristol and Bath Theatres from January to March 1835. His biographers describe this as a venture in management, which is not strictly correct since both theatres already had a lessee, and Mrs. M'Cready, at least, was not allowed to sub-let without permission of the Proprietors. It is more probable that Macready made private arrange-ments with "Jemmy" Woulds and Sarah M'Cready, perhaps paying them a fixed sum while taking responsibility for organising the season and receiving the ticket-money.

Macready packed the programme with stars – first and foremost him-self, of course, but also his current leading lady, Mrs. Maria Lovell, the character comedian. William Dowton, and the opera singers, Mr. and

Mrs. Wood. Shakespeare alternated with other favourite Macready roles : Virginius, William Tell, Werner and Sardanapalus, spiced with 18th Century comedy and operas by Rossini and Auber. In Bristol the houses were on the whole excellent; Macready wrote to his friend Gaspey at the beginning of March that they had been playing "to considerably above £100 each night, and the *boxes greatly taken* for the remaining nights".[76] For *The Jealous Wife*, despite the company's imperfect command of the text and the prompter's disposition audibly to supply "the word" in the midst of Macready's best-thought-out pauses, there was a packed house – Richard Smith estimated it as at least £180.[77]

Bath, it is clear, did not respond to the same extent, even though there were usually only two performances there each week as against four in Bristol. Macready was not long in wishing he were rid of his agreement, and during March he terminated it. Had he been content with Bristol only, the tale might well have had a different ending, but that *ignis fatuus*, "the re-union of the Bath and Bristol theatres", proved as disappointing when captured as it seemed desirable in the pursuit.

The choice of repertoire, like the engagement of stars, reflected the incessant attempt to ascertain popular box-office appeal and meet it, whatever form it might take. William Charles Macready obtained for his stepmother, as he had for his father, an early opportunity of producing what serious plays were being brought out in London : Mrs. M'Cready's Benefits saw the first performances in Bristol of Bulwer Lytton's *Richelieu* and *Money*, Leigh Hunt's *A Legend of Florence* and Marston's *The Patrician's Daughter*. Sheridan Knowles and Macready, and to a lesser extent Charles Kean, Butler, Denvil and James Anderson, included new dramas in their starring engagements without very much success in most cases. Though lavish in the space they devoted to the productions, the Bristol critics were acutely aware of the deficiencies of many of the plays themselves. Bulwer Lytton's *The Sea Captain* was roundly, but not unfairly, condemned.

A more washy composition, collected from different sources, and unrelieved except in two instances by brilliancy of thought and felicity of diction, we never witnessed . . . The story (if such it can be called) reminded us forcibly of Boz's inimitable sketch of the melodrama at Greenwich.[78]

Scarcely any of these works, except some of those by Knowles and Lytton, entered the everyday repertory; bluntly, few of the plays and fewer of the Stock Company actors were good enough to inspire the necessary enthusiasm in an apathetic audience.

Shakespeare almost disappeared from the repertory. The enormous success of Vestris' production of *A Midsummer Night's Dream* at Covent

Garden in 1840 did persuade Mrs. M'Cready to bring out a close imitation at Bristol early in 1841, but this ran for only a week, and to diminishing houses, despite general praise. The terms of that praise are significant :

Fantastical we allow it [the play] to be; but varied and amusing in incident, and rich in poetical beauty, it at the same time opens a field for artistical embellishment such as few legitimate dramas will admit of.[79]

The appeal of "artistical embellishment" was similarly exploited by Charles and Ellen Kean in 1845. "*Macbeth* and *Richard the Third* are announced, which will be produced with all the splendid dresses and appointments used on the revivals of the tragedies at Drury-Lane, and which cost Mr. Kean as much as 500 *l.*"[80] Both productions laid claim to correct period reproduction as well as picturesque stage effect, though "it was much to be regretted that the bungling of the scene shifters [in *Macbeth*] should have marred the effect of the change from the blasted heath to a moonlight view in Scotland."[81]

But, as the *Mercury* had pointed out, few "legitimate dramas" gave opportunities for the colour and show so beloved by the average theatregoer. To compensate for this there was a marked increase in pseudo-historical spectaculars. In *Jane of the Hatchet* the expectant audience was promised "SIXTY WOMEN IN ARMOUR".[82] To display the costumes in *The Jewess* to better effect, a platform was built from the stage to the Pit, down which the processions paraded. The *Bristol Gazette* waxed lyrical over the effects :

The procession of the Cardinals, with all the ceremonial grandeur of the Catholic Church – the entree of Emperor Sigismund, in a complete suit of steel armour, flashing with radiance, and attended by a numerous suite of bowmen in mail, mace-bearers, officers, and dignitaries, mounted on horses, also clothed in steel – the whole cortege forming a body of upwards of *one hundred* persons . . . and the scenery beautiful throughout, but, perhaps not to be surpassed is the final view of the immolation of the Jewess, where the perspective is so admirably managed that the distant throng of spectators (on canvass) actually seem as much parts of a living and breathing reality as the animated figures in front.[83]

It was such productions, alternating with a series of dramatisations, mainly of Dickens, and numerous short-lived domestic pieces, which formed the bulk of the main pieces in the programmes. There were scattered performances of the classics, particularly in 1842 and 1843 when the young James Bennett was making his way in the company, but it is a sad comment on Bristol's taste that by far the most popular play of the period was a drama taken from Ainsworth's *Jack Sheppard*, which to the disapproval of the moralists ran for eighteen nights in eight weeks in 1839-40.

In 1840 Sarah M'Cready tried the attraction of pieces with local plots : a Surrey drama, *John Duddlestone, the Breeches and Corset Maker of Bristol,* and later the same month Featherstone's *Cooke's Folly.** Neither could by any stretch of the imagination be called successful. They were followed by a local opera, with more tragic consequences. *Lundy in the Olden Time,* with music by Cornelius Bryan, organist of St. Mary Redcliffe and the Lord Mayor's Chapel, was rehearsed for performance in March 1840. During a break at one rehearsal, Bryan, walking up and down the stage abstractedly, fell down an open trap used for raising scenery and so injured his spine that, despite immediate medical help, he died next day. So, sadly, the opera had only one performance, on 27 March, for the Benefit of Miss Bryan, the librettist (presumably the composer's sister or daughter).[84]

The trend away from the old-style five-act main piece meant that the "entertainments" grew correspondingly longer. It became normal rather than exceptional for the programme to include main piece, interlude and afterpiece, the last-named almost invariably a farce. Alternatively, to prolong the stage life of an expensive novelty, it might be transferred to the end of the bill after its initial run, to tempt more spectators at half price.

The multitude of stars also had its effect on the repertoire, for by now many of the minor theatres were encouraging their own dramatists, and stars like Mrs. Fitzwilliam, Ben Webster, Mademoiselle Celeste and the Jim Crow entertainers had each a special repertory. The resultant demands on the Stock Company were considerable; during a seven night engagement of Celeste and Webster in July 1842 twelve different pieces were presented, of which only one (*Speed the Plough*) could fairly be called a stock comedy; two (*The Woman Hater* and *A Lover by Proxy*) were completely new, and only one of the others had been produced since the last engagements of these particular stars.

The drama, legitimate or otherwise, was by no means the only attraction provided by the Theatre Royal. Many of those antipathetic to playgoing, either on moral grounds or from distaste at the fare provided, regarded music as at the same time less open to objection and more genteel. This bias was already becoming evident by the end of M'Cready's management, and had been reflected also in the repertoire of his successors, but none of them exploited it to the same extent as Sarah M'Cready. Probably at no time before or since has a Bristol audience had so many opportunities of hearing the greatest musical performers of the day – from Grisi[85],

---

* Three years later Mrs. M'Cready brought out an Easter Pantomime on the same local legend, called *Harlequin Hobbledy Gobbledy,* which proved rather more to local taste.

Pasta, Madame Garcia and Adelaide Kemble to Ole Bull and the Strauss Band. "Vocal and instrumental concerts" were organised; Promenade Concerts occupied the autumn recess in 1841, 1842 and 1843, involving the flooring over of the Pit and the closing in (presumably by a false ceiling, for acoustical purposes) of the stage.[86]

But pre-eminently there was opera : some English Opera in the shape of Balfe's earlier works, *The Maid of Artois* and *The Siege of Rochelle*; the occasional revival of ballad operas; but most often the works of the Italian composers, Rossini, Bellini and Donizetti. Mr. and Mrs. Wood were the first to introduce *Norma* to Bristol, claiming (incorrectly) that it was for the first time on the English stage.[87]

The ever-popular former Bristol singers, Emma Romer and George Stansbury, were frequent visitors, one of their best-loved vehicles being Donizetti's *Love Spell* (*L'Elisir d'Amore*). Its first performance in Bristol in September 1839 was somewhat marred by the behaviour of the pony engaged to draw the quack doctor on to the stage in his chaise. The animal, petrified by the flare of the footlights and the noise of the orchestra, baulked :

The Doctor remonstrated, but being an indifferent whip, his entreaties only served to urge the animal against a woodland side scene, which he would have uprooted, together with a village church which occupied the front view, had not the Chorus opportunely come to his assistance.[88]

Stansbury was a great favourite in his home city; Richard Smith wrote in the *Bristol Mirror* :

It would be absurd to say that [he] has either a good voice or plays well, yet he dodders through the acting and the singing so as to come through with flying colours. We confess that we believe there is a little sneaking kindness towards him, and a sort of little favouritism, so that the audience cannot help being pleased with his honest Bristol-looking face.[89]

Despite all the emphasis on stars, spectacle and opera, it should not be thought that the Stock Company was entirely negligible. In Mrs. M'Cready's first season the leading lady was Harriet Faucit, thought by some to have been unjustly overshadowed by her more famous sister, Helen. Mr. and Mrs. Frank Matthews, among the leading comedians of the mid-Victorian stage, joined the company in April 1834 and became very popular. Frank Matthews as Old Rapid (in *A Cure for the Heartache*) was deemed by the *Bristol Mirror* "never . . . excelled either upon these boards or elsewhere".

Another scion of the Glover family, Edmund, was leading man in 1835-6 and 1839-40; no doubt it was his presence, and that of her

daughter, Mrs. J. Bland, which encouraged Mrs. Glover to come down
and play Mrs. Oakley to his Oakley in *The Jealous Wife*, and Elvira to
his Rolla in *Pizarro*.* Founding a family connection with the Theatre
Royal, Bristol were Ben and Sarah Terry, from the Liverpool Theatre,
who joined the company for two seasons in December 1843, during which
period Kate Terry was born. Mrs. Terry was little more than a "super,"
but Ben Terry was given some quite good character parts, and occasionally contributed an entr'acte song, not always fully appreciated.

Mr. TERRY . . . warbled forth a doleful ditty, described in the bills as a "favourite song", accompanying himself on the guitar. This gentleman *may* be a good
singer, but we fear that with the Bristolians his acquirements are not very highly
appreciated.[90]

Bristol gave the popular low comedian, Edward Wright, his West End
opening. Joining the company in January 1837 after a successful engagement at Birmingham, he was immediately acclaimed. "He has a life – a
buoyancy – a relish for fun quite enough for all who do not wish to see
either overstep all propriety."[91] He was engaged at the St. James's Theatre
in the autumn of that year, but continued to spend a goodly portion of
the following summers with his old friends in Bristol.

The 1838-9 season saw for its initial months the engagement of one Mr.
Lee Moreton "from the London Theatres" (a decided exaggeration). This
was no other than the young Dion Boucicault, who played Irish and
other extravagant comedy parts, such as Mantalini in *Nicholas Nickleby*
and Le Beau in *As You Like It*, to the great satisfaction of the "Gods".
He also brought out (unlicensed) one of his earliest plays, a farce called
Lodgings to Let.

It is one of the plotless *bagatelles* which serve to make us laugh for half an
hour, and then wonder for an hour afterwards at what it is we have been laughing; in a word it is a tolerable vehicle for many bad jokes, some good ones – a
few new, still more old . . . The trifle is not without merit, but we venture to
prophesy that both the pruning knife and polishing brush must be liberally
applied to it before it will become a popular farce.[92]

It was played in Bristol four times, and Ben Webster, who was starring at
the time, was sufficiently impressed to consider putting it on at the Haymarket.

Perhaps the most important engagement in its consequences for the
Bristol theatre, however, was that of James Henry Chute in September

---

* Edmund Glover, junior (presumably Edmund's son), was juvenile lead in
1854-5.

1839. He had already wide experience in the provinces, including Bristol under Brunton (see p. 102) and the Lincoln and York circuits, and wherever he went he made friends. Billed as "from the Theatre Royal, Dublin", he opened on 2 September as Laertes to the Hamlet of the former Bristol leading man, Butler, now of Drury Lane. Chute was a skilled fencer, a talented though not very strong singer, a lively and robust actor and a resourceful and energetic Stage Manager. For five years he divided his time between Bristol and Dublin, till circumstances finally fixed him in Bristol.

It was in 1842 that Mrs. M'Cready's daughter Mazarina ("Maggie") made her stage debut, first in Cardiff and later in Bristol. Understandably rather lacking in confidence and technique at first, she had an appealing sincerity. "There is a great natural earnestness about her acting, and a depth of feeling in parts so unforced as to seem more the spontaneous effect of genuine impulse than of mere acting."[93] James Anderson, the young Drury Lane actor who had played juveniles for Macready, came down for her Benefit in March 1844 and took her off as his leading lady on a tour of the provinces. Returning to play for her mother's Benefit in May, a great improvement was noted, "her movement on the stage being much more free from stiffness and embarrassment than it was".[94] On 28 October the same year she was married to Chute at St. Margaret's Westminster, and so began a partnership of nearly thirty years, and a theatrical dynasty of nearly a century.[95]

Chute's consequent virtual absorption into the management of the Theatre Royal helped to overcome a personal disadvantage faced by Sarah M'Cready. Though a woman manager was no novelty in the provincial theatre, a woman stage-manager was almost unthinkable (an attitude persisting into the 20th Century). A good deal of the practical business of production was necessarily delegated to the current stage-manager, and some were by no means satisfactorily conscientious. Indeed, Sarah M'Cready's first manager, Chaplin from Drury Lane, seems from the playbills to have stayed only one night. William Charles Macready, trying to dragoon the company into an intensive rehearsal of *Sardanapalus*, deplored the inactivity of Mude, Chaplin's successor. "There was no head to give impulse and energy to the limbs of the concern, and I felt annoyed to see this woman's money thrown away by the supineness and apathy of those whom she was paying."[96] Spasmodic complaints of over-long pauses between individual pieces, and even between acts, occur throughout the first ten years of Mrs. M'Cready's management and support a general impression of some lack of drive in stage direction in the early years.

"Mrs. Mac", like her husband, became popularly typed as a theatrical "character". John Coleman recalled her as "a very eccentric and sibylline old lady" and she had an eye like a hawk for any sign of extravagance, watching every sixpence expended on supers.[97] But this was a matter of hard necessity in the financial circumstances of her management, and coupled with it was a great financial probity. Not once in nearly twenty years' management was she behind with her rent or her actors' salaries, though more than once pay-day left her with her own purse empty. She gave generously to charity and opened her theatre for numerous benefit performances, making only £30 house charge.

The pattern of performances adopted by Mrs. M'Cready closely followed that established by her late husband; a main season beginning on Boxing Day, running four or five nights a week and ending with Benefits for the principal members of the company in April and May. The theatre would then be closed, save for occasional short lets, until the Autumn season, which usually lasted all September and sometimes, if a particularly attractive star were available, for part of October. The opportunity to engage Ducrow and his equestrian troupe in 1835 extended the season till mid-November, but this was a solitary instance.

Patronage was rare, though the Masons gave occasional bespeaks, and the Mayor almost always patronised one or more nights. Very properly, John Kerle Haberfield, Treasurer to the Proprietors from 1838, exerted himself in Mrs. M'Cready's cause when Mayor, and sold tickets to the value of fifty guineas or more. Mrs. M'Cready could also capitalise on political feeling, members of the Beaufort and Berkeley families bespeaking rival performances. In the General Election of January 1839 the respective candidates from each family mustered their supporters on different nights in the same week, to the great advantage of the box-office, the Hon. F. H. F. Berkeley's night yielding £140 and the Duke of Beaufort's £160.

These, unfortunately, were exceptional occasions; but almost the only ones when a substantial assembly could be expected in the Dress Boxes. A reduction in the Upper Box price to 3s. from the end of August 1843 onwards encouraged popular attendance there, but the theatre's main support came from Pit and Gallery. Mrs. M'Cready maintained the reduced Gallery price of 1s. instituted by Bellamy in 1833, and at the beginning of the 1837-8 season onwards she brought the Pit entrance down to 2s. Rowdy the Gods and Pittites certainly were on occasion – a performance of La Sonnambula in 1839 was interrupted by a free fight in the Pit over a "lady" – but they were at least loyal. Wisely, one night when there was a particular crush in the Gallery, Mrs. M'Cready allowed some of the overflow into the upper side Boxes without extra charge.

In any case, the behaviour of those in the Boxes was not always any better. Drunken youths interrupted James Wallack's performances in 1834 and there were complaints of the throwing of pennies into the Pit (one cut a woman's eye), and even fireworks. Against the remonstrance of the Box-keepers, young bloods insisted on smoking cigars, which "has the effect of keeping many ladies away who otherwise would be found warm patronesses of the drama."[98]

The abolition of the September Fair in 1838 removed the influx of country visitors for whom the autumn season had originally been designed to cater. The September opening was too well established to be dropped, but increasingly from the summer of 1843 onwards this and other short engagements outside the main season were advertised at "Half Price from the commencement of the Performance."

If the Bristol theatre was in difficulties, however, the Bath theatre was far worse off. After Woulds relinquished management in 1839 there was a succession of short-lived lessees : Davidge, Newcombe and Bedford, Hoy and Hooper, the last-named terminating his tenancy in March 1845. When the rising American tragedian, Edwin Forrest, visited Bristol the following month, Mrs. M'Cready hired the Bath Theatre for one night so that he might act there. Finally she made proffer for, and was granted, a five-year lease of the Theatre Royal, Bath, with the proviso by the proprietors that each season should not average less than ninety nights.[99] From September 1845 the Bath and Bristol theatres were once again run as a circuit – but with one great change : from now onwards Bristol was the dominant partner.

Five

1845–1853

The obvious economic advantages of combining the Bath and Bristol theatres into one circuit again were unfortunately almost cancelled out by the parlous state of theatricals in Bath. The chaos and the bankruptcies of the past six years had produced an apathy so profound that it would have taken energy and capital far greater than Sarah M'Cready possessed to revive an interest in theatricals in what had once been acknowledged the centre of fashion and culture in the West. The "ninety performances" clause in the lease was easier to insert than to carry out satisfactorily; although Mrs. M'Cready started by extending her autumn season, and devoting alternate nights in the winter to Bath and to Bristol, hard economics forced her to limit the Bath theatre nights to two a week – and if there were no star there might be only a Saturday night performance.

In Bristol the depression showed no signs of lifting. Doggedly Sarah M'Cready continued to pay her rent, maintain a respectable Stock Company and engage as many and varied stars as opportunity allowed, but only rarely was there the house she deserved, even at her own Benefit. To a considerable extent the lack of support was due to the effects of the crisis in Bristol's trade. The contemporary press is full of the failures of mercantile houses and banks; Bristol's port facilities had fallen so far behind what was needed that the city rapidly lost all the advantages which might have accrued from the building of the *Great Western* and *Great Britain*, while it was too early for the expanding railway network to have very much compensatory effect.

Sarah M'Cready herself was aging; she was 55 at the time she took the Bath lease, and the impression one gathers is of a woman increasingly fatigued by an unrewarding struggle, and now lacking either the personal or the material resources to overcome public apathy. The Bristol press was sympathetic and appreciative of her difficulties; their notices are on the whole remarkably lenient. But occasionally the undoubted drop in standards is starkly revealed :

It is very seldom that we visit the Bristol Theatre, for, excepting a "star" now and then, there is nothing to tempt one to leave a comfortable fire side for a dingy old place, every year getting more and more gloomy – scenery, with every inch of which we are familiar, and tired withall, – "property" dresses claimed as the property of moths, – boxes clear of occupants, – and pit, the forlorn hope of an orange-woman, – gallery, noisy, if there are enough half-price sixpences to make a row, – actors dispirited having nobody to play to . . .[100]

Save for the provision in December 1847 of a new act-drop by Thomas Grieve of Drury Lane (representing "a magnificent curtain of scarlet cloth and gold, lined with white satin, and a medallion of Orpheus surrounded by the Thracian maidens"), no improvements to or redecorations of the theatre were carried out by the lessee. The Proprietors were no more moved; they declined the expense of a public water supply and were only reluctantly persuaded to take advantage of a local sewerage extension to connect the theatre premises to mains drainage.[101]

Major spectacles almost vanished from the repertoire, save for special productions at Easter and Christmas. During this period there was an Easter pantomime almost every year; the first Christmas pantomime, however, seems to have been tried out initially at Bath in December 1850 and transferred to Bristol the following month. This "new comic harlequin-ade" was titled *Harlequin Templar, or, Richard Coeur de Lion taking in Bristol on his way to Palestine*, "arriving in Bristol *en route* – carpet-bag and all – by parliamentary train, and being entertained by the Mayor and Aldermen, whom, in acknowledgement of their courtesy, he favours with some rather free criticisms of their city and its inhabitants".[102] Though the houses were disappointing at first, it took the public fancy sufficiently for the opening to be revived as an afterpiece at Easter.

The following Christmas brought an instructive diorama, *Our Native Land*, painted by Grieve, Telbin, Absolon and J. Herring, sen., and displayed to appropriate music; this was succeeded by an elaborate extravaganza, *The Three Princes*. In 1852-3 the Bristol season started for the first time with a run of its own pantomime (*Queen Mab*), preceded by an assortment of stock pieces, and the pattern of Christmas theatricals in Bristol was set.

Apart from the establishment of the pantomime, the principal characteristic of the theatre programme of this period is diversity. At one end of the spectrum was a prestige production in 1845 of a version of Sophocles' *Antigone*, with Mendelssohn's music, done with some approximation to historicity. Dialogue was accompanied by a flute, the "plastic attitudes," which, we are told, characterised the acting of the Greeks were also tolerably observed; the stage was fitted to resemble the vestibule of a palace, the floors being covered in imitation of tesselated marble; and there were likewise the logeum, or pulpitum, and the altar for the principal characters, used to distinguish the rank of the characters, and the sunk orchestra for the chorus.[103]

Without a star, however, it failed to attract, though according to Rennie Powell the Gallery produced a vociferous call for the author at the final curtain.

At the other end of the scale were the recurrent revivals of domestic dramas such as *Susan Hopley** and *Jane Lomax*, which was said to be founded on local events; and a reproduction of *Jack Sheppard*. Towards the end of the period *The Corsican Brothers*, first produced for Mrs. M'Cready's Benefit in April 1852, caught on, but the only play to have a real run – a play which in various guises would be exploited as a refuge for impecunious managers over the next sixty years – was *Uncle Tom's Cabin*, first presented in Bristol in an adaptation by James Henry Chute on 1 November 1852.[104]

Into this production went all the resources of the theatre; as sheer spectacle it was the most elaborate for many years, with "a series of new scenes by Mr. J. S. Lennox [actually I. S. Lenox], from the Theatre Royal, Birmingham, who . . . promises to be the best scenic painter that we have had at this theatre for some years".[105] Added to this was the vast interest already aroused by Harriet Beecher Stowe's novel, the performance of the play evoking a wave of popular emotion against negro slavery no less genuine for being sentimental:

George Harris, and *Eliza*, and *Tom*, and *Aunt Chloe* carry the audience along with them, and every vantage point they attain is sure to bring down thunders of applause, whilst the iniquities of *Haley* are regarded with horror and disgust, which were on Thursday night, most unequivocally expressed by numbers among the auditory, who in one of the most exciting scenes broke forth into a yell of execration.[106]

Drama was of course only one component of the programme; music, as before, played an important part, with all kinds of instrumentalists, musical groups and opera soloists visiting the theatre. A former leading soprano of the company, Miss M'Mahon, returned with her husband,

* "Why despise the 'short and simple Annals of the Poor?' among which will be found some of the most Interesting Events and heart-rending Scenes of rural Life . . . Alas! how little do the Rich, revelling in wealth and luxury, know of the cares and troubles, the miseries and deprivations under which the Poor labour; and yet behold their patent suffering!" – Playbill of *Susan Hopley*, 8 March 1847.

Donald King, in Balfe and Bellini in 1849, and Emma Romer continued her regular visits, but the outstanding stars undoubtedly were the great tenor, Sims Reeves, who sang in *La Sonnambula*, *Lucia di Lammermoor* and *I Puritani* in February 1850, and above all the "Swedish Nightingale," Jenny Lind.

The engagement of Jenny Lind in September 1847 had the same overwhelming impact in Bristol as elsewhere. Chute made special arrangements for the booking of seats, the prices of which were quintupled; "no more Tickets will be issued than the several places will conveniently accommodate." Even so, when it came to the night of 27 September, "by six o'clock [the Concert was due to begin at eight] the pressure against the gallery door became so great that it gave way, and a number of persons thus prematurely gained admission". Standing room for several hundred was provided on the stage, and a barricade erected round the platform from which Jenny Lind and the other performers, Signor and Madame Lablache, Madame Solari and Michael Balfe, were to sing. The crush was so immense as to arouse fears of collapse, and this tension was felt by some to have adversely affected the diva's singing.

However, despite this, and the last-minute absence of Madame Lablache (through illness) and Madame Solari (unexplained), the whole occasion was an overwhelming success.[107] Thus encouraged, Chute the following year negotiated for a further engagement of Jenny Lind, this time with the Opera Company of Her Majesty's Theatre, in *La Sonnambula*. Announcements had already appeared when the promoter, Cockram, advertised a Jenny Lind concert at the Victoria Rooms, Clifton, on the same night, and, despite protests, Chute had to give way.[108]

The duplicity of John Knowles, Jenny Lind's manager, on whom the blame fell for the cancellation of the promised opera, was not, unfortunately, unique. Mrs. M'Cready found herself in similar difficulties over the Danseuses Viennoises, who after attracting delighted notices during an engagement in November 1845 were billed again three months later, but failed to arrive :

Mr. Simpson, the Manager of the Liverpool and Birmingham Theatres, had "farmed" the *Danseuses Viennoises* of their directress, Madame Weiss, for a term of one month, and was to pay 1,000 *l.* for their services . . . but, owing to some dispute with Madame Weiss, he has been compelled to make compensation to the several managers with whom he has broken faith.[109]

Mrs. M'Cready accepted the compensation, and was able to engage the dancers for the following month.

It was during this period that ballet as a serious art first made a real impact on theatregoers. Starting with Fanny Elssler's engagement in

1843, the next ten years saw almost every great danseuse of the time appearing in Bristol. Cerrito paid two visits, in August 1844 and August 1847; Taglioni came in October 1845, Flora Fabbri in August 1846, and Rosati in September 1848. These visits, as will have been noticed, took place in the autumn season, which was normally a half-price period, and tickets had to be raised above even the standard full price. This was not helpful to attendances, and criticisms of the exorbitant fees alleged to be charged by the ballerinas were repeated with emphasis.

Even in the main season and at normal prices a full house could not be counted on. Coming after Macready's farewell visit, at the end of January 1850, Carlotta Grisi herself failed to attract. For her first performance, which included extracts from *Esmeralda*, "in truth there was but a miserable attendance."[110] With rare generosity, however, Grisi danced one further night without charge to help Mrs. M'Cready, a gesture very much appreciated.

Repeatedly Mrs. M'Cready was told by the press that to draw any houses at all she must maintain a continuous succession of stars. The resultant list contained the usual engaging miscellany of attractions, of which perhaps the oddest were the Female American Serenaders (Mesdames Cora, Woski [*sic*], Yarico, Rosa, Miami, Wamba and Jumba, according to the playbills), who appeared in August 1847, and Madame Wharton's Walhalla Exhibition. These young ladies in their "poses plastiques" occupied the theatre for the whole of November 1849, their repertoire ranging from "Lady Godiva" (which predictably "drew down the unanimous applause of a most numerous assemblage") to "The Angel Talking with Adam."

Among the most popular of the light entertainers were Mlle. Celeste, a regular visitor from 1834 onwards, and Mrs. Fitzwilliam, who delighted her audience by adding a special verse to her popular song, "Old Rosin the Beau", to celebrate Bristol's new status as a free port at the beginning of 1849 :

> Then with gold ships shall come in such thousands,
> Sure the reason you all ought to know;
> They've made a FREE-PORT of Old Bristol,
> Because she should rosin the beau,
>   The beau, the beau,
> Because she should rosin the beau;
> For who will count up all the duties,
> When with gold-dust they rosin the beau.[111]

Madame Vestris paid a farewell visit with her husband, Charles Mathews the younger, in March 1847, delivering a delightful curtain speech in which she commended to the audience her "junior partner," who would in future "undertake the travelling department."[112] Edward Wright maintained his links with Bristol, and turned down three offers of paid engagements to play free for W. H. Angel's Benefit in October 1848.

Less predictable was the public's response to the more serious actors and actresses. Charlotte and Susan Cushman played Romeo and Juliet in September 1846 to a good house :

> Miss C.'s forte lies in the grand, the terrible, and the majestic, rather than in the tender, loving, and pathetic . . . Miss Susan Cushman's *Juliet* was a beautiful piece of acting . . . The applauses, the yet more flattering silent attention with which Miss Susan Cushman's effort on Monday was received, proved how triumphantly she overcame the obstacles in her way.[113]

But James Anderson and Helen Faucit continued to be more respected than supported, and Fanny Kemble, with Charles Kemble Mason as her leading man, after a postponement due to illness played two nights in the summer of 1847 to miserably thin audiences. She wrote to her friend Hal that "the house at Bristol the first night was wretched, my share of it only £14."[114] A more deserved failure seems to have been that of George Owen, one of the first of the touring provincial tragedians :

> We witnessed his personation of *Macbeth*: Macbeth did "murder sleep," and Mr. G. Owen did murder Macbeth, and that too most effectually. He certainly had got his part perfectly by heart, and there ends all that we can say in his favour.[115]

Still the only constant attraction among the classical actors was William Charles Macready. His engagements drew most of the best critical writing of the period,[116] and for once critical and popular admiration coincided. In 1847 his Benefit was an overflow. His farewell engagement in January 1850 aroused a depth of feeling which no other actor had evoked in Bristol during the century, for the Bristol critics possessed a genuine appreciation of his aims as an actor : his insistence that a character should be "not only a great piece of acting [but] a consistent and harmonious whole,"[117] and his moral purpose. "He has not been the mere actor seeking only the ephemeral gratification of his audience, but . . . regarding the drama as an instructive art."[118] Bristol audiences have always needed an object on whom to focus attachment, whether manager or actor, from Powell and Dimond to Peter O'Toole and Denis Carey. William Charles Macready had provided this focal point for many years, and it was at least partly the void created by his retirement that enabled the young Stock Company actor, George Melville, to make his name in Bristol.

Not that Macready, or any other star, was exempt from the ill behaviour of part of the audience. Even during his last performance of Lear, a party of young officers in one of the stage boxes smuggled in their black terrier and tried to make it bark at Macready in his best scenes. Complaints about smoking and throwing away live matches continued, and so did occasional rowdyism : one galleryite threw a bottle into the Pit and injured a lady's arm, and "strange to say, although Mr. Artaud, the stage manager, immediately came forward and offered a reward of £5, for the apprehension of the unmanly ruffian, the delinquent was allowed to escape."[119] Henry Mayhew, journalist, humorous writer and social historian, made such a hash of his one-man entertainment that "the occupiers of the gallery expressed their disapprobation with more candour than politeness" – or, in John Coleman's blunter phrase, Mayhew had to "turn tail and bolt for his life amidst the storm of derisive cat-calls."[120]

Despite all that has been said of the decline in overall standards, it should not be thought that the theatre lost all hold on Bristolians. Individual members of the company, especially, as usual, among the low comedians, had a considerable following. W. H. Angel and Stephen Artaud (both of whom interspersed their regular engagements at Bristol with appearances at London theatres, including Drury Lane) were a well-loved pair, both capable of rich character comedy; Angel's was the broader and Artaud's the drier humour, and they made admirable foils for each other. In addition, Artaud coached the Bristol Amateur Dramatic Society, who rewarded him with an additional Benefit.[121] He was also an energetic Stage Manager in the last years of Sarah M'Cready's management.

That most unreliable of theatrical memoir-writers, John Coleman, joined the Bristol-Bath Company as leading man at Christmas 1848 and stayed for two years, during the first of which not a single mention of him was made in the Bristol press – not even of his Richard III, which he claims was so controversial. It was not until his second season, when he played the chief supporting roles to Macready during the latter's farewell engagement, that he obtained any critical notice. His Macduff attracted much praise, in which a faint note of surprise is detectible :

We did not conceive that he possessed such histronic abilities as he exhibited in the scene where he received intelligence of the murder, by the usurper, of his wife and children; it was extremely well done, and much applauded.[122]

His Othello, to Macready's Iago [Plate 14] in which, according to Coleman, the audience got up and cheered, was unanimously regarded by the press as totally inadequate : "ill-conceived, ill-acted, and ill-dressed".[123]

Much more important was the engagement of Coleman's successor, George Melville [Plate 16]. Unlike Coleman, he quickly aroused critical interest, and, while his Macbeth was only partially successful, his Hamlet won prompt and widespread support, especially from the occupants of the cheaper parts of the house – a support which never deserted him in thirty years. With Melville's arrival Shakespeare once more came back into the standard repertory, and his popular success was the first important step in attracting audiences back to a Stock Company without a star.[124]

In the last two years of Mrs. M'Cready's management, indeed, the first signs of the turning of the tide can be detected. It is no disparagement of her magnificent achievement as manageress to say that a major factor in this was the passing of effective control of the theatre into younger and livelier hands, those of her son-in-law, James Henry Chute, and her Stage Manager, Artaud. For nearly twenty years, in the face of continual difficulties and disappointments, Sarah M'Cready had kept the theatre open for its full season; she had enabled the Proprietors to remain solvent at whatever cost to herself; she had provided for Bristolians opportunities of seeing and hearing almost every dramatic and musical experience available to the provinces. When compared with the record of other provincial theatres – indeed, of the London Patent Theatres themselves – the extent of this achievement may be more fully appreciated.

That in doing all this she had prematurely worn herself out is little wonder. In May 1852 she was reported alarmingly ill, and, though she temporarily rallied, she collapsed with bronchitis in the New Year and died on 8 March 1853.

In her will she expressed "my earnest hope that the Proprietors of the Bristol Theatre in consideration of their old Tenant and that my Property in the Theatre is of a kind which is only available on the Spot will consent to receive my said Son-in-Law Mr. Chute as Tenant thereof in my stead for the benefit of my daughter and grandchildren"; a hope the Proprietors had no hesitation in fulfilling.

NOTES

[1] *Bristol Gazette*, 4.9.1817.

[2] *Bristol Journal*, 4.10.1817.

[3] *Bristol Mirror*, 21.2.1818.

[4] See Committee Minutes, 30.5. and 27.6.1818. It was not until May 1841 that the Proprietors received their one and only dividend on Watson's estate, amounting to £25 3s.

[5] *Bristol Mercury*, 12.10.1818.

[6] *ibid.*, 28.12.1818.

[7] *Bristol Mirror*, 3.4.1819.

[8] M'Cready's *Prospectus* of 6 March 1819.

[9] K. M. D. Barker: Better than fiction? *Theatre Research/Recherches Théâtrales*, X, 2, 86-8.

[10] *Bristol Mercury*, 5.4.1819.

[11] *Bristol Observer*, 18.5.1820.

[12] *Bristol Mercury*, 21.2.1825.

[13] F. C. Wemyss: *Theatrical Biography*, Glasgow, 1848, Ch. VI.

[14] *Bristol Mirror*, 26.5.1821.

[15] See *Bristol Journal* and *Bristol Mirror*, 7.4.1821.

[16] Certainly he could: this was Michael Atkins, son of the well-known Belfast and Derry manager of the same name under whom the elder M'Cready himself had acted. (See W. S. Clark: *The Irish Stage in the County Towns*, 1720-1800, Oxford, 1965.) Macready's letter is in the William Macready Collection, Harvard Theatre Library.

[17] *Bristol Observer*, 22.4.1819.

[18] See obituary notice in *Bristol Mercury*, 12.3.1853.

[19] *Bristol Gazette*, 7.2.1822.

[20] *Bristol Mercury*, 26.12.1825.

[21] K. M. D. Barker and J. Macleod: The McCready prompt books at Bristol, *Theatre Notebook*, 4, 4, 76-81.

[22] *Bristol Gazette*, 9.3.1826. The scenery was mainly by Whitmore and Walter Donaldson, the machinery "by, and under the direction of" Donaldson. In his *Recollections of an Actor* (London, 1865) Donaldson dates his first engagement at Bristol as 1826, but in fact he joined M'Cready in November 1824 and stayed till the summer of 1827.

[23] *Bristol Gazette*, 3.4.1824.

[24] R. Powell: *The Bristol Stage – Its Story*, Bristol, 1919, p. 35.

[25] *Bristol Gazette*, 25.11.1819. The playbill of 22 November 1819 assigns "The Queen's Library" to Brown and "A Grand Gothic Scene and Gallery" to Finlay.

[26] Lease to William Charles Macready and Richard Brunton; see for transcription and comments A Bristol Theatre Royal Inventory, in *Studies in English Theatrical History*, London, 1952, pp. 98-113. In itemising the contents of the theatre room by room it also provides invaluable evidence of the internal arrangements of the theatre at this period.

[27] *Bristol Observer*, 11.12.1822.

[28] *Bristol Mercury*, 28.3.1825.

[29] *ibid.*, 30.4.1827.

[30] In *The Thespian*, 24. and 31.3.1823.

[31] *Bristol Gazette*, 4.9.1828.

[32] Among these are notices of his Richard III (*Bristol Journal*, 1.1.1820), Coriolanus (*Bristol Journal*, 8.4.1820), Virginius (*Bristol Observer*, 1.2.1821) and Macbeth (*Bristol Observer*, 5.2.1823); and articles in *The Thespian* (3. and 10.2.1823).

[33] *Bristol Journal*, 2.9.1826.

[34] *Bristol Gazette*, 14.2.1828.

[35] *Bristol Mercury*, 20.9.1819. and *Bristol Journal*, 25.9.1819.

[36] *Bristol Observer*, 21.9.1820.

[37] *Bristol Mirror*, 13.11.1819.

[38] *Bristol Gazette*, 18.11.1819.

[39] *Bristol Mirror*, 29.11.1828.

[40] *ibid.*, 30.12.1820.

[41] Playbills, 26.12.1821, 18.11.1822, 22.12.1823 and 2.3.1844; *Bristol Mercury*, 29.12.1823 and 29.11.1824; *Bristol Gazette*, 25.11.1824.

[42] *Bristol Mirror* and *Bristol Journal*, 30.12.1826.

[43] All Victorian accounts of George McCready infer that he was the legitimate son of William M'Cready and Sarah Desmond. though in the 1820's he seems to have been passed off as M'Cready's nephew; however,, he was born at Langholm, Dumfriesshire, on 8 July 1814, a period when M'Cready's company (including Miss Desmond) was certainly playing in that area, but seven years before his putative parents married. George was apprenticed a surgeon and gained membership of the Royal College of Surgeons on 30 May 1836. He served as medical attendant on the steamship *Great Western*, and then enlisted in the the 52nd Regiment of Foot

as Assistant Surgeon on 23 August 1839. He transferred to the 31st on 7 August 1840 and died at Barrackpore, India, on 2 October 1846 of infective hepatitis. In September 1850 Mrs. M'Cready was sent a medal "in commemoration of his gallant conduct in the campaign of the Sutlej." (Information from MOD Army, the Royal College of Surgeons; *Bristol Mirror*, 16.3.1839 and 7.9.1850; see also W. Toynbee (ed.): *The Diaries of William Charles Macready*, London, 1912, Vol. I, p. 322.)

[44] *Bristol Gazette*, 16.4.1829.

[45] Committee Minutes, 18.5.1829.

[46] Penley, *op. cit.*, p. 122.

[47] *Bristol Mercury*, 19.5.1829.

[48] K. M. D. Barker: The first English performance of Byron's *Werner*, *Modern Philology*, 66, 4, 342-4.

[49] *Bristol Journal*, 30.1.1830.

[50] *Bristol Gazette*, 11.2.1830.

[51] Committee Minutes, 8. and 12.3.1830.

[52] *Bristol Gazette*, 30.9.1830.

[53] *Bristol Mercury*, 5.10.1830.

[54] F. A. Kemble: *Record of a Girlhood*, London, 1878, Vol. 3, pp. 36 *et seq.*

[55] *Bristol Gazette*, 28.7.1831.

[56] General Meeting Minutes, 10.5.1832.

[57] Details of the alterations have been drawn from accounts in the Richard Smith Collection; *Bristol Liberal*, 24.9.1831; *Bristol Mirror* and *Bristol Journal*, 8.10.1831; *Bristol Mirror*, 22.10.1831 and *Bristol Gazette*, 27.10.1831. See also Committee Minutes, 5.10.1833.

[58] *Bristol Mirror*, 22.10.1831.

[59] Richard Smith Collection.

[60] See *Bristol Mirror*, 13.10.1832, and Toynbee, *op. cit.*, Vol. I, pp. 2-3.

[61] *Bristol Mercury*, 1.6.1833.

[62] Committee Minutes, 12.10.1833.

[63] *Bristol Mirror*, 19.10.1833.

[64] Committee Minutes, 13.1. and 15.4.1834.

[65] *Bristol Gazette*, 15.5.1845.

[66] *Bristol Mirror*, 16.12.1835; *Bristol Mercury*, 26.12.1835; and Playbill, 28.12.1835.

[67] Letter of 9.5.1838 in Trustees' Collection.

[68] Richard Smith Collection.

[69] *Bristol Mirror*, 28.8.1841.

[70] Account Book.

[71] *Bristol Times* and *Bristol Mirror*, 21.12.1844.

[72] *Bristol Journal*, 13.4.1839.

[73] Information from Charles Kean's Account Books transcribed by Dr. Glen Wilson.

[74] *Bristol Times*, 3.10.1840.

[75] *Bristol Mercury*, 6.5.1843.

[76] Quoted in W. Archer: *William Charles Macready*, London, 1890, pp. 90-1.

[77] Toynbee, *op. cit.* Vol. I, p. 218; *Bristol Mirror* 7.3.1835.

[78] *Bristol Times* 14.3.1840.

[79] *Bristol Mercury*, 20.3.1841. Compare the account here and in the *Bristol Mirror* of the same date with the descriptions of the Vestris revival in G. C. Odell: *Shakespeare from Betterton to Irving*, New York, 1920, Vol. 2, pp. 223-5, and see also Playbill of 15.3.1841.

[80] *Bristol Mercury*, 1.3.1845.

[81] *ibid.*, 15.3.1845.

[82] Advertisement, *Bristol Mirror*, 9.1.1841.

[83] Playbill, 15.4.1836; *Bristol Gazette*, 14.4.1836. The scenery was by C. J. James.

[84] *Bristol Journal*, 21.3.1840. The script of *Lundy* was submitted for licensing but has unfortunately disappeared from the Lord Chamberlain's Collection in the British Museum.

[85] At one concert organised by the famous impressario, Laporte, Grisi failed to arrive, having been "double booked". One of the Bristol magistrates, McBayne, who was among the disappointed audience, was prepared to indict Laporte for obtaining money on false pretences, but the promised complainants did not come forward when the court sat. (*Bristol Gazette*, 30.5.1839.)

[86] See Playbill, 15.11.1841, and *Bristol Mercury*, 22.10.1842.

[87] Playbill, 21.9.1841. The first performance in English had been given at Drury Lane on 24 June 1837.

[88] *Bristol Times*, 28.9.1839.

[89] *Bristol Mirror*, 28.9.1839.

[90] *ibid.*, 13.4.1844.

[91] *Bristol Advocate*, 14.1.1837.

[92] *Bristol Mercury*, 23.2.1839.

[93] *Bristol Times*, 7.1.1843.

[94] *ibid.*, 25.5.1844.

[95] The Chute link with the Bristol theatre was finally broken only by the death of Mrs. James Chute, a director of the Prince's Theatre, in 1931.

[96] Toynbee, *op. cit.*, Vol. I, pp. 176-7.

[97] J. Coleman: *Players and Playwrights I Have Known*, London, 1888, Vol. I, p. 79; Powell, *op. cit.*, p. 52.

[98] *Bristol Mirror*, 11.1.1845.

[99] *Bristol Mirror*, 5.7.1845, quoting *Bath Chronicle*.

[100] *Bristol Journal*, 5.4.1851.

[101] Committee Minutes, 15.3. and 11.11.1848.

[102] *Bristol Mercury*, 18.1.1851.

[103] *ibid.*, 20.9.1845.

[104] Chute produced a number of (unlicensed) dramatisations in Bristol; his version of *Don Caesar de Bazan* had been staged in February 1845.

[105] *Bristol Mercury*, 23.10.1852.

[106] *ibid.*, 27.11.1852.

[107] There are very full and lively accounts in all the local papers, especially *Bristol Gazette*, 30.9.1847, and *Bristol Journal* and *Bristol Mercury* of 2.10.1847. H. E. Cooper, the able leader of the theatre orchestra, so impressed Jenny Lind by his tactful and competent accompaniment that she recommended him for appointment as leader of the band at Her Majesty's Theatre, then the home of grand opera. (See *Bristol Journal*, 23.10.1847.)

[108] See the acrimonious debate in *Bristol Journal* and *Bristol Mercury*, 4. and 11. 11.1848, and Bristol Gazette, 9.11.1848.

[109] *Bristol Mirror*, 21.2.1846.

[110] *Bristol Times*, 2.2.1850.

[111] *Bristol Mirror*, 20.1.1849.

[112] Quoted in full in *Bristol Gazette*, 11.3.1847.

[113] *Bristol Gazette*, 17.9.1846.

[114] F. A. Kemble: *Records of Later Life*, London, 1878, p. 191.

[115] *Bristol Mirror*, 15.2.1851. Two years later Owen had risen no higher than the "heavy business" at Worthing. See M. T. Odell: *More About the Old Theatre, Worthing*, Worthing , 1945, p. 32.

[116] See, e.g., *Bristol Gazette*, 14.1.1847 (Hamlet); *Bristol Mercury*, 23.1.1847 and 8.1.1848 (Macbeth); and *Bristol Times*, 8.1.1848 (Wolsey).

[117] *Bristol Gazette*, 14.1.1847.

[118] *Bristol Mercury*, 12.1.1850.

[119] *Bristol Gazette*, 11.11.1852. As early as August 1846 Mrs. M'Cready had had to include in her advertisements: "No Smoking allowed within the walls of the Theatre."

[120] *Bristol Journal,* 12.5.1849; J. Coleman: *Fifty Years of an Actor's Life,* London, 1904, p. 499. The engagement took place in Coleman's first Bristol season, not, as he infers, his second.

[121] The publication of 1846 of an engraving of Artaud as "Trotty" Veck in *The Chimes* bears witness to his popularity. See *Bristol Mirror,* 25.4.1846.

[122] *Bristol Gazette,* 10.1.1850.

[123] *ibid.,* 17.1.1850.

[124] From Boxing Day 1851 to the end of the season on 10 May 1852 the only visitors were the child prodigies, Kate and Ellen Bateman.

1. The facade of the Theatre Royal in 1804-5. One of a group of drawings prepared for James Winston's *Theatric Tourist* and now in the Mitchell Library, Sydney.

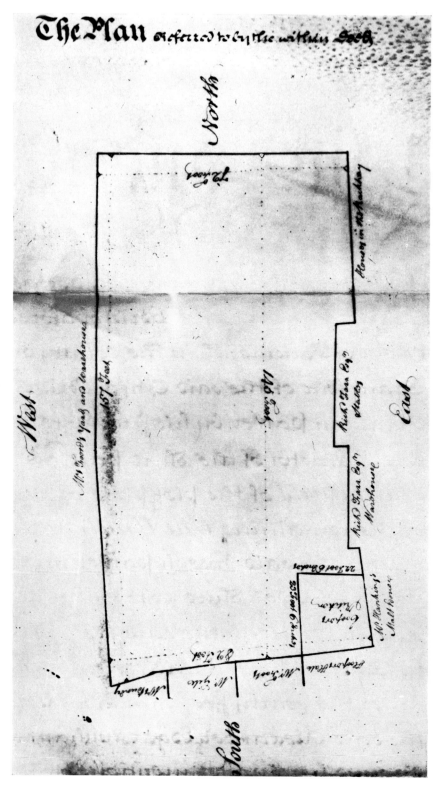

2. Ground plan of the Theatre site, attached to the deed of conveyance from Mrs. Bethia Richards and others to the Theatre Proprietors, dated 23 October 1764. Theatre Royal Trustees' Collection, Bristol City Archives.

3. Auditorium of the Richmond (Surrey) Theatre prior to demolition in 1884.
This theatre was designed by James Saunderson and opened the year before the
Bristol theatre. Richard Southern Accession, Theatre Collection, Bristol University.

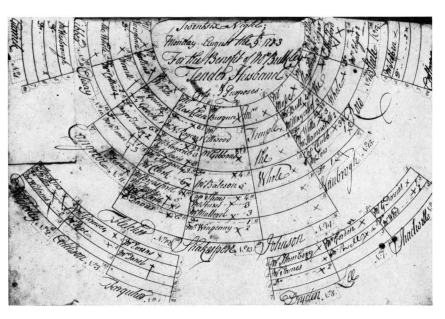

4. A sheet from one of the early Box Books, preserved in the Richard Smith Collection,
Bristol Reference Library.

5. The back of the Theatre Royal showing the original dressing rooms and recess backstage, a unique survival of theatre architecture. Photographed by Mr. G. W. Nash shortly before demolition in 1970, and reproduced by permission of the Victoria & Albert Museum.

6. View of the Theatre Royal auditorium taken just before closure in 1970, showing the Corinthian pillars flanking the former Stage Boxes and the reeded pilasters of the Dress and Upper Circles. Photograph : Derek Balmer.

8. William Wyatt Dimond (?1750-1812) and Tryphosa Wallis (1774-1848) as Romeo and Juliet, parts which they played in Bristol on 4 April 1796. Engraving by F. Bartolozzi from a painting by E. Shirreff (1796), reproduced by permission of the Trustees of the British Museum.

7. Memorial to William Powell, erected in 1771 and restored by his daughter in 1811, sited in the north wall of Bristol Cathedral. Photograph by Tudor, Facey & Miller; reproduced by permission of the Dean and Chapter of Bristol Cathedral.

9. William M'Cready the elder (1754-1829), Manager of the Theatre Royal, Bristol, from 1819 to 1829. Engraving by W. Ridley from the miniature by Halpin, reproduced by permission of the Trustees of the British Museum.

Theatre-Royal, Bristol.

Signor Il Diavolo Antonio,

At the instance of several Ladies and Gentlemen, is induced to appear again on the

CORDE VOLANTE,

In the THEATRE-ROYAL, BRISTOL, which he purposes doing

On FRIDAY Evening next, the 25th June, 1819,

For His Benefit,

When will be presented, SHAKESPEARE's TRAGEDY of

Richard the Third.

Richard........ .... Mr. BOOTH

Who has volunteer'd his services to his Friend SIGNOR ANTONIO, on the occasion.

King Henry.......... .... Mr. CRESWELL §	Earl of Richmond.................. Mr. PRIOR
Duke of Buckingham, Mr. GLADSTANES; §	Prince Edward...... .... Miss PARR
Duke of York .. Miss NEWTON § Catesby.. Mr. LASCELLES §	Lieut. of the Tower, Mr. DARLEY
Tressell .... Mr. HOOPER § Ratcliff... Mr. JOHNSON §	Tyrrel............... Mr. BENNETT
Lord Stanley.... Mr. MANDERSON § Norfolk... Mr. RIVERS §	Dighton.............. Mr. PLASANTS
Lord Mayor...... Mr. NEWTON §	Officer...... .... Mr. LEWIS
Lady Anne.............. Mrs. NEWTON §	Dutchess of York....... .... Mrs. MARA
And the Queen..................... Miss DESMOND.	

END OF THE PLAY,

SIGNOR IL DIAVOLO ANTONIO,

To show his unequalled Elegance and Ease

ON THE CORDE VOLANTE,

Will, when the Rope is in full swing, accompany the Orchestra on the CASTANETS in " La Folie d'Espagne."

SIGNOR ANTONIO, on this night must crave the kind indulgence of the Audience, to allow his omission of that part in his performance where strong exertion is required.

After which a COMIC SONG, by Mr. NEWTON.

In the course of the Evening,

MADAME ANTONIO will Sing A FAVOURITE AIR.

(As sung by MADAME CATALANI) being her first appearance in Public.

The whole to conclude with the revived PANTOMIME of

ROBINSON CRUSOE.

Robinson Crusoe... Mr. JAMES JONES ‡	Friday's Father.............. Mr. LEWIS
His Man Friday... Mr. LASCELLES ‡	Principal Savage............ Mr. DARLEY

Savages, Messrs. Johnson, Plasants, &c. &c.

A British Captain... Mr. RIVERS

TICKETS to be had of SIGNOR ANTONIO, 34, Queen-Square, at ROUTH & JAMESON's, Printing-Office, at the WHITE LION HOTEL, Broad-Street, and of Mr. COZENS, at the Theatre where places for the Boxes may be taken.

10. *Amende Honorable*. After wounding the tight-rope performer Il Diavolo Antonio in a pistol duel, Booth played Richard III for the Benefit of "his Friend". Theatre Collection, Bristol University.

Theatre=Royal, Bristol.

For the BENEFIT of

Mr. Macready,

And the *LAST NIGHT* of his Performing.

NEVER ACTED.

The MANAGER has the honor of announcing that

On MONDAY EVENING, January 25, 1830,

A Tragedy entitled

WERNER;

Or, THE INHERITANCE,

FROM THE PEN OF LORD BYRON,

Will be submitted, on its first representation, to the judgment of a Bristol Audience.

The SCENERY will be New and Appropriate, as well as the DRESSES, in which no expense will be spared to do all possible justice to the reputation of the NOBLE AUTHOR.

The SCENERY Painted by Mr. SMITHES and Assistants.—The DRESSES by Mr. SMITHES and Assistants.

Werner..........................Mr. MACREADY

Ulric....Mr. MASON | Baron Stralenheim.....Mr. F. WILTON | Idenstein (Intendant of the Old Palace)....Mr. EDWARDS
Gabor (an Hungarian)...........Mr. BRUNTON | Fritz (Valet to Stralenheim)........Mr. SELBY
Henrick..Mr. SMYTHES | Erick...Mr. CHEW | Ludwig....Mr. MARTIN | Rodolph...MURRAY | Rodolph..Mc.C JONES
Gabot (an Hungarian)...........Mr. McHEW | Servant of the Old Palace.........Servants of Stralenheim.
The Prior Albert.....Mr. BUTLER | Servants of Siegendorf, Hunters, &c. Miss GLIDDON.
Josephine. (Wife of Werner)........Miss MAILLARD | In Stralenheim.

A WAINSCOTTED HALL, in a RUINED CASTLE.
A CORRIDOR.
A Tapestried Chamber.——A Vaulted Passage.
An Apartment in the Castle of Siegendorf.

After which, Shakespeare's Petic Comedy of

Catherine and Petruchio.

Petruchio......Mr. MACREADY, his first appearance in that character in this Theatre
Baptista.....Mr. C. JONES | Gremio........Mr. GARDNER | Biondello.....Mr. F. WILTON | Music Master....Mr. SELBY
Tailor....Mr. EDWARDS | Pedro.....Mr. MURRAY | Gregory....Mr. MARTIN | Nathaniel....Mr. SMYTHES
.......Mr. CHEW | Nicholas.....Mr. BRUNTON | Curtis.......Mr. BUTLER
Catherine.......Mrs. SELBY | Bianca.......Miss GLIDDON | Curtis........Mrs. SOUTHBY

To conclude with the Grand Pantomime called

PEROUSE.

Champanzee (an Animal of the Desolate Island)...................Mr. ESHER
Perouse.....................Mr. EDWARDS
EUROCLYDON, (Son of Perouse).....................Miss UMBER
Perouse (The Navigator).........Mr. SELBY
Congee (Servant to Madame Perouse)..Theodore (Son of Perouse)....Mr. SELBY
Madame Perouse.....................Mr. SELBY. HONEY

NATIVES OF A NEIGHBOURING ISLAND.

Harko (Sailor to Umba)....Mr. EDWARDS | Tetane............Mr. MURRAY | Puyepaw....Mr. MURRAY
Umba.....................Mr. CHEW | Tetane............Mrs. FIELD

Nights of Performing this week—MONDAY, WEDNESDAY, THURSDAY, & FRIDAY.

Tickets for the Pit and Gallery to be had at the Office of the Bristol Mercury, 9, Narrow Wine-Street.

Somerton, Printer, Mercury-Office, 9, Narrow Wine-Street.

13. Peeling off the stuccoed canvas over one of the Dress Circle box-fronts revealed this painted wooden panel, dating from 1835. This and another similar panel are now on display in the Dress Circle lobby. Richard Southern Accession, Theatre Collection, Bristol University.

15. Ellen Terry as Hector Melrose and Kate Terry as "Mrs. Terrorbody" in *Home for the Holidays*, played by them at their first joint Benefit in Bristol, 28 November 1862. Photograph: Victoria & Albert Museum.

14. A wash drawing by Moyr Smith of William Charles Macready as Iago and John Coleman as Othello, parts they played in Bristol during Macready's farewell engagement on 14 January 1850. Originally reproduced in Coleman's *Fifty Years of an Actor's Life* and rephoto-

18. Andrew Melville I (1853-96), manager, of the Theatre Royal, Bristol, from 1881 to 1892. Photographs of George and Andrew Melville kindly supplied by Andrew Melville III.

16, 17. Above, George Melville (1824-98), one of the most popular leading actors ever engaged in Bristol. His performance in *East Lynne* (right) marked the centenary of the Theatre Royal. (The woodcut on the playbill, in Bristol Reference Library, shows the death of Little Willy.)

19. The façade erected by the Proprietors in 1902, as drawn for the *Bristol Evening News* of 2 January 1903. This frontage was demolished in 1970.

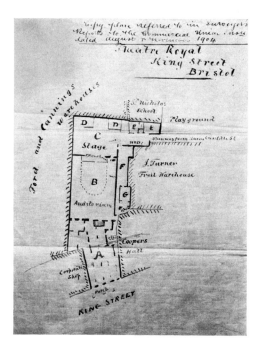

20. Ground plan of the Theatre Royal attached to a Fire Insurance policy of 1904 in the Theatre Royal Trustees' Collection, Bristol City Archives. The plan includes the following key:

A and B	Entrances to Pit, Circles and Gallery, Offices, Bill Store and Cloak Rooms and Lavatory, Auditorium, Boxes and Refreshment Bars.
C, D.D., E.E., F and G	Building of the Stage, Band Store, Old and New Dressing Rooms, Scene Painting Room, Carpenters Shop (containing one double bench) and Passages.

21. Sketches of members of Muriel Pratt's Repertory Company in Arthur Skemp's *Guenevere*, produced on 2 November 1914. Reproduced from *Bristol Playgoer*, November 1914, by permission of the Bristol Playgoers' Club.

22. The finale of *Dick Whittington*, pantomime for 1910-1. On the extreme right is the Stage Manager, Mr. Lake, and next to him Crosby and Walker. Photograph from contemporary postcard in the possession of Mr. Edward Goulding ("Dan Jacques"), then Assistant Stage Manager at the Theatre Royal.

23. The auditorium of the Theatre Royal in the early 1930s, showing the three rows of stalls in front of the benched pit.

24. The auction of the Theatre Royal on 28 January 1942. Photograph: *Bristol Evening Post*. Original negative destroyed; rephotographed by Veronica Stanley.

25. The Watch in a post-war Messina, led by Warden Dogberry (William Devlin) and a rustic Verges (Kenneth Connor) in Hugh Hunt's 1947 production of *Much Ado About Nothing*. Photograph: Desmond Tripp.

26. Cyrano (Peter Wyngarde) completes his Ballade by pinking the Vicomte de Valvert (Philip Anthony) in a duel at the Hôtel de Bourgogne. This photograph, from John Hale's 1959 production of *Cyrano de Bergerac,* shows part of Patrick Robertson's "theatre within a theatre" set. Photograph: Desmond Tripp.

27. Princess Marina drinks a toast to the future of the Theatre Royal after the Bicentenary Gala Performance on 2 June 1966. Right is Val May, Artistic Director of the Bristol Old Vic, and left are electrician Ken Vowles and chief engineer Ernest Peppin. Photograph: *Bristol Evening Post.*

Part Four
Indian Summer

Mr. Chute . . . combines rare taste for scenic display with great judgment, and thus he saw at once that it was not sufficient to merely decorate the theatre in the highest style of fashion, without placing before the public pieces, the sterling merit of which is rendered still more apparent by the general acting ability of the corps.

Bristol Times, 24.9.1853.

I see no reason why Bristol should not . . . possess a building which would be a credit to the city, and do away with that horrible den in King Street, which street, I may add, has long since become one of the back slums of the town.

"R.A.D." in *Western Daily Press,* 4.11.1863.

One

1853-1862

"Our governor is a fine looking man, deep in the chest, broad in the shoulders – well set up, twinkling eyes – that can be severe – broad massive forehead and large moustache. His hands are Frenchy in their action, and he is never seen without a pair of gloves – which I am told by the old hands he has never been known to put on."

This letter from the young actor, William Rignold, to his father, written when he joined the Stock Company in the autumn of 1859,[1] gives a vivid picture of James Henry Chute in his middle years. The members of his companies soon discovered that matching the impressive physique was a knowledge of the stage and a care for all that was best in the theatre which was quite exceptional, and to which Marie Wilton, Madge Robertson and Ellen Terry all pay tribute.

Chute should undoubtedly be reckoned among the great provincial theatre managers. His experience as a Stock Company actor provided him with contacts all over the British Isles, and gave him the close friendship of men like Edward Compton and Charles Kean.* Fortunate in the exceptional continuity of management in the Bristol Theatre Royal, he fostered a family atmosphere which encouraged former members to renew their contacts, both through personal engagements and through their children. His administrative competence was of an equally high order : the pattern of efficient stage and house management he set was still being quoted with approval by Seymour Hicks in 1910.[2]

* It was no doubt Chute's friendship with Kean which led to the engagement for one night of "Miss Marlowe" as Jessica in *The Merchant of Venice* on 28 May 1858. "She played with as much confidence as one would like to see in a young lady of refined and modest feeling, and she read the little fragmentary bits of which the dialogue is made up with intelligence and care." (*Bristol Mercury*, 29.5.1858.) "Miss Marlowe" was in fact the temporary stage name of Patty Chapman, Mrs. Charles Kean's niece, who was being tried out in the part at Bristol prior to assuming it in the June production at the Princess's.

But above all Chute had the vital quality of being able to identify himself with the most influential section of Bristolians, the successful middle-class businessmen : his conservative outlook, scrupulous morality and commercial respectability appealed directly to them. It is no surprise to find Chute joining the newly-formed Rifle Volunteer Corps and being appointed Sergeant of No. 1 Company; and so able and popular did he prove that every year the Corps bespoke a performance at his theatre at least once in the season, an occasion guaranteed to produce an overflow even at enhanced box prices. This local identification was reflected in Chute's concept of his theatre : not just as the home of a struggling hack company which could only be made respectable by a succession of stars, but as an artistic, and a moral, force of intrinsic value; a company whose productions, while they might be inspired by the best in the metropolitan theatre, would be worth seeing for their own sake.

At the time of Sarah M'Cready's death a second instalment of *Uncle Tom's Cabin*, highlighting the death of Little Eva, was in preparation, and the momentum of its success, even greater than that of the earlier version, carried the season forward to its close. The last night was devoted to a Benefit for the new manager, an eminently satisfactory occasion "with the exception of a slight interruption caused by a gentleman in the dress circle being seized with a fit".[3]

Chute had the courage of his convictions; abandoning the penny-pinching caution which had become second nature to Mrs. M'Cready, he risked almost all his resources in a thorough renovation of the theatre during the summer vacation. Knowing the demand for spectacle, he over-hauled the stage machinery and enlarged the stage by roofing over the yard behind the theatre which had been leased by Mrs. M'Cready, turning it into "an added stage and dressing rooms". He seems to have intended to follow this up by demolishing the rooms either side of the back-stage recess, as was done in 1970 – indeed, the *Bristol Gazette* implies that this was in progress when the season began. However, a succession of leases during and after Chute's management continue to list the "rooms on stage" and their fittings exactly as in 1829, while an insurance schedule of 1862 (quoted in Committee Minutes) itemises separately the fact that

The Stage of the Theatre adjoins and lies open to a building the property of the Trustees of Mrs. J. H. Chute erected at the back of the Theatre part of which building forms a continuation of the Stage of the Theatre and other part contains dressing and other rooms applied to theatrical purposes.

It would appear, then, that Chute used additional depth behind the recess (32 feet, according to the *Bristol Mercury* of 30 July 1853), flanking it with extra dressing rooms. These were certainly needed, for the old understage dressing rooms had long been annexed by the Band, while the Stock Company was larger than ever before. Besides these amenities, Chute completely renewed the whole of the gas fittings (towards the cost of which the Proprietors allowed him £50 off his rent) and laid on "The COMPANY'S WATER with Fire Mains".

In the new scheme of decoration the ceiling of the theatre was divided by radiating lines into segments ornamented with allegorical figures representing the four elements and four seasons, designed by I. S. Lenox, the scene painter, and painted by him and his assistants. The fronts of the boxes were redecorated by Edkins & Son and presented "a chaste and elegant appearance, the prevailing colours being lemon, French grey and white, with occasional illuminations in scarlet and gold." Grieve and Telbin produced a new act-drop which "represents a Grecian plain studded with ruins far and near of temples and aqueducts, while what appears to be the ruins of an amphitheatre graces the scene".[4]

Undoubtedly in the long term this expenditure, amounting to over £616, constituted a valuable, indeed an essential, investment by Chute, but meanwhile by the end of the first season he found himself desperately short of money, for, as he ingenuously wrote to the Proprietors, "expense after expense crept in and one necessity begat another till I found myself fairly in for it." He had hoped that the Committee would take responsibility for the costs incurred in laying on mains water, and for the whole of the front of house gas lighting, but all they would offer was another £50 towards the latter, which Chute reluctantly accepted.[5]

At the end of the 1854-5 season the lease was due for renewal and to his disgust the Proprietors insisted on increasing the rent by £100 to £350. Chute

remonstrated against this advance, on the grounds that he had been, on the whole, a loser by the last season, that the rent of £250 was only what was paid in the most palmy days of theatrical success, whilst his enterprise alone prevented the establishment being shut for some years, and thus thrown profitless on the hands of the proprietors. He further stated that he had expended nearly £1000 in decorations, &c.

The increase was principally instigated by one of the Committee, Isaac Riddle, who claimed that "if Mr. Chute would not give the advance, parties in London were prepared to do so", and in order not to lose all benefit from his considerable outlay Chute could do no other than agree.[6] Almost certainly this episode provided him with the first important stimulus towards acquiring a theatre of his own.

Such irritations did not prevent Chute from making further improvements in the Theatre Royal. He widened the stage by three feet in

September 1854, obtained permission to put backs to the seats in the lower boxes in 1856, and in 1858 put forward more important proposals for a separation of the Pit and Gallery entrances, a highly necessary safety precaution, which he carried out that autumn.[7] In 1861 Chute finally persuaded the Proprietors to let him lease both theatre and adjacent houses for eight and a half years from October at a yearly rent of £400, and thenceforth the property was always treated as a whole.

Chute also turned his attention to the organisation of the season, and here again he determined to break with the past. Because of the increasing number of both operatic and theatrical companies who were beginning to tour as almost complete units during the summer,[8] Chute was often able to let the theatre without risk to himself during part of August. The traditional September opening, a relic of the days of the St. James's Fair, was prolonged into mid-December. After a break in which to rehearse the pantomime intensively, the main season began on Boxing Day and ran till about mid-May (including Benefits), with extra nights at Whitsuntide and occasional subsequent bookings. Thus, juggling with the various attractions of stars, novelties, opera and pantomime, Chute kept his theatre open for almost ten months of the year, which enabled him to reduce admission prices almost uniformly to the old half-price scale: Dress Boxes 3s. (Second Price 2s.); Upper Boxes 2s. (Second Price 1s. 6d.); Pit 1s.; Gallery 6d.

The size of the company Chute maintained allowed him when necessary to run performances at both Bath and Bristol on the same night, but Bath was very much the junior partner.* Bristol saw the first run of the pantomime and major novelties, and, when stars came, they normally played four nights at Bristol as compared with two at Bath.

Striking out boldly in his first full season, Chute brought out only a fortnight after the opening a detailed reproduction of Charles Kean's revival of *Macbeth* at the Princess's the preceding February, down to the antiquarian notes attached to the playbill. George Melville was the Macbeth, Mrs. Chute his Lady; both gave interesting though uneven performances, but it was the remarkably high standard of the staging – made more respectable by the association with Kean's name – which drew the comment, and, no doubt, the crowds:

When the curtain drew up in the first scene in which the witches appear, the stage was so darkened that it was impossible to distinguish more than shadowy forms haggard and wild, and thus the illusion was heightened . . . The night view of Iona was one of the sweetest moonlight scenes we ever witnessed, and called

* Chute had managerial links with Bath before he took the theatre, having leased the Assembly Rooms in 1848, but he gave up the Rooms after ten years; see *Bristol Times* for 2 October 1858.

forth the merited applause of the audience . . . An important change is also made in the scenery representing Macbeth's Castle at Inverness and Dunsinane, where instead of a front view of the castle gates, we get a side view, the whole of the stage being made available as a court-yard, while the back scenery represents a mountainous country.[9]

In February 1854, after the pantomime, a similarly elaborate copy of the Princess's *King John* (Kean's first great "historical revival" of two years previous) was put on the Bristol stage.

The success of these and other classical productions, however much helped by extensive scenery and historical costume, could not have been sustained without strong leading actors. Here the enormous popularity of George Melville counted for much. It is difficult to gauge just how good Melville really was, for he clearly had that personal magnetism associated with the gallery idol, which inspires intense partisanship, but is unfortunately destructive of self-criticism. The most crucial of Melville's faults was inability to develop; the praise and criticism of his acting in his earliest days is essentially the same as that dealt out twenty years later.

He does not distinguish sufficiently between what should be declamatory and what colloquial, and thus, when he should enunciate a passage with quiet emphasis, he frequently bursts forth into a fury, and appears to lose sight of his author, and only study how to gain the applause of his audience.[10]

The influence of the audiences' uncritical adulation led to difficulties for other leading actors. At the beginning of the 1853-4 season, Chute engaged Walter Montgomery, whose range of parts was similar to Melville's, with a view to alternating them in Othello and Iago. But at Montgomery's first performance of Othello Melville failed to appear, "under the impression, we hear, that he should be playing second to Mr. Montgomery." However, not improbably influenced by the unexpected success of Harcourt Bland, who had played Iago at short notice, Melville changed his attitude, and soon he and Montgomery were playing in double harness with apparent smoothness.

The following season, Melville being engaged at Birmingham, Chute hired Walter Shelley, from Edinburgh, as his leading man. Unfortunately his Shylock was deemed "anything but good, falling immeasurably short of that of his predecessor, Mr. W. Montgomery"; in Macbeth "he had no idea of the part, and did not appear even to have made a guess at it. He had but one indiscriminate way of shouting through every passage".[11] Similar objections were made to his King John. These were the unanimous reactions of the box critics; the gallery made their viewpoint even clearer. Before Shelley could speak a word on his first entry, he was "assailed by vulgar clamours and cries for another performer." Deeply and understandably hurt, Shelley resigned his engagement early in October, after writing an indignant letter to the *Bristol Mercury*. The next week Melville was back, his re-appearance "hailed by the playgoers with much satisfaction".

It needed an actor of Melville's or Montgomery's appeal to make a major classical revival pay over an extended run, and after *King John* there was no further production of this type till one of *A Midsummer Night's Dream* in October 1858 – also in imitation of Kean, who had staged it two years previously. Its beauty was acclaimed :

> The scenery is to the full as beautiful [as Kean's], the mechanical and dioramic effects as brilliant and striking, the dresses as characteristic, costly, and elegant, the appointments as ample and complete, the groupings as chaste and classical, and the *tout ensemble* such as some twenty years ago or more no one would have dreamt of attaining.[12]

The attendances, however, were disappointing; Chute took warning, and thereafter Shakespeare became largely incidental to the repertory, and increasingly the preserve of the visiting star.

Shakespeare, of course, was not the only author whose plays enjoyed spectacular success at the Princess's. *Faust and Marguerite* (first brought out by Kean in April 1854) was reproduced in Bristol in October 1857, and aroused much controversy :

> Some people say that it is profane to personate angels at a theatre, whilst others say that if the play points a good moral, as it certainly does in this case, it cannot be objectionable. At any rate, it is a drama which must impress the mind, at times, even with religious awe, especially when the machinery is so complete and excellent as it is in this instance.[13]

The "Faust light" (an early application of limelight) was so much admired that Chute made use of it immediately for the statue scene from *The Winter's Tale*, and four years later in *The Angel of Midnight*.

The emergence of the sensation play also absorbed much of the resources hitherto invested in classical revivals. Such playwrights as Edmund Falconer, and, pre-eminently, Dion Boucicault, purveyed mingled thrills and spectacle on a scale which made mere drama seem an anticlimax. Chute was able to obtain a licence from Boucicault to produce *The Colleen Bawn* from late February to Easter 1861, and it ran for four weeks without a break. *Peep o' Day*, produced on 24 March 1862, was staged almost every night till the season ended on 16 May, except for Benefit nights and a week's engagement of Mr. and Mrs. Charles Kean.

Chute advertised that he had been in direct communication with Boucicault, and would therefore be able to produce *The Colleen Bawn* "with all the Original Scenic Effects and Mechanical Contrivances . . . and with the same completeness as in London, the whole appliances of the Theatre being directed towards this object".[14] The scenery was a triumph for George Gordon :

The "Water Cave", the scene of the attempted murder of the Colleen Bawn,* is an exquisite picture which startles the audience, not by any wonderful display of tinsel grandeur or rolling canvas, but by its charming simplicity, its quiet, solemn beauty . . .[15]

With all this emphasis on scenic effect, it is not surprising that Christmas pantomime became an important part of the programme; within only a few years of its introduction Bristolians were taking it for granted as part of their Christmas tradition. On the annual pantomime all the skill of painters and machinists was lavished, especially on the transformation scenes. After the meeting of demons at the beginning of *Valentine and Orson*

The view now becomes gradually transformed to "The Valley of Flowers in the Island of Bloom and Beauty" . . . Golden palm trees, bearing fruit of rubies, emeralds, and sapphires, tower majestically from the earth, flowers of the richest hues deck the ground, and a river of crystalline waters, which appears to flow from the very back of the stage, keeps up a ceaseless ripple.[16]

In contrast, the humour was often decidely crude; indeed, it occasionally met with criticism at the time :

The general public don't like to see even a pantomime infant stripped naked and thrust into a monster's mouth, nor do they think it pleasant to have their lungs filled with a nauseous gas, for the sake of seeing a few crackers explode at the heels of a Chinaman.[17]

But where all was bustle, action, glitter and kaleidoscopic colour there was no time to brood on niceties.

Large numbers of extras were always hired for the pantomime. For *The Babes in the Wood*, in 1858, Chute was rash enough to advertise for "A Host of Children, between 7 and 9 years of age", who should apply at the Theatre the next Saturday afternoon. Apply they did, in their hordes :

The doors were literally besieged, and not only were the passages impassable by mere civilians, but General Chute himself had the greatest difficulty in forcing a passage to his green room. When he did get there such a din arose as

---

* Coming immediately after a dramatisation of Wilkie Collins' *Woman in White*, Boucicault's drama was irreverently christened by the wags "The Woman in Wet."

has seldom been heard. "Take me!" cried one; "Am I big enough for a soldier?" bawled another; "Do 'ee, sir, have this nice little boy!" shouted an anxious mother; until at length the gallant General was so bewildered that he was obliged to threaten that he would turn on the cold water hose, and so cool the ardour of the whole force.[18]

Finally the selection was made, and the well-drilled little recruits made their contribution both to the pantomime and to the exchequer of many a poor local household.

An important part of the pantomime's appeal, of course, was local, and Chute exploited this fully. Local allusions, mainly satirical, were *de rigueur* in the opening scenes of Demons and Fairies; local shops were portrayed (doubtless for a consideration) in the scenery, and local views adorned the Harlequinade, and sometimes the dramatic opening as well.

The manager's shrewd eye for the topical was not confined to the pantomime. When Lord John Russell came down to open the New Athenaeum in Bristol in October 1854 Chute profited by the interest aroused to stage Russell's *Don Carlos*.[19] He introduced into Charles Reade's *Gold* a scene puffing a local emigration agency, though so clumsily that on the advice of the press he cut it (and a good deal more) out again. When the Rifle Volunteer Corps created some furore by complaining to the newspapers about the choice of their officers, the style of their uniform, and the organisation of their parades, Chute produced a delightful burlesque, probably adapted from Edward Stirling's *The Rifle Volunteers,* with Emily Thorne (sister of Sarah Thorne of Margate) as the dashing Captain.

> The humour of the piece is concentrated on Mr. [Arthur] Wood's address to the awkward squad, whom he instructs not to obey any order, if there should be the least inconvenience attendant upon its execution.[20]

The Corps, not wihout a sense of humour, included the piece in the programme of their next Bespeak.

The waves of patriotism aroused by the Crimean War and later the Indian Mutiny were aslo reflected not only in the pantomime but in the standard repertory. In the anxiety to promote the status of the French as our noble allies in the Crimea, the spectacle of *The Battle of the Alma* ended with nothing less than "an apotheosis of Napoleon the 1st and Wellington smiling benignantly on the conquerors". *The Battle of Agincourt* (adapted from Shakespeare's *King Henry V*) was produced the next month to bring out the analogies between the Battles of Agincourt and Inkerman. "Any apparent want of regard for the character of our French allies," the historically squeamish were reassured, "is cured by a prologue and epilogue, in which the different circumstances of France in

1415 and 1854 are contrasted, and the unjustifiable character of the English king's aggressive war exposed."[21]

The demands of the repertory dictated the composition of the company, but here again Chute showed his acumen. "Gaffs" and tavern music halls were springing up all over Bristol during the 1850s, and circuses were becoming larger, more elaborate and more frequent. There was nothing to be gained by trying to compete with these types of entertainment, and it was in the interests of middle-class respectability not to try. At the other extreme, the tendency to tour in large and viable groups instead of as individual stars, just perceptible in drama, was becoming the rule rather than the exception in opera, the so-called Dublin, London, National, and Harrison & Pyne Opera Companies, as well as the Italian Opera, touring regularly. Sensibly Chute concentrated on supplying the remaining needs : on increasing the acting strength of his company and expanding the ballet into a respectable (though of course by to-day's standards woefully amateur) corps.

Some of Chute's engagements proved to be unforeseeably fortunate. When Robert Wilton joined the Bristol Company as a small part actor in the autumn of 1850, it could hardly have been prophesied that his eleven-year-old daughter, Marie, would become a brilliant comedienne. She made her Bristol debut as Fleance in *Macbeth* on 26 September 1853, but the first part she recalled playing was that of the Sprite of the Silver Star in the 1853-4 pantomime, *Harlequin World of Flowers*, in which she was

discovered high up in the clouds, prettily dressed in pale blue silk and spangles, my long hair hanging in large waves over my shoulders. As I was lowered by machinery, which every now and again gave an uncomfortable jerk, I was conscious of an anxious look upon my face . . . I was instructed to come down with a happy smile on my face, but the expression must have resembled the fixed stare one sees on a photograph after the victim's long and tedious sitting.[22]

The pretty Sprite was favourably noticed, and went on to play a variety of youthful parts, particularly the boy Henri in *Belphegor the Mountebank*, a favourite vehicle of Charles Dillon. On his visit in April 1855 she argued with both him and Chute over her business in the scene where the Mountebank discovers his wife has deserted them, sensing that it would be both more realistic and more effective if Henri's tears and murmured prayers formed an audible background to his father's reactions.[23] She won her point when, at a test rehearsal, she actually made Chute weep. After the performance Dillon promised that, if ever he had a London theatre, he would offer her an engagement, and so he did, Marie Wilton leaving Bristol in the autumn of 1856, though she returned more than once as a star or to play for her father's Benefit. In view of her later almost exclusive dedication to comedy, it is noteworthy that she several times played Ophelia in Bristol with "affecting simplicity," and even attempted Adrienne Lecouvreur.

Miss Margaret Robertson – Dame Madge Kendal to be – again became a member of the Bristol Stock Company only because her parents, who in more prosperous times had run the Lincoln circuit where Chute had been an actor, were now employed by him. The accounts of Madge Robertson's early days in Bristol, both in T. E. Pemberton's biography and her own memoirs,[24] are totally unreliable. She certainly did not play Little Eva in 1854-5 (the child prodigy, Clara St. Casse, was specially engaged); it was October 1858 when she first appeared in the part, and even in 1860 she was deemed not to be the equal of Miss St. Casse. During her first four years she acted mainly children's roles, the most highly praised being her Arthur, in *King John,* "a piece of careful and correct acting, which exhibits great promise."[25]

It was some years after Melville ceased to be a member of the Stock Company before Chute made another lucky hit in his choice of leading man, but in Charles Vincent, who joined the Company in 1857, and Arthur Stirling (1859), he secured two competent actors who made some mark in the Victorian theatre. Vincent was praised as "a valuable addition to the *corps,* especially in gentlemanly parts, for which he is most adapted," while Stirling impressed as "an experienced and finished actor; he has a naturally powerful but musical voice, which, assisted by ready elocution soon made him a favourite with his audience." Both, however, were outshone in popular favour by their leading lady, Louisa Cleveland (Mrs. Charles Vincent), who remained in Bristol for most of the period 1857 to 1861. She had an unusual range :

An artist, but snatching a charm beyond the rules of art, her conceptions of the sublime and beautiful are classical, polished, and unlaboured. But her tragedy is not finer than her comedy, and she is equally captivating in burlesque. We have seen the house in tears at the former, and bursting with laughter at the latter.[26]

In October 1859 Chute secured the services of the Rignold brothers, William and George, the second generation to play at the Theatre Royal, their father having been a dancer in M'Cready's companies of 1824-5 and 1827-8. They were noticed with moderate praise as Claudio and Don John in *Much Ado*; both were versatile, William making a great success as Hardress Cregan in *The Colleen Bawn* and George even attempting the Giant Gorgibuster in *Jack and the Beanstalk,* in which he "adds new charms nightly to that somewhat forbidding, but, withal, popular character."[27] They were in fact at this stage unpretentious and hardworking utilities, who were content sometimes to play quite small parts for experience, and who steadily improved in technique and range during their engagement.

No Bristol Stock Company would have been complete without its comics. John Rouse, who played from 1851 to 1859, was a broad comedian much in the John Reeve tradition, who had occasionally to be reproved for going beyond the mark, contriving in *The Unfinished Gentleman* "by a coarseness and vulgarity we have never noticed in his acting on any former occasion, to disgust nearly every one of the audience."[28] He was succeeded by Arthur Wood from the Plymouth Theatre, whom Bristol at once took to its heart.

Perhaps the most enduring favourite with the audience, however, was William Fosbrooke, "Funny" Fosbrooke, as he was nicknamed, who became a veritable institution. In the Second World War old playgoers were still recalling his name, and his descendants live in Bristol yet. Fosbrooke, who like Chippendale seems to have played comic old men from boyhood, acted Pantaloon in the Harlequinade every year until in *Valentine and Orson* (1857-8) a trick was mis-timed, and instead of being somersaulted from his revolving chair to the back of the scene, he was thrown heavily to the floor and concussed. Though he lived to play for another forty years, it was a long time before he would trust himself again in pantomime.

Chute's eye for casting was not impeccable, but some, at least, of the failures may be assigned to a praiseworthy desire to break out of the straitjacket of Stock Company typecasting, and give his actors encouragement to develop beyond their ordinary range. Some, like the young Rignolds, Marie Wilton, and later Madge Robertson, profited by this; others lacked the ability, or were too inhibited by tradition, to take advantage of the opportunities. The inevitable limitations faced by Chute were appreciated, and the markedly higher overall standard of acting aroused favourable comment.

Chute was a theatrical businessman with a strong sense of responsibility. He was very willing to avail himself of stars, but his years of management show a noticeable diminution in engagements of mere popular entertainers. He made an exception for the Bristol Clown, James Doughty, whose performing dogs were an attraction in November 1854. Doughty's Benefit on 15 November introduced in the part of Violante in *The Wonder*, a Miss Herbert: none other than the future "beautiful Miss Herbert" of the St. James's, a native of Bristol, who thus made her stage debut under the not too dignified auspices of an animal-trainer whose family kept a Cider House where women and children were not admitted.

But most of Chute's stars were fairly strictly legitimate, and included Gustavus Vaughan Brooke, Charlotte Cushman and Samuel Phelps. Phelps had a rather unhappy introduction to Bristol in April 1855; his luggage (costumes, wigs and props) went astray on the railway, and he was consequently "greatly annoyed and excited by the occurrence, so much so indeed as to quite unnerve himself for the part [of Macbeth] . . . much to the damage of the exchequer".[29] Despite his publicised inheritance of Macready's mantle, he failed to inherit his success with Bristol audiences, whose support was disgracefully poor. It is to be feared that the emotional and boisterous style of Melville had spoiled local taste for Phelps' more cerebral acting. On the other hand, audiences were selective enough to discriminate against the rant of a Mrs. W. C. Forbes, "the Eminent Tragic Actress . . . Of the principal Theatres in America," and her immediate successor, the improbably-named McKean Buchanan.

Charles Dillon's appearance as Belphegor has already been mentioned; it was an engagement which involved a good deal of upset because it coincided, not only with a visit of the Dublin Opera Company to the theatre, but with a concert version of *Antigone* at the Victoria Rooms, for which (the number of competent orchestral players in Bristol being limited) the services of some of the theatre band were needed. Had Dillon been willing to make up a double bill with the Opera Company, playing Belphegor in the second half, all could have been arranged but he peremptorily refused to play second to any opera company. "He was in the bill for first fiddle, and first fiddle he would be."[30] The Opera Company's performance had therefore to be cancelled at the last moment.

In lighter vein, the ageless Celeste continued her periodic visits, and so did Charles Mathews, whose impeccable comedy technique enchanted audiences in Bristol as elsewhere. Perhaps the comedian with the greatest cause to remember Bristol, however, was the "eccentric Baronet", Sir William Don. He had taken to the stage in a laudable desire to earn money to free himself and his estate from debt; he had little natural talent, but capitalising on his exceptional height and thinness was an acceptable droll in some types of farce. With his actress wife, Emily Saunders, he played a reasonably successful engagement in Bristol in November 1857, but as he stepped into his cab to be driven to the railway station he found himself arrested by a "gentleman in black" and spent the next fortnight in Bristol's Debtors' Prison. Undeterred, he made friends with the Governor and

with his meerschaum between his lips, and tranquilly puffing the soothing leaf, he strolled up and down his narrow domain, and enlivened the seclusion of the place and those in it with his powers of anecdote and passages of adventure.[31]

Released on bail, he played a week at Birmingham and returned to Bristol for a Benefit performance, at which he gave a curtain speech entirely in character :

"Before concluding, I wish to give a bit of advice to the fast young gentlemen present, and I am sure there are too many before me. – (Laughter.) . . . If you can't afford to keep a horse and want to go fast, take a second-class ticket and 'go to Bath'. – (Laughter.) – Keep out of debt . . . Dear young gentlemen, take this long monumental warning before you . . ."[32]

Stars, however, even bankrupt stars, cost money, at a time when normal seat prices were continuing to drop. The friendship between the Keans and Chute did not prevent the former exacting their full star rates on their visit in April 1860, and these involved raising the admission to almost twice the standard price, 5s., 3s., 2s. and 1s. – and no second price. The result, in money-conscious Bristol, was predictable : the houses were poor and the result a loss.

This was indeed a problem which increasingly faced Chute. A concession continued speedily becomes assumed as a right, and so with Chute's original reductions in admission; the public soon came to forget that they had ever been other than the norm, and consequently resented what they saw as a burdensome increase. The Theatre might be growing more respectable, but it was not yet an institution for which prestige prices would be paid.[33]

This attitude did not apply to the higher walks of grand opera. When Giulia Grisi and Mario were announced for October 1856 Chute took out the pit benches and put in a false floor and numbered stalls – the first time, apparently, this now standard booking device had been used in Bristol. The prices (8s. 6d. in the Dress Boxes and Pit Stalls, 5s. in the Upper Boxes and 2s. 6d. in the Gallery) seem to have been paid without a murmur. (Indeed, when similar prices were put into effect in 1859 it was noted that the "Gods," having had to pay half a crown, were markedly less rumbustious.) There was, of course, quite an element of snob appeal, reflected in the amount of space used by the *Bristol Times* to describe the ladies' dresses at a performance of *Gli Ugonotti* in December 1853, and not all the audience were fully knowledgeable. One lady spent much of a performance of *The Barber of Seville* audibly enquiring why "All is lost" (from *La Sonnambula*) had not yet been sung.

This was the period of the emergence of Verdi, whose *Traviata* caused a great sensation. Introduced to Bristol by the London Opera Company in March 1857, the opposition of the moralists was at first dismissed as a storm in a teacup. But opinion later hardened, and not only

147

the morals but the construction and music of the opera came under fire. The *Bristol Advertiser* described it as

this notorious and obnoxious opera . . . The subject is unfit for stage representation; the treatment is sickly and unnatural. The music can hardly be excused. It is poor from beginning to end. The whole work cannot boast one single entrancing melody – one single commanding or memorable passage.[34]

It is unnecessary to say that such broadsides did not prevent *La Traviata* entering the regular repertory of the touring opera companies; it was, however, many years before Verdi's popularity overtook that of Bellini and Rossini.

All things considered, in the Spring of 1862 Chute could look back with some satisfaction on his achievements in making the theatre both popular and respected. True, its site was increasingly disadvantageous, and his box audience, largely resident in the north-western suburbs of Clifton and Redland, was still reluctant to make theatre-going in King Street a regular habit, but the appointments of the theatre and the good repute of company and manager were generally held to be adequate compensation. Then the first serious blow fell. On the eve of Good Friday, 1862, the Bath Theatre Royal caught fire.

Charles Kean, who was in Bath at the time, telegraphed to Chute, who "immediately took a special train to Bath, and arrived to see what a few hours previously had been one of the most elegant buildings in the city now reduced to four bare walls".[35]

Two

1862–1867

Chute personally lost several hundreds of pounds' worth of scenery, props and costumes in the Bath fire. In a wave of sympathy, the Bristol Amateurs gave a Benefit performance for him, at doubled prices, at the beginning of May, and some of the citizens of Bath subscribed to present him with a handsomely chased silver tankard and set of silver dessert knives and forks. In May, too, plans for a new theatre (the competition for the design of which was won by C. J. Phipps, one of the most prolific of all theatre architects) were announced, and four months later work began, the theatre being opened on 4 March 1863.

Meanwhile Chute was thrown back on the resources of Bristol alone, and for the first time performances were regularly given on Saturday evenings. Since this was pay-night for the city's workers there was some apprehension about the type of audience which might be attracted, and the degree of its sobriety, but, though the choice of plays was usually modified to suit their assumed tastes, there seems to have been no real trouble, and even after the opening of the new Bath theatre some Saturday performances were still given in Bristol. The general success of Chute's management was unimpaired by the complications introduced by the disaster at Bath.

A gradual change in the organisation of the London theatres caused Chute to modify the composition of his company until it came to resemble some of the better repertories of today. Up to his last year at the Theatre Royal he relied very little on individual stars, though he retained a weakness for provincial tragedians, and of course he could not afford to miss the opportunity of engaging national figures such as E. A. Sothern as Lord Dundreary, Madame Ristori in *Medea* and Kate Bateman in *Leah*. He even interrupted the run of his pantomime for a farewell visit from Mr. and Mrs. Charles Kean in 1867. The supply of opera companies dropped off considerably, so that complete touring companies were now virtually restricted to the short run of the pantomime in Bath, or to the late summer and early autumn. Instead Chute reinforced his Stock Company by securing established London actors and actresses in between their metropolitan engagements, for visits which might last for weeks or even months and so enable them to participate in rather than dictate the repertory, without identifying themselves with the provinces. Former Stock Company leading actors were especially glad of this type of contract, and Melville, James Bennett, Arthur Stirling and William Rignold took frequent advantage of it.

Chute's most important acquisition in this way was Kate Terry who, having found herself *de trop* in the St. James's Company after the summer of 1862, toured temporarily in one of those "scratch" London companies which were a feature of the period, and was snapped up by Chute to be his leading lady for the autumn season. With her came her younger sister, Ellen, then fifteen, whose engaging, not to say mischievous, personality was ideally suited to the mythological extravaganzas of the Broughs. Her Cupid in *Endymion** and Dictys in *Perseus and Andromeda*, set against the more ladylike charms of Kate in the heroines' parts and the brilliant dash of Henrietta Hodson as the heroes *en travestie*, made these two productions the hits of the season. In the eleven weeks of the sisters' 1862 engagement only eight evenings failed to include one or other of these pieces.

Ellen had never previously played in burlesque and was at first rather disconcerted at finding herself, as a utility member of a Stock Company, expected to tackle everything :

I told the stage manager I couldn't sing and I couldn't dance. His reply was short and to the point. "You've got to do it," and so I did it in a way – a very funny way at first, no doubt. It was admirable training, for it took all the self-consciousness out of me to start with. To end with, I thought it capital fun, and enjoyed burlesque as much as Shakespeare.[36]

Such conditions were less favourable to Kate Terry, whose main vehicles as leading lady were revivals of *Peep o' Day, Faust and Marguerite* and *Giselle*. It was not till the sisters' second visit in the early autumn of 1863 that Kate had the opportunity of playing the lead in a new play of importance, or of appearing regularly in a classical part – that of Ophelia, which she had during the preceding months been performing to the Hamlet of Fechter and was now to act in Bristol to the rather different concep-

* "Everything is so lightly done that at the end we could not feel very much surprised if *Cupid* were to take wing and fly away." (*Western Daily Press,* 30.10.1862.)

tion of George Melville. The triumph, however, was the same in both cities.

Despite the limited opportunities given her in Bristol, Kate Terry gained great admiration from her audiences for the delicacy of her playing. "Ladylike" is a frequently-repeated adjective, and praise of an actress could hardly be higher at that time. T. E. Pemberton records a sad story of a local shopboy, so carried away by his infatuation for Kate Terry that in the face of all discouragement he kept sending her expensive presents which ultimately led him into embezzlement; the details are confirmed by the accounts of the Magistrates' Court hearing in the Bristol press.[37] It is noteworthy that not the slightest reflection was made at any time on Kate herself.

The 1863 engagement ended more happily. Tom Taylor visited the sisters just before their joint Benefit in October, and reported to his wife :

I have seen at least ten boxes disposed of since my arrival! . . . Kate has received a gold bracelet, set with a horse-shoe of pearls, & Nelly a pretty gold pencil-case, with the enclosed letter which Nelly allows me to send for your perusal, & says she 'does not think it is at all bad for a chemist'.[38]

On their last two nights the sisters played Portia and Nerissa in *The Merchant of Venice*, and Beatrice and Hero in *Much Ado*. Hero was undoubtedly the most successful of the few straight parts which Ellen Terry played in these two early engagements, and the unforced pathos and natural charm she lent the character were widely praised.

Bristol was always loyal to the Terrys. When they returned as stars in March 1867 the *Clifton Chronicle* noted that "the whole [city] has been wild about them during the last two weeks" – and this despite the wretched melodramas in which they played and a heavy blizzard almost blocking all traffic.

The Rignold brothers were the chief male supports of the Company during 1862 and 1863, William developing into a juvenile lead of great appeal, capable of accepting criticism and improving his performance accordingly, as was noted in the case of his Bob Brierly in *The Ticket-of-Leave Man*. George began to specialise in the heavier parts, his Claudius being much more subtle and kingly a villain than usual, though his greatest triumphs were as Hawkshaw the Detective (which brought him an offer from the Olympic) and in 1865 as The Softy in *Aurora Floyd*.

His assumption of the silly laugh of idiotcy rose to the highest point of acting, but not a whit inferior was the diabolical and artful trickery which characterised the sly and fiendish malice of the revengeful, half-witted stable-help . . . He introduces a great amount of what is technically known as "business", and the introduction in all cases is particularly judicious. By this means the audience are enabled to grasp those connecting links which in *The Softy's* mind lead him to the perpetration of his great crime.[39]

Charles Coghlan, who played a wide variety of parts alongside the Rignolds, was in some ways an actor born out of his time. Scrupulous over his make-up and dress for every character, he was the antithesis of the personality actors who dominated the stage. Such qualities as his were particularly attractive to the architect and aesthete, Edward Godwin, who contributed free-lance theatre criticisms to the *Western Daily Press* from October 1862 to November 1864. Godwin coupled Coghlan with Kate Terry as actors who "made one at times quite lose the persons in the characters,"[40] though he was not blind to Coghlan's limitations.

Mr. Coghlan has knowledge incomparably greater than that usually thought to belong to the so-called professors of his art, and he is careful to *use* this knowledge in the development of the character he portrays, but there is at times a forcedness which seems to me to spring from a lack of sympathy with the character and the situation . . . In a word, we want – what we rarely or never get – more poetry.[41]

After almost suddenly blossoming as Cinderella in the 1862-3 pantomime,[42] Madge Robertson became entrusted with increasingly responsible parts, and during the next two years her development as an actress was rapid. In March 1864 she played Virginia to James Bennett's Virginius, and the *Bristol Times* claimed that "a better Virginia than Miss Robertson we have not seen. She gave a charming picture of the young, innocent schoolgirl." By September she was acting Portia to Bennett's Shylock "with a grace and womanly dignity which struck us as beyond her years and experience."[43] Buckstone engaged her as leading lady for his new theatre in Bradford, and she left Bristol amid general regret in December 1864.

Though the Stock Company never quite regained the standard of these years, during the next three seasons it included Fanny and Carlotta Addison (recruited, like Kate Terry, from a touring company), Jane Rignold, a sister of George and William, and W. H. Vernon, a versatile juvenile lead quickly snapped up by London managements.

With a company containing artists of this calibre, it may seem surprising that during the whole of this time there was mounting criticism of its standards, so that, when discussing a possible Tercentenary production of Shakespeare, a correspondent of the *Western Daily Press* could say, with general approval, "By all means let the Bristol actors take part, but leave it not to them alone." This criticism was, however, only one manifestation of a much wider restlessness among the more educated section of the audience, including the generality of newspaper critics of the day. They were, for example, becoming more sensitive to the "improvements" of Shakespeare embedded in the traditional prompt-books used by Chute; the old gags in the Church scene of *Much Ado* were recognised and questioned by the *Clifton Chronicle,* and the Shakespearean hotchpotch which was Cibber's version of *King Richard III* was analysed with some sharpness by the *Western Daily Press.*

To some extent Chute was the victim of his own early success and the standards he himself had set. Twenty, even ten, years before no one would have remarked, even had they noticed, the re-use of stock scenery. But when, in a sketch called *Paganini Redivivus,* produced in September 1865, Chute brought out a scene painted by George Gordon the preceding year, it was immediately identified by the *Western Daily Press* critic with the dry comment: "The scene is supposed to be the ruins of an old abbey near Florence, but we have yet to learn that Tintern Abbey is in Italy."[44] At the same time, the growth of the long run system in the London theatre established a degree of care in mounting, and polish in playing, which showed up the inevitable deficiencies of a Stock Company whose members had still to a great extent to provide their own dresses,[45] whose scenery had to meet the demands of a wide repertory,[46] and whose actors might still have to learn three major new parts within five nights to suit a star.

No one expressed this increasing discontent with the resultant improvisations more freely than Edward Godwin, who wrote under the heading "Theatrical Jottings" and the motto

> "I must have liberty,
> Withal, as large a charter as the wind,
> To blow on whom I please."

In his stress on the need for artistic consistency, even above historicity, in decor, acting and music he anticipated in his own way the viewpoint of his more famous son, Edward Gordon Craig.[47]

A controversial figure from the outset, Godwin finally precipitated the warmest public debate yet on the standards of the Bristol theatre. In September 1864 Kate Terry accepted a four week engagement, sharing leading parts with James Bennett. Their joint appearances ensured a much higher proportion than usual of classical and other serious drama, which unfortunately the considerably weakened company of that season was unable to support adequately. *Romeo and Juliet,* with a raw and graceless new juvenile, J. G. Rosiere, as the hero; Bennett, a fine Othello or Virginius, as Mercutio; and the noisy melodramatist George Yates as Friar Lawrence, drew a notice of such infuriated protest from Godwin[48] as verged on the libellous, and one which, however accurate in its artistic criticisms, certainly earned the riposte by Chute which announced a new production, *Monomania, or, Softening of the Brain* :

With a view to insure efficient representation, the Manager hopes that he will be able to prevail upon the celebrated "THEATRICAL JOTTINGS" to undertake the principal character.

The "pictorial illustrations" were to comprise a series of buildings designed by Godwin which had aroused varying degrees of controversy in Bristol.[49] Rennie Powell says that Chute even threatened to include a picture of one of them, which had suffered cracks across the frontage due to subsidence, on a cloth in the pantomime under the caption "This is the House that 'Jottings' built!"[50]

Tremendous argument was aroused, and it can hardly have comforted Chute that, while most contributors felt that the terms of Godwin's notice were excessively violent, they supported the general tenor of his criticisms, while the *Western Daily Press* editor uncompromisingly refused to retract any part of Godwin's article when Rosiere protested. Looking back over a hundred years, however, one can see that at the back of what superficially was often destructive criticism was something much more constructive : a largely unformulated but growing realisation of what the theatre could contribute to the aesthetic life of a city – in the widest sense to its education. Chute had begun to demonstrate this, and what emerges over and over again is disappointment at his apparent failure to live up to the standard he had himself set.

This particularly applied to the repertoire. Here it has to be admitted – and was admitted freely even by Godwin – that like any commercial manager Chute was limited by what his audience would pay to see, but it was also contended that he might have done more to elevate its taste. Certainly during the period when his company was at its strongest the programme contained a disappointing proportion of lurid pieces like *Laid Up in Port*, which Godwin neatly summarised as containing "amongst a great deal of minor villainy, one seduction, one abduction, one murder, and a lot of righteous slaughtering, as a matter of course, in the final scene."[51] *The Trail of Sin*, *Lady Audley's Secret*, *Aurora Floyd* and *The Fool's Revenge* pandered to similar tastes, and against such pieces Tom Taylor's *Ticket-of-Leave Man*, Buckingham's *Faces in the Fire* and Robertson's *Society* were hailed almost as classics.

There was no doubt, however, that it was the sensation pieces which drew the crowds, especially when all the scenic resources of the theatre were devoted to their production. A localised version of Boucicault's *The Streets of London*, called, of course, *The Streets of Bristol*,[52] was decked out by George Gordon and Horn with local scenery, including the exterior of the Theatre Royal, and the Drawbridge in winter, which attracted "night after night quite a *furore* amongst the audiences, who do not satisfy themselves until they have called the enterprising lessee, Mr. Chute, and Mr. Gordon himself, before the curtain". Later Gordon improved even on this success "by the introduction of miniature cabs, &c., which are driving along the Quay at the end of Clare Street, and give a life to the locality."[53] Arthur Stirling was specially engaged for four weeks to play Trumper, but the play was continually revived with other actors in the part.

It was not inappropriate that on the centenary of the Theatre Royal the principal actor should be George Melville (visiting with a "scratch company" including Marie Henderson, future wife of George Rignold, and the Australian actress, Josephine Fiddes). It was, unfortunately, equally appropriate that the play should have been *East Lynne* [Plate 17].

A commonplace excuse for the failure of the Box audience to support Chute's better class productions was that they were deterred by the behaviour of the gallery – "the caprice of the 'gods', which is a regular nuisance to the respectable and paying portion of the audience."[54] The gallery could certainly be obstreperous, especially when, crammed in their hundreds in semi-darkness with the heat from the gas-lighting rising steadily, they were faced with having to sit through a condensed version of *The Lady of Lyons* before they could get to the pantomime. But only a few months later, when this same play was put on as a main piece on a Saturday night, the gallery paid it most respectful attention. "The toiling crowd," condescended the *Western Daily Press,* "have human hearts if their intellects be somewhat dull, and the true touch of nature makes that crowd kin to a higher life than that which they ordinarily share."[55] It was loyal, too; but at a shilling a head – frequently only sixpence – it would not make a theatre pay.

It is impossible to be sure when the conception of a theatre of his own, in the more fashionable Clifton area, first became a definite project in Chute's mind. There was a good deal of public pressure from time to time; as early as March 1861 "Young Hamlet" had written to the *Western Daily Press* to demand a theatre for Clifton which would give its inhabitants "a most healthy and almost necessary intellectual feast near their own homes." The glories of the new Bath Theatre pointed up stark comparisons with the increasingly outmoded King Street house; throughout 1863 various suggestions of floating a company and acquiring a site were put forward (accompanied by vigorous protests from the opponents of the theatre, who deemed it "an institution which panders to the lusts and passions of mankind," and a warm and loyal defence of Chute's management by Charles Coghlan). The discussions about the Shakespeare Tercentenary Celebrations in Bristol revived the debate in 1864; indeed, it came almost to be assumed that a second theatre would be built. It was even suggested, when it was clear that the Bath Theatre was proving a liability to Chute of which he was anxious to rid himself, that a Clifton and a central theatre might be run in circuit : eloquent tribute to the dichotomy between Clifton and Bristol.

By September 1866, Chute, who had resolutely abstained from any kind of comment, let it be known that he was negotiating for a site in Park Row. Outline plans of the financing of the proposed theatre were announced in November,[56] and in the Theatre Royal pantomime of *Robin Hood*, one of the scenes was a representation of the New Theatre, which a large board informed the public would be opened on 14 October 1867. C. J. Phipps, architect of the Bath Theatre Royal, designed the new Bristol theatre also.

Chute did not neglect the Theatre Royal while his plans were maturing; in 1862 he had the theatre repainted, the prevailing tints being lemon, pale mauve, ruby, white and gold. The following season Grieve and Telbin provided a new act drop containing a view of Lisbon, seen through the warm haze of a summer's day, with groups of peasants and mules in the foreground, and presided over by a bust of Shakespeare.[57] In 1864 the comforts of both audience and actors were improved; one row of dress circle seats was removed and the remainder respaced; both seats and backs were covered with crimson turkey cloth, and stuffed with horsehair. Similar alterations were made in the upper boxes. Behind the scenes, dressing rooms and greenroom were improved, and the machinery over-hauled.[58]

There was no intention of giving up the Theatre Royal; in August 1867 it was announced that Arthur Wood, the popular low comedian, would manage it on Chute's behalf. Meanwhile, before the new theatre was ready for occupation, there were touring attractions to be housed : a London Dramatic Company headed by Charles Dillon and a former Bristol leading lady, Juliet Desborough; and for two weeks from 16 September, the St. James's Theatre Company under Louisa Herbert. Several of the company – Miss Herbert herself, Mr. and Mrs. Frank Matthews and W. H. Vernon – were already well known in Bristol, but the leading juvenile, despite family links with the city,[59] was new to its theatre. He was Henry Irving, touring after his first successful London engagement in such parts as Hastings, Captain Absolute and Joseph Surface. "Despite a stiffness of figure and a cold inexpressive visage, Mr. Irving is an excellent player," commented the *Bristol Times & Mirror* of the last-named impersonation, and the *Western Daily Press* was even more enthusiastic.

This was the last engagement before Chute moved his headquarters to the New Theatre in Park Row; a final sprinkle of starshine before the Theatre Royal's inevitable eclipse.

NOTES

[1] Quoted in Powell, *op. cit.*, p. 113.

[2] S. Hicks: *Twenty-Four Years of an Actor's Life*, London, 1910, p. 48.

[3] *Bristol Gazette*, 26.5.1853.

[4] Details of Chute's alterations will be found in *Bristol Mercury*, 3.9.1853; *Bristol Gazette*, 8 & 15.9.1853; *Bristol Times*, 17.9.1853. The continued separate existence of the back extension of the theatre is confirmed by a ground plan appended to an underlease of an adjacent yard dated 24 October 1877 in the Trustees' Collection.

[5] Committee Minutes, 10. and 11.5.1854.

[6] *ibid.*, 10.5.1855 and *Bristol Times*, 12.5.1855. Riddle showed himself consistently antagonistic towards Chute and, though he was usually overborne by his colleagues, he provided a continual irritant in the relations between Lessee and Proprietors.

[7] Quoted in Minutes erroneously dated 13.5.1858 but certainly not earlier than 2 June 1858, the date of Chute's letter.

[8] The first instance in Bristol, apart from the Italian Opera, seems to have been the visit of the Haymarket Company in September 1850.

[9] *Bristol Times*, 1.10.1853. Lenox and I. Gilbert were the scene-painters.

[10] *Bristol Mirror*, 7.10.1854.

[11] *Bristol Mirror*, 23.9.1854 and *Bristol Times*, 30.9.1854.

[12] *Bristol Mercury*, 30.10.1858. William Gordon, of the Princess's, designed the Bristol scenery also, and painted it with the help of his son, George (who became Lenox's chief assistant and eventually succeeded him), Lenox and John Watson. See Playbill, 27.10.1958.

[13] *Bristol Mirror*, 10.10.1857.

[14] *Bristol Gazette*, 28.2.1861.

[15] *Bristol Mirror*, 2.3.1861.

[16] *Bristol Mercury*, 2.1.1858.

[17] *Western Daily Press*, 26.12.1860.

[18] *Bristol Mercury*, 18.12.1858.

[19] *Bristol Mirror*, 28.10.1854; *Bristol Times*, 4.11.1854. This was a version of Schiller's *Don Carlos*, puffed as though it were an original play.

[20] *Western Daily Press*, 5.11.1859.

[21] *Bristol Mercury*, 16.12.1854.

[22] *Mr. and Mrs. Bancroft – On and Off the Stage*, London, 1886, p. 27.

[23] *ibid.*, p. 32.

[24] T. E. Pemberton: *The Kendals: A Biography*, London, 1900; *Dame Madge Kendal, by Herself*, London, 1933.

[25] *Bristol Mirror*, 13.10.1860. Her first appearance in Bristol was as Pastime (a very small part) in the 1857-8 pantomime of *Valentine and Orson*.

[26] *Bristol Advertiser*, 26.9.1857; *Bristol Times*, 1.10.1859; *Bristol Mirror*, 12.2.1859.

[27] *Western Daily Press*, 15.1.1862.

[28] *Bristol Mirror*, 3.6.1854.

[29] *Bristol Mercury*, 28.4.1855.

[30] *ibid.*, 14.4.1855.

[31] *Bristol Times*, 28.11.1857.

[32] *Bristol Mirror*, 12.12.1857.

[33] This is reflected in the level of actors' salaries, which showed a gradual rise over those of the 1820's, but were still barely equal to those of a century before. Powell, *op. cit.*, pp. 51-3, says that Melville received £3 3s. weekly and Arthur Stirling £3 10s. while the leading ladies had £3. The "second leads" averaged £1 10s. to £2. Lenox, as chief scenic artist, had a salary of £2 15s. a week and a Benefit; the conductor of the orchestra £2 2s. and a Benefit. Highest paid was the Clown, who received £2 10s. a week during rehearsals, and £5 during the run of the pantomime, as well as a Benefit which was always packed.

[34] *Bristol Advertiser*, 16.5.1857.

[35] *Western Daily Press*, 19.4.1862.

[36] E. Terry: *The Story of my Life*, London, 1908, p. 41. This book and Chapter III of Pemberton's *Ellen Terry and her Sisters* provide considerable detail about the 1862 engagement (which Ellen misdates 1861). See also K. M. D. Barker: The Terrys and Godwin in Bristol, *Theatre Notebook*, XXII, 1, 27-43.

[37] T. E. Pemberton: *Ellen Terry and her Sisters*, London, 1902, p. 66.

[38] Letter of 8.10.1863 in the Tom Taylor Collection, British Theatre Museum.

[39] *Western Daily Press*, 21.4. 1865.

[40] *ibid.*, 24.11.1862.

[41] *ibid.*, 19.9.1864.

[42] This production had a record run of eight weeks against the usual four or five; it was also notable as the first Bristol pantomime in which the use of masks was left off by the main characters, so that "the points are brought out with much greater effect than they possibly could be were the dialogue spoken behind a coloured sheet of pasteboard". (*Western Daily Press*, 26.12.1862.)

[43] *Bristol Times*, 19.3.1864; *Bristol Mercury*, 24.9.1864.

[44] *Western Daily Press*, 13.9.1865.

[45] Tom Taylor describes Kate Terry's dress as Portia "made up . . . under stress and difficulty which had no Venetian character and was not becoming – a black velvet casaque, with gold lace, with a blue skirt ornamented by a large pattern in white & silver that might have done very well with a body to match but which 'swore' at the velvet". (Letter of 9.10.1863 in the Tom Taylor Collection, British Theatre Museum.)

[46] In a production of *Romeo and Juliet*, Friar Laurence's cell was said to be "in one scene of Peterborough Cathedral, and in the other a kind of *Renaissance* Registrar's Office". (*Western Daily Press*, 24.11.1862.)

[47] Godwin's criticisms of this period are discussed in K. M. D. Barker: The Terrys and Godwin in Bristol. It was, however, not through his journalistic activity but in his capacity as Secretary of the Bristol Shakespeare Society, for whom he arranged readings, that Godwin met Ellen Terry. See Dudley Harbron: *The Conscious Stone*, London, 1949, Ch. III; this account must, however, be accepted with some reservations, as Harbron appears to have relied on information supplied by the Bristol City Librarian, and does not give references in detail. A number of his statements and assumptions relating to the Bristol theatre are quite inaccurate.

[48] *Western Daily Press*, 5.10.1864.

[49] *ibid.*, 7.10.1864. The advertisement was repeated in every Bristol paper for a fortnight.

[50] Powell, *op. cit.*, p. 63. But this may have been only *esprit de l'escalier: The House that Jack Built* had been the pantomime the previous year.

[51] *Western Daily Press*, 21.10.1862.

[52] This Bristol version was allegedly prepared by Stirling Coyne, author of *Fraud and Its Victims*, on which *Les Pauvres de Paris*, Boucicault's immediate model, was based. See *Bristol Mercury*, 5.11.1864, and *Western Daily Press*, 8.11.1864.

[53] *Bristol Mercury*, 12.11.1864; *Western Daily Press*, 17.11.1864.

[54] "A.H.F." in *Western Daily Press*, 18.3.1863.

[55] *Western Daily Press*, 1.4.1863.

[56] Chute, determined to be entirely his own master, raised the whole sum of over £18,000 from personal resources and private loans in units of £100, to be repaid by lot at various dates between 1875 and 1882, and bearing interest at 6 per cent. For full details see *Bristol Times & Mirror*, 13.5.1867.

[57] *Bristol Mercury*, 16.8 and 26.9.1863.

[58] *Western Daily Press*, 26.8.1864, and Playbill, 29.8.1864.

[59] See L. Irving: *Henry Irving*, London, 1951, p. 35 *et seq.*; and Froom Tyler: *A Note on Irving*, Bristol, 1931.

Part Five
Struggle for Survival

The Royal . . . has a history that should make every student of drama anxious to see it inhabited by more *actual* beings than that cheery old ogre, Melodrama, and the more pleasant but unreal fairy, Pantomime.

Bristol Playgoer, 9.1.1914.

The fact has to be faced: the Theatre Royal has had its day, or, rather, night.

Bristol Times & Mirror, 23.2.1924.

One

1867-1881

When Arthur Wood re-opened the Theatre Royal on 7 November 1867 it was with a very respectable Stock Company, including Arthur Stirling, Charles Coghlan, Jane Rignold and Wood himself, and a programme ranging from *Othello* to *The Castle Spectre*. It seems to have been assumed that each of the two Bristol theatres would serve a separate geographical area :

> There is plenty of room, we are sure, for two well-managed Theatres in a city the size of Bristol, but what was wanted by the denizens of Clifton and the surrounding district was a "dramatic temple" which they could visit without the long and tedious journey down into town, and back again, being enforced upon them.[1]

The two theatres were run in close conjunction at first, members of the companies playing at either theatre (or even both on the same night) according to the requirements of the programme. Unfortunately there was insufficient support for an old-fashioned repertory, eked out with newer farces, in what was only too obviously a second-string theatre, and notice after notice bemoans the thin houses.

A home-made pantomime with an interminable title, *Little Tom Tucker and the Fine Lady of Banbury Cross, or Harlequin Taffy the Welshman and the Old Woman who Lived in a Shoe and Little Silver Bell the Fairy*, was staged at Christmas. In a spirit of economy, the diorama *Our Native Land*, first brought out 26 years previously, was resurrected, but aroused little enthusiasm :

> The exhibition of the panorama without a word being said occupies too much time, and has a tendency to create impatience . . . The painting is good, but people in the midst of mirth are not disposed to study the fine arts without some sort of enlivening lecture.[2]

163

The pantomime moved to Bath after 10 January and two more nights wound up the season. In mid-February, Marie Wilton's London Comedy Company played *Caste* for a fortnight, travelling to Bath on Wednesdays and Saturdays; at the beginning of March came the Beni-Zoug-Zoug Arabs (a team of acrobats), followed by the Grand English Opera Company in *Faust* and *Il Trovatore*; and the theatre was then closed without explanation for over seven months.

Chute had overstrained his resources. At the beginning of April the Committee of Proprietors received "a notification that Mr. Chute the Lessee had been obliged to place his affairs in the hands of Messrs. W. H. Williams & Co. with a view to making an arrangement with his Creditors". In the summer of 1868 Chute at length rid himself of the incubus of the Bath Theatre, and though, perhaps out of sentiment, he continued to lease the Theatre Royal, Bristol, it was put only to intermittent use. There were no more Christmas pantomimes; there was indeed no predictable pattern of opening at all, though January and February (when pantomime engrossed the New Theatre audiences) were usually well booked.

A good cross-section of contemporary theatrical entertainment, however, could still be enjoyed. The Theatre Royal was recognised as an ideal venue for the more intimate social comedies of T. W. Robertson; *Caste* and *School* were particularly popular, and the former on its performance on 31 January 1870 was the first play to constitute a full bill in itself at the Theatre Royal, "in consequence of the length of the comedy, and the fact that it contains all the elements of pathos and humour which usually go to make up a Dramatic Performance."[3] The companies sent out under Richard Younge, and later Craven Robertson, visited the Theatre Royal regularly and, except in February 1878, when the acting was unusually weak, drew large houses. It was Younge's company which was playing in Bristol in February 1871 when T. W. Robertson's death was announced; the last night's performance was cancelled as a mark of respect.

Another sure attraction was H. J. Byron's light farcical comedy, *Our Boys,* and from 1876 to 1880 Duck's "Our Boys" Company visited King Street each January playing this and other pieces by Byron. *Married in Haste* had its first provincial representation in Bristol on 24 January 1876, while *Widow and Wife,* an attempt at something more serious, was produced for the first time on any stage on 11 September of the same year. Byron's protestations in the preliminary advertisements that his play was "essentially a Drama", not a "comic production, such as 'OUR BOYS', &c." reminded one critic of Robson's "Ladies and Gentlemen, this is not a comic song!'" which prefaced his rendering of *Villikins and his Dinah.* Altogether *Widow and Wife* was pronounced a poor melodrama, resorting too frequently to limelight and slow music, and not even the presence in the cast of the Bristol comedian and ex-manager, Arthur Wood, could make it successful.

Also well suited to the intimacy of the Theatre Royal were the early plays of W. S. Gilbert, who was considered far more seriously as a dramatist than he is now.

When Mr. Gilbert writes a play he does more than furnish an hour or two's amusement; he adds to the literature of the day . . . To use a form of expression that was once popular, Mr. Gilbert is a poet among dramatists and a dramatist among poets.[4]

Pygmalion and Galatea, *The Wicked World* and *Broken Hearts* enjoyed great vogue, the cast of the latter introducing to Bristol Florence Terry, younger sister of Kate and Ellen, as Lady Vavir. The unsuccessful *Ne'er-do-Well*, rewritten as *The Vagabond*, had its first provincial performance in Bristol in April 1878.[5]

The well-implanted idea that the King Street stage was too small for the increasingly elaborate effects required by sensation plays may have accounted for the small number of such pieces staged there in this period, and the relative lack of success of many of them. The less spectacular *East Lynne*, however, generally drew crammed houses, and during Wilson Barrett's visit in November 1873, when Barrett himself played Archibald Carlyle and Caroline Heath Lady Isabel, on many evenings people had to be turned away from the theatre. One highly successful sensation drama was Romaine Callender's *True as Steel*, in which the hero was in danger of being crushed under a Nasmyth hammer, in a scene described as "The Interior of the Iron Works by Night, universally pronounced the most marvellous and realistic Scene ever presented on the British Stage". But a lesser realism could prove just as fascinating to an unsophisticated audience. Albery's *Two Roses* included "the introduction of real soda-water, which is drunk by the hero amidst the profound attention of the house."[6]

Although major musical companies generally preferred the New Theatre, the rage for opera bouffe did not entirely pass the Theatre Royal by. Offenbach's *The Grand Duchess* was staged in January 1870 by a company led by Emily Soldene, "a lady of prepossessing appearance and excellent vocal ability", but she had to share the honours with a former Bristol Stock Company favourite, Maria Cruise, who played Wanda. "Her welcome by the audience was sincere and hearty, for Bristol is very conservative in its friendships, and rarely forgets old faces."[7] *Genevieve de Brabant* was brought out three years later, and the famous duet of the "bold gendarmes" was "encored until the vocalists declared 'they had sung out all they knew'."[8] For such engagements even the Dress Circle was almost full.

The notorious *Pink Dominos* visited the Theatre Royal in January 1878, and the alleged naughtiness of the scenes at Cremorne Pleasure Gardens aroused much controversy. The *Western Daily Press* thought it "only fair to say that anything really compromising in its situations has been avoided with great ingenuity"; the *Bristol Times & Mirror* summed up:

> "The Pink Dominos," to those who go to a theatre for a good laugh, without much minding what amuses them, is an attractive piece no doubt, but at a time when there is so much talk about elevating dramatic taste and improving the general tone of stage production it will, perhaps . . . not go a great way towards the promotion of these desirable ends.[9]

Others, less moderate, showered the cast with earnest tracts calling upon them "to reform ere it be too late," to the great disgust of the leading comedian, Alfred Maltby.

Even a few major stars might still be seen in King Street: Madame Ristori, Wilson Barrett and Caroline Heath, G. H. Macdermott, the Haymarket Company supporting John Baldwin Buckstone on his rather pathetic farewell tour in 1877. On the last night Buckstone, who was 75, understandably found the part of Tony Lumpkin almost too much for him, and after his curtain speech he had to ask to be excused from appearing in the afterpiece. Besides drama and opera bouffe, there were occasional visits of Grand Opera companies of a moderate standard, one of which engaged the Band of the Bristol Artillery Volunteers to accompany the Soldiers' Chorus in *Faust*.[10]

Generally speaking, indeed, the fare at the Theatre Royal was very similar to that available at the New Theatre, though on a less lavish scale and provided almost entirely by touring companies. The radical disadvantage was that there were simply not enough of these companies yet to fill up the year, and the theatre would be opened and closed quite unpredictably. Occasionally Chute was able to sublet to a so-called manager, as he did in January 1872 to Henry Loraine, father of the well-known American actor, Robert Loraine. Loraine started quite successfully with Charles Osborne's *The Face in the Moonlight*, but support quickly fell away, and on the following Monday

> The few persons assembled . . . had to depart without witnessing the performance announced. The reason for there being no play, as stated by Mr. Dornton, one of the company, was that Mr. Loraine, the leading actor, was unwell.[11]

No more was heard of Loraine's company, and it is to be feared that there was not only no play but no manager. Fortunately other sublessees were more reliable.

Nevertheless, the fact remains that, with the theatre open for less than half the year, it must have been a losing proposition, and it is surprising that Chute twice renewed his lease. On the second occasion, in 1874, there was some opposition from the Proprietors themselves, led by Chute's old enemy, Isaac Riddle, and, though a new lease for seven years was eventually granted, the Proprietors had to insist on Chute's undertaking repairs to the City Architect's specifications "and to complete the same by the 30th September next and that in default thereof the necessary measures must be taken."[12] What repairs were necessary is not recorded; the audience only noticed that "the whole of the front of the auditorium has now been re-gilded and re-decorated, and the house now presents an extremely pretty appearance. It always was very cosy and comfortable."[13]

Things soon deteriorated again, and although after James Henry Chute's death on 23 July 1878 his sons, George and James Macready Chute, took over the lease, it was clear they were not really interested in continuing to run an uneconomic theatre for sentiment's sake.[14] As a first step, in the summer of 1880 they suggested that the Proprietors might like to buy from them the land at the back of the stage which they had been using for many years, but they wanted £700 for it, and this the Proprietors would not entertain. Instead, the Proprietors' Secretary was told to enquire whether the Chutes intended to renew their expiring lease and "to request them to remove from the premises the old Properties and other rubbish which had accumulated there". Correspondence, with ominous reference to "the Dilapidations," dragged on into the spring, but no agreement could be reached, and discussion was broken off with a threat to sue the Chutes for the cost of necessary repairs to the theatre, £210 being eventually accepted in settlement.

However, the Proprietors were not left tenantless for long. Within a fortnight they had a letter from the popular actor George Melville, on behalf of his son, Andrew,

applying for a Lease and stating the terms to which he would agree – and it was Resolved that a Lease be granted . . .[15]

A tradition had been broken; a new and very different one was to be established.

Two

1881–1894

Andrew Melville [Plate 18] belonged to the new generation of commercial managers. Possessed of tremendous energy and extrovert ebullience, despite the diabetes which sapped his strength and ultimately killed him at the early age of 43, he built up a chain of theatres, some owned, some leased, in South Wales, Glasgow, the Midlands, London and the South Coast.[16] When he took over the Bristol theatre he already had four theatres in South Wales, but, leaving these for the time being largely to managers, he embarked enthusiastically on the rehabilitation of the Theatre Royal, Bristol, the plans being prepared by the ubiquitous C. J. Phipps and T. Pope, the City Architect. "Some idea of the renovation may be gained by the fact that the structural changes and ornamentation will involve an expenditure of about £3000."[17] The Proprietors allowed Melville the first year's rent (£400) and another £300 from their reserve fund towards the cost of "structural and other repairs, alterations, improvements, decorations and embellishments inside and out"; but Melville himself must have contributed by far the largest share.[18]

The alterations he made gave the Theatre Royal substantially the auditorium we see to-day. The stage was cut back by five feet to its present position; plain proscenium doors, topped with niches containing ornamental vases, flanked the shallow forestage.* The under-stage machinery was overhauled to include "three new 'bridge' traps, three 'star' traps, and a 'vampire' trap".[19] For the comfort of the audience, "Phipps' patent chairs" were substituted for "the old-fashioned divisioned seats" in the boxes; backs were provided to the benches of the pit and gallery. It is to Melville also that we owe one of the most outstanding features of the auditorium, the star studded ceiling.

In the centre is a new ventilator, 9 ft. in diameter, most elaborately decorated

---

* These can be seen in the photograph of *Dick Whittington* [Plate 22].

and gilded, and enclosed in a heavy gilt moulding. In each corner is a handsomely designed medallion, enriched with gilding. The proscenium is entirely new, the colour being French grey, with rich gilt mouldings and elaborate ornamentalism . . .

Around [the ventilator] the groundwork of French grey or blue, is fretted with gold stars, and outside these are diagonal enrichments faced with gold frieze.[20]

If anything the result must have been even lovelier then than now, with its effect of a twilight sky seen through the shimmer of gas lighting.

Additionally, Melville succeeded in leasing for three years the yard at the back of the theatre which his predecessors had found so useful; a draft lease of 1 December 1881 gives the area as 60 ft. by 32 ft., and describes it as including "the erection or build^g now standing and being upon the s^d Plot of Ground and forms [sic] Painting, Scene & Dressing Rooms and other conveniences to the said Theatre".

On 5 December 1881 Andrew Melville opened the Theatre Royal with his ever-popular father, George, in *The Duke's Motto*.

The first words he speaks to his followers are, "I see you know me," to which someone in the gallery replied, "Rather!"[21]

George Melville followed this success with a revival of *Hamlet*, always the most admired of his performances in Bristol; he ended his season on 17 December to be followed by his manager-son, under the stage name of "Mr. Emm", in some low comedy parts.

It is to be regretted, however, that the pieces chosen for representation had no pretensions to literary merit, and were of a class which, although popular amongst a small portion of theatre-goers, will not attract the class of audience which this pretty little theatre ought to have.[22]

Andrew Melville was not disposed to concern himself unduly with literary merit, or with any particular class of audience, provided sufficient numbers came to his theatre. His biggest financial successes in the early years were undoubtedly the pantomimes, the first of which was put on without a single working day's closure. Not surprisingly, it proved so under-rehearsed, and so over-provided with "more people almost than they could find room for . . . more scenery than they could work, and more dresses than they could use" that the opening matinee was in danger of having to be cancelled, and the first few nights verged on the chaotic.

Melville's pantomimes (he staged one every Christmas up to 1889-90, and frequently – less the Harlequinade – at Easter and Whitsuntide as well) were forerunners of a type which can still be found in the provinces to-day. The artists were drawn very largely from the music hall, a cause of regret to some, but, as the *Clifton Chronicle* pointed out,

Managers know full well who our best song-and-dance people are; and what is pantomime without these features? Are not many of the best of our opera-bouffe artistes ascendants from the halls, and do we not get all our catchy pantomime songs from the same source?[23]

Speciality acts were lavishly introduced, the plot being so contrived as to provide some semblance of an excuse – a celebration at a King's court or in a Sultan's harem – for their display, and the artistes were frequently changed during the run. Local allusions were still considered essential, and the Bristol journalist A. J. Levy was employed on several of the scripts.

The earlier pantomimes were roaring successes, especially those in which Emm appeared himself, whether as one of the characters or in the guise of a 20-stone Columbine. *The Three Jacks* (1882-3) ran till 3 March, and the advertisements include a "Notice to Country Visitors" :

> The Pantomime now concludes at about 7 minutes to 11, and as the Return Excursion Trains start from the Joint Station at 11.20 . . . this affords ample opportunity of enjoying this remarkable Pantomime from the rise of the curtain at 7.30 to its descent at 10.53 (no interval).[24]

Melville regarded it as a challenge at least to equal the run of the New Theatre pantomime; he would even mount a second edition for a single week in order to avoid defeat. When *Aladdin* was staged in 1887-8 he countered his rival's publicity with some of his own :

> Mr. MELVILLE distinctly contradicts the statement made in an advertisement issued by the management of the Park-row Theatre, that "the universal opinion" is that their Pantomime is "far and away the best seen in Bristol for many years". Thousands are of the opinion that ALADDIN, at the Theatre-Royal, King-street, is the better of the two Pantomimes now being played in Bristol.[25]

For several years Melville outbid the Chutes for the services of William Fosbrooke, a great draw in such different comic parts as Tinbad in *Sinbad the Sailor*, Dame Crusoe, and one of the Babes in the Wood. As Dame Crusoe his make-up and costume were so good "that the audience requires oral demonstration of his identity before greeting him with that hearty applause which his appearance invariably invokes".[26]

Rivalry between the two Bristol theatres was not confined to pantomimes; Melville was altogether decidedly provocative in his relations with the Chutes. It was almost certainly he who stirred the Proprietors into belatedly protesting against the title "the New Theatre Royal" for the Park Row Theatre, an insistence which led to its being rechristened from July 1884 "The Prince's Theatre". He ostentatiously closed his theatre on Ash Wednesday, while the Park Row theatre stayed open : "This being a

THEATRE ROYAL, the Law renders Closing Compulsory on ASH WEDNES-
DAY." He even ran his own production of *Uncle Tom's Cabin* to antici-
pate a revival by the Chutes, who hinted publicly (but quite unjustly)
that he was going to plagiarise the James Henry Chute version, so
"morally dealing with stolen property".[27]

During the first few years of his management, Andrew Melville spent a
good deal of time in Bristol, acting with various Special Companies in
such plays as *The Wandering Jew* and *The Streets of London*. The touring companies engaged by him provided mixed fare; though strong drama
increasingly predominated, light comedy was provided by Charles Col-
lette's Company and opera bouffe by Kate Santley in *La Mascotte*, and
Joseph Eldred's No. 2 Company in Offenbach and Lecocq. Grattan and
Eldred's *Follies of a Day* was given its premiere in Bristol on 16 October
1882 and drew good notices. Even Ristori once more graced the Theatre
Royal stage later the same year, playing Queen Elizabeth and Lady Macbeth in English.[28]

In his curtain speech on the last night of *The Three Jacks* Emm refuted
rumours that he was about to sell out by announcing that he had "just
purchased one-fifth of the freehold"[29] of the Bristol theatre. "I have grown
to like the town, its streets, its people, in fact everything about it but its
taxes, and these I cannot bring myself to regard with affection."[30] But unfortunately for Bristol Melville soon became immersed in the acquisition
of more theatres, among others the Grand Theatre, Birmingham (built for
him, and opened in November 1883); the St. James's, Manchester, in
1884; and the Grand Theatre, Derby, in 1886. Inevitably his personal
contacts with the Bristol Theatre became fewer and fewer, and he had to
rely on his local agent, H. A. Forse.[31] By January 1884 Melville was nine
months in arrears with his rent, and thenceforth he had considerable
difficulty in meeting his obligations. The Proprietors were not over-
sympathetic to his pleas of bad times, however well justified, "his losses
being solely due, in the opinion of the Committee, to want of personal
attention on his part."[32]

It was not, of course, easy to keep up good standards of house and
stage management through a succession of touring engagements ranging
from farce to Shakespeare, and from grand opera to melodrama. Typical
conditions found by one such touring company are graphically described
in his autobiography[33] by Seymour Hicks, who at the beginning of his
acting career was engaged as Assistant Stage Manager at thirty shillings
a week for Yorke Stephens' production of *Mr. Barnes of New York*, which
visited Bristol at the end of August 1888. Only three weeks earlier the
Bristol Times & Mirror had commented on deficiencies in the staging of
Passion's Slave,

for instance, the display of a dirty gauze curtain at the end of the third act, owing to the front lights not being turned down in time, and the letting down of the baize curtain before the end of the piece,

and this was unfortunately typical rather than exceptional.

Although even by 1884 the Theatre Royal was becoming known for the proportion of sensational melodramas it included in its programme, it was not for several more years that such plays, varied occasionally by opera bouffe and even more rarely with "comedy-oddities" such as *Fun on the Bristol* and *Muldoon's Picnic,* really began to dominate the repertoire, and eventually replace the Christmas pantomime. There were quite a number of touring grand opera companies still, though the only one which attracted really good support, for no special apparent reason, was Arthur Rousbey's in April 1888, Mozart's *Marriage of Figaro* in particular drawing a crowded house. Hermann Vezin remained faithful to the King Street theatre, bringing respectable companies in September 1890, November 1892 and May 1894. The most notable visitors to the Theatre Royal in this period, however, were F. R. Benson and John Martin Harvey, in each case as a young actor just trying himself out in management, and having to accept the Theatre Royal as a step towards the Prince's.

Benson brought his "Celebrated Shaksperian and Old English Comedy Company" to the Royal in mid-October 1884, only the second year of the Company's existence. The *Western Daily Press* commented on Benson's Hamlet :

His rendering of the part, though differing in many respects from that of several well-known actors, was consistent and clever; the principal soliloquies were well delivered; and in several of the scenes – and notably his interview with the players and the play scene – his acting was very natural and effective.[34]

The company received very fair support in a programme which included *She Stoops to Conquer* (with G. R. Weir as Tony Lumpkin) and *Rob Roy.*

It is doubtful whether the engagement meant anything particular to Benson, but Martin Harvey to the end of his life remembered his appearance at the Theatre Royal on 9 July 1888, for it was the first – indeed at that stage the only – engagement of a troupe recruited largely from Irving's Lyceum Company under the joint management of Martin Harvey, William Haviland and Louis Calvert, who each nominated a proportion of the plays in the repertoire.

We started with *Othello*. Oh! the glory of that first night! the thrill of looking through the curtain and seeing people in front – an audience who had actually paid to see us act! the ancient, musty smell of that little theatre itself whose boards – perhaps the very same boards – had been trodden by Garrick, Kean,

Mrs. Siddons and Macready! the astounding fact that there was applause at the end of each act! and, then, the night when it came to our turn – Miss de Silva's and mine – in *Ruy Blas*, with Louis Calvert as "Don Salluste", and Haviland as "Don Caesar de Bazan" (a perfect performance)! Can you wonder that after waiting so long to express ourselves and now being actually called before the curtain at the end of the play to receive the applause of the house, we were hysterical and that, after the curtain finally descended, we fell into each other's arms with tears – tears of incredulous amazement and joy.[35]

Martin Harvey, like the other members of the company, was well reviewed, especially for his Cassio; the good notices brought offers of more provincial engagements; and the King Street theatre saw Martin Harvey no more till the days of the Preservation Appeal in 1942.

As the attraction of the theatre narrowed in scope it drew rather different audiences. They were not necessarily less well behaved; though there was occasionally rowdyism in the gallery, when a drunk interrupted a performance of *The Wages of Sin* in November 1882 there was general applause at a request from the stage for his removal. On another occasion a political allusion to Ireland made in a song in the burlesque of *Brum* "aroused a Fenian spirit located in the gallery which was at once drowned by the cheers of the larger portion of the audience."[36] What is discernible is a growing, and sometimes rather endearing, lack of sophistication; it is at this period that the spontaneous hissing of the villain becomes an established reaction. Powerful acting too met its reward; Miss A. Goward as the maniac wife, Bertha, in an adaptation of *Jane Eyre* was so realistic in the drawing room scene that several ladies had to leave the house.

The support of his audience, once the impetus supplied by Andrew Melville's personal presence was removed, proved intermittent. The *Bristol Times & Mirror* put this down to a plethora of revivals of threadbare pieces, and it is true that certain titles recur again and again : *Uncle Tom's Cabin* (rapidly becoming an excuse for a sort of enlarged Christy Minstrel show), *East Lynne, Proof*, Boucicault's Irish plays and *It's Never Too Late to Mend,* for example. But some of these were still the most dependable draws of the repertoire, especially the two first-named.

Realism was the order of the day, more especially effects involving "real water". *Saved from the Streets* advertised "Extraordinary Effects, including Real River of Real Water, with Real Boats, Real Swimming, &c., &c. A portion of the Stage converted into a Huge Tank."[37] But sometimes these contrivances failed of effect; when "Professor Johnson, the Man-Fish" gave a swimming display in a similar tank, "owing . . . to the condition of the water it was impossible to observe all the performances closely,"[38] and one suspects this was not unique. Unfortunately, too, companies visiting the Theatre Royal after May 1886 were further limited in staging the sensation scenes which melodrama demanded by the loss of the yard behind the theatre, Ford and Canning, the owners, refusing to renew the lease despite the representations of the Proprietors on Melville's behalf.

Melville also faced increasing competition from the expansion of the music hall. The old Alhambra (1870) was reopened as the Star (later Tivoli) in September 1890, the People's Palace in Baldwin Street, was built two years later, and the Empire, Old Market Street, a year after that. Here was cheap, lively entertainment competing for much the same clientele but providing far greater comfort than anything the Royal could offer.

In an attempt to encourage attendances Melville made various altera-tions in the prices and booking arrangements. The cutting back of the forestage of course severely restricted the view of those sitting at the side of the Dress Circle, so that Melville deemed it wise to reduce the prices for the side seats from the standard 3s. to 2s. The Upper Boxes were uni-formly 1s. 6d. the Pit 1s. and Gallery 6d. It was possible to reserve some seats in the Dress Boxes, while the extra (i.e. early) doors system, giving priority to those queueing for unreserved seats at a small premium of 6d. (3d. for the Gallery), was also established during 1882.[39] Second price remained a frequent device to encourage audiences, especially in the sum-mer, but for the more expensive touring productions – the rare Shake-speare weeks, grand opera, and sometimes opera bouffe – it might be abolished, or Box prices might be raised to 4s. and 3s. in the Dress Circle, 2s. in the tier above. From 22 September 1884 a second price for the Pit of only 6d. was introduced, following the example of other large towns such as Birmingham, "and in making the experiment in Bristol, Mr. MELVILLE hopes it will be acceptable to those who cannot conveniently attend at the commencement of the performances at 7.30."

But of improvements to the amenities of the house there were none. A number were mooted at various times, in particular the provision of a separate refreshment bar, but whenever the Proprietors suggested that Melville should share the cost the discussions faded away. By June 1887 he was already proposing to give up his lease and transfer it to Moss of the Edinburgh and Newcastle Theatres, "but as they required to be at liberty to terminate any Lease in the event of interference by the Lord Chamber-lain no arrangement was come to."[40] Finally in March 1893 Melville, by now a sick man, applied to transfer his lease to John Barker of the Grand Theatre, Nelson, offering to guarantee the new lessee's rent for the first five years. Barker had brought his tour of *The Forty Thieves* to the Theatre Royal the preceding week and, according to his first night curtain speech on 1 May, "he then fell in love with the old house. He then decided to buy the place off Mr. Melville, and make it as comfortable as he could."

It was not to be quite so simple, however, for Ford and Canning, whose warehouses now adjoined the Theatre on two sides, offered £3,500 to buy the building "with prompt vacant possession subject to Mr. Melville's existing tenancy". In a last spurt of fighting spirit Melville offered £50 more; but a valuation by Henry Daniel put the minimum price at £4,000, "and were it my own – considering alike its present surroundings, the offers made for rental, and the future prospects – I should not care to sell it for under Four thousand five hundred pounds". This sum apparently no one would offer, so Barker received a 21-year lease at the same rent and on the same terms as Melville had held the property.[41]

Despite an initial promise that he would spare no expense, Barker's management was only a poor imitation of Melville's. One of his first engagements, *Icebound*, had its effects sarcastically described as "glimpses into residences that might be imagined palatial, and white washed coves that with an equal stretch of the imagination might be looked upon as ice of the most approved two days' thaw type . . . The second act elicits a race scene with several paste board horses and one live thoroughbred, which is in great favour with the gallery."[42] The Christmas production, *Androcles and the Lion*, was advertised as a pantomime, but it was much nearer an extravaganza with music hall interludes, into which so nearly tragic a plot fitted very awkwardly indeed.

By May 1894 Barker was so far behind with his rent that the Committee of Proprietors had twice had to distrain, and called upon a disconcerted Melville to honour his guarantee, retaining his current dividends as a shareholder while he sought to make an arrangement to protect himself.[43]

Barker at first offered to purchase the theatre for £4,000, then suggested the transfer of his lease to Ernest Carpenter of the Darwen Theatre and Carpenter's solicitor, Leonard Broadbent. Melville, surprisingly, affirmed his willingness to continue his guarantee of rent; Barker withdrew his offer to purchase (which one suspects was little more than a piece of kite-flying) and was given permission to terminate his lease. Even before the Committee had recorded its decision the *Clifton Chronicle* of 6 June reported the transfer as an accomplished fact :

Mr. Carpenter will enter into possession at once, and residing in Bristol will devote all his energies to the management.

Three

1894–1909

It was not long before the programme at the Theatre Royal assumed a routine of pantomime and melodrama. In his first few years as manager Ernest Carpenter did provide some variety: an occasional burlesque or musical comedy; Edmund Tearle's company in Shakespearian tragedy and Knowles' old drama of *Virginius*. He even revived the idea of a Stock Company for the summer months of 1895-7, and again in 1900 and 1901, though, influenced by the organisation of the touring system, plays were now produced on a weekly basis. Significantly the repertory looked back to the 1860s, with *The Colleen Bawn*, *The Shaughraun*, *East Lynne*, *The Ticket-of-Leave Man* (Carpenter himself playing Hawkshaw or Bob Brierly) and *Driven from Home* as its chief attractions. Carpenter paid considerable attention to the mounting of his productions, and in his companies he introduced two long-standing favourites to the Bristol public: Matt Wilkinson and Sam Livesey (father of Barry, Jack and Roger).

Such experiments, however, soon ended. In a curtain speech at his Complimentary Benefit in July 1903 Carpenter explained that he had found

they liked the drama at the old house, and he was loath to attempt to launch out in a lighter and more mirthful direction. He did make the experiment a few years ago, but everybody expressed a preference for the drama.[44]

"The drama" meant, effectively, melodrama, sometimes of a very crude and lurid nature. The hairbreadth escapes from cremation, circular saw, Nasmyth hammer, flood or express train are now a matter for joke, however they may once have been regarded, but sensation was not confined to such episodes. In *Under the Czar* the hero, Yeroslaff, was hanged (and resuscitated) before the audience; in *Lady Satan*, billed as a "comedy-drama", "there was a harrowing scene when the heroine was thrashed by a jealous rival and tortured with hot irons with a view to driving her mad

176

in the presence of her lover"; and even the hardbitten critic of the *Times & Mirror* was inspired to protest at the flogging of a child on stage in *The Black Mask*. Fortunately not all realism was so unpleasant. *The World's Verdict*, in September 1895, advertised "Real Ducks on Water, Pigeons, Rabbits, &c.", and "real water" effects retained their popularity.

The response of the largely working class audiences became conditioned by this type of fare. Not content with hissing, one woman "rose from her seat in the pit and roundly cursed" the villains in Wills's *Jane Shore*. The relatively serious drama, *The Manxman*, adapted by Wilson Barrett from Hall Caine's novel, was staged by a good company in September 1896, but the audience "which enthusiastically greeted many of the strong situations and features of the performance . . . not only failed to grasp the signification of many of the subtler details, but entirely misconstrued them."[45]

The nature of Carpenter's audience also inevitably affected in time the price structure of the house. The turn of the century saw the building up of the commercial resources of Bristol to a new high level, but this wealth was still based on cheap labour, and unemployment was a major problem in Bristol as elsewhere.*

For the 1898 pantomime, "In consequence of the great demand for Shilling Seats in former Pantomimes, Mr. CARPENTER has decided to REDUCE the UPPER BOXES to 1s.," and only four months later another advertisement proclaimed : "The whole of the Lower Circle is now 2s. being the Best 2s. Seats in Bristol." By 1902 the standard prices were 2s. in the Centre Dress Circle (2s. 6d. unreserved or 3s. reserved for the pantomime), 1s. 6d. in the Side Circle; 1s. Upper Circle and Pit; and 6d. Gallery. In August 1906 the Pit was reduced to 8d. and the Gallery to 4d. : "The Public want good Entertainment at Popular Prices, and we intend to MOVE WITH THE TIMES !" It can be no coincidence that the following month audiences were being encouraged to see a production of *The Coal King* by the offer of a raffle for free bags of coal.

The chief source of patronage in this period came from the various football clubs. A song, "Play up, Bristol," was introduced into Carpenter's first pantomime;[46] the following year there was a "Football night" under the auspices of six Clubs; and in *The Football King*, staged in November 1896, part of a Cup Final was displayed with "well-known local gentlemen" appearing as referees. In 1897 there was even a Football Harlequinade to *Puss in Boots*, in which members of the Bristol Football Club took part.

---

* The *Western Daily Press* of 25 April 1905 commented on the timeliness of the play *The Poor Must Live*, "with the bitter cry of the unemployed and the complaint of rising rates that have of late been voiced in the city", and local allusions were introduced to point this.

Publicity for the Theatre Royal was certainly varied, if not always artistically refined. A Brass Band of Real Indians paraded through the streets whenever Hardie & Van Leer's production of *On the Frontier* came to Bristol; when Frederick Melville (son of Andrew) sent his company in *The Ugliest Woman on Earth*, "A carriage and pair with two liveried men on a box, and with the figure of a woman whose head was concealed by a large black veil, attracted great attention in the city," and a beauty competition was also held in conjunction with the engagement. To draw attention to the burlesque, *Aladdin Condensed*, in June 1898, Jehan Bedini, "equilibrist and juggler" in the company, "undertook to catch on a fork, attached to his head and the back of his neck, turnips thrown from the [Clifton Suspension] Bridge, while he stood on the roadway beneath. He succeeded in catching six turnips, one landing safely on the fork at the back of his neck" – a feat for which he was loudly cheered by the crowd who assembled to watch.[47]

Though certain plays seem to have had an almost timeless appeal, the programme taken as a whole reflects changes in the focus of popular interest as the 19th Century drew to a close. In turn the death of Gordon and the subsequent campaign by Kitchener in the Sudan, the Matabele War and the Boer War were drawn on for a series of military dramas of the late 1890s, interspersed with recurrent productions dealing with Nihilist plots and secret police in Tsarist Russia; while the comparative peace of the first decade of the 20th Century brought about a retreat to Ruritania. But wherever the scene might be laid, on land, on (or even under) the sea, the basic plot and the emotional appeal to the audience varied little. The temptations of London and the wiles of women were exhaustively exploited by the Melville brothers, and they never failed to attract an audience.

Ernest Carpenter also revived to some extent the pantomime glories of the Theatre Royal, laying considerable emphasis on attractively-painted scenery, but even more on broad (but "family") comedy.* Dave O'Toole and Edwin Garth were two of his most popular Dames, and Carpenter engaged a notable series of knockabout duos in Karr and Kooney, Sandford and Lyons, and Crosby and Walker – the last-named being better known later as Syd Walker, "Radio's Junk Man" of Second World War fame.[48] The introduction of speciality acts was confined to characters in

---

* *Robinson Crusoe* (1904-5) was advertised as follows:
"Pretty! Funny!! and Refined!!!"
"IMPORTANT! – Mr. Carpenter desires particularly to draw attention to the refined character of this production. Although screamingly funny, it is wholesome and harmless, and is essentially a Pantomime that families and children can be brought to in safety . . ."

Western Daily Press, 2.1.1905.

the show (though on Benefit nights artists from the Prince's and from the local music halls would contribute extra entertainments), while the Harlequinade became shorter and shorter and after 1903 was dropped altogether. The choice of subjects was narrowed down almost exclusively to that handful of tales which we still associate most readily with pantomime : *Aladdin, Robinson Crusoe, Sinbad the Sailor, The Babes in the Wood, Red Riding Hood, Puss in Boots, Dick Whittington* and *Cinderella*. By means of the introduction of a second edition with new songs and business, the pantomime now usually extended into March, and was for Carpenter, as for Melville, the money-spinner of the year.

In the midst of the series, however, there was a break. Carpenter was not content with one Bristol theatre, but had built and opened in February 1898 the Queen's Theatre, Swindon, and later the same year took over the lease of the Empire Music Hall in Bristol. To this much larger theatre he transferred his Christmas "annual" in 1899, and the *Times & Mirror* reported that "it is now almost sure that the Theatre Royal will be the scene of pantomime no more."[49] However, a premature and disastrous attempt to introduce twice-nightly variety caused Carpenter to give up the lease of the Empire in the spring of 1900; next Christmas Bristol playwright and actor-manager, Frank Dix,[50] provided a five-week production of *Sinbad the Sailor*, and thereafter Ernest Carpenter and his actress wife, Jessie, concocted the book and lyrics themselves.

Within limitations, Carpenter was an efficient and conscientious manager. He not only kept the Proprietors up to the mark in repairs to the structure and roofs[51] and in external decorations, but himself contributed a number of improvements. The Upper Boxes were reseated with tip-up chairs for the pantomime of 1895-6, the Pit benches were padded five years later. The most important advance instituted by Carpenter, however, was the provision of electric lighting instead of gas – a change which the management carried out in the autumn of 1905 without closing the theatre for a day.

In addition to the increased safety that the installation must ensure, its facility of control is of tremendous assistance to the stage manager in obtaining the many effects in which a shade of light or gloom may make or mar a scene; and with the magnificent switchboard that is now in course of completion the footlights or battens can be controlled almost to the degree of a lamp.[52]

Meanwhile, in 1897 it was reported that the King Street houses forming the façade of the Theatre Royal were in a dangerous state, complicating the question of the ground lease held from the Corporation and due to expire in 1919. The Proprietors would have liked to acquire the freehold, but the Corporation were willing to consider this only if another similar property, preferably commercial, could be offered in exchange, and this the Proprietors were unable to find. In 1899 the houses had to be shored up, and it was not till April 1900 that the Corporation agreed to grant the reversion of the land forming the King Street frontage subject to a fee-farm rent and "the expenditure of not less than £1,800 in the execution of buildings on the land according to Plans to be approved by the Corporation."[53]

It was just at this time that Ernest Carpenter applied to transfer his lease to his father, Frederick, in consequence, no doubt, of his own expanding activities in management. After much bargaining, and the withdrawal of Broadbent, an agreement was drawn up on 20 January 1902 by which the Proprietors were allowed access to the premises to carry out their agreement with the Corporation, "the Landlords hereby undertaking that the said Works shall be so carried out as not to interfere in any way with the business of the said Theatre". On completion of the work, the old lease would be surrendered, and a new one made out to Frederick and Ernest Carpenter jointly for 21 years at £500 p.a. for the first fourteen years. As compensation for giving up their own right to determine at the end of that period, the Proprietors exacted a rent of £600 for the last seven years.

The alterations did not go through smoothly. Mr. W. Skinner, the architect, first produced plans on 26 May 1902 "when it appeared that the proposed Elevation did not extend across the entire front", and when the tenders for the reconstruction of the frontage, and for the renovation of the interior, were opened "it was found that the lowest Tender for the former far exceeded the amount stipulated by the Corporation . . . and that the lowest tender for the repairs and decoration was also too high". Skinner was able to prune the specifications and an amended tender by H. H. Forse of £1,800 for the new buildings and £575 for the internal work was accepted.

The Theatre was shut for the month of July, during which time additional cloakrooms were constructed, the gilding of the interior was renewed, and the gallery ceiling further raised; while "the quaint timbered house at the entrance has been taken down, after standing more than 300 years, and some of the oak was found to be as sound as if it had been recently placed there".[54] In evidence six years later it was stated that "the gables, the upper part, and the front wall were pulled down," but that in the new building the old foundations were used 'and considerably strengthened.'[55] With a façade of Bath stone, and a cantilevered iron portico [Plate 19], the resultant building, opened in January 1903, provided not only access to the theatre but modern offices for the management.

The existing Royal Patent was due to expire in 1903, but just as they were about to apply for a renewal the Proprietors learned that Carpenter had been summoned on eleven charges under the Licensing Acts. It was common practice for him to gather his cronies round him after the performance ended, holding convivial and boisterous gatherings in the Dress Circle Bar until the small hours,[56] and the Proprietors had already issued several warnings to Carpenter about them. But since everyone, from the manager to the Chief Constable, was anxious that the application for the Patent should not be prejudiced, the magistrates accepted Carpenter's unlikely plea of ignorance that his "Royal" theatre was subject to the law of the land, and merely fined him two guineas and costs.[57]

The Lord Chamberlain, however, was much less interested in the peccadilloes of the management than in the safety of the artists and audiences. The report of his Surveyor, Frank T. Verity, made on 15 June 1903, ran to eight foolscap pages, and pointed out, *inter alia*, that there was only one exit to each part of the house except the Pit; that nearly all the doors opened inwards; that the O.P. Dressing Rooms possessed no means of egress from the theatre other than across or under the stage; and that there was "absolutely no separation in the Fire risk between the Stage and the Auditorium the division being a lath and plaster partition there being a brick wall only between the Orchestra and the Cellar under the Stage." The gangways in the Upper Boxes were only fifteen inches wide, and even in the Dress Circle the centre gangway was under three feet; there was no secondary lighting system and fire appliances were exiguous. On receipt of this report, the Lord Chamberlain's office wrote firmly to the Proprietors

to ask whether you are prepared at once to carry out alterations, and if so, by what date they will be completed, because unless this is done the Lord Chamberlain feels that he will be obliged to treat the theatre as seriously in default and not merely to refuse to advise the regrant of the Patent, but to take such immediate steps as he may be advised to put an end to a condition of things that is reported to him as dangerous.[58]

To meet the most urgent of these requirements the Proprietors – already heavily overdrawn – had to pay £500, for the erection of a fire curtain involved rebuilding the proscenium arch (and trimming one side of the proscenium doors); and then a further £650 for new dressing rooms on the Rackhay site, to replace those deemed dangerous for the artists.* In consideration of the Proprietors' expenditure of nearly £4,000, Carpenter agreed to an increased rent of £600 for the first fourteen years of his lease and £700 for the last seven.

* A ground plan attached to an Insurance proposal of 1904 shows the resultant layout of the theatre [Plate 20].

These improvements, however, met only the most urgent demands of the Lord Chamberlain, and when checking on their provision in November 1903 Verity found he had to make clear to the Proprietors

that, in the event of the Company deciding to apply for a new Patent, a detailed list of requirements will have to be served upon them, and they will have to submit plans to the Lord Chamberlain showing the manner in which the requisites could be complied with.[59]

Since these included the provision of alternative exits to all parts of the house, which the buildings then surrounding the theatre made impossible, and since the City Police were quite satisfied with what had been done, Ernest Carpenter successfully applied instead for a local licence in May 1904, telling the magistrates that "as a citizen of Bristol, he was anxious to come before the local authorities rather than obtain a licence from the Lord Chamberlain."[60] The Patent was accordingly allowed to lapse and the Theatre Royal was, strictly, Royal no longer.

To meet their expenditure the Proprietors were able to arrange a mortgage for £3,500 at 4½ per cent. with Mr. T. H. R. Winwood, a descendant of an early Proprietor.[61] They were mildly worried that a new warehouse being built to the west of the theatre in the summer of 1906 might interfere with light and air, and began correspondence with the owner, Murphy, to limit its height and persuade him to finish the wall facing the theatre with white glazed bricks; Murphy found it more profitable to spin out negotiations while he completed the building, let it to a haulier and warehouseman called Burgess, and eventually pay £105 compensation to the Theatre Royal Proprietors. When, however, Burgess started loading up the warehouse with grain on 14 December, he was warned that "the building never would stand the weight . . . Only the next day, December 15th, the theatre people were terrified, and in great agitation, as cracks were appearing. Doors and windows were jammed and would not open, and the building was dragged down some three inches."[62] After negotiations spread over more than a year had proved abortive, the matter was taken to court and Murphy was fined £300 and costs. No further subsidence appearing, the Proprietors were content to patch up the cracks with concrete fillets and put off proper re-instatement indefinitely.

All these matters were complicated by the death of Frederick Carpenter only two days after the amended lease to Frederick and Ernest Carpenter had been signed on 8 January 1904. Carpenter left all his real and personal estate to his widow, Emma, who therefore became officially co-lessee with their son, Ernest. Shortly afterwards, Ernest Carpenter moved to Brighton (where he had acquired a theatre) leaving his able manager, W. F. Crowe, in charge at Bristol, and in 1907 he leased the Lyceum Theatre in London, which had been a music hall since the glory of Irving had departed from it, but which he ran with H. R. Smith as a melodrama house. Crowe was called from Bristol to take over house management and H. C. Alty took his place.

Ernest Carpenter, unfortunately, was not physically strong, and suffered from a "severe internal malady". In rehearsing his 1909 Christmas pantomime at the Lyceum for thirteen hours at a stretch he overtaxed himself, collapsed, and died on the eve of the production.[63] Eight months previously the *Times & Mirror* had surveyed his achievements very fairly, pointing out that the limited choice of theatres in a provincial city normally caused the audiences to demand variety of fare.

It is possible, however, to educate them in a groove, and that is what has really happened at the Theatre Royal. The house was not in a very flourishing condition when Mr. Carpenter assumed control, and he did not at once find a royal road to favour. Neither can it be claimed for him that he has exactly restored its ancient glories. Yet he has succeeded in doing what others had failed to do there – he has gathered round him a profitable clientele, for whom he caters in a manner which they know well how to appreciate.[64]

Four

1910-1924

The death of Ernest Carpenter removed the last vestiges of stability from the management of the Theatre Royal. Despite his apparent success his estate was valued at only just over £350. His interest in the theatre lease passed to his wife, Jessie; after the pantomime his younger brother, Frederick, took over the practical running of the theatre. Frederick Carpenter, with no personal commitment to restrict him and no financial resources to aid him, proved a sharp-witted and plausible manager with no perceptible policy other than to keep the theatre's head above water if he could : he was contemptuous of any criticism of his repertoire based solely on aesthetic considerations.[65]

The pantomimes continued on the same lines, Jessie Carpenter supplying the book, and first-rate artists might still be seen at the Theatre Royal during the Christmas season. Judith Espinosa, of the famous ballet family, arranged and took part in the dances for *Robinson Crusoe* in 1909-10 and 1915-6. Crosby and Walker were the making of *Dick Whittington* in 1910-11, for which "the final scene (Outside the Guildhall) has been prepared on a gorgeous scale for the Theatre Royal"[66] – as may be seen from the postcard photograph made of it [Plate 22]. The following year the comics were the up-and-coming pair, Naughton and Gold, as the Robbers in *The Babes in the Wood*.

They are to be classed among the cleverest pair of comedians that can be recalled in the Theatre Royal pantomimes . . . Their funniest scene is in the forest, where for about half an hour they keep the audience in roars of laughter with a duel, boxing match, and other absurdities. Their dancing, too, is quite exceptional.[67]

They returned again for *Aladdin* in 1913-4 to equally enthusiastic notices.

184

Touring companies continued the staple fare outside the pantomime period, mostly exploiting the catchpenny sensations of the day; in 1913 there were six plays on the White Slave Traffic in as many months. There was occasionally something serious : Derwent Hall Caine in a production of *The Christian* (based on his father's famous novel) in December 1911, and Rex Beach's *The Barrier,* which treated its theme of mixed marriages in a responsible fashion. Frederick Carpenter was generally more willing to experiment than his brother had been, though how far this was a positive policy and how far a matter of opportunism is open to question. However, he did book Alexander Marsh and his Shakespeare Company in November 1910; there were touring productions of *The Belle of New York* (which attracted crowded houses) and *Floradora* in 1912, and further experiments with weekly repertory in the summer months, with emphasis on the more modern types of melodrama.

Repertory was becoming the watchword of the progressives in the theatre. The Bristol Playgoers' Club, founded in November 1911, was pledged to work towards its establishment in Bristol, and there was therefore great excitement when Carpenter announced the engagement for a fortnight in December 1913 of Miss Horniman's Company from the Gaiety, Manchester, including Lewis Casson, Sybil Thorndike, Eliot Makeham and Muriel Pratt.

This is an announcement of great moment to us, if we deserve the name of Playgoers; nay, we go as far as to say that this is a test of us as Playgoers,

declared the Editor of the November edition of the *Bristol Playgoer,* the Club's monthly magazine.

The main production was Houghton's *Hindle Wakes,* blending delightful North Country comedy with its problem "Should Fanny marry Alan?" which was blazoned on the posters outside the Theatre Royal. An audience by no means made up entirely of Playgoers gave it a mixed reception :

The cheaper parts of the house . . . entirely spoilt the first act by ill-timed laughter. Indeed, the more grave the crisis the louder were the guffaws.[68]

In *Candida,* produced during the second week, Lewis Casson's Marchbanks so irritated one member of the audience that "the stillness of the auditorium was broken . . . by a penetrating voice calling upon someone to wring his neck!"[69] Galsworthy's *Silver Box* received more critical acclaim than popular support, but the careful realism of both play and production was appreciated, if sometimes lightheartedly :

We never remember seeing a police court scene better played or more faithfully represented. The only person to arrive late was one of the reporters. It quite reminded one of our local police court.[70]

Artistically, the engagement was a triumph, and triggered off considerable discussion about the possibility of restoring the glories of the historic King Street house by establishing there a repertory company on Manchester lines. As "Gordon" in the January *Bristol Playgoer* pointed out :

It is not too large, an advantage from every point of view to a repertory house; and it has a history that should make every student of drama anxious to see it inhabited by more *actual* beings than that cheery old ogre, Melodrama, and the pleasant but unreal fairy, Pantomime.

Ironically, while Bristol was extolling Manchester as a model, the Gaiety was going through one of its crisis periods, which led to the resignation of Lewis Casson and several other members of the company, including Muriel Pratt, who had played Fanny in *Hindle Wakes* and Prossie in *Candida* during the Bristol visit. She started a company of her own, and in February 1914 Carpenter announced that he had booked her for a three-weeks' season in May, despite doubts whether it was a wise choice of dates "when the Spring evenings are inducing most people out of doors." Carpenter probably felt it was so poor a time that he had nothing to lose and might just possibly pick up something instead.

He was certainly in need of a windfall, for, like all live theatres, the Royal was finding the going increasingly hard. When Frederick Carpenter became manager Bristol had two theatres, three music halls and seven cinemas, and the number of the latter rapidly increased. Of the music halls, the Tivoli had given up in 1903, and the People's Palace gradually became devoted entirely to films;[71] Sir Oswald Stoll built two Hippodromes, one in Bedminster which opened in 1911 but was converted as a cinema in 1915, and one in St. Augustine's Parade which opened as a Variety house in December 1912. Attempts by the halls to secure stage licences were invariably bitterly opposed by both the Prince's and the Theatre Royal, on the grounds that the business they were doing simply would not stand further competition. "It is no secret that neither can afford to lose any considerable proportion of its patrons," Carpenter said frankly.

In November 1910 Carpenter had put up a colossal bluff to the Proprietors, proposing to raise £15,000 capital, buy up the Theatre Royal and some adjoining property, "bringing the Theatre up to date and making the principal entrance in Queen Charlotte Street on a site for which he was now negotiating all of which might necessitate the rebuilding of the whole or greater portion of the Theatre."[72] The Proprietors continued discussions all through 1911, despite the fact that by September of that year Carpenter had not paid the quarter's rent due at midsummer, but finally the scheme was abandoned. It is difficult to believe it was anything more than a front to induce some confidence in Carpenter's solidity as a manager.

Undeterred by his failure, Carpenter submitted to the Committee of Proprietors a list of "absolutely necessary" improvements to the old theatre :

Raise the roof over the stage, so that we may be able to lift our cloths without rolling, as is done everywhere else.

At present we are greatly handicapped; for it means that we have to employ stage hands all the year round, and specially at Pantomime time, and visiting companies complain seriously about the damage done to their cloths, and some of them will not visit us on that account.[73]

Remove the Circle Bar to the room at the top of the stairs . . .

Reseat the Circle completely . . .

Redecorate the interior . . .

Put in additional Heating Apparatus . . .

Estimating that this would cost at least £1,500, Carpenter offered to pay half in return for a new lease for twenty-one years at £600 per annum with an option of purchase on the terms already arranged.

With a heavily mortgaged theatre and the rent income already uncertain, it was hardly possible for the Proprietors to undertake major alterations. Indeed, a steady stream of repair bills was gradually exhausting the reserve intended for the reinstatement of the front buildings, which was never actually carried out. However, the Committee did agree to contribute £50 towards a much modified scheme, whereby the Bar was moved in the manner suggested, the old Bar in the foyer being converted to the sale of tea, coffee, cocoa and Oxo. A much-needed overhaul of cloakroom and sanitary provisions was made during the summer, and a new heating system installed by George Crispin & Co. Shelter in the side yard for the Early Doors queue also met with a welcome. Progress on all these alterations was punctuated by distraints for overdue rent, unsuccessful requests for its reduction, and finally an arrangement for weekly payment.

It is against this background of near-insolvency that Muriel Pratt's attempt to found a Bristol Repertory Theatre must be viewed. For her experimental three-weeks' season in May 1914 she made a positive attempt to link up with the Bristol Playgoers' Club and attract a better class audience, altering the starting time from 7.30 to the more fashionable 8 p.m., reseating the Pit and raising the price of seats there to 1s. 6d., and including in her programme the winning entry for the Playgoers' one-act play competition (*Reuben's Wife,* by George Holloway).[74]

It was indeed a magnificent three weeks, the repertory consisting of four curtain-raisers and five full-length plays, one of which was Violet Pearn's poetical drama, *Wild Birds,* produced for the first time. The authoress had written the heroine's part especially for Muriel Pratt out of admiration for her beautiful voice, and the play was rapturously received. Harley Granville Barker had intended to be at the first night, but sent his apologies in a rousing letter read to the audience by Noel Spencer, Miss Pratt's producer :

Business and nothing but business keeps me, most unfortunately, from being with you on Tuesday, to see and applaud the new play, and to wish you personally a real and permanent success in your work there . . . For quite surely Bristol – the Metropolis of the West – will soon be as little able to imagine itself without its own repertory theatre as now it could without its library, museum, swimming baths, and public parks . . . If I were a Bristolian I'd get up in the theatre and say, "Confound to-morrow and the day after. Here's a company and a repertory theatre started – alive. Let's do the obvious thing. Let's keep it alive from to-day onwards."[75]

A company which also included Brember Wills, Douglas Vigors and Clive Carey (already showing his musical gifts) could hardly fail to make an impact, and a questionnaire circulated by Muriel Pratt during her season revealed such enthusiastic support that she obtained an option for the following spring from Fred Carpenter. The *Times & Mirror* sounded a warning about depending on paper promises :

The Bristol public are a peculiar lot to cater for, and it would require an extremely attractive repertory week to stand up, for instance, against "The Girl from Utah", a return visit of "The Marriage Market", and the latest Edwardes and Courtneidge successes.[76]

Unheeding, enthusiasts in the Playgoers' Club, led by Guy Tracey Watts and Professor Arthur Skemp of Bristol University, pushed forward the scheme, and a public meeting, addressed by Lena Ashwell, was held in the Theatre Royal on 1 July to promote an autumn season of sixteen weeks. Muriel Pratt, who had no capital, stood firm that she needed guaranteed ticket sales of £1,600 before undertaking such a season, and the Secretaries of the Playgoers' Club organised an appeal.

By mid-July the press announced that "the repertory season is to be an accomplished fact". Even the Theatre Royal Proprietors limited their dividend in order to contribute towards renovating the auditorium. The Treasurer, in a burst of enterprise, snapped up a bargain lot of 126 tip-up seats for £26.15s.6d, which were used to reseat the Upper Circle, and, except that Carpenter was again behind with his rent, all seemed set fair.

And then came the outbreak of the Great War, announced by Lodge Percy from the stage of the Theatre Royal where his company was playing *Under Two Flags*. During the initial hysteria, opinion on supporting a "luxury" like the theatre was sharply divided, even in the Playgoers' Club, where President Dr. Barclay Baron was finally asked to resign over the issue.[77] However, a canvass of supporters revealed a five to one majority in favour of continuing the season, the renovation of the theatre also went forward.

Besides the new seats in the Upper Circle, green leather stalls replaced the padded benches of the Pit, and an entrance to them was made through the Dress Circle[78] – but "though the stalls are now on the ground floor, Miss Pratt wishes it to be known that evening dress is optional." The walls, the ceiling, and most of the woodwork were cleaned and redecorated, and a new act drop specially painted. Prices for the new season were 3s. and 2s.6d. for the Stalls and for the Centre Dress Circle; 1s. 6d. for the Side Circle; Upper Circle 1s. and Gallery 6d.

Brember Wills, Clive Carey and Susan Claughton remained in the company; the most important newcomer was Muriel Pratt's husband, the actor-producer W. Bridges Adams (later an outstanding director at Stratford on Avon). On 31 August 1914 Miss Pratt inaugurated her Bristol season with a revival of *Wild Birds* and a specially-contributed Prologue by John Masefield.[79] She worked on a weekly basis, with a repertory of challenging quality and variety. The Rousseau-esque romanticism of *Wild Birds* was followed by Galsworthy's *The Pigeon,* produced to bring out its original dream setting; a melodrama, *Subsidence*; and Housman and Granville Barker's *Prunella*, one of the greatest successes of the season. On 26 October the premiere of Masefield's *Philip the King* took place, though owing to delay in submitting the script to the Lord Chamberlain the first performance had to be organised as a private one.[81] Set at the period of the Armada and written in rhymed verse, it was much admired, though Masefield was felt to be at his best, as one would expect, in his descriptions of the sea. The play was partnered by Lascelles Abercrombie's odd little comedy, *The End of the World,* which was a complete failure, and contributed to the thin houses experienced.

The following week provided yet another premiere, this time a blank verse play on the King Arthur legend by Professor Arthur Skemp, called *Guenevere* [see Plate 21]) The company were able to use the Burne-Jones designs, and borrow some of the actual armour, for Irving's *King Arthur,* and Bridges Adams' effective use of lighting and drapes set these off admirably. The acting was uneven; the *Western Daily Press* said tactfully that Clive Carey "played Lancelot fairly well – but he is really a Galahad," and a contributor to the November *Playgoer* complained that neither Carey nor Muriel Pratt (Guenevere) "evinced the least appreciation of how verse should be spoken," but "seated themselves on a bench and chatted airily of their passion and their ailments." This criticism brought an angry protest from Skemp in the next issue.

But, despite the undoubted artistic success, support was spasmodic, even from the Playgoers' Club. It was necessarily an uphill task to win a completely new audience for the Royal, one prepared to listen and think and feel, as it had not done – indeed, had had but little opportunity of doing – for many years. Despite the introduction of more modern comedies in the latter part of her programme, Muriel Pratt was in dire straits financially, and her affairs were in great confusion, while Carpenter was under continuous pressure for his rent, having sent a cheque which the Bank declined to honour.[82]

A further blow fell: in order to keep her company together over the pantomime period Muriel Pratt applied for a temporary licence of the hall at the Grand Spa hotel to put on children's plays. Opposed by both the Prince's and the Theatre Royal Proprietors (though not, to his credit, Fred Carpenter), the application was turned down out of hand. There was a storm of protest from playgoers, 1,500 signing a petition at the theatre, and the Rev. Lewis Johnson of David Thomas Memorial Church wrote to the press delightfully:

The Church in its history continually prays God to bless our Magistrates by giving them grace to execute justice and to maintain truth. Probably we have not prayed fervently enough; for one would not like to suggest the horrid alternative that our Magistracy is past praying for. Anyhow, the grace sought after has certainly not fallen upon them in their recent decision regarding Miss Muriel Pratt's application for a dramatic licence.[83]

All was in vain, and Miss Pratt went on tour, while Carpenter took out the stalls again and ordered a huge Union Jack as curtain for this year's pantomime, *Jack and the Beanstalk,* which starred Bobbie Comber as Billy Buttons.

Muriel Pratt returned on 12 April 1915 to find Emma Carpenter on the verge of bankruptcy. Relations were so strained that the Proprietors even arranged to impound Miss Pratt's rent of £24 a week, from which they disbursed £8.10s. to Fred Carpenter for his managerial services and to meet rates and taxes.

As a compromise with wartime taste, Miss Pratt's season consisted almost entirely of comedies ranging from *Mrs. Gorringe's Necklace* to *The Doctor's Dilemma;* additionally she ran special 4.45 matinees of

Candida, Masefield's *Nan* and *Therese Raquin.* But, as so often happens, compromise succeeded no better than adherence to principle. The comedies chosen made just the sort of demands on technique, polish and pace which weekly repertory is least well organised to provide. Predictably, notice after notice complained of slowness on the first nights, and the most earnest supporters dropped away. Years afterwards Muriel Pratt disclosed[84] that her takings during her three seasons had averaged about £100 a week, representing the bare minimum guarantee she had originally required; and when it is remembered that, of this, £24 went on rent and the rest had to pay a company of about a dozen, its ancillary staff, and the production costs of a weekly repertory, including a number of costume plays, it will be appreciated how little margin there was.

Incredibly, Miss Pratt was not discouraged. Mrs. Carpenter went bankrupt on 31 May; with no assets but her interest under the lease and a mortgaged annuity, she was living as a paying guest at the home of her solicitor's father, "receiving on an average Two pounds a week out of the Receipts of the Theatre." Miss Pratt applied to the Proprietors for a three-year lease, offering a rent of £600 a year, but the Proprietors postponed consideration, thinking that a better offer was coming from a mysterious London syndicate, and the opportunity was lost.

So died a most courageous experiment, a casualty primarily of the Great War, but also of public apathy and dubious commercialism. For, as it turned out, the Proprietors' delaying tactics cost them dearer than they could have imagined. Mrs. Carpenter's Trustee in bankruptcy, Mr. C. H. Tucker, without reference to the Proprietors, proceeded to assign the lease to a company calling themselves Bristol Theatres Ltd., whom it proved impossible to dislodge.[85]

The man behind this syndicate was an irrepressible and quite unscrupulous theatrical confidence trickster, known in the theatre as Cecil Hamilton Baines, though his real name was William Francis Jackson. He had been declared bankrupt twice already, and sentenced on various occasions for fraudulent representation.[86] With no real resources save an infinite capacity for bluff, he kept the Theatre Royal going after his fashion for eight more years. After one manager had had a nervous breakdown and a second resigned, Baines took over management himself at a salary of £5 a week (£10 during the pantomime run) and 10 per cent. of net profits — but, as he admitted with cheerful ingenuousness when he was once again declared bankrupt in 1922, "there had been no profits, net or gross, unfortunately." It is clear from the Minutes that the Proprietors suspected the *bona fides* of Bristol Theatres Ltd. from the beginning, but proof was another matter, and their opponents cleverly gave them no opportunity to raise the matter in Court. After nearly four years of expensive and frustrating legal actions. the Proprietors succeeded in obtaining arrears of rent, but had to resign themselves to the fact that the control of the theatre was effectively out of their hands.

With brief interludes for miscellaneous touring companies (it is doubtful whether many reputable managements would have accepted dates) Baines divided the year between his pantomime season and a "Theatre Royal Repertory Company" (with the old favourite, Matt Wilkinson, as low comedian), whose seasons usually began with *East Lynne* and continued with patriotic and domestic dramas, increasingly advertised as "For Adults Only". These performances were, with rare exceptions, twice nightly.[87] The prices on the first introduction of this system in March 1916 were reduced to Centre Circle, 1s.; Side Circle 9d.; Upper Circle, 6d.; Pit, 4d. and Gallery, 2d. with a small extra charge for Early Doors. Thus even a packed house would bring in barely £30; no wonder there were no profits!

So disgusted were the Committee with the situation that they obtained the consent of the Proprietors as a whole to sell the theatre, and in August 1919 they advertised its forthcoming auction.[88] Out of pure mischief, Bristol Theatres Ltd. promptly inserted a counter-advertisement claiming that they had acquired a new central site "for the erection of one of the best Drama Houses in the country", to be opened at Christmas 1924.

> Until then the Theatre Royal will be carried on as usual, and at the expiration of the present lease, the whole of the fixtures [which belonged, of course, to the Proprietors, not the lessees], together with several pantomimes, will be offered for sale by public auction.

This superficially serious announcement led to some speculation about the future of the Theatre Royal as a building; but even the sympathetic *Times & Mirror* could only suggest that it might make a good boxing hall.[89]

On 25 September the auction took place, but the highest bid was only £9,850, not approaching the reserve price of around £12,500. A subsequent private offer fell through on the grounds that the rent charge of £37.10s. had not been included in the particulars; suspicion that this was a mere pretext is confirmed by the mention of Mr. Harry Rossiter as the purchasers' nominee, for Rossiter was Hamilton Baines' father-in-law.

Over the next few years the state of the building went from bad to worse. Two years' wrangle over unsafe electrical wiring reached no satisfactory conclusion; in July 1920 it was reported that there had been flooding in the Dressing Rooms; six months later the Secretary told the

Proprietors that "the General Manager of the Lessees had phoned him on the 31st December last informing him that the water was coming through the Roof of the Gallery and that unless seen to at once they would have to close down the Theatre." In October 1921 a major emergency arose, for the Magistrates refused to renew the licence unless an additional exit were made from the Gallery, and it was estimated that this, though practicable, would cost between £500 and £600. The Bank refused point-blank to grant an overdraft, the lessees were totally unco-operative, and, as the Proprietors reluctantly realised, any attempt to coerce them "would only be throwing good money away after bad."[90]

Then, only a matter of days before the temporary licence was due to expire, the resident manager at the Theatre Royal, J. Windsor Stevenson, located an old staircase to the gallery, boarded up and covered with plaster, but adaptable at a relatively small cost.[91] In view of this dis-covery a provisional three-month licence was granted, and was confirmed in February. The alterations cost over £200 and their architect told a disgruntled Committee of Proprietors "it was cheap at the price con-sidering the price of materials and labour and could not be got for less elsewhere."

A month later Hamilton Baines went bankrupt, offering eventually 5s. in the £. His examination disclosed an incredible succession of projected enterprises, mainly catering and theatrical, none of them with the remotest vestige of financial or organisational backing; which did not prevent Baines from trying to make himself out an injured victim of circumstances.[92] Bristol Theatres Ltd. was of course technically unaffected but it was clear that the situation there, too, was desperate. Two dis-honoured cheques were followed by a distraint by the Proprietors in June 1923.

Paradoxically, some of the most worthwhile engagements for many years were made during this period. The Chelsea Players gave an interesting week of Shakespeare in July 1921, including the rarely-produced *Measure for Measure,* and a month later Edward Irwin, well known in the provinces for his brilliant acting in Vachell's *Quinneys,* brought Galsworthy's *The Skin Game* for twice nightly performances. Doris Brookes, previously a popular Stock Company leading lady, included a night of *A Doll's House* in an otherwise pedestrian week's repertoire.

Baines' most surprising capture, however, was Ben Greet. Presumably a company inured to school and church halls was glad enough to book a theatre of any kind (their earlier Shakespearean performances in Bristol had been at the Zoological Gardens); and Greet had known the Royal since February 1891 when he toured Grundy's highly successful drama, *A Village Priest,* with himself and A. E. W. Mason in the cast.[93] The experimental week at the beginning of March 1922 was unexpectedly successful. The initial production of *Macbeth* "was witnessed by a large and appreciative audience, the better parts of the house being crowded, while the popular parts of the building were also satisfactorily filled".[94] Special facilities were offered to parties of school children, who supported the matinees in their scores. By Friday, there was an overflow for *The Tempest.* The company's fidelity to the text, simplicity of staging and level standard of acting won high praise throughout the week.

In a final curtain speech Ben Greet announced that his company would be returning three weeks hence for a fortnight (eloquent testimony to the hand-to-mouth arrangements for booking on both sides) and this time his company included among its minor players Flora Robson, whose first part seems to have been Nerissa in *The Merchant of Venice,*[95] and who won special mention for her Bianca in *Othello.* Surprisingly, the least popular performance was *Twelfth Night,* but a three-and-a-half hour *Hamlet* brought the engagement to a triumphant conclusion on the eve of Shakespeare's birthday. Ben Greet promised if he came again "he would give the whole of 'Hamlet' without any 'cuts'. It would last about five hours."[96]

Baines could see the possibilities of an occasional venture into classical repertory, and after the 1922-3 pantomime he organised a Grand Shakespearian Festival, opening with Ernest Milton, fresh from his Old Vic triumphs, as Shylock in *The Merchant of Venice* for a fortnight, followed by competent productions of *The Taming of the Shrew* and *Othello.* Several former members of the Chelsea Players and Ben Greet's Company were in the supporting casts, but the audiences were disappointing,[97] and after a few weeks of Grand Guignol and revue the Repertory Company resumed its twice nightly showings of *East Lynne, The Neglected Wife,* and *If Those Lips Could Only Speak.*

The end was abrupt. The artists in the 1924 pantomime of *Dick Whittington* had accepted lower salaries than usual on the promise of a twelve-week run, but on 30 January Mrs. Hamilton Baines, the chief debenture holder of Bristol Theatres Ltd., lost patience and put in a Receiver, who took over the takings. Because, apparently, of other outstanding liabilities, and despite the vigorous endeavours of the resident manager, Frank Riego, the Receiver paid only half the week's salaries on 2 February, and failed to produce the remainder as promised on the following Monday morning. The Company put on Monday night's show on a commonwealth basis, the Receiver himself guaranteeing payment to the Corporation Electricity Department (which was threatening disconnection for a long overdue bill) for the electricity used that night.

But when the salaries remained unpaid on Tuesday, and the supply was cut off as the result of the Receiver's telling the Department it would not be wanted, the company gave up, and it was left to their Union representatives to fight a strenuous, but ultimately successful, battle for the outstanding salaries.

Thus was the curtain rung down on the Old Theatre pantomime, a unique finale, and one which will long be remembered by those who took part in the final scene.[98]

Twelve of the principals decided to stay in Bristol and work up parts of the pantomime into a twice nightly entertainment appropriately titled *Carry On!* Successive evenings were patronised by Bristol University students and the Bristol Beer, Spirit and Wine Trade Association, but public support was not forthcoming for this courageous venture, which "folded" after only a week.

While the Proprietors frantically negotiated for the sale of the theatre there was much speculation about its future. The repertory idea was once more canvassed, but the Little Theatre had only just been established in the converted Lesser Colston Hall and so pre-empted that possibility. Harlequin in the *Times & Mirror* wrote sadly :

A good many sentimental folk – and I am not unsentimental – are fond of harping on the glories of the "Old", but it is impossible to get away from the fact that the surroundings of the Theatre Royal are all against its becoming a popular place of amusement now . . . The fact has to be faced: the Theatre Royal has had its day, or, rather, night.[99]

Five

1924-1943

It is not surprising that even well-wishers tended to write off the Theatre Royal as a going concern. Quite apart from its recent financial history, it had deteriorated appallingly as a building – leaking, filthy, and cluttered with empty beer bottles. The Proprietors' Secretary reported gloomily "that the premises as a whole were in a shockingly dirty state – refuse being piled up anywhere – some of it rotting", and orders were given for a thorough cleaning, "otherwise the Theatre if shown to any prospective buyer in its present condition would never sell".[100]

Enquiries were not lacking; Sir Oswald Stoll negotiated for some time with a view to obtaining the transfer of the licences to the Hippodrome, but his prospective purchaser of the building itself withdrew.[101] Despite widespread advertising it was not until November 1924 that, through the agency of the local firm of Tricks & Son, a tenant was found : Douglas Millar, formerly London manager for Robert Courtneidge. He accepted a fourteen year lease at a rent of £600 p.a., increasing by £50 yearly to a maximum of £900 p.a., with an option to purchase at £10,000 at any time within the first ten years.[102]

Millar had a likeable blend of shrewdness and sentiment, revelling in the legendary glories of his theatre and quite uncritical about them.[103] A martyr to rheumatism, he told the Licensing Magistrates that "after a breakdown in health, following his long experience with the stage, he had obtained the lease of the theatre in order to settle down to a tolerably quiet life." This somewhat naïve hope was not fulfilled.

Cleaning, rewiring, decorating and reseating the theatre (including taking out two rows of pit benches to give more leg room) cost Millar not less than £2,000 – in itself a commentary on the dilapidated state of the building. On Boxing Day 1924 the Theatre Royal reopened with the pantomime of *Aladdin,* starring Winifred Ward and Will Gane, with Karr and Kooney the knockabouts. Determined to assert the prestige of the Royal (and, no doubt, recoup his expenditure), Millar boldly raised prices to a maximum of 4s. 9d. for reserved Centre Dress Circle seats down to 6d. for unreserved places in the Gallery (Early Doors 1s.). Telegrams of good wishes from Robert Courtneidge, Ben Greet, and Bristol's Little Theatre, among many others, testified to the renewed hopes of Douglas Millar's wellwishers, and the pantomime earned excellent notices, running until 21 March.

With this encouragement, at the beginning of March 1925 Millar exercised his option to buy, finally beating the Proprietors down to £8,500 in view of their need for ready money to repay the executors of the mortgagee, Ricketts Winwood, who had just died. On 10 March Millar's deposit note for £850 was received; on 6 May the sale was completed and the Theatre Royal passed out of the hands of Bristolians after 160 years.[104] In fact, though this is nowhere mentioned in the Minutes, the purchase money was put up jointly by Robert Courtneidge, Milton Bode and Millar, who remained as manager.

While negotiations proceeded, Millar carried out a ballot among his patrons to establish the future policy of the theatre: drama, comedy, musical comedy or revue, once or twice nightly. The resultant figures showed an overwhelming majority for drama (2,151 votes), followed by musical comedy (1,356); only 240 people voted in favour of twice nightly performances. Accordingly, Millar engaged a Repertory Company under G. Carlton Wallace in a programme mainly consisting of domestic and patriotic dramas, but also including *The Christian* and *Called Back*. Despite the voting, by mid-May Millar had to revert to twice-nightly performances, reducing the price-range from the original "6d. to 2s. 6d." to "4d. to 2s." By the end of the season

although the excellence of the acting and the completeness of the mounting have been enthusiastically acknowledged, it must be admitted that the financial result has disappointed Mr. Millar, and he can only conclude that unrelieved melodrama has not a sufficient following in Bristol to be remunerative.[105]

Accordingly, Millar changed his policy to the booking of touring companies, aiming at a far higher standard than ever before. The Irish Players opened with the premiere of Laurence Cowen's *Biddy* on 3 August, the cast including Maire O'Neill, Arthur Sinclair and Fred O'Donovan. The Lord Mayor and Lady Mayoress were in the audience. Subsequent engagements ranged from *Anna Christie* to Frank Forbes-Robertson in his uncle's great success, *The Passing of the Third Floor Back*, and included two contrasted plays from the up-and-coming dramatist, Noel Coward: *Hay Fever* and *The Vortex*. The *Western Daily Press* was pleased to note of the former that "there is not a line to ruffle the feelings of the most susceptible," which certainly could not be said of *The Vortex*;

> It is difficult to believe that the degenerate and decadent collection of people portrayed in this amazingly clever though unpleasant play can be said to mirror truly the state of society as a whole,

sniffed the same critic.[106]

Encouraged by the response, Millar obtained permission in October to replace the front benches of the Pit by three rows of stalls, separated by a partition from the rest of the Pit : these came into use at the end of the month [Plate 23]. Ben Greet paid what proved to be his last visit at the end of November, and introduced Stanford and Thea Holme (then Thea Johnston) and Ernest Hare to Bristol audiences in a programme interrupted by the closure to mark the funeral of Queen Alexandra.

Millar's second pantomime, *Sinbad the Sailor*, with the 22-year-old George Lacey as Tinbad,[107] and Constance Studholme as Fairy Queen, was rated even higher than *Aladdin*, and more touring productions, mainly of a lighter type, brought the season up to the beginning of May 1926, when Millar was to produce for two weeks the musical play, *Young England*, acted by the cream of Bristol amateur talent.[108] It was a personal venture by Millar, but with high-level patronage promised for almost every night it seemed a sure success. The B.B.C. arranged to broadcast the entire performance on 11 May, the first time a complete show had been transmitted in the West. But the outbreak of the General Strike paralysed transport and virtually killed the production; the financial loss to Millar was crippling, and the residual effect on theatre audiences hardly less disastrous. Frank Forbes-Robertson, returning at the end of May, told his audience in a curtain speech "that this time the attendance had fallen to less than a quarter the numbers reached previously. Unless the houses improved later in the week . . . it would be impossible for him ever to visit Bristol again."[109]

Little wonder that after the summer closure Millar reverted to twice-nightly, three-day repertory by one of Frank H. Fortescue's companies – who became principal providers of the fare at the Theatre Royal for the next fifteen years. In October, however, by a long-standing arrangement, the Theatre Royal housed quite the most remarkable musical event of its long life, when a nucleus of professional singers (including Steuart Wilson, Louise Trenton and Dorothy D'Orsay) backed by local choruses and theatrical ballet, took part in a three-week festival almost entirely devoted to English opera. The main conductor was Dr. Adrian Boult; guest conductors included Dame Ethel Smyth, whose *Entente Cordiale* was given its first performance on 20 October, and Vaughan Williams, who presided over a programme including *The Shepherds of the Delectable Mountains* and his folk-ballet, *Old King Cole,* on 30 October. The most outstanding success, however, was the production of Mozart's then little known *School for Lovers (Così fan Tutte)* in E. J. Dent's translation. Later *The Times* was to claim :

> It was this success at the Theatre Royal, Bristol, which induced Mr. Johnstone Douglas to put it on for a run later at the Court Theatre in Sloane Square, a run which brought it back into the consciousness of Londoners who had quite forgotten that *Così fan Tutte* was one of Mozart's major operas.[101]

The season aroused widespread interest, quite as much outside Bristol as in it. The lingering local reputation of the Royal probably still militated against fashionable attendance to some extent, snobbery extending to a reluctance to take up the Gallery seats, which were only a shilling. But by the third week attendances had much improved, and in a message read on the last night the organiser, Dr. Napier Miles of Kings Weston (descendant of a former Bristol M.P. who had been an enthusiastic patron of both amateur and professional theatricals), reported ruefully "If the houses had only been consistently fuller during the first week the financial result would be considerably better"[111] – a comment applicable to many a subsequent production in Bristol.

Millar followed the opera season with a new play by a local solicitor and great theatre lover, Francis Habgood, called *False Dawn.* It was a not very original romantic melodrama, and the acting was extremely uneven (not improved by under-rehearsal), but Millar scored a great personal success in the part of Angelo Nasari, a violin-maker : "a cameo of intense and artistic acting that it will pay all playgoers to visit the Royal to see".[112] Its production typified Millar's initiative and his desire to identify the theatre with local interests as much as possible; he did a good deal of work for amateur societies and let the Theatre to them for major productions.

It was after Christmas 1926 that things began to go seriously wrong again. An influenza epidemic hit Bristol, and affected the pantomime takings so badly that Millar took the show off on 12 February. Afterwards he admitted that this was an error of judgment, for *Puss In Boots* was widely considered the best of his pantomimes to date, with George Lacey in his first Dame part. "Lacey's dame is one of the cleverest bits of fooling one could wish to see. His dresses are as exceptional as he is himself."[113] No sooner had irrevocable arrangements been made for ending the run than business picked up and the last fortnight brought near-capacity houses, but the loss on a particularly lavishly costumed production was considerable.

Millar took no further risks. From henceforth Repertory Companies under various managements filled up the year with dramas reminiscent of the Hamilton Baines days : *Why Girls Go Wrong, Flaming Passion, Was She to Blame?* Occasionally something a little better was attempted : in the summer of 1927 the Company from the Elephant in Southeast London included detective plays, Boucicault's *Shaughraun* and Henry Arthur Jones's *The Middleman* with Millar himself as Cyrus Blenkarn. But the successes of the year were *Maria Marten,* kept on for two weeks of twice-nightly performances, and *Mademoiselle from Armentieres,* which on the Saturday brought "the most people he [Douglas Millar] has ever squeezed into the Theatre Royal."[114]

T. Morton Powell ran a company from July to December 1928, beginning with light farcical comedies, such as Jones's *The Hypocrites,* and dramas of the order of *The Christian* and that old stand-by, *A Royal Divorce,* but, in the words of the company's juvenile, George Dare, "this type of play did not suit the rather rough and unsophisticated audience who patronised the theatre in those days, and the fare was soon changed to the more popular melodrama."[115] However, there were some productions of interest, including one by Millar himself of a new play by local journalist, Froom Tyler, *The Winged Ship,* in November 1928.

The position was complicated too by the fact that at least some of the audience for melodrama was not a genuine one. Students and young professional men could pick up half-price tickets at public houses in the neighbourhood and went to the theatre more in joke than earnest;[116] a sort of theatrical slumming, encouraging the exaggeration of the proverbial responses to melodramatic characters and situations, which probably did as much to undercut Douglas Millar's attempts to make the Theatre Royal a venue for serious playgoers as any real deterioration in popular taste.

In July 1929 Millar sold out his share in the Royal to Courtneidge and Bode, though he continued resident manager for two years more. In March 1931 he made one last bid to improve the prestige of the Theatre Royal, running his own weekly repertory on a once-nightly basis. The company included Paul Lorraine (later a stalwart of the Little Theatre Company) and the repertoire was mainly composed of Victorian favourites such as *The Silver King, The Three Musketeers* and *The Ticket-of-Leave Man.* Within a few weeks, however, Millar was "overwhelmed with letters begging him to return to the former system of two performances every evening"; he bowed to the demand, but after two months gave up altogether.

Ostensibly to celebrate the Theatre Royal's 165th birthday, in 1931, but actually as a personal benefit for Millar himself, an all-star matinee was organised at the Prince's Theatre by its manager, Mr. T. C. P. Hickson, on 5 May. Cicely Courtneidge, Jack and Claude Hulbert, Shaun

Glenville and Dorothy Ward, joined in a programme launched by a speech from Sir Frank Benson. Millar's disappointment over the Theatre Royal was widely known and appreciated, and there was some speculation again about the future of the building, this time on the lines of its use as primarily a theatre for amateurs. However, Courtneidge and Bode decided to keep the Royal going, and William King, who had been running the Leicester theatre for Milton Bode, replaced Millar in December 1931.

Under King, revue, which had made occasional appearances for some years back, became the established fare during most of the year. These "super revues at cinema prices" (4d. to 1s. 3d.), as may easily be imagined, were second-rate "girlie" shows rejoicing in such titles as *Spicy Bits, Yell of a Night* and *Legs and Laughter*, and their attractions were eked out by local talent competitions and "Gala Joy Nights" in the summer months. Broad comedians were, after the "girls," the mainstay of the entertainment, among the most frequent visitors being Sandy Lauri, Wal Butler (also a popular pantomime artiste) and Freddy Fitts and Irene Rose, who settled in Bristol on retirement. George Fearon, taking up a booking for *Ridgeway's Parade* "on spec.," found that even at cinema prices there was difficulty in raising an audience, and so many tickets were sent out to local hospitals and factories to paper the house that it was almost impossible to make a show pay. His own flair for publicity, and the co-operation of the local press, overcame this, and packed houses were the rule for *Ridgeway's Parade* from its first visit in 1932 to its last in the summer of 1939.[117]

The most successful of the Theatre Royal's shows were as ever the pantomimes, especially those produced by Bristol music hall comedian, Randolph Sutton : *Cinderella* in 1935-6, *Jack and the Beanstalk* in 1937-8 (in which a revolve was used apparently for the first time on the Theatre Royal stage), and the first wartime pantomime, *Babes in the Wood*, which ran with a minimum of three matinees a week until the end of March. In all of these Sutton not only produced and took one of the characters, but also gave songs from his music-hall act in evening dress. During the intermediate years Frank H. Fortescue provided the pantomimes (as he did many of the revue companies), and in 1938-9 he secured Harry Tate, a shadow of his former self but still a substantial "name", as an additional attraction in *Little Bo-Peep*.

The death of Milton Bode on 10 January 1938 left Robert Courtneidge sole proprietor till his own death on 6 April 1939. For the time being, even after the outbreak of war, their executors continued running the Theatre Royal; indeed, with the bombing of the Prince's on the night of 24 November 1940, it provided the only live Christmas show that year, *Red*

Riding Hood. Rehearsed in air raid shelters and financed on a sharing basis, it was warmly welcomed and ran till 15 March. Announced to follow it was the optimistically-titled revue, *Happiness Ahead*, but the blitz of 16-17 March so disrupted services in central Bristol that, though the theatre itself, miraculously, was undamaged, it had to close.[118] At the end of March a scratch drama company sponsored by Frank H. Fortescue reopened the theatre with *Forbidden Fruit*

> For ADULTS Only
> 2.30 and 6 o'clock Daily . . .
> *You can get home at nights Before Dark.*

But this token effort petered out after a month, the last advertised productions being of *East Lynne* and *Sweeney Tod* [*sic*]. Once more the Theatre Royal was closed, and once more it seemed doomed to extinction.

However, not all appreciation of the theatre's potential had been lost during the past decade. In 1935 Herbert Farjeon made a valiant effort to arrange a festival of Eighteenth Century plays, produced by Tyrone Guthrie, which would reawaken interest in the old building, but Bode and Courtneidge refused to entertain the idea.

Three years later, George Fearon, impressed by the standards of the Rapier Players in the face of the difficult conditions of the Little Theatre, and mindful of his own success in bringing Clifton to King Street, suggested in *Theatre World* that the Royal should be taken over, by civic action or private patronage, as the home of the repertory company.[119] The suggestion stimulated a good deal of discussion, though the current reputation (and physical state) of the Theatre Royal was such that few really conceived it a practical possibility. Nevertheless, the idea of the Royal becoming "Bristol's Old Vic" (as Mrs. Blanche Rogers prophetically suggested)[120] was revived in the public consciousness, and when it was announced that the theatre would be sold by auction on 28 January 1942 this ambition mingled with historical and architectural arguments in the surge of feeling which led to the building's preservation.

The Council for the Preservation of Ancient Bristol was the most active body concerned, setting up a special committee, and negotiating with Mr. C. H. W. Davey of the Metal Agencies Company, who were known to be interested in buying the building as a warehouse. On behalf of the Company Mr. Davey very generously offered to put up the necessary purchase money to a limit of £12,500, provided

that he should appoint the agent to bid for the property; that fees and costs should be a first charge on any fund raised by the C.P.A.B., and that the latter assumed responsibility for all outgoings. Without specifying any time limit for the repayment of the advance it was hoped that a substantial payment would be made within three months and, in the unlikely event of the necessary funds not being raised, the property should be reconveyed to the Metal Agencies Company.[121]

Meanwhile a Bristol businessman, Mr. S. Kay, had suggested in a letter to the press that a public company of local residents should be floated to buy the theatre, and he called a meeting at the Grand Hotel on 21 January, rather to the embarrassment of the C.P.A.B., who felt bound to disclose something of what was afoot. Inevitably this became distorted by wishful thinking, and the statement was publicised that an anonymous Bristolian was prepared to buy the Royal "and either present it to the National Trust or hand it over to a civic trust" – a misinterpretation Colonel Mark Whitwill had to correct in the press.[122]

Through letters by Herbert Farjeon and W. Macqueen Pope published in *The Times*, the fate of the Theatre Royal, Bristol, became a national matter. The B.B.C. made a recording of the auction, which in the end took only $7\frac{1}{2}$ minutes, Messrs. Chas. A. Tricks securing the property on behalf of the Metal Agencies Co. for £10,500, overbidding Mr. John Hare of the Eastville Greyhound Stadium by £500.[123] [Plate 24]. On 31 March the Lord Mayor, Alderman E. T. Cozens, launched a preservation appeal for £25,000, any unneeded portion of which would be invested in War Bonds. The Preservation Fund Committee at that time hoped to replace the 1902 frontage with something more in keeping, and, after restoring the theatre as a whole, vest it in the National Trust with a local committee of management.

At a crowded meeting held in the theatre itself on 1 May, Robert Donat made a rousing appeal, describing the Royal as "slightly battered, but still immensely strong, teeming with tradition, reeking with atmosphere, and rejoicing in its own fundamental vitality." Perhaps the ghost of Macready, Kemble or Kean was still lurking in the gloom of the wings, he mused, wondering if the old thunder run were still working. A pause; and the long roll broke over the audiences' heads as shot was released down the chute of the run.[124]

An Appeal Committee was set up in London as well as Bristol, and donations at first came in promisingly, but after a month or so tailed off. In particular, scarcely any Bristol business houses contributed, although Sir Francis Cowlin, of the Bristol building firm, a descendant of the Edkins family, not only sent a donation but provided essential maintenance free. To obtain further publicity, the theatre was opened for talks by, among others, the City Librarian, Rupert Siddons (great-great-grandson of Sarah Siddons) and Sir John Martin Harvey. Michael Redgrave, born and educated in Bristol, whose father, Roy Redgrave, had brought his company to the Royal in 1898 in *Black-Eyed Susan*, visited the theatre while on tour and called on the Lord Mayor with a generous gift.

By the autumn of 1942 only about £4,000 had been raised and it was proving extremely difficult to obtain licences for even essential repairs. But the possibility of keeping the Royal as a live theatre was growing. J. Baxter Somerville and Peter Hoar opened negotiations with the Committee in September, but these were abandoned when at the beginning of October the Council for the Encouragement of Music and the Arts (a wartime body which became established as the Arts Council of Great Britain) made specific proposals for a lease. C.E.M.A. offered to put the theatre in working order and maintain it, provided the actual purchase price was covered; this was done by bank overdraft* guaranteed personally by members of the Preservation Fund Committee, the sum so raised enabling the outstanding debt to the Metal Agencies Company to be repaid.[125]

The lease[126] was for a period of 21 years from 11 November 1942, determinable on six months' notice after the end of the war, at a rent of £300 p.a. plus the interest on the overdraft secured by the Committee. Profits were to be devoted to the cost of renovation, repayment of the balance of the purchase money, and a reserve fund for future productions. Further, the lessees were

> Not to make or permit to be made any alterations in or additions to the said premises either external or internal without the previous consent in writing of the Trustees and in particular to preserve the architectural and other characteristics of the building full regard being paid to its traditions and past history . . .
>
> AND the Lessees also agree that the historic portions of the building shall be open to the public at such times during the day time when no performances or rehearsals are being given . . .

Both these clauses caused future friction, epitomising the difficulties inherent in balancing the claims of architectural preservation and commercial theatre practice.

At the end of 1942 a formal declaration of trust was made by the group of citizens most concerned in saving the theatre and subsequently as guarantors for the purchase overdraft† whereby trustees for the building were appointed under the chairmanship of Mr. Wilfrid Leighton, a man of the greatest tenacity of purpose, clarity of mind and integrity. By the creation of this Trust the ownership of the Theatre Royal returned to the citizens of Bristol, little as most of them had done to help in the achievement.

* A mortgage was substituted in 1944.
† Messrs. Wilfrid Leighton, Ellison Fuller Eberle, E. J. Taylor, Mark Whitwill, F. C. Burgess, F. M. Burris and Sir Foster G. Robinson.

At the beginning of 1943 Lewis Casson, then Drama Director of C.E.M.A., announced the appointment as resident manager of T.C.P. Hickson, formerly of the Prince's, and under the supervision of the architect, J. Ralph Edwards, renovations and redecorations to the value of £8,000 were undertaken. The pit benches and leather stalls were removed, the floor slightly raked, and the whole turned into stalls; the slips of the gallery were cut off, some of the wooden benches (very doubtfully labelled "original 18th Century") being left as show-pieces. Gallery theatre-going was also made more comfortable by alternate rows being turned into back rests – up to this time each row was used for seating, which helps to account for the fact that even in 1942 the theatre was advertised as holding about 1,140 people. The auditorium was repainted in green and gold, a colour scheme thought to approximate to that of the original Georgian interior – though of course it was being applied to late Victorian decorations.

By the summer of 1943 the theatre was ready for opening by C.E.M.A. with an Old Vic Company in *She Stoops to Conquer*, and on 11 May 1943 Dame Sybil Thorndike, dressed as Mrs. Hardcastle, came before the curtain to deliver Herbert Farjeon's charming (if historically inaccurate) Prologue to an invited audience of civic dignitaries and contributors to the Preservation Fund.[127] Only one sadness marred a truly historic occasion : the death on the very eve of re-opening of Douglas Millar, whose love for the Theatre Royal and frustrated hopes for its artistic standards would have found their fruition with this renaissance.[128]

NOTES

[1] *Bristol Gazette,* 17.10.1867.
[2] *Western Daily Press,* 27.12.1867.
[3] Advertisement in *Western Daily Press,* 31.1.1870.
[4] *ibid.,* 28.3.1876.
[5] See notices in *Bristol Times & Mirror,* 11.4.1878 and *Western Daily Press,* 12.4.1878.
[6] *Western Daily Press,* 21.4.1876.
[7] *ibid.,* 11.1.1870.
[8] *ibid.,* 4.2.1873.
[9] *Western Daily Press* and *Bristol Times & Mirror,* 15.1.1878.
[10] *Bristol Times & Mirror,* 21.6.1871. The military often gave their patronage to the Theatre Royal during this period, the building of Horfield Barracks having led to the regular stationing of a series of regiments in the city.
[11] *Western Daily Press,* 23.1.1872.
[12] Committee Minutes, 30.7.1874.
[13] *Bristol Times & Mirror,* 13.10.1874.
[14] Chute had also kept a regular Stock Company going at the Park Row theatre until his death; his sons disbanded it and concentrated on booking touring companies.
[15] Committee Minutes, 30.5.1881.

[16] Much invaluable background information on the Melville family, including portraits of George and Andrew, has most generously been given me by their descendant, Andrew Melville, who is engaged in writing the history of the family.

[17] *Western Daily Press*, 23.8.1881.

[18] Committee Minutes, 6.9.1881. The Account Book shows actual expenditure by the Proprietors of £571 10s. 9d., of which Melville later repaid £300.

[19] During his second pantomime Melville put in some additional traps (see *Clifton Chronicle*, 31.1.1883); he made no other alterations to the theatre during his twelve-year tenancy.

[20] See *Western Daily Press* and *Bristol Evening News*, 3.12.1881, and *Clifton Chronicle*, 7.12.1881. Photographs of the ceiling, invariably dated far too early, have been reproduced in Southern, *Georgian Playhouse*, Plate 27; Little, *op. cit.*, p 9; and *The Story of the Theatre Royal, Bristol*, Bristol, 1966, p. 7.

[21] *Bristol Times & Mirror*, 6.12.1881.

[22] *Bristol Evening News*, 20.12.1881.

[23] *Clifton Chronicle*, 31.12.1884.

[24] *Western Daily Press*, 13.1.1883.

[25] Advertisement in *Bristol Times & Mirror*, 2.1.1888.

[26] *Clifton Chronicle*, 6.1.1886.

[27] See advertisements in *Western Daily Press* of 14. and 15.2.1884. It is perhaps as well Melville was unaware that this version of Chute's had never been licensed by the Lord Chamberlain – though for that matter neither were his own pantomime scripts.

[28] See *Western Daily Press*, 1. and 4.12.1882. According to Rennie Powell (*op. cit.* p. 61), Ristori's terms were so exorbitant that the Chutes declined to engage her; when she played at the Theatre Royal it was to "practically empty benches". However, the *Press* records that, though the audience for her Elizabeth was "not large", the house was crowded for her Lady Macbeth.

[29] He presumably meant one-fifth of the shares; according to H. A. Forse (*Bristol Times & Mirror*, 2.1.1899), Melville held eleven shares in all. See also note 43.

[30] *Clifton Chronicle*, 7.3.1883.

[31] Forse was also a member of the Committee of Proprietors of the Theatre Royal; a building contractor by trade, he was a keen amateur singer, and enlivened numerous charity performances with his rendering of "When Other Lips" and similar operatic ballads.

[32] Committee Minutes, 14.1.1884 and 14.5.1885. Probably Melville's cash resources were being pre-empted by the financing without outside assistance of the Birmingham and Derby theatres.

[33] Hicks, *op. cit.*, Ch. III.

[34] *Western Daily Press*, 14.10.1884.

[35] *The Autobiography of Sir John Martin Harvey*, London, 1933.

[36] *Clifton Chronicle*, 21.6.1882.

[37] *Western Daily Press*, 30.6.1890.

[38] *ibid.*, 4.12.1883.

[39] Playbill of 13/14.10.1882 and *Western Daily Press*, 30.11.1882. Few playbills and programmes remain for this period, and newspaper advertisements do not always include full particulars, so that it is not possible to be sure exactly when these changes were made.

[40] Committee Minutes, 27.6.1887.

[41] Committee Minutes, 13.3. and 12.4.1893; General Meeting Minutes, 27.4.1893.

[42] *Western Daily Press*, 16.5.1893.

[43] Committee Minutes, 10.5.1894. These Minutes confirm that Melville was currently the largest shareholder, and it was even suggested that he should be nominated as one of the Theatre's Trustees, "but the suggestion was withdrawn on the Solicitor's pointing out that it would be better to defer the appointment until Mr. Melville's connection with the lease of the Theatre should be at an end."

[44] *Bristol Evening News,* 31.7.1903.

[45] *Bristol Times & Mirror,* 22.9.1896. A vivid article on audiences of this period was contributed by Jim Harris to the *Bristol Evening Post* Theatre Royal Bicentenary Supplement under the title "Cheers and Tears at the Old Gaff."

[46] *Clifton Chronicle,* 6.2.1895. Two rather jejune verses were recalled and quoted in *Western Daily Press,* 5.5.1931.

[47] *Western Daily Press,* 17.6.1898.

[48] See *Bristol Evening World,* 24.1.1945.

[49] *Bristol Times & Mirror,* 9.1.1900.

[50] Dix had three of his plays premiered at the Bristol Theatre Royal: *True Till Death* on 13 July 1896; *Held in Terror* on 21 June 1897; and *Delivered from Evil* on 27 March 1899. The last-named was reproduced several times by touring companies.

[51] There was dry rot in the Dress Circle in May 1896, and in May 1908 the timbers of the Upper Circle were reported to be giving way. See Committee Minutes of 14.5.1896 and 1. & 8.5.1908.

[52] *Bristol Times & Mirror,* 3.10.1905. The following week the auditorium, too, was lit by electricity, "with the happiest results."

[53] Committee Minutes, 10.5. and 26.7.1899, 2.4.1900; see also J. Latimer: *Annals of Bristol in the Nineteenth Century,* Bristol, 1902, p. 94.

[54] *Western Daily Press,* 5.8.1902.

[55] *ibid.,* 1.7.1908.

[56] Lively reminiscences of these sessions were published in the *Bristol Evening Post* of 12.10.1942.

[57] *Bristol Evening News,* 6.3.1903, and correspondence in Lord Chamberlain's Office.

[58] Undated letter, c. 17.6.1903, from Lord Chamberlain's Office to Chilton & Son, Solicitors for the Proprietors.

[59] Letter from F. Verity to Lord Chamberlain dated 30.11.1903.

[60] *Bristol Evening News,* 9.5.1904.

[61] Committee Minutes, 28.12.1904 and 8.2.1905. The Minutes describe Winwood as descended from one of the *original* Proprietors, but Thomas Winwood did not acquire his share (by purchase from Joseph Harford) till March 1777. See the "Register or Memorandum of the Several Assignments of Shares of the Original Proprietors" in the Theatre Register Book.

[62] *Western Daily Press,* 1.7.1908.

[63] *Bristol Times & Mirror,* 24.12.1909, First and Second Editions.

[64] *ibid.,* 19.4.1909.

[65] See Carpenter's article in the *Bristol Playgoer,* No. 8, December 1913.

[66] *Western Daily Press,* 26.12.1910.

[67] *Bristol Evening News,* 27.12.1911. An article on Naughton and Gold's early experiences in the theatre was included in *Bristol Evening News,* 25.1.1912.

[68] *Western Daily Press,* 2.12.1913.

[69] *Bristol Playgoer,* No. 9, January 1914.

[70] *Bristol Times & Mirror,* 11.12.1913.

[71] The Palace, later the New Palace, Cinema is now the Gaumont, Baldwin Street.

[72] Committee Minutes, 23.11.1910.

[73] This remained a drawback until the alterations of 1970-1. Presumably by 1912 the grooves had been removed, though they are listed in the schedule to the lease of 1904, the latest one remaining in the theatre's archives.

[74] *Bristol Times & Mirror,* 19.5.1914. Holloway became a well-known local actor, especially on West Region Radio.

[75] Quoted in *Western Daily Press,* 20.5.1914.

[76] *Bristol Times & Mirror,* 30.5.1914.

[77] Bristol Playgoers' Club Minutes, 21.9.1914.

[78] This more genteel way of gaining entry to the Pit had been mooted for the Oratorio season as far back as 1793 (*Bristol Mercury*, 18.3.1793 &c.), and was used on various occasions in the 19th Century for concerts and opera. The centre panel of the Dress Circle was hinged and latched to form a practicable door.

[79] Quoted in *Western Daily Press*, 1.9.1914. This prologue was also used by the Liverpool Repertory Theatre when re-opening on 19 September 1914 (G. Wyndham Goldie: *The Liverpool Repertory Theatre 1911-1934*, Liverpool, 1935, p. 101). It does not, however, appear in Masefield's collected works.

[80] In this production Arnold Ridley, author of *The Ghost Train*, then a Bristol undergraduate, made his first stage appearance. (*Bristol Times & Mirror*, 13.11.1926.)

[81] Information from W. Bridges Adams in a letter to the author. This production antedated by just over a week that at Covent Garden produced by Granville Barker and designed by Charles Ricketts.

[82] Bristol Playgoers' Club Minutes, 6.12.1914 and 4. & 25.1.1915; Proprietors' Committee Minutes, 30.9.1914. According to the Bristol Playgoers' Club 25th Anniversary History, *Bristol Playgoers' Club 1911-1935*, at the close of the season "a full call had to be made on the Guarantors."

[83] Letter in *Western Daily Press*, 10.12.1914.

[84] In a speech to Bristol Rotary Club, reported in *Western Daily Press*, 8.3.1921. It was Rotary who in 1923 leased the Lesser Colston Hall and started Bristol's Little Theatre.

[85] Mrs. Blanche Rogers, later prominent in the Bristol Kyrle Society, claimed that she launched a private appeal, with the co-operation of Rotary, for the purchase of the Theatre Royal as a Repertory Theatre, but that before any effective organisation could be set up "a London syndicate had bought the theatre over our heads". (*Bristol Evening Post*, 25.8.1938 and 19.1.1942.)

[86] *Bristol Evening News*, 26.11.1924.

[87] The twice nightly system seems to have been introduced by Frederick Carpenter for a summer repertory season in 1911, and then abandoned until the spring of 1916; Bristol Theatres Ltd. reverted temporarily to once nightly, but after *Red Riding Hood* in 1916-7 the twice nightly arrangement became standard. It was even tried for pantomime in 1917-8, but this proved a failure and was never repeated.

[88] *Bristol Times & Mirror*, 16.8.1919. This first advertisement contained no estimate of capacity; a second notice on 30 August described the theatre as "having seating accommodation for 1,500, and further standing room for several hundreds". Caution – and belated respect for safety regulations – caused the Proprietors to modify this figure to "SEATING ACCOMMODATION for 981" (no mention of standing spectators) in their advertisement on 13 September.

[89] *Bristol Times & Mirror*, 23.8.1919.

[90] Committee Minutes, 15.10.1921.

[91] *Western Daily Press*, 6.12.1921. The provenance of this staircase is uncertain; it may well have been the original (1800) gallery staircase, which was probably blocked up when "an entire new staircase . . . for giving access to the gallery" was constructed as part of the 1881 alterations (*Western Daily Press*, 23.8.1881; see also *ibid.*, 3.12.1881).

[92] *Bristol Evening News*, 10.3.1922; *Western Daily Press*, 13.4.1922.

[93] W. Isaac: *Ben Greet and the Old Vic*, London, 1964, p. 36; *Clifton Chronicle*, 18.2.1891.

[94] *Bristol Times & Mirror*, 7.3.1922.

[95] *ibid.*, 11.4.1922. Janet Dunbar in her biography *Flora Robson* (London, 1960) says she made her first appearance as Emilia in *The Winter's Tale*, but this was not staged until the Thursday of this second engagement.

[96] *Western Daily Press*, 24.4.1922. The company returned in November 1925, but *Hamlet* was not included. See page 198.

[97] Mrs. E. Brean, who was a dresser at the Theatre Royal at this time, told me that one night Milton played to an audience of four in the pit.

[98] The events are fully set out in the Bristol newspapers of 6, 7 and 8 February 1924. The lamentable history of Bristol Theatres Ltd., as revealed at the first meeting of the creditors, is recorded in *Bristol Times & Mirror*, 9.8.1924.

[99] *Bristol Times & Mirror*, 23.2.1924.

[100] Committee Minutes, 1.5.1924.

[101] *ibid.*, 13 & 17.2.1924. It may have been this client who proposed turning the Theatre Royal into a bacon factory, as reported by Miss M. E. Board in *The Story of the Bristol Stage*, London, n.d. (1926), pp. 48-9.

[102] Committee Minutes, 24.11.1924. The lease is no longer extant.

[103] The recurrent story that John Barrymore's parents held their wedding reception on the stage of the Theatre Royal seems to have originated with Millar.

[104] Committee Minutes, 10.3. and 7.5.1925. Each shareholder received just over £108 for his £100 share.

[105] *Western Daily Press*, 22.6.1925.

[106] *ibid.*, 15.9. and 20.10.1925.

[107] A short article on George Lacey was included in Stage Notes in *Bristol Times & Mirror*, 13.2.1926.

[108] Thus Millar anticipated by twenty years the efforts of the Bristol Guild of Players.

[109] *Bristol Times & Mirror*, 2.6.1926.

[110] *Times*, 23.1.1942.

[111] *Bristol Times & Mirror*, 8.11.1926.

[112] *Western Daily Press*, 9.11.1926.

[113] *ibid.*, 28.12.1926.

[114] *Bristol Times & Mirror*, 20.12.1927.

[115] Letter from George Dare to the author.

[116] Information from Mr. Alan Reynolds of Bristol University and Bristol playwright, Mr. Edward Purchase.

[117] Information from George Fearon modified by evidence from contemporary press. The Royal was not, of course, the only Bristol theatre in difficulties during the slump of the 1930's; the Hippodrome became a cinema in October 1932, not returning to live shows until August 1938; the Little Theatre collapsed in the summer of 1934, and Ronald Russell, who took over in January 1935, faced a further crisis in May the following year, the theatre being saved only by the generous action of a small number of financial guarantors (*Bristol Evening World*, 9.5.1936). Even the Prince's found itself in trouble, trying summer variety in 1935 with reduced prices but failing to recruit enough worthwhile "turns" (*Western Daily Press*, 5.3.1935; *Bristol Evening Post*, 1. & 15.6.1935).

[118] The Theatre Royal escaped remarkably lightly during a period in which much of central Bristol was gutted by air attack. The roof was damaged by blast on 3 January 1941, but quick action by firewatchers prevented incendiary bombs from taking hold. Dressing rooms were flooded during efforts to save an adjacent building which was on fire. (W. Leighton: *The Preservation of the Theatre Royal, Bristol, and Matters Relating to the Building 1942-60*, Bristol, 1961, privately circulated. I am indebted to Mrs. Leighton for permission to quote from the copy of this monograph given me by her late husband.)

[119] G. Fearon: The Repertory theatres – Bristol, *Theatre World*, August 1938.

[120] Letter to *Bristol Evening Post*, 25.8.1938.

[121] Leighton, *op. cit.*

[122] *Bristol Evening World*, 21. & 23.1.1942.

[123] *Bristol Evening Post*, 28.1.1942, and *Western Daily Press*, 29.1.1942. Hare claimed that the group he represented would have maintained the Royal as a living theatre.

[124] *Bristol Evening Post*, 1.5.1942; *Times*, 2.5.1942.

[125] Leighton, *op. cit.* The account given by Charles Landstone in *Off-Stage* (London, 1953, pp. 43-4) has many inaccuracies.

[126] Since C.E.M.A. as a body had no legal power to enter into such an agreement, the lease was made out in the names of individual members. This curious position was rectified in 1948. (Leighton, *op. cit.*)

[127] Prologue printed in *Bristol Evening Post* of 12.5.1953.

[128] *Western Daily Press,* 11.5.1943.

Part Six
Renaissance

"Making it our endeavour, first and last,
To serve the present and deserve the past."
Prologue by Herbert Farjeon
on the re-opening, 11 May 1943

Nothing can compare with King Street . . .
Sixty Thousand Nights, I, 1(A)

One

1943-1954

In the first two years of C.E.M.A.'s tenancy of the Theatre Royal a fairly wide variety of touring companies (many of them under the auspices of C.E.M.A. itself) were available for booking, and some of these brought classical and modern plays of a high standard. Priestley's *Desert Highway* was given its first performance on 14 December 1943, the audience including Sir James Grigg, Minister for War. Other notable visitors included the Norman Marshall Company and Basil Langton's Travelling Repertory Theatre. It was with the latter that Ann Casson, daughter of Sybil Thorndike, played her first Saint Joan in January 1945 at Bristol, carrying the sword used by her mother in the original production. Lewis Casson produced and played Warwick.

The Ballets Jooss and the Ballet Rambert did much to increase knowledge of and enthusiasm for the dance in Bristol, and were always popular; and Robert Atkins, then director at Stratford on Avon, brought a number of Shakespeare productions of varying quality but invariable honesty of approach. The initial outlay on renovating the building was recouped completely by C.E.M.A. from the profits (not least the bar profits) of the early seasons.[1]

With the end of the war, came the cessation of many of the special tours, and it became more and more difficult to obtain companies of standing. There was no lighting console, and the restricted stage facilities of the Royal, in particular the low cat-walk and the lack of flying room, hampered the handling of scenery.[2] A certain languor replaced the initial enthusiasm, and even Alec Clunes with the London Arts Theatre Company (visiting unfortunately just before the 1945 General Election) was miserably supported, despite a vigorous and moving *Hamlet* and a racily stylish production of Farquhar's *The Constant Couple*. The latter won the dubious distinction of being preached against by a local Nonconformist minister, the Rev. E. T. Garrington; his chief ground, apparently (since he admitted he had not seen the play), was a local theatre critic's description of its dialogue as "delightfully bawdy."[3]

The next season started well with Freda Jackson's superb performance as the evil, battening "ma" of *No Room at the Inn*, but rapidly tailed off, and criticisms of uneven acting and amateurish production became frequent. A system of "two seats for the price of one" was briefly tried on Monday nights to improve the size of audiences, but it was clear that the first impetus had been lost.

On 11 December 1945 Charles Landstone, then Assistant Drama Director of C.E.M.A., announced that the Old Vic organisation would set up a resident repertory company in Bristol under the direction of Hugh Hunt. Partly because it was uncertain whether Bristol would support adequately a three-weekly repertory, and partly because there was still some demand for the variety that touring companies (especially the ballet companies) could bring, plays were to be run for a fortnight in Bristol followed by a week at Bath or Weston-super-Mare.[4] The Bristol Arts Club organised a meeting in support a month later, addressed by Mr. Hunt, who stressed that the Old Vic intended to complement, not rival, the work of the Rapier Players at the Little Theatre.

The Bristol Old Vic Company, led by William Devlin and Pamela Brown, and including Faith Brook, Yvonne Mitchell and Kenneth Connor, opened on 19 February 1946 with Farquhar's *The Beaux' Stratagem*. Thus began what was claimed to be the first experiment in decentralising the theatre and in fostering the new provincial audiences which it was believed had been created by the war-time tours. Christopher Hassall's prologue defiantly claimed :

> By your good leave, we're yours – not passing through,
> As certain of our friends are wont to do,
> *En route*, they hope, for Shaftesbury Avenue.

The predictable initial wave of enthusiasm was sustained through the two subsequent productions : the premiere of *Jenny Villiers*, a charming but much overpraised play by Priestley, set in a Theatre Royal, and *Macbeth*, in which Hugh Hunt as producer and William Devlin as Macbeth first showed their finest and most characteristic qualities.

The first setback came with Chekhov's *The Seagull*, sensitively produced, well acted, but poorly attended. It was to be some years before Bristol's blind spot for Ibsen and Chekhov (encouraged, unfortunately, by some imperceptive newspaper criticism) was overcome, and at the time Hugh Hunt, still getting on terms with Bristolians and himself exquisitely tuned to the subtleties of the Russian dramatists, received a rude shock, which the lukewarm reception of Denis Johnston's savagely powerful drama about Dean Swift, *Weep for the Cyclops,* did nothing to soften. He even hinted that, if support did not improve, the second Bristol Old Vic season might be the last, a suggestion which aroused more antagonism than anxiety.[5]

There was little real danger; the Bristol Old Vic was too obviously putting down its roots in the city. A supporters' club was launched in July and packed the theatre to overflow; the establishment of a Theatre School with classes for amateurs as well as professional stage training was announced in June as part of the Old Vic Theatre Plan, and on 21 October 1946 was opened by Laurence Olivier. It occupied a converted warehouse in Queen Charlotte Street, opposite the stage door entrance; its first Director was Edward Stanley, formerly producer of Perth Repertory Company.[6]

In the second season touring companies were virtually abandoned and all productions ran for three weeks in Bristol. The Bristol Old Vic also made its first appearance in London; *Tess,* an adaptation of Hardy's novel by Ronald Gow with his wife, Wendy Hiller, in the name-part occupied the New Theatre for a week in November 1946 while the London Old Vic were in Paris.

The second half of the season started in January with *King Lear,* Devlin's shattering performance in the title role and Robert Eddison's steel-cold Edmund outstanding in a production whose implacable drive and complete control of atmosphere overcame some very dubious casting in certain lesser roles; and in March Hunt brought out Vivian Connell's controversial *Throng o' Scarlet,* with Kenneth Connor as the stable-boy, Mikey, revealing depths of pathos which the London stage has never allowed him to repeat. It ended with an enchanting "contemporary" *Much Ado,* in which the wiles of Don John were foiled by the Messina ARP and Home Guard ("Have a care that your pikes be not stolen!") led, in Conrad Voss Bark's phrase,[7] by "Mr. Devlin as a lion in warden's clothing and Mr. Connor as a bleat behind" [Plate 25]. The following season included the world premiere of Peter Watling's *Rain on the Just* (4 November 1947), the first play produced by the Bristol Old Vic to be taken up for production in the West End.

For all his occasional maladroitness in personal relations, and an uncertainty in handling comedy which could result in strident lapses of taste, Hugh Hunt as a director was always utterly individual and exciting; his productions at their best were brilliant in their creation of atmosphere and orchestrated with the subtlety of a virtuoso. Bristol's theatregoers took him to their hearts without perhaps ever fully establishing a mutual understanding. When it was announced[8] that he was to be appointed a

Director of the London Old Vic Company, as part of their ambitious post-war reorganisation, there was a wrenching sense of loss, and the ovation which greeted him on the opening night of his last production as Bristol Director (a maddeningly uneven *Romeo and Juliet*) is unlikely to be forgotten by anyone present.

Hunt was succeeded in mid-season by his Assistant Director, Allan Davis, who had recently proved that his talents were not restricted to pantomime by a remarkable production of *Winterset*. He was unfortunate in having to succeed a director of so powerful a theatrical personality, and doubly unfortunate in being the victim of the theatre's first major post-war crisis.

Since the expenditure incurred in renovating the theatre for the 1943 re-opening, no further major improvements had been made, though the age of the building, coupled with the patchwork maintenance of the preceding sixty years, meant that expensive *ad hoc* repairs might at any time become necessary.[9] There had been several improvements in the amenities: a new heating system in 1944; the removal of the Upper Circle Bar so that the clinking of bottles no longer punctuated the play; and in 1948 the construction of an improved Box Office "by closing up an old, and no longer used, exit passage" for which a compensating exit was provided.[10]

Later in 1948, however, following a serious fire at the Bristol Hippodrome, the authorities were moved to tighten up considerably the fire regulations at other local theatres. Ironically, the very requirements on which the Bristol police were now insisting were largely those which Carpenter had avoided carrying out in 1903 by giving up the Patent in favour of a local licence : additional exits, fire-proof partitions and safer secondary lighting. The theatre shut rather earlier than usual, on 10 June 1949, to enable the necessary alterations to be carried out.

But early in August the press discovered that all work on the site had stopped – with part of the roof removed and only covered by a tarpaulin – and no official explanation was forthcoming.[11] The general rumour was that "the alterations are . . . costing far more than was anticipated", though this was denied by Miss Glasgow, the Secretary General of the Arts Council. Then a fortnight later, without warning or, apparently, any prior local consultation, the entire remaining theatre staff, including the manager, Mr. T. C. P. Hickson, were given notice ("A normal business safeguard", said the Arts Council). Though it was by now clear that uncertainties over costing were indeed the major issue, there was still no open statement of the situation, and Bristol playgoers made their feelings known in unmistakeable manner.

Criticism was directed quite as much at the Arts Council's deplorable handling of the situation as at the propriety of the decisions taken. It was accompanied by a new proud possessiveness about the achievements of the Bristol Old Vic and the glorious history of the Theatre Royal, though even the most confident proponents of a public appeal were shaken when the figure of £20,000 was eventually given. All this found front-page voice in the local press, and was backed by national papers from *The Times* to the *Daily Worker*. If more irony were needed, it could be found in the announcement during this period that the Arts Council had paid back to the Trustees the last instalment of the mortgage debt on the Theatre.[12]

In the end the Arts Council agreed to meet the cost (which according to Landstone, was in fact very close to the first estimates) and the alterations were completed by the end of the year. They included a new sprinkler system, the substitution of electricity for gas in the secondary lighting, and the blocking up of many doorways between auditorium and backstage. One result of this was to make the proscenium doors unusable, another was to stop the old access to the thunder-run by way of the flies. Most important, four new exits were made from the O.P. side of the auditorium on to neighbouring land owned by the G.P.O., over which rights of way were negotiated.[13]

The Royal finally re-opened on 23 January 1950 with *As You Like It*. During the rest of the truncated season Allan Davis played safe (and most successfully so) with a programme very heavily weighted towards comedy, which hardly did justice to his versatility as a producer. An able company included among its minor actors Dorothy Tutin, fresh from R.A.D.A., and Denis Cannan, whose comedy, *Captain Carvallo*, was given its premiere by the Bristol Old Vic on 14 March; the rights were almost immediately snapped up by Laurence Olivier and it was brought out at the St. James's later the same year. The final production, Vanbrugh's *Provok'd Wife*, was put on for a week at the Bath Festival, where the Archdeacon of Bath directed a sermon against it,[14] but this time Bristol accepted Restoration comedy without clerical protest.

At the end of the season Allan Davis left the Bristol Old Vic, to the regret of many who felt that circumstances had prevented him from showing his true quality, but the crisis of the closure had substantial compensations. Apart from rallying the supporters of serious theatre to a fresh loyalty, it had also aroused the practical interest of Bristol Corporation.

Section 132 of the Local Government Act (1948) enabled Local Authorities to use money from the rates to promote the arts, and the possibility of exploiting this to help the Royal had been widely mooted. The Arts Council themselves openly invited local participation when they made their statement on the resumption of work at the Theatre.[15]

In May 1950 the Colston Hall Management and Entertainments Committee proposed to the City Council a £5,000 grant towards improvements and £1,500 a year for three years to meet insurance and similar running costs, a proposal accepted with the proviso that the Corporation should have two representatives on the Theatre Management Committee.[16]

The £5,000 enabled the Management Committee during the summer of 1951 to undertake extensive reseating and improve the rake of the Dress Circle seats, as well as to instal a more efficient heating system. The plasterwork decoration on the Dress Circle was regilded, and amber parchment shades gave a rather better impression of period than the cheap white bell-type lampshades which had preceded them.[17] In the summer of 1953 "several thousands" were spent on a new fire curtain, an extra dressing-room exit and redecoration of the gallery and foyer.[18]

Bristol could hardly have been more fortunate in the choice of Allan Davis' successor: Denis Carey, who, after a slightly uncertain first season, won both the lasting affection and the respect of his audiences and did more than anyone else to make the Bristol Old Vic popular in the best sense of the word, constantly campaigning for the total involvement of his public. "If one loves a thing and cares so much that it hurts, one criticises it, one fights for it, one exults in it."[19]

Hugh Hunt had established a purist policy of classics alternating with completely new plays; Denis Carey varied this by introducing a number of the more worthwhile West End successes: Fry's *The Lady's Not For Burning* and *Venus Observ'd*, T. S. Eliot's *Cocktail Party* and Grahame Greene's *The Living Room*, for example. On the whole he was not fortunate in his selection of serious new plays, but it was his encouragement which nurtured the happy series of entertainments by Dorothy Reynolds and Julian Slade, beginning with *Christmas in King Street*,[20] of which the most famous was of course *Salad Days*. This near-end-of-season frolic for the summer of 1954, which went on to create a new record for West End runs at the Vaudeville, from the financial terms of the contract enriched the Bristol Old Vic by some £40,000 all told, and enabled them not only to buy up some land to the east of the Theatre for a future extension but to put £7,000 towards new premises for the Bristol Old Vic Theatre School in Clifton.[21]

Many Bristolians would unhesitatingly rank highest Carey's production of *The Wild Duck* in April 1953, with its precise proportioning of every dramatic element from downright farce to deepest tragedy, but apart from *Salad Days* it was probably *The Two Gentlemen of Verona* which did most to make the Bristol Old Vic's name a national one. Slightly fantasticated but never distorted, the Forest of Milan was infused with the spirit of that other Shakespearian forest in which "they fleet the time carelessly, as they did in the golden world". Brought to the London Old Vic in February 1952, it was so popular that the company had to return at the end of the summer season. Yet it was in many ways quite uncharacteristic of Denis Carey's productions, which were usually most conspicuous for their scrupulous realism.

During his engagement with the Bristol Old Vic, Carey directed the great majority of the seasons' plays, and during many of those for which a guest producer was employed in Bristol he himself was directing at Stratford or in London. It is not surprising, therefore, that his fourth season showed some failure of grip and repetitiveness of technique. With modesty and self-analysis rare in his profession, Carey himself admitted this.[22] But by the time of his departure, the Bristol Old Vic was unassailably established not only in its own city but as a name to be reckoned with nationally and internationally.

This was the more important because the earlier plans for the expansion of the Old Vic's activities had collapsed and the future relations of the Bristol Old Vic with its "parent" would clearly have to be rethought. The Bristol Theatre School, for example, was now in quite a different position from that originally envisaged, and the new Principal, Duncan Ross,[23] could look forward to a greater degree of independence.

The two-way ladder by which it was envisaged that London would send promising beginners to Bristol, where they might be entrusted with bigger parts, while the best of Bristol's Company could expect to move up to the London Old Vic after a few years,[24] was expressive of a relationship which both sides, perhaps, were beginning to feel irksome – even though it had made the careers of such actors as Paul Rogers and John Neville.

At the same time the bias of management was gradually shifting towards local control. The introduction of two Corporation representatives on the Management Committee in 1950 was the first step and, despite a reduction of £500 in their annual grant to the Theatre Royal in January 1953, it was clear that the Corporation of Bristol were beginning to feel a proprietary interest in both theatre and company.[25]

In March 1952 the Arts Council, pursuing its new policy of withdrawing from direct control of theatres, obtained the Trustees' consent to sublet to the Old Vic Trust, while retaining representation on the board of management and continuing their financial support.[26]

Co-operation with the University was also growing. Sir Philip Morris, Vice-Chancellor of the University, was Chairman of the Management Committee from the beginning (and happily continued even after his retirement from the University), and the University Drama Department, itself a pioneer in its field, shared staff and technical resources with the

Theatre School to their common benefit. The opening in 1951 of the University Drama Studio, designed by Richard Southern, greatly increased production facilities, and end-on courses for Drama students deciding on a theatre career were soon being planned.[27]

The Trustees, too, several of whose original members had died, negotiated a new scheme with the Charity Commissioners whereby the remaining Trustees were joined by representatives of local and national bodies likely to have an informed interest in the building, such as the National Trust and the Council for the Preservation of Ancient Bristol, as well as the City Council and University of Bristol.[28]

Superficially all these developments may have appeared to be little more than nominal changes; but in fact they constituted the first hints that a new management structure would eventually have to be created.

Two

1954-1966

John Moody, who succeeded Denis Carey, was at the time of his appointment Drama Director for the Arts Council, and so had already an intimate knowledge of the Bristol Old Vic. He deliberately broadened the repertoire of the Company still further to include more modern plays from abroad:[29] up till now Anouilh had been almost the only contemporary foreign dramatist whose work had been seen in Bristol. Probably Moody's most exciting capture was the Swiss musical, *Oh! my Papa!* *(Feuerwerk)*, which, in a lively production by Warren Jenkins, was transferred to London almost immediately after its original run in April 1957; unfortunately its first night in London was disrupted by a gallery claque and it failed to establish itself. Arthur Miller's *The Crucible,* also produced by Jenkins, had its first British performance in Bristol on 9 November 1954, and both this play and Angus Wilson's *The Mulberry Bush* (September 1955) were later taken up by the Royal Court.

The prestige of the Bristol Old Vic, and the range of acting opportunities its repertory could offer, continued to attract players of quality to the Theatre Royal. Former ballerina Moira Shearer graced the company in the autumn of 1955, her performance in Giraudoux's *Ondine* being probably her best. Her leading man was Eric Porter, playing for a second Bristol season,[30] who produced two performances of great intensity in his Volpone (December 1955) and King Lear (February 1956) – the latter worthily marking the tenth anniversary of the Bristol Old Vic. Peter O'Toole, who joined the company in the autumn of 1955 as a small-part player, very rapidly won promotion, and during the following season brought back that special tense excitement among audiences which can be detected in the accounts of earlier actors like Powell, Elliston and Melville.

The management did not neglect the maintenance of the theatre, though the results were not always appreciated. In September 1955 the redecorated foyer, papered in cream with narrow broken vertical black stripes, and with a black-painted ceiling, aroused a furore, Alderman R. F. Lyne (a former Chairman of the Bristol Old Vic Theatre Club) claiming it induced in him "shock and nausea". Much of the subsequent criticism arose merely from conventional distaste for anything modern, but even so, in defending his choice, Philip James of the Arts Council seemed unduly to stress the differences in period between foyer and auditorium, ignoring the possibility of trying to minimise them and build up a unified theatre atmosphere. However, patrons were able to recover from the initial impact in new and more comfortable stalls, replanned either side of a central aisle with a cross-passage between the Pit exits, an arrangement which made movement in and out of this part of the auditorium much easier.[31]

In January 1959 Moody announced his resignation to devote himself to his other great love, opera, and was succeeded by John Hale.[32] Hale gave a preliminary taste of his quality by his production in May 1959 of Rostand's *Cyrano de Bergerac*. His designer, Patrick Robertson, capitalised on the perfect architectural relation of auditorium with stage by building the set of the Hôtel de Bourgogne as a continuation of the theatre's Dress and Upper Circles : a breathtaking triumph of classical perspective [see Plate 26].

Unfortunately this achievement was never again quite matched, though the level of competence was high, and a gay and full-blooded *Comedy of Errors* at the beginning of July 1960, with the tuneful assistance of Cy Grant, recalled agreeably Denis Carey's *Two Gentlemen*. Of the new plays produced by John Hale, *The Tinker*, by Laurence Dobie and Robert Sloman, was transferred for a run in London with its original cast shortly after the Bristol premiere in November 1960 – the first straight play to achieve this.[34]

A less happy precedent was set by the arrangement with H. M. Tennant Ltd. under which the first British performance of Anouilh's *The Rehearsal*, already scheduled for West End production, was given a prior-to-London three weeks' run in Bristol with its full West End cast in March 1961. Delightful as it was to see such actors as Robert Hardy, Alan Badel, Phyllis Calvert and Diana Churchill together, this was merely using the Theatre Royal for touring purposes; it had nothing to do with any idea of creative local theatre and was criticised by the Arts Council accordingly.[35] However, for some years it remained an isolated lapse of policy.

Val May, John Hale's successor, came to Bristol from the Nottingham Playhouse with a reputation for creating just that quality of repertory teamwork on which the Bristol Old Vic prided itself.[36] Like Denis Carey before him, he took some months to play himself in; it was not until the production of *War and Peace* in February 1962 that he really made his mark. As a producer his genius thrives on complex technical problems; the more complex they are, the surer appears his grasp of the play's essentials; and Piscator's adaptation of Tolstoy's epic, with its use of narrator, projected slides and models, was something then new and stimulating, though as usual it took the first week for Bristol to realise it. Given a showing at the Old Vic Theatre in the summer, it made such an impression that it was transferred for a limited run to the Phoenix.[37]

It can hardly have been easy to give undistracted attention to artistic matters when organisational problems of all kinds were becoming acute. The last months of John Hale's appointment had been bedevilled by a crisis of confidence between the Bristol Old Vic Theatre School and the Theatre Management Committee, which led to the resignations of the School Principal, Duncan Ross, and his Technical Lecturer, Michael Ackland. A quite disastrous subsequent appointment prompted more resignations the following Spring.[38]

During the same period the Royal said goodbye to two well-known figures : Charles Landstone (who had been succeeded as General Manager by Nat Brenner in 1959 but who had continued as Clerk to the Management Committee) finally broke his formal link with the Bristol theatre in July 1961, and Tom Hickson, resident manager since 1943, gave up his post a year later, Michael Ashford taking his place.

Besides these personal losses there were far more fundamental anxieties. Rises in production costs had been so sharp during the preceding few years that by July 1961 the Little Theatre was in serious difficulties, and at the Royal it was calculated that an average of 90 per cent. attendance every performance was necessary merely to break even.[39] But the annual grant from the Corporation to the Theatre Royal had been cut to £250 (partly on the grounds that the profits from *Salad Days* made more help unnecessary), a paltry "token" of support which aroused vigorous and public criticism from the local press and the Bristol Old Vic itself.[40]

Finally, hanging over the Company and the Trustees of the Theatre was a double uncertainty. The Arts Council's 21-year lease was due to expire in 1963 and it was already known two years previously that they would not renew it. The Old Vic as a theatrical organisation was near disbandment with the establishment of the National Theatre; it was certainly in no position to underpin its "younger brother" in Bristol and was suspected of having an increasing disinclination to do so even if it could.[41] Administratively and artistically the Bristol Old Vic had been becoming progressively more independent over the past years; now complete independence would clearly be thrust upon it, but the necessary financial subvention – not least the question of responsibility for the Theatre Royal building – was still uncertain.

Talks between the Arts Council and the Trustees began in December 1961. The upshot was a proposal put forward by the Council Entertainments Committee (who had early been drawn into the discussions) that the Corporation should lease the Theatre Royal from the Trustees from 1 April 1963, at an annual rent of £800. For the year 1963-4 they proposed a further grant of £2,500 (£1,000 of which, together with half of any trading profits, would go to a building fund). The Theatre would then be sublet to a new non-profit-distributing company, the Bristol Old Vic Trust Ltd., with representatives from the Corporation, the University, and the Royal Victoria Hall ("Old Vic"), which would be responsible for the Theatre School as well as for the company at the Theatre Royal. Financial security would be guaranteed by the Corporation.*[42]

Hardly were these proposals accepted than the Rapier Players, the Corporation's tenants at the Little Theatre since 1935, gave notice to terminate their tenancy the following June. Staunchly independent of subsidy, they had seen their reserves gradually eaten away by rising costs, despite increased public support, and they now calculated that they would need a further £3,000 a year to break even.[43] Despite public outcry, it was obvious from the outset that the scales were weighted against them. The Entertainments Committee, while agreeing to talks with the Rapier Players, took umbrage at the manner in which notice had been given, and at the very first subsequent meeting Alderman Chamberlain, Chairman of the Committee and a member of the Bristol Old Vic Trust, stated:

Various alternatives have already presented themselves to us, perhaps not the least interesting of these is that the Little Theatre and the Theatre Royal should combine to form a unit capable of presenting the widest range of dramatic entertainment.[44]

Ronald Russell, managing director of the Rapier Players, commented on this that he would be "extremely surprised if we were asked to withdraw the notice" and on 21 February 1963 he and Alderman Chamberlain issued a joint statement:

The parties have now agreed that it will not be possible to devise a plan which will be wholly acceptable to both sides.

* Suspicious Councillors were reassured that it was highly unlikely the Arts Council would withdraw their financial support – and, if they did, "there was protection in the fact that there would be a yearly lease." (*Bristol Evening Post*, 4.9.1962.)

The following month the Entertainments Committee put forward just the plan adumbrated at the outset by Alderman Chamberlain, whereby the Bristol Old Vic Trust would take over the artistic direction of the Little as well as the Royal; an arrangement unique in the English provincial theatre and opening up most exciting possibilities.[45]

As a result of the consequent internal reorganisation Nat Brenner, who had served the Bristol Old Vic since 1950, when he came as Denis Carey's Stage Director, moved to the Theatre School. His wide experience of every aspect of the theatre, and his temperament, engagingly blending humorous cynicism and passionate enthusiasms, were precisely what was needed to restore sanity and stability in a difficult situation, and make the School once more a vital part of the Bristol Old Vic. He and David Phethean, the Resident Producer for the Little, became Assistant Directors to Val May, and actors and producers formed a common pool for both theatres. The ramifications of the new organisation meant that the Trust required a first-class all-round administrator as General Manager, whom they found in Douglas Morris, who had previously been responsible for some of the Bristol Old Vic tours abroad.

Artistically, independence thrust the Bristol company into ever greater public prominence. As the only actors now bearing the Old Vic's name, they greatly extended the scope of their touring, sending a company under Denis Carey to India, Pakistan and Ceylon in 1963. There were two more West End transfers in the autumn of 1962 : *Fiorello!* (a musical biography of "Fiorello" La Guardia) and Keith Waterhouse and Willis Hall's *All Things Bright and Beautiful.* Unfortunately both met sharp criticism in London and came off after short runs, but these disappointments were more than compensated by the success the following spring of *A Severed Head,* an adaptation by J. B. Priestly of Iris Murdoch's novel. As was expected from the outset,[46] its Bristol cast moved to London en bloc – but the leading members had almost all been specially recruited for the occasion, the regular members of the company taking only supporting roles.

The season ended with the first British performance of Anouilh's *Hullabaloo* – as it turned out, an appropriate enough title. Mark Dignam had been engaged to play the leading part of the General, but unluckily had to withdraw through illness within ten days of the opening, and Christopher Benjamin, who had been with the Company all season, took over the part. Panicking, Anouilh's agent attempted to ban the press from the first night; whereupon the Bristol critics to a man circumvented the ban by attending as paying theatregoers, considering the attempt an unwarranted slur on the Bristol Old Vic's standards. In the event Christopher Benjamin received a well-deserved ovation for his performance, and the agent had the belated grace to withdraw his useless embargo.[47]

The following year, 1964, was of course the Shakespeare Quatercentenary, and its celebration in Bristol was in marked contrast with the attempts of a hundred years previous which had comprised a fancy dress ball, some penny readings, and at the Theatre Royal a programme of extracts supplemented by a farce called *Shakespeare at Home on his Tercentenary*, full of "execrable puns and vile rhymes", in which "the reverenced form of Shakespeare" was shot up through a trap door.

For the Quatercentenary ample amends were made. The Bristol Old Vic produced at the Royal a tragedy (*Othello*), a history (*King Henry V*) and a comedy (*Love's Labour's Lost*), presenting them in repertory for three weeks after their initial runs; thus giving a two-months' programme of Shakespeare which played to over 80 per cent. capacity. Additionally, at the Little Theatre there was a joint bill of the pre-Shakespearean comedies of *Gammer Gurton's Needle* and *Ralph Roister Doister*, followed by a production by the School of Marlowe's *Edward II*, while the Drama Department of the University provided a fascinating series of Tudor moralities and interludes and other Elizabethan plays.[48] It was the most valuable piece of co-operation yet accomplished, and further distinction was lent by Princess Marina, patron of the Old Vic, who paid a special visit on 27 April to see *King Henry V* with Richard Pasco in the name-part.

Following the Bristol season the company took the three Shakespearian productions on an exhausting but triumphant tour of Europe throughout the summer and most of the autumn; though again there was a price to be paid locally in lack of continuity, since an almost completely new Bristol company had of course to be recruited for September 1964.

Two more West End transfers formed part of the next season's programme, *Portrait of a Queen* (March 1965), in which Bristol welcomed back Dorothy Tutin, and in April Frank Marcus' black farce, *The Killing of Sister George*, which gave Beryl Reid a new opportunity in straight theatre which she took with both hands.*

The Theatre Royal's bicentenary year brought past, present and future into happy association and national prominence. It opened with the knowledge of two solid West End successes keeping the Bristol Old Vic's name to the fore in London, and the anticipation of a tour of Canada and the United States, an invitation arising from the enormously successful European tour of 1964. In March the first hints were given of the scheme for a theatrical precinct in King Street, linking the Theatre Royal and Coopers' Hall, a project significant of the new civic acceptance of drama

---

* "What a shame," murmured an elderly lady to me on the first night, "that when you do get a play with an all-women cast it couldn't possibly be performed by a Townswomen's Guild!" There was a twinkle in her eye.

generally, as well as embodying the hope that the historic Royal should have a setting more worthy of it.[49]

But past and present came together most memorably in the bi-centenary production, *Sixty Thousand Nights*, of which, as the programme put it, the Theatre Royal was the setting and the star. A script which aimed at portraying many of the greatest actors who had played on the Royal's stage, together with some of the turning-points in the Theatre's history, could easily have become little better than a name-dropping local pageant; as created by George Rowell and shaped by Val May it was a magnificent embodiment of living, and total, theatre. No painstaking accuracy of historical detail could have improved on its imaginative truth in recording the richness and variety of the theatre's life. Julian Slade's score included some delicious period pastiche for the set pieces from Bickerstaff's 18th Century musical farce, *The Padlock*, and, almost a century later, Brough's *Endymion*.[50]

The actual date of the bicentenary, 30 May, unfortunately fell on Whit Monday, so the gala performance, attended by Princess Marina and followed by a Civic Reception, was postponed to 2 June. [See Plate 27]. A sense of occasion can never have been more deeply felt in all the two hundred years of the Theatre Royal's history, and when the audience reluctantly dispersed it was possessed not only with a euphoric complacency arising from the achievements of the past, but a renewed devotion to establish the future.

> Dear Theatre, long may you
> Be a House with an ever-open door
> And may your actors take the floor
> For sixty thousand nights
> Or more![51]

NOTES

[1] C.E.M.A. Report for 1944, summarised in *Bristol Evening World*, 20.4.1945.

[2] The Trustees, on the advice of John Summerson and Richard Southern, refused a request by C.E.M.A. in 1945 to have the fly-galleries taken down; later they agreed to the removal and storage of the cat-walks. (Leighton, *op. cit.*, p. 14.)

[3] *Bristol Evening World,* 30.7.1945 *et seq.*

[4] Bristol newspapers, 12.12.1945. According to Landstone (*op. cit.*, p. 47), the Old Vic had been approached before the 1943 reopening, but were at that time unenthusiastic.

[5] *Bristol Evening Post,* 27.6.1946; see also programme note, "What about Tchechov?" in the programme of *Keep in a Cool Place* (14.5.1946+). Subsequent correspondence took place in the *Post,* 29.6. to 9.7.1946.

[6] See programme notes in programmes for *Twelfth Night* (5.6.1946+) and *The Playboy of the Western World* (23.10.1946+); also *Bristol Evening Post,* 3. & 22.10.1946.

[7] *Western Daily Press,* 9.4.1947.

[8] *Times,* &c., 23.12.1948. The announcement of Hunt's successor was not made till mid-February.

[9] Landstone, *op. cit.,* p. 134, recalls that one evening manager T. C. P. Hickson "found that the dress circle seats were sinking gracefully into the Stalls Bar" and £2,500-worth of stanchioning had to be put in.

[10] Alterations recorded in Leighton, *op. cit.,* p. 14; Programme of 29.10.1945; *Bristol Evening World,* 6.11.1945; Landstone, *op. cit.,* p. 136. The disused exit was almost certainly the old stage door.

[11] Landstone, *op. cit.,* p. 136, says it was the unexpected bill for the Box Office alterations of the previous year which brought about the standstill.

[12] See *Bristol Evening Post, Bristol Evening World* and *Western Daily Press* for August and September 1949. The whole story is set out in Landstone, *op. cit.,* pp. 134-8, and briefly in Leighton, *op. cit.,* p. 15.

[13] See *Western Daily Press,* 18.7.1949 and 17.1.1950; *Times,* 1.9.1949; *Bristol Evening Post,* 6.12.1949. In February 1950 the *Bristol Evening World* reported that the timbers of the thunder run were rotting and £20 must be found if it were to be repaired.

[14] *Bath & Wilts Chronicle,* 22.5.1950.

[15] See, for example, *Western Daily Press,* 1.9.1949, and Bristol newspapers, 9.9.1949.

[16] *Western Daily Press,* 18. & 24.5.1950.

[17] Programme, 3.9.1951; *Vic-Wells Association News-Sheet,* October 1951; Leighton, *op. cit.,* p. 16.

[18] *Bristol Evening Post,* 6.7.1953.

[19] Programme note to *The Taming of the Shrew,* 21.5.1951.

[20] Christmas 1952-3; revived 1958-9.

[21] *Times,* 27.6.1956. It was proposed that certain rooms in the new premises should be named after Denis Carey, Julian Slade and Dorothy Reynolds; Miss Reynolds, however, having strong views on acting schools generally, declined the compliment.

[22] *Times,* 1.5.1954.

[23] Ross succeeded Edward Stanley in the summer of 1954 (*Western Daily Press,* 11.6.1954).

[24] *Bristol Evening Post,* 9.7.1953.

[25] *Western Daily Press,* 14.1.1953.

[26] *Times,* &c., 28.3.1952, and Leighton, *op. cit.,* p. 17. Charles Landstone, on officially leaving the Arts Council in 1952, continued General Manager of the Theatre Royal under the Bristol Old Vic till the autumn of 1959.

[27] See *Times,* 25.6.1956. The successful completion of a degree including Drama at Bristol carried exemption from one year of the School's two-year acting or technical course. In 1962 it was even proposed that the Old Vic might give one-year contracts to up to four such students every year (*Bristol Evening Post,* 11.9.1962); the idea was not proceeded with.

[28] The organisation of the Trustees is set out on page 2 of their pamphlet, *The Story of the Theatre Royal, Bristol* (1972).

[29] See *Theatre World,* January 1955.

[30] Eric Porter's first season had been with Denis Carey two years previously.

[31] *Bristol Evening Post,* 6. to 15.9.1955.

[32] *Times,* &c., 20.1.1959; *Western Daily Press,* 9.6.1959. Hale was appointed Director of Productions with Nat Brenner as his General Manager – a division between artistic and administrative responsibilities which has continued and sharpened.

[33] As such it was probably rivalled only by Alan Barlow's setting for Leonov's *The Apple Orchards* in April 1948, which by clever use of perspective gave apparently infinite depth to the stage.

[34] Programme, 29.11.1960. The film, *The Wild and the Willing,* was later based on this play.

[35] See *Bristol Evening Post,* 11. & 15.3.1961; *Sixteenth Annual Report of the Arts Council of Great Britain, 1960-1,* pp. 21-2. The pros and cons closely parallel those relating to the introduction of the star system into the Stock Companies of the 19th Century.

[36] "The Nottingham Playhouse in the latter part of the fifties, reached the highest standard of acting and direction under its director Val May that in the writer's opinion was ever attained by any repertory theatre in the country during that decade," wrote John Fernald in *Sense of Direction* (London, 1968, p. 171, n.). See also Val May's own programme note, 4.9.1961.

[37] *Bristol Evening Post,* 3. & 7.2.1962; 30.4. and 21.6.1962; and London Old Vic programme, 14.6.1962.

[38] Duncan Ross felt that the over-representation of London interests on the Theatre Management Committee, coupled with unsatisfactory financing arrangements, had prevented the School from becoming truly independent in the way which earlier developments had promised. Despite the provision of new premises in Downside Road, Clifton, opened in June 1956, the School still lacked a proper studio theatre of its own, and had no assured income beyond that from students' fees. See *Bristol Evening Post,* 15. & 16.5.1961, 2. & 10.6.1961; and *The Stage,* 15.6.1961.

[39] *Bristol Evening Post,* 11.7., 25.11. and 30.12.1961.

[40] The grant had been cut to £250 from 1956-7 onwards and was in any case to be used for the upkeep of the theatre and not for the production expenses of the Bristol Old Vic. I am indebted to Alderman F. G. W. Chamberlain for letting me have particulars of the grants made by the Corporation from 1950 onwards. See *Bristol Evening Post,* 23.10. and 30.12.1961; 3., 9., 14. & 15.5.1962.

[41] Professor Glynne Wickham of the University Drama Department was particularly outspoken in his views. See *Bristol Evening Post,* 23.10.1961 and 15. & 31.5.1962, and G. W. G. Wickham: *Drama in a World of Science,* London, 1962, pp. 88-92.

[42] Full details are set out in *Bristol Evening Post* and *Western Daily Press* of 28.8., 4., 10. & 12.9.1962.

[43] *Times,* 9.11.1962; *Bristol Evening Post,* 7. & 10.11.1962.

[44] *Bristol Evening Post,* 15.11.1962.

[45] *ibid.,* 21.3. and 10.4.1963. Such an arrangement was not, of course, novel in Bristol, but the precedent, the common management of the New Theatre (Prince's) and the Royal from 1867 to 1881, was hardly happy. The same danger, that the smaller theatre might be treated as an inferior "second string", was very obviously apparent, and indeed it was some years before a really consistent policy was worked out. During the initial debate the Council was told that "the plays at the Little would be 'more in the lighter vein' " (*Bristol Evening Post,* 21.3.1963) to encourage the retention of Rapier Players' supporters. Val May (*ibid.,* 27.7.1963) declared for "a broad liberal policy" aimed at attracting younger Bristolians to the theatre, which after some trial and error showed signs of succeeding. The repertoire at the Royal was unaffected.

[46] *Bristol Evening Post,* 27.4.1963.

[47] *ibid.,* 25. & 29.5. and 1.6.1963.

[48] For accounts of these, see *New Theatre Magazine,* V, 2 and G. W. G. Wickham: *Shakespeare's Dramatic Heritage,* London, 1969, pp. 30-9.

[49] *Bristol Evening Post,* 17. & 18.3.1966.

[50] The fame of both Theatre and Company was reflected in the number of descriptive articles (of very varying standards of historical accuracy) and reviews in national as well as local newspapers and periodicals, e.g. *Times,* 25. & 30.5 and 6.6.1966; *Guardian,* 30.5. and 3.6.1966; *Illustrated London News,* 14.5. and 11.6.1966.

[51] *Sixty Thousand Nights,* I, 1 (D).

Bibliography

(excluding articles in periodicals, &c.)

(*Anon.*): *An Address to the Citizens of Bristol*. Bristol, 1766 (reissued 1773).

Archer, William: *William Charles Macready*. London, 1890.

Arts Council of Great Britain: *Annual Reports 1-21*. London, 1945-1966.

(Bancroft, Squire and Marie): *Mr. and Mrs. Bancroft On and Off the Stage*. London, 1886.

Banister, Douglas: *Life of John Reeve*. London, 1838.

Barker, Kathleen M. D.: *The Theatre Royal, Bristol: The First Seventy Years*. 3rd Edn. Bristol, 1969.

do.: *The Theatre Royal, Bristol: Decline and Rebirth*. Bristol, 1966.

Bernard, John: *Retrospections of the Stage*. London, 1830.

Bingham, Frederick: *A Celebrated Old Playhouse. The History of Richmond Theatre*. Richmond (Surrey), 1886.

Board, M. E.: *The Story of the Bristol Stage, 1490-1925*. London, n.d. (1926).

(Bridges, Lord, *et al.*): *Help for the Arts: A Report to the Calouste Gulbenkian Foundation*. London, 1959.

Byrne, M. St. Clare (ed.): *Studies in English Theatrical History*. London, 1952.

(?Champion, R.): *The Consequences of a New Theatre, to the City of Bristol*. Bristol, 1765.

(?*do.*): *Bristol Theatre*. Bristol, 1766.

Coleman, John: *Players and Playwrights I Have Known*. London, 1888.

do.: *Fifty Years of an Actor's Life*. London, 1904.

Cordova, Rudolph de (ed.): *Dame Madge Kendal, by Herself*. London, 1933.

Council for the Encouragement of Music and the Arts: *The Arts in Wartime*. London, n.d. (1944).

Curwen, Samuel: *Journals and Letters* (ed. G. A. Ward). London, 1842.

Dickens, Charles: *Memoirs of Joseph Grimaldi* (ed. R. Findlater). London, 1968.

Donaldson, Walter: *Recollections of an Actor*. London, 1865.

Downer, Alan S.: *The Eminent Tragedian – William Charles Macready*. Harvard, 1966.

Dunbar, Janet: *Flora Robson*. London, 1960.

Dunlap, William: *Memoirs of George Frederick Cooke*. London, 1813.

Dyer, Robert: *Nine Years of an Actor's Life*. London, 1833.

Everard, E. Cape: *Memoirs of an Unfortunate Son of Thespis.* Edinburgh, 1818.

(Genest, John): *Some Account of the English Stage.* Bath, 1832.

Harbron, Dudley: *The Conscious Stone.* London, 1949.

Henderson, John (ed.): *The Bristol Old Vic Company: a record of two seasons.* London, 1947.

Ireland, John: *Letters and Poems by the late Mr. John Henderson.* London, 1786.

Isaac, Winifred: *Ben Greet and the Old Vic.* London, 1964.

Jenkins, Richard: *Memoirs of the Bristol Stage.* Bristol, 1826.

Jordan, Dora: Correspondence in Henry Huntington Library.

Kemble, Frances A.: *Record of a Girlhood.* London, 1878.

do.: *Records of Later Life.* London, 1882.

Landstone, Charles: *Off-Stage.* London, 1953.

Latimer, John: *Annals of Bristol in the Eighteenth Century.* Bristol, 1893.

do.: *Annals of Bristol in the Nineteenth Century.* Bristol, 1902.

Leacroft, Richard: *The Development of the English Playhouse.* London, 1973.

Lee, Henry: *Memoirs of a Manager.* Taunton, 1830.

(Leighton, Wilfrid): *The Theatre Royal, Bristol, 1766-1942.* (Bristol, 1943.)

do.: *The Preservation of the Theatre Royal, Bristol, and Matters Relating to the Building 1942-1960.* (Bristol, 1961; privately circulated.)

Little, Bryan: *The Theatre Royal: the beginning of a Bicentenary.* Bristol, 1964.

Little, D. M., and Kahrl, G. M. (eds.): *Letters of David Garrick.* London, 1965.

Macready, William Charles: *Reminiscences* (ed. F. Pollock). London, 1866.

Martin Harvey, John: *The Autobiography of Sir John Martin Harvey.* London, 1933.

Mitchell, Yvonne: *Actress.* London, 1957.

New Bristol Guide. 2nd Edn. Bristol, 1800.

Pemberton, T. E.: *The Kendals: A Biography.* London, 1900.

do.: *Ellen Terry and her Sisters.* London, 1902.

Penley, Belville S.: *The Bath Stage.* London/Bath, 1892.

Powell, Rennie: *The Bristol Stage – Its Story.* Bristol, 1919.

Raymond, George: *The Life and Enterprises of Robert William Elliston.* London, 1844.

Robinson, Mary: *Memoirs of the late Mrs. Robinson, written by herself.* London, 1801.

Rosenfeld, Sybil: *Strolling Players and Drama in the Provinces.* Cambridge, 1939.

Rowell, George R., and Slade, Julian: *Sixty Thousand Nights.* (In *Plays of the Year,* London, 1967.)

Siddons, Sarah: *Reminiscences of Sarah Kemble Siddons.* Harvard, 1942.

Southern, Richard: *The Georgian Playhouse.* London, 1948.

Terry, Ellen: *The Story of My Life.* London, 1908.

Toynbee, W. (ed.): *The Diaries of William Charles Macready.* London, 1912.

Trewin, J. C.: *John Neville.* London, 1961.

(Trustees of the Theatre Royal): *The Story of the Theatre Royal, Bristol.* Bristol, 1966 and 1972.

Watts, Guy Tracey: *Theatrical Bristol.* Bristol, 1915.

Wemyss, F. C.: *Theatrical Biography.* Glasgow, 1848.

Wickham, G. W. G.: *Drama in a World of Science.* London, 1962.

Williamson, Audrey M.: *Paul Rogers*. London, n.d. (1956).

do., and Landstone, Charles: *The Bristol Old Vic: The First Ten Years.* London, 1957.

Winston James: *The Theatric Tourist*. London, 1805. Also ms. collections relating thereto in Harvard Theatre Collection, Birmingham Public Library and Johannesburg Public Library.

Young, Julian C.: *Memoir of Charles Mayne Young*. London/New York, 1871.

OTHER PRINCIPAL COLLECTIONS OF MATERIAL

Bristol Central Library: Richard Smith Collection (5 vols.) of playbills, &c., relating to Bristol Theatres; J. H. Chute's guardbooks of Theatre Royal playbills, 1853-1868; miscellaneous collection of playbills and programmes; Michael Edkins' Account Book.

Bristol City Archives: Trustees' Collection of legal documents relating to the Theatre Royal; playbills, promptbooks &c.; Minute and Account Books of the Proprietors, 1764-1925; correspondence by the late Mr. Wilfrid Leighton relating to the Theatre Royal.

Bristol University: Miscellaneous collection of playbills and promptbooks; Minute Books &c. relating to post-World War II period.

British Museum: Playbills 1769-1848 (4 vols., callmark PB 203-6).

Smaller playbill collections in Birmingham Library Shakespeare Collection, Folger Shakespeare Library and Harvard Theatre Collection.

Local newspapers in Bristol Central Library and British Museum Newspaper Library, Colindale.

Appendix

Special Engagements of Performers at the Theatre Royal, Bristol, 1779–1868

This Appendix includes all touring companies, individual performers or groups of performers (actors, musicians, dancers and entertainers) given special engagements at the Theatre Royal, Bristol, during the period 1779–1868 when the Stock Company system was in operation. In the few cases where such performers appeared with earlier companies these engagements have also been included; but appearances after January 1868 have been omitted. I am grateful to Mr. Ivor Guest for help in identifying a number of the artists concerned.

The term "special engagement" has been used to cover both "star" performances and the type of short-term engagements described on page 150, a few examples of which may be traced earlier than Chute's management, especially during the Autumn seasons of William and Sarah M'Cready (see, e.g., under James Woulds). Where the performers were also at any time members of the Stock Company the dates of these engagements also have been given. A question-mark before an initial date indicates that this is the first appearance which can be documented, though earlier ones are possible; similarly, a question-mark before a final date indicates that this is the last known performance of that engagement, though it is possible that later performances took place.

Concerts or appearances at Benefit performances have not normally been included except where performers were entitled to inclusion on other grounds. A very few exceptions have been made of particularly famous artists, e.g. Nicolò Paganini and Jenny Lind.

Performers appearing with touring companies have been included only under the title of the company, except where they also secured personal engagements or were former Stock Company members, when they are also listed individually, with cross-references. Thus a few actors and singers, e.g. J. F. Cathcart and Giulia Grisi, may be found twice.

Main entries will be found below the name under which the performer first appeared in Bristol (e.g., details of all Mrs. Glover's appearances will be found under "Betterton, Miss Julia"). Cross-references, however, are always provided.

SC Stock Company
* Special engagement

Abbott, William (Actor)   1789-1843
   (SC) 30.9.1805-14.7.1806; (SC) 29.9.1806-20.7.1807; (SC) 28.9.1807-3.8.1808;
   (SC) 3.10.1808-31.7.1809; (SC) 2.10.1809-30.4.1810; (SC) 5.10.1810-22.7.1811;
   (SC) 4.10.1811-?1.7.1812; *2.-14.9.1829.
Adams, the Misses E., H. and S. (Dancers)
   *18.-30.10.1805.
Addison, Miss Carlotta (Actress)   1850-1914
   *29.8.-9.9.1864 (Addison's Co.); *10. & 11.4., 5. & 12.5.1865; (SC) 26.12.1865-
   27.4.1866.
Addison, Edward Phillips (Actor)   1808-1874
   (SC) ?29.8.-29.10.1838; *21.8.-1.9.1854 (Princess's Theatre Co.); *29.8.-9.9.1864
   (Own Co.); *5. & 12.5.1865.
Addison, Miss Fanny (Actress)   1847-
   *29.8.-9.9.1864 (Addison's Co.); (SC) 24.10.-16.12.1864; (SC) 29.12.1864-
   16.5.1865; (SC) 18.9.-19.12.1865; (SC) ?8.1.-2.5.1866.
Addison's Company
   *29.8.-9.9.1864 (E. P. Addison [q.v.], Ashley, Best, Stephen Bishop, David Evans
   [q.v.], Jervis, Payne Family [Frederick, Harry and W. H. Payne and Mademoiselle Esther], Master Pitt; Miss Carlotta Addison [q.v.], Miss Fanny Addison
   [q.v.], Mrs. Manders, Miss Gertrude Melvin [q.v.], Miss Ward; and various
   members of the Stock Company).
African Opera Troupe
   *2. & 3.6.1865 (Will Anderson, C. Blamphin, J. Eglinton, La Feuillade, Herbert,
   Louis Lindsay, Montgomery, G. Robinson, Harry Templeton).
Albertazzi, Madame Emma, née Howson (Singer)   1814-1847
   *17.8.1843 (Concert) (with Mademoiselle Howson, her sister).
Aldridge, Ira Frederick (Actor)   1807-1867
   *1.-3.2.1826 (as Keene); *23.3.-1.4.1830; *16.1.1832; *16.-27.3.1846; *8.-
   18.2.1847; *15.-22.5.1850.
Alexandre (Ventriloquist)   1799-
   *7. & 14.1.1823.
Alsop, Mrs. Frances, née Daly/Jordan (Actress)   1782-1821
   *15.-29.1.1816.
van Amburgh, Isaac A. (Animal Trainer)   1812-1865
   *5.-8.6.1840.
Anderson (Harlequin)
   *13.-?16.4.1846; *24.12.1866-8.2.1867.
Anderson, "Professor" John Henry (Conjuror)   1815-1874
   *24.6.-8.7.1844; *17.-31.3.1851.
Anderson, James Robertson (Actor)   1811-1895
   *16.-22.1.1844; *20.2.1844; *7.-15.3.1844; *26.1.-2.2.1846; *3.-5.3.1856; *21.-
   25.10.1861; *1.-13.12.1862.
Angel, Miss Louisa (Actress/Singer)
   *4.-8.12.1854; *25. & 26.2.1856; *7. & 8.4.1856; *15.8.1856; (SC) 26.12.1856-
   30.1.1857; *17.-26.9.1860.
Angel, W. H. (Actor)
   (SC) 5.4.-16.6.1824; *22.5. & 8.6.1840; (SC) 31.8.-?14.10.1840; (SC) ?30.12.1840-

?3.5.1841; (sc) ?21.9.-8.10.1841; (sc) ?31.12.1841-?2.5.1842; (sc) 11.-?.7.1842; (sc) ?1.9.-?3.10.1842; (sc) ?2.1.-?5.6.1843; (sc) ?31.8.-9.10.1843; (sc) (sc) 26.12.1843-20.5.1844; (sc) 29.8.-?7.10.1844; (sc) ?28.12.1844-19.5.1845; (sc) 2.-4.6.1845; (sc) 1.9.-?13.11.1845; (sc) 26.12.1845-25.5.1846; (sc) 1.-4.6.1846; (sc) ?8.9.-2.11.1846; (sc) 26.12.1846-18.5.1847; (sc) ?-11.10.1847; (sc) c. Dec. 1847-?28.4.1848, 17.7.1848; (sc) c. Sept. 1848-23.10.1848; (sc) ?28.12.1848-7.5.1849; *22.10.1849; *27.11.-8.12.1854; *25. & 26.2.1856; *7. & 8.4.1856; *15.8.1856; (sc) ?6.-30.1.1857; *17.-26.9.1860.

Antonio, "Il Diavolo" (Tight-rope performer)
*3.-?7.11.1817; *12.-16.1.1818; *31.5.-25.6.1819; *9.-18.1.1822; *26.12.1831-2.1.1832.

Archer, Thomas (Actor)   1789-1848
*30.8.-24.9.1824.

Artis, Master Frederick (Child prodigy)
*27.6.1859.

Asbury (Dancer/Pantaloon)
*20.4.-1.5.1840; (sc) ?2.1.-?29.4.1843; (sc) ?31.8.-29.9.1843.

Assiote or Assiotti, Mademoiselle (Dancer)
*31.8. & 7.9.1846 (Flora Fabbri's Co.); *24.3.-?3.5.1848; (sc) ?5.10.-c. Dec. 1852; (sc) 27.12.1852-?25.4.1853.

Atkinson, Miss Emma (Singer)
(sc) 16.12.1828-15.5.1829; *3.-10.3.1834; (sc) 27.12.1837-14.5.1838; (sc) 26.12.1838-?6.5.1839.

Ayton, Miss Fanny (Actress/Singer)   1806-1832+
*8.3.1827 (Concert); *10.-12.12.1828.

Baker, The Brothers (Sprites)
*26.12.1867-10.1.1868.

Balfe, Michael William (Singer/Composer)   1808-1870
*3.-14.9.1838; *6.-10.4.1840; *25.8.1842 (Concert); *17.8.1843 (Concert); *27.9.1847 (Concert).

Balfe, Mrs. Lina, née Rosa (Singer)   1808-1888
*6.-10.4.1840.

Balls, J. S. (Actor)   1799-1844
(sc) ?31.8.-21.9.1821; (sc) 26.12.1821-14.6.1822; (sc) 2.-27.9.1822; *7.-10.9.1840; *22.-29.3.1841; (sc) 26.12.1843-?9.5.1844.

Bannister, John (Actor)   1760-1836
*20.7.1807; *4.-21.12.1809; *19.11.-3.12.1810; *27.7.1812.

Barnes, Mrs. (Actress)
*10. & 26.12.1787.

Barnett, Master John (Singer)   1802-1890
*26.2.1816.

Barnett, Morris (Actor)   1800-1856
*4.-7.4.1837; *7.-11.10.1850.

Bartlett (Pantaloon)
*30.8.-7.9.1830.

Barton, John Henry (Actor)   ?1802-1849
(sc) 22.11.1824-6.6.1825; (sc) 29.8.-23.9.1825; (sc) 7.12.1825-27.4.1826; *19.-23.1.1835; *23. & 25.2.1835; *23., 27. & 31.3.1835; *13.-28.2.1845.

Bateman, Miss Ellen (Actress)   1844-1936
*5.-13.2.1852; *5.3.1852.

Bateman, Miss Kate (Actress)   1843-1917
*5.-13.2.1852; *5.3.1852; *11.-15.12.1865.

Beatrice, Mademoiselle (Marie Beatrice Binda) (Actress)   1839-1878
*26.2.-9.3.1866.

Beckett (Dancer)
*2.-?26.9.1839.

Bedford, Paul John (Actor/Singer) ?1792-1871
(sc) 7.10.1816-30.6.1817; *20.9.1826; *22.5.1840; *12. & 14.4.1841; *15.-
26.2.1858.
Bedouin Arabs (Acrobats)
*26.-31.12.1836.
de Begnis, Giuseppe (Singer) 1793-1849
*20.2.1823 (Concert); *11.12.1823 (Concert); *3.2.1825 (Concert); *13., 20. &
24.2.1829, 5. & 6.3.1829 (Own Co.); *5.-16.10.1835 (Own Co); *21.9.1837.
de Begnis' Company
*13., 20. & 24.2.1829; 5. & 6.3.1829 (de Begnis and Pupils of Royal Academy of
Music, viz.: Isteghi Brizzi [q.v.], Hodges, A. Sapio [q.v.], E. Seguin; Miss Brom-
ley, Miss Childe); *5.-16.10.1835 (de Angioli, de Begnis [q.v.], Bennett [q.v.],
Chevallos, Destre, Galli, de Meric [14.10. only], Scotto [14.10. only], Venefra
(Dancer), Zotti; Sga. de Angioli, Sga. Faustini [14.10. only], Sga. Grandi, Miss
Waters).
Belfille, Mrs. Anne, née Burdett (Actress) -1789
*28.10.1782.
Benjamin (Strong Man)
*30.10.-1.11.1826.
Bennett (Singer)
(sc) 25.-28.10.1831; (sc) ?30.1.-?15.2.1832; *13.5.1833; (sc) 26.12.1834-
20.2.1835; *5.-16.10.1835 (de Begnis Co.).
Bennett, George John (Actor) 1800-1879
*31.10.-10.11.1854.
Bennett, James (Actor) -1885
(sc) ?17.1.-?2.5.1842; (sc) ?30.12.1842-?8.5.1843; *7-18.3.1864; *18.4.-
2.5.1864; *16.9.-4.11.1864; *23.10.-3.11.1865; *19.11.-7.12.1866; *6.12.1867.
Betterton, Miss Julia (later Mrs. Glover) (Actress) 1781-1850
(sc) 21.9.1795-5.8.1796; (sc) 28.9.1796-28.7.1797; (as Mrs. Glover:) *21.9.-
5.10.1821; *17.5.1823; *28.1.-3.2.1840; *16.-23.9.1844.
Betts, Miss Louisa (Singer) -1867
*27.11.1828 (Concert); *17.-27.5.1836.
Betty, William Henry West (Actor) 1791-1874
*21.-30.4.1806; *5.12.1806-12.1.1807; *25.4.-16.5.1808; *17.2.-2.3.1812; *6.-
20.4.1812; *8.2.-4.3.1813; *27.3.-17.4.1815.
Biggs, Miss B. (later Mrs. Grove) (Actress)
*28.9.1801; (as Mrs. Grove:) (sc) 6.10.1807-18.7.1808; (sc) 12.10.1808-
24.7.1809; (sc) 4.10.1809-18.7.1810; (sc) ?6.11.1811-unknown date.
Bishop, Madame Anna, née Riviere (Singer) 1810-1884
*22.-26.3.1847.
Bishop, Thomas (Singer)
*27.4.1842; *?9.-?21.9.1842; *5.-7.6.1844; *2.-14.9.1844; *22.-26.3.1847.
Blake, Miss (Singer)
*18.5.1819 (1st appearance any stage); (sc) 30.8.-17.9.1819.
Blanchard (Animal trainer)
*16.-24.4.1846 (with his dog, Hector).
Blanchard, Thomas (Pantaloon) ?1787-1859
*29.4.-9.5.1823 (with son, Master Blanchard).
Blewitt—see Chute, John Coleman
Blissett, Francis (Actor) 1741-1824
(sc) 10.6.-16.9.1776; (sc) ?15.-?22.3.1779; (sc) 19.4.-31.5.1779; (sc) 4.10.1779-
29.5.1780; (sc) 25.9.1780-5.6.1781; (sc) 10.9.1781-15.7.1782; (sc) 23.9.1782-
?6.6.1783; (sc) ?29.9.1783-19.7.1784; (sc) 20.9.1784-25.7.1785; (sc) 3.10.1785-
17.7.1786; (sc) 2.10.1786-23.7.1787; (sc) 3.10.1787-21.7.1788; (sc) 19.9.1788-
24.7.1789; (sc) 21.9.1789-?30.7.1790; (sc) ?1.10.1790-?29.7.1791; (sc)
?2.11.1791-?1.8.1792; (sc) 24.9.1792-29.7.1793; (sc) 30.9.1793-4.8.1794; (sc)

?6.10.1794-?24.7.1795; (SC) 21.9.1795-8.8.1796; (SC) 26.9.1796-7.8.1797; (SC) 25.9.1797-?20.7.1798; *8. & 29.11. & 20.12.1802; *3. & 17.1.1803; *6.6.1804; *11.3.1805; *22.4.1805; *3.7.1805; *4.4.1808; *21.11. & 19.12.1808; *2.4.1810; *19.4. & 19.5.1813; *16.6.1813.

Boai, Michael (Entertainer)

Boai, Madame (do.)
   *17.-21.1.1831 (with German Minstrels); *23.-25.4.1838.

Bochsa, Robert Nicholas Charles (Harpist)   1789-1856
   *29.11.1827 (Concert); *21.9.1837; *27. & 28.9.1838.

Boleno Family of Acrobats
   *24.9.-1.10.1846 (Boleno, G. Boleno, Milano Boleno; Mademoiselle E. Davie, Mademoiselle Morice).

Booth, Junius Brutus (Actor)   1796-1852
   *12.5. & 30.6.1817; *16.-19.9.1817; *17.5.-28.6.1819; *6.-10.2.1826.

Booth, Miss Sarah (Actress)   1792-1867
   *1. & 8.5.1815; *30.8.-8.9.1821.

Borrani (Singer)
   *22. & 24.9.1845; *15.-26.9.1857 (London Grand Opera Co.); *9.-13.2.1857 (London Grand Opera Co.).

Bradbury, Robert (Clown)   1774-1831
   *15.-19.5.1820.

Braham, Charles (Singer)   1823-1884

Braham, Hamilton (Singer)
   *30.12.1843; *2.-10.2.1845.

Braham, John (Singer)   1777-1856
   *5.-19.2.1810;   *13.1.-10.2.1812;   *12.-30.10.1812;   *12.6.1818 (Concert);
   *23.1.1823 (Concert); *30.12.1824 (Concert); *3.-11.1.1825; *28.1.1825;
   *5.-12.1.1829;   *28.12.1830-3.1.1831;   *27.-29.1.1831;   *3.-10.3.1834;   *11.-18.9.1837; *31.1.-2.2.1838; *23.12.1839 (Concert); *30.12.1843 (Concert); *2.-10.2.1845.

Braid, George Ross (Actor)   1812-1878
   (SC) 26.12.1837-14.5.1838; (SC) ?27.9.-c. Oct. 1838; (SC) ?1.9.-8.10.1841; (SC) ?31.12.1841-?2.5.1842; *23.-27.9.1850 (Haymarket Co.); *5.-7.11.1850 (Haymarket Co.).

Brizzi, Isteghi (Singer)
   *13., 20. & 24.2.1829 (de Begnis Co.); *27. & 28.9.1838; *19.8.1840 (Concert); *21.9.1843 (Concert); *3.9.1845 (Concert).

Bromhead, Miss (Singer)
   *12.-21.12.1825; (SC) 10.4.-29.5.1826.

Brooke, Gustavus Vaughan (Actor)   1818-1866
   *29. & 31.3.1854.

Brough, Lionel (Actor)   1836-1909
   *?30.9.-1.10.1841.

Brunton, Miss Anne (Actress)   1769-1808
   (SC) 25.4.-13.6.1785; *8.5.1786.

Bryson Children, The (Musical prodigies)
   *27.4.-11.5.1789.

Buchanan, McKean (Actor)   1823-1872
   *4.-8.4.1849.

Bucher (Flautist)
   *10.4.1834; *7.5.1834.

Buckstone, John Baldwin (Actor)   1802-1879
   *23. & 24.7.1840; *13.1.1843; *13.-31.3.1843; *10. & 11.9.1846; *8.-19.1.1849.

Bull, Ole Borneman (Violinist)   1810-1880
   *12.6.1837 (Concert).

Bunn, Alfred (Manager)   1798-1860
   *3.4.1850.

Burke, Master Joseph (Actor/Singer)   1818-
    *27.9.-1.10.1824; *7.-25.3.1825.
Butler, Samuel (Actor)   ?1797-1845
    (sc) 20.1.-14.6.1824; *1.-12.2.1836; *9.-13.1.1837; *2.-6.9.1839.
Byrne, Miss Eleanor (Singer)   -1821
    *23.2.-2.3.1820.
Campbell, Mrs.—see Wallis, Miss Tryphosa.
Campbell's Minstrels
    *19.-23.7.1860 (Bond, Joseph Crocker, H. Drummond, C. H. Fox, Gough, Walter
    Neville, Master J. Ritter, West).
Caremoli, Mademoiselle (Singer)
    *27. & 28.9.1838.
Catalani, Madame Angelica (Singer)   1780-1849
    *20. & 27.2.1809 (Italian Opera Co.); *4.-15.2.1825; *10.11.1828 (Concert);
    *27.2.-3.3.1829.
Cathcart, James Faucit (Actor)   1828-1902
    (sc) 29.12.1846-?19.3.1847; *21.8.-1.9.1854 (Princess's Theatre Co.); *9.-
    20.4.1860; *25.-28.1.1867.
Caulfield, H. E. (Actor)
    *20. & 27.2.1804; *4.10.-5.11.1804; (sc) 9.10.1805-2.7.1806.
Celeste, Madame Celine (Actress)   1814-1882
    *17.-21.3.1834; *18.-26.9.1834; *12.-16.3. & 21. & 23.3.1838; *1.-9.9.1841;
    *3. & 10.3.1842; *11.-18.7.1842; *1.9.1842; *27.2.-10.3.1843; *25.-29.9.1843;
    *6.-10.1.1845; *18.-25.5.1846; *7.-18.5.1855; *22.10.-2.11.1855; *27.-
    31.10.1856; *15.-26.2.1858; *28.2.-4.3.1859; *9.-13.5.1859; *13.-17.5.1861;
    *17.-21.2.1862; *17.-21.3.1862; *23.-28.2.1863; *28.11.-9.12.1864; *6.-
    17.2.1865.
Cerrito, Fanny (Dancer)   1817-1909
    *29. & 30.8.1844; *30.8.1847.
Chalon (Conjuror)
    *21.-24.1.1823.
Chap (Maître de ballet)
    *17. & 18.10.1826 (with pupils); *27.10. & 3.11.1826 (with pupils).
Chapman, Miss Patty (Actress)   ?1830-1912
    *28.5.1858 (as Miss Marlowe); *9.-20.4.1860 [with sister, Miss N. Chapman];
    *23.-28.1.1867.
Chappell (Pantaloon)
    *26.12.1853-27.1.1854.
Chapuis, Mademoiselle Adele (Dancer)
    *31.8.-7.9.1846 (as Mademoiselle Adele; Flora Fabbri's Co.); *30.8. & 3.9.1847.
Charles, Miss (Actress)
    *20., 21. & 28.3., 4. & 5.4.1843.
Chatterly, William Simmons (Actor)   1787-1821
    (sc) 2.10.1811-?20.7.1812; (sc) 28.9.1812-?21.7.1813; (sc) 27.9.1813-5.8.1814;
    (sc) 26.9.1814-12.7.1815; (sc) 27.9.1815-27.5.1816; (sc) 7.10.1816-26.5.1817;
    *14.-22.6.1820.
Chatterly, Mrs. L.—see Simeon, Miss Louisa.
Childe, Mrs. (Singer)
    *12.-28.10.1812.
Chinese Jugglers from the Court of Pekin
    *21. & 25.-27.9.1821; *2.6.1824 (one only).
Chute, John Coleman (Actor)   1818-1913
    (sc) Sept. 1841; (sc) 21.9.1842 et al.; (sc) ?31.8.-?29.9.1843; (sc) 29.8.-
    30.9.1844; (sc) ?14.1.-?14.2.1850 (as Blewitt); (sc) 1.4.-?June 1850 (as Blewitt);
    (sc) ?14.1.-?8.5.1851 (as Blewitt); (sc) 9.-11.6.1851 (as Blewitt); (sc) ?13.10.-
    2.12.1851; (sc) 20.9.-14.12.1852 (as Blewitt); (sc) ?10.1.-23.5.1853 (as Blewitt);

(sc) 19.9.-16.12.1853; (sc) 4.1.-12.6.1854; (sc) 18.9.-18.12.1854; (sc) 28.12.1854-19.6.1855; (sc) 2.10.-14.12.1855; (sc) ?7.1.-19.5.1856; *13.-17.8.1860 (Melville's Co.).

Clarke, Miss (Rope-dancer)
*27.12.1821-8.1.1822; *15.-21.9.1824; *26.12.1834 & 5.-13.1.1835 (as Mademoiselle Clarkini).

Cleaver, Miss (Actress)
*28.8.-8.9.1837; *7.-?13.5.1845.

Clement, Master (Violinist)   1780-1842
*10.1.1791.

Cleveland, Miss Louisa (Actress)   -1902
*27.8.-11.9.1857 (Leigh Murray's Co.); (sc) 21.9.-21.12.1857; (sc) ?29.12.1857-3.5.1858; (sc) 12.-20.5.1858; (sc) 13.9.-17.12.1858; (sc) 30.12.1858-9.2.1859; *6.5.1859; (sc) 17.9.-14.12.1860; (sc) 24.12.1860-9.5.1861; *1.-13.12.1862.

Cline (Tight-rope performer)
*26.4.-3.5.1826.

Coates, Robert ("Romeo") (Amateur)   1772-1848
*10.12.1816.

Coleman, John (Actor)   1831-1904
(sc) ?28.12.1848-7.5.1849; (sc) ?7.1.-6.5.1850; *9.-18.12.1861.

Coleman, "Picaninni" (Actor)
*8.-12.3.1841.

Colinson, Mademoiselle (Dancer)
*1.-5.6.1857 (Drury Lane Ballet Co.); (sc) 20.9.-19.11.1858.

Collins, Miss Clementina Hayward (Actress)
*20.1. & 10.2.1794.

Collins, John (Actor/Singer)   1804-1874
*1.-7.9.1840.

Coney (Mime/Animal trainer)
*10.-16.4.1828 (with his dog, Bruce).

Conway, Frederick Bartlett (Actor)   1819-1875
(sc) 6.7.1840 et al.; *16.-27.9.1861.

Conway, Mrs. Sarah, née Crocker (Actress)   1834-1878
*16.-27.3.1861.

Conway, William Augustus (Actor)   1789-1828
*25.9.-9.10.1815; *24.3.1817; *23.-30.3.1818.

Cooke, George Frederick (Actor)   1756-1812
*18.12.1801; *5.4.1802; *30.8.-13.9.1802; *24.3. & 7.-18.4.1806; *15.-24.6.1808; *28.11.-12.12.1808.

Cooke, Miss Harriet (later Mrs. Waylett) (Actress/Singer)   1798-1851
(sc) 2.10.1816-30.6.1817; (as Mrs. Waylett:) *14.-21.9.1829; *12.-16.2.1838; *2.-6.4.1838; *1.-8.10.1838; *14.-18.9.1840; *21.-26.4.1841; *29.1.-2.2. & 9.2.1844.

Cooke, Master Henry (Child actor)
*15. & 16.9.1841; *2.-21.9.1842.

Cooke, Thomas Potter (Actor)   1786-1864
*7.-14.2.1831.

Cooke, Thomas Simpson (Singer)   1782-1848
*26.9.-31.10.1814 (with Mrs. Cooke); *23.1.-27.2.1815; *4.2.1816; *25.8.-3.9.1817 (with Mrs. Cooke).

Cooper, Miss Adeline (Singer)
(sc) 31.8.-?14.10.1840; *25.2.-1.3.1841.

Cooper, John (Actor)   1790-1870
*25.-29.8.1834; *11.1.-5.2.1847.

Corri, Mrs. Anna, née Adami (Singer)   1799-1867
*2.-?9.9.1844.

Corri, Master Haydn (Singer) ?1844-?1876
 *30.6. & 1.7.1859.
Corri, M. (Clown)
Corri, Mrs. (M.), née Davis (Columbine)
 *31.3.-18.4.1823.
Corri, Patrick (Singer) 1820-1876
 *22.-26.3.1847; *28.1.-5.2.1856 (English Opera Co.); *6.-7.3.1856 (English Opera Co.).
Corri, P. Haydn (Singer) 1785-1860
 *2.-?9.9.1844.
Corri, Miss Rosalie (Singer) 1803-1876
 *20.-28.3.1821.
Courtenay (Piper) -1794
 *14.-18.10.1793.
Coveney, Miss (Singer) ?1818-1838
 *2.-9.4.1829.
Cowell, Samuel Houghton (Entertainer) 1820-1864
 *30.6. & 1.7.1859.
Coyne, Gardiner (Actor)
 *15.-26.10.1866; *25.3.-5.4.1867.
Craven, Henry Thornton (Actor) 1818-1905
Craven, Mrs. (H. T.) (Actress)
 *11.-15.9.1865.
Creswick, William (Actor) 1813-1888
 *13.5.1839 (billed as 2nd app.); *29.8.-18.9.1843; *22.5.1848.
Curioni, Alberico (Singer) 1785-1875
 *8.3.1827 (Concert); *29.11.1827 (Concert); *21.9.1837.
Cushman, Miss Charlotte (Actress) 1816-1876
 *6.-10.10.1845; *14.-22.9.1846; *1.2.1848; *16.-20.10.1848; *28.2.-2.3.1855; *12.-14.12.1855; *7.11.1856.
Cushman, Miss Susan (Actress) 1822-1859
 *14.-22.9.1846.
Cushnie, Mademoiselle Annie (Dancer)
 *20.11.-1.12.1854 (with sister Therese); *1.-12.10.1855 (Drury Lane Ballet Co., with sisters Hannah and Therese); *19.-27.5.1864 (Swanborough Burlesque Co.).
Cuthbert, Miss I. (Actress/Singer)
 (sc) ?29.12.1849-6.5.1850; (sc) 2.9.-?Oct. 1850; (sc) ?Dec. 1850-12.5.1851; (sc) 7.10.-?28.11.1851; (sc) ?Dec. 1851-?22.3.1852; *27.8.-11.9.1857 (Leigh Murray's Co.).
Danseuses Viennoises (Directress: Josephine Weiss)
 *3-14.11.1845; *23. & 24.2.1846.
Davidge, George B. (Actor) 1793-1842
 (sc) 7.-16.6.1813; (sc) 27.9.1813-8.8.1814; (sc) 26.9.1814-10.7.1815; *28.1.-1.2.1839.
Davison, Mrs.—see Duncan, Miss Maria.
Davis's Equestrian Troupe
 *22.11.-17.12.1824 (Bolton, W. Brown, Darnley, Davis, W. Davis, Fillingham, Freelove, Jones, Lightfoot, Makeen, Pearce, Smith, Southby, Steadman, Williams, Yates; Miss Darnley, Mrs. Fillingham, Miss Lightfoot, Mrs. Makeen, Miss Peter, Mrs. Yates).
Dawson, Master (Child prodigy) ?1799-
 *16.10. & 1.-8.11.1805 (with sisters Misses Dawson, S. Dawson and J. Dawson [16.10.1805 only] and father [6. & 8.11.1805 only]).
"Deani, Herr" (Dean) (Clown)
 *26.12.1856-29.1.1857; *26.12.1857-29.1.1858; *8. & 9.9.1859.
Decour (Acrobat)
 *31.8.-8.9.1821.

D'Egville, Peter (Dancer)
(sc) 10.6.-13.9.1776; *16.1.1792; *12.6.1797.
D'Egville, Miss Fanny (Dancer)
D'Egville, Master George (Dancer)
D'Egville, Miss Sophia (Dancer)
*16.1.1792 (Fanny and George); *12.6.1797 (Fanny and Sophia).
Delavan (Clown)
*26.12.1853-31.1.1854; *16. & 17.2.1854 (with dog Nero and pupils); *26.12.1854-31.1.1855 (with his wife [29.-31.1.1855 only] and his sons [31.1.1855 only]).
Delavanti (Singer)
27.2.1850 ?et al.
Delvoir, Master (Juvenile Pantaloon)
*26.12.1853-27.1.1854.
Denvil, Henry Gaskell (Actor)   1804-1866
*7.-11.9.1835; *4.-22.1.1836.
Desarais (Animal trainer)
*9.-27.1.1854 (with dogs and monkeys).
Desborough, Miss Juliet (Actress)   1837-1892
*21.8.-1.9.1854 (Princess's Theatre Co.); (sc) 19.1.-27.5.1863; *2.-13.9.1867 (Charles Dillon's Co.).
Deulin Family (Pantomimists)
*1.-16.4.1850 (Caldi, Deulin, J. Deulin, Charles Stilt, Master Stilt, Mademoiselle Theodore).
Dickons, Mrs. Maria, née Poole (Singer)   c.1770-1833
*2.-16.1.1809; *3.4.1809; *1.-15.1.1810; *4. & 5.7.1814.
Dillon, Charles (Actor)   1819-1881
*9.-20.4.1855; *30.11.-4.12.1857; *14.-18.3.1859; *2.-13.9.1867 (Own Co.).
Charles Dillon's Company
*2.-13.9.1867 (C. W. Barry, Blythe, Charles Dillon [q.v.], R. Edgar, E. Fossett, Haywell, C. Horsman, C. Jones, Mondyar, Murray, J. Seyton, Taylor, E. M. Warde; Miss Juliet Desborough [q.v.], Miss Edgar, Miss Harwell, Miss Hemmings, Mrs. C. Horsman, Miss Johnson, Miss Lawrence, Miss Leigh, Miss Lilley, Miss F. Wallis, Miss Warde, Miss Watkins, Miss Webster).
Dimmon (Acrobat)
*5. & 9.9.1823.
Distin Family (Sax-horn players and vocalists)
*19.-21. & 30.10.1840; *11. & 12.8.1845; *26.8.1846; *10.6.1847; *11. & 14.8.1848; *15.2.1850; *6.10.1851.
Dohler, Theodor (Pianist)   1814-1856
*27. & 28.9.1838.
Don, Sir William Henry, Bart. (Actor)   1825-1862
*20.-24.4.1857; *9.-17.11.1857; *7.12.1857; *15.-19.3.1858; *14.-18.2.1859.
Don, Lady—see Saunders, Miss Emily.
Dorus-Gras, Madame Julie Aimée Josephe (Singer)   1805-1896
*1.10.1840.
Doughty, James (Clown)   1818-1913
(sc) 26.12.1838-?6.5.1839; *26.10.1840; *9.11.1840; *6.-15.11.1854 (with dogs); *24.12.1861-7.2.1862 (with dogs).
Dowton, William (Actor)   1764-1851
*3.6.1816; *25.8.1817; *3.-11.5.1819; *17.5.1823; *12.-16.1., 26.-30.1., 6.2., 16.-20.2., 2.-16.3.1835.
Driver, William (Harlequin)
*26.12.1859-8.2.1860.
Drury Lane Ballet Company
*1.-12.10.1855 (Milano, W. Seymour; Miss Ada Barnes, Miss Craven, Mademois-

elle Annie Cushnie [*q.v.*], Mademoiselle Hannah Cushnie, Mademoiselle Therese Cushnie, Miss Jackson, Miss White); *1.-5.6.1857 (Edouard, Harry Sonne, E. W. Veroni; Mademoiselle Caerson, Mademoiselle Colinson [*q.v.*], Mademoiselle Copeland or Copelarde, Mademoiselle Edal or Eval, Mademoiselle Huddart, Mademoiselle Leverson, Mademoiselle Lloyd, Mademoiselle Marie [*q.v.*], Mademoiselle Stanley, Mademoiselle Taylor, Mademoiselle E. or J. Taylor).

Ducrow, Andrew (Equestrian/Acrobat)   1793-1842
*19.-28.12.1814 (as "Young Ducrow"); *25.3. & 1.4.1816 (as "Young Ducrow"); *15.3.-19.4.1824 (Ducrow's Equestrian Troupe); *3.11.1826 (Ducrow's Equestrian Troupe); *10.-13.11.1835 (Ducrow and West's Riding Troupe).

Ducrow and West's Riding Troupe
*19.10.-13.11.1835 (Avery, Bullock, Fillingham, Foster, Frazer, Rice, W. West, Widdicombe; Miss Blackett, Madame Simon; Andrew Ducrow [*q.v.*] and Miss Louisa Ducrow [from 10.11.1835]; with Les Quatre Antipodeans [up to 6.11.1835] and the Chinese Wonders [9.11.1835]).

Ducrow's Equestrian Troupe
*15.3.-9.4.1824 (Buckley, Cope, Dainey, Andrew Ducrow [*q.v.*], J. Ducrow, Fillingham, Hillar, Lyon, Mackintosh, Smith, Tomkins, Vollar, Webb, Widecomb, Yates; Mrs. Burrow, Mrs. Frazer). *16.10.-3.11.1826 (Fillingham, Pope, Sanders, Sherlock, Watkins, Widecomb, Yates; Master Partleton [*q.v.*] and Master H. Partleton [from 26.10.1826]; Andrew Ducrow [*q.v.*] [3.11.1826 only]).

Duncan, Miss Maria (later Mrs. Davison) (Actress/Singer)   1783-1858
*22. & 26.6.1812; *28.9.-5.10.1812; (as Mrs. Davison:) *24.4.1815; *10.-21.2.1823; *27.2.-10.3.1824.

Dunn, T. C. (Actor)
*26.12.1837-5.1.1838; *19.-22. & 30.3.1838.

Durand, Charles (Singer)   ?1824-1904
*5.-23. & 30.3.1855; *9.-20.4.1855; *2.-13.3.1857 (Grand National English Opera Co.); *12. & 15.5.1857 (Grand National English Opera Co.); *2.-12.2.1858 (National English Opera Co.); *12.-23.2.1866 (Grand English Opera Co.); *13.-24.5.1867 (Grand English Opera Co.).

Duville (Harlequin)
*24.12.1861-7.2.1862.

Dyer, Miss (later Mrs. Haigh) (Singer)
*2.-13.3.1857 (Grand National English Opera Co.); *12. & 15.5.1857 (Grand National English Opera Co.); (as Mrs. Haigh:) *22.-26.3.1858; (as Madame Haigh-Dyer:) *31.8.-4.9.1863 (Rosenthal Grand Opera Co.); *30.11.-1.12.1863 (Rosenthal Grand Opera Co.).

Eburne, Miss Margaret (Actress)   1829-1903
*10.6.1861; (sc) 30.9.-24.12.1861.

Edwin, Mrs. Elizabeth Rebecca, née Richards (Actress)   c.1771-1854
(sc) 11.10.1797-?25.7.1798; (sc) 24.9.1798-29.7.1799; (sc) 23.9.1799-21.7.1800; (sc) 22.9.1800-3.7.1801; (sc) 4.9.1801-?2.7.1802; (sc) 30.8.1802-?4.7.1803; (sc) 19.9.1803-9.7.1804; *27.9.-20.10.1806; *14.4.-12.5.1819.

Egan, Pierce (Actor/Dramatist)   1772-1849
*17.-19.3.1835.

Elephant of Siam (Mademoiselle D'jek; trainer: M. Huguet)
*12.-19.4.1830; *3.-7.5.1830.

Ellar, M. (Harlequin)
*24.4.-?3.5.1848.

Ellar, Thomas (Harlequin)   1780-1842
*3.11.-5.12.1814; *6.-27.11. & 18.12.1815; (sc) 13.11.1816-17.3.1817; *30.8.-11.9.1824; *30.8.-7.9.1830.

Elliott (Actor)
*11.-14.3.1834; *27.12.1834-14.1.1835.

Elliston, Robert William (Actor)   1774-1831
(sc) 25.4.1791; (sc) ?14.10.1793-?28.7.1794; (sc) ?13.10.1794-?24.7.1795; (sc)

21.9.1795-8.8.1796; (sc) 5.10.1796-7.8.1797; (sc) ?2.10.1797-?25.7.1798; (sc) 24.9.1798-26.7.1799; (sc) ?4.10.1799-?23.6.1800; (sc) 29.9.1800-6.7.1801; (sc) 31.8.1801-?2.7.1802; (sc) 3.9.1802-29.4.1803; (sc) 19.9.1803-7.5.1804; *20.-29.11.1809; *5.-19.3.1810; *10.-21.12.1810; *18.-25.2.1811; *4.-18.11. & 2.12.1811; *13.6.1814.

Elphinstone, Miss Emma (Actress)   ?1808-1881
*26.9.-?5.10.1837; *6.-31.1.1840.

Elssler, Fanny (Dancer)   1810-1884
*1. & 17.5.1843.

Elsworthy, Miss Maria (Actress)   1825-1879
*3.-5.3.1856.

Emery, John (Actor)   1777-1822
*26. & 27.2.1821.

English Opera Company
*17.-28.9.1855 (B. Bowler, Helder [i.e. Whitworth, q.v.], Holder, George Honey [q.v.], Power, St. Albyn [q.v.], J. A. Shaw, Oliver Summers; Miss Hodson, Mademoiselle Nau, Miss M. Stanley, Miss Emily Weymouth).
*28.1.-5.2.1856 (Bowler, Coleman, P. Corri [q.v.], Gledhill, Gould, Green, J. Martin, St. Albyn [q.v.], Shaw, Oliver Summers; Miss Emma Cowlrick, Miss Hodson, Mademoiselle Nau, Miss Kate Warrington).
*6. & 7.3.1856 (B. Bowler, Coleman, P. Corri [q.v.], Gledhill, Gould, Green, St. Albyn [q.v.], J. A. Shaw, Oliver Summers; Miss Hodson, Mademoiselle Nau, Miss Kate Warrington).

Ethiopian Serenaders
*8. & 9.9.1846 (Germon, Harrington, Pell, Stanwood, White).
*12.-14.7.1847 (Bowter, Palmer, Sefton, Sweeny, Walford).
*2.-12.10.1848 (Briggs, Everton, Irwin, Juba, Ludlow, Pell, Valentine).

Evans, David (Actor)
(sc) 12.9.-16.12.1853; (sc) 30.7. & 20.8.1855; (sc) ?18.9.-13.12.1855; (sc) 26.12.1855-19.5.1856; (sc) 29.9.-15.12.1856; (sc) 26.12.1856-5.5.1857; (sc) 21.9.-21.12.1857; (sc) 26.12.1857-3.5.1858; (sc) 13.7. & 3.8.1858; (sc) 6.9.-16.12.1858; (sc) 27.12.1858-20.5.1859; (sc) 13.-27.6.1859; (sc) 8. & 9.9.1859; 26.9.-16.12.1859; (sc) 26.12.1859-30.5.1860; (sc) 24.9.-14.12.1860; (sc) 24.12.1860-24.5.1861; *18.8.-3.9.1862 (Stirling's Co.); *29.8.-9.9.1864 (Addison's Co.).

Everett, George (Actor)   ?1823-1881
*21.8.-1.9.1854 (Princess's Theatre Co.); *9.-20.4.1860; *23.-28.1.1867.

Fabbri, Flora (Dancer)
*31.8.-7.9.1846 (with Bretin, W. H. Payne, Ridgeway, T. Ridgeway; Mademoiselle Adele [Chapuis, q.v.], Mademoiselle Louise [q.v.], Miss A. Payne; and Her Majesty's Theatre Corps de Ballet - Misses Assiote [q.v.], Ada Barnes, Lee, Moreton, Motte and Presdee).

Fabri (Singer)
*10. & 11.5.1825.

Fane, Miss Marie Blanche (Actress)   -1858
*10.-14.3.1851.

Farrell, Henry (Actor)
(sc) 29.9.-16.12.1856; (sc) 30.12.1856-29.4.1857; (sc) 21.9.-21.12.1857; (sc) 29.12.1857-22.4.1858; (sc) 13.9.-17.12.1858; (sc) ?30.12.1858-20.5.1859; (sc) 13.-15.6.1859; (sc) 26.9.-16.12.1859; *19.-27.5.1864 (Swanborough Burlesque Co.).

Farren, William (Actor)   1786-1861
*13.3.1835; *27.-31.8.1838; *16.-23.9.1844.

Faucit, Miss Helen Saville (Actress)   1815-1898
*28.8.-2.9.1843; *5.-9.10.1846.

Faust (Sprite)
*24.12.1863-5.2.1864.

Fawcett, John (Actor)   1769-1837
   *4.5.1812; *5. & 7.7.1813; *12.-16.9.1825.
Featherstone, Miss Isabella (later Mrs. Paul) (Singer/Entertainer)   1833-1879
   *2.-27.10.1854; (as Mrs. Paul:) *3.-14.8.1857.
Female American Serenaders
   *16. & 17.8.1847 (Mesdames Cora, Jumba, Miami, Womba, Woski and Yarico).
Fernandes (Lyre-player)
   *10.3.1800.
Feron, Miss Elizabetta (Singer)
   *30.9.-18.10.1811; *11.-17.3.1828.
Field, Henry (Pianist/Singer)   -1848
   *20.2.1823 (Concert); *11.12.1823 (Concert); *22.1.1824 (Concert); *19.5.1824;
   *16.6.1824;   *3.6.1826; *11.10.1826; *5.10.1827; *13., 15. & 17.3.1828;
   *20.5.1828; *12., 14. & 16.12.1831 (Concerts).
Fisher, Miss Catherine (Child actress)   1792-
   *9. & 30.12.1805 & 27.1.1806 (with her father, a Harlequin [30.12.1805 only]);
   *26.5.1806.
Fisher, Miss Clara (Child actress)   1811-1898
   *18.5.1818; *2.-13.9.1822; *1.-13.9.1823; *12.-22.2.1826.
Fitzgerald (Conjuror)
   *23. & 24.4.1840.
Fitzwilliam, Mrs. Fanny Elizabeth, née Copeland (Actress)   1801-1854
   *16.-20.1.1837; *5.-9.10.1840; *9.-13.1.1843; *13.-31.3.1843; *18.-20.7.1843;
   *11.4.1844; *10. & 11.9.1846; *28.10.-2.11.1847; *8.-19.1.1849.
Flexmore, Richard (Dancer)
   *9.12.1811-1.1.1812; *30.8.-3.9.1825.
Foote, Miss Maria (Actress)   1798-1867
   *27.8.-26.9.1817; *21.3.1825; *14.-18.4.1825; *5.-9.9.1825; *24.2.-1.3.1826;
   *19.-23.3.1827; *18.-22.2.1828; *15.-22.9.1828; *10.4.1829; *8.-15.2.1830;
   *17.-21.2.1831.
Forbes, Mrs. (W. C.) (Actress)
   *28.3.-1.4.1859.
Fornasari, Luciano (Singer)   ?1808-1846
   *27.8.1844 (Concert); *3.9.1845.
Forrest, Edwin (Actor)   1806-1872
   *14.-18.4.1845.
Fosbrooke, William (Actor)   1830-1898
   (SC) ?11.10.-2.12.1851; (SC) 2.-23.2.1852 et al.; (SC) 27.12.1852-?25.4.1853;
   (SC) 19.9.-16.12.1853; (SC) 26.12.1853-6.6.1854; (SC) 18.9.-18.12.1854; (SC)
   26.12.1854-15.6.1855; (SC) 1.10.-14.12.1855; (SC) 26.12.1855-19.5.1856; (SC)
   29.9.-16.12.1856; (SC) 26.12.1856-29.4.1857; (SC) 21.9.-21.12.1857; (SC) 26.12.
   1857-28.5.1858; (SC) 6.9. & 13.9.-14.12.1858; (SC) 27.12.1858-20.5.1859; (SC)
   13.-15. & 27.6.1859; (SC) 26.9.-16.12.1859; (SC) 4.1.-30.5.1860; (SC) 3.10.-14.12.
   1860; (SC) 24.12.1860-17.5.1861; *18.8.-3.9.1862 (Stirling's Co.); (SC) 21.9.-
   18.12.1863; (SC) 31.12.1863-17.6.1864; *29.8.-9.9.1864 (Addison's Co.); (SC)
   16.9.-16.12.1864; (SC) 26.12.1864-26.5.1865; *14.-16., 22. & 23.6.1865 (Melville-
   Rouse Co.); (SC) 11.9.-19.12.1865; (SC) 26.12.1865-2.5.1866; *21.5.-1.6.1866
   (Melville's Co.); (SC) 17.9.-19.12.1866; (SC) 24.12.1866-10.5.1867.
Franks (Singer)
   (SC) 28.8.-26.9.1834; *18.9.1837; *6.-10.4.1840.
Frazer (Singer)
   *25.2.-1.3.1841.
Frederico, Francis (Harlequin)
   *27.12.1852-?18.1.1853.
French Opera Comique
   *28.5.1850 (Bugnet, Chateaufort, Josset, Lac, Soyer; Mademoiselle Charton,

Mademoiselle Danhausser, Mademoiselle Guichard, *et al.*).

Galer, Eliot John Norman (Singer)   1828-1901
  *15.-26.9.1856; *9.-13.2.1857 (London Grand Opera Co.); *27.8.-7.9.1860
  (Opera in English); *20.-23.9.1864.

Gallaway (Harlequin)
  *26.12.1828-16.1.1829.

Garcia (Pantaloon)
  *11.-15.9.1827.

Garcia, Madame Eugenia (Singer)   1818-1880
  *5.-7.6.1844; *5.-12.9.1845.

Gattie, Henry (Actor)   1774-1844
  (sc) 8.10.1804-15.7.1805; (sc) 30.9.1805-14.7.1806; (sc) 1.10.1806-17.7.1807;
  (sc) 28.9.1807-8.8.1808; (sc) 3.10.1808-31.7.1809; (sc) 2.10.1809-23.7.1810;
  (sc) 3.10.1810-22.7.1811; (sc) 2.10.1811-?20.7.1812; (sc) 28.9.1812-6.7.1813;
  *30.8.-24.9.1824.

George, Miss Amelia Angelica (Singer)   1803-
  (sc) 4.1.-14.6.1822; *9. & 23.1. & 20.2. 1823 (Concerts); *11.12.1823 (Concert);
  *22.1. & 4.3.1824 (Concerts); *3.2.1825 (Concert); *29.12.1825 (Concert);
  *7.3.1827; *17.5.1827; *25.3.-27.5.1833.

Georgette, Mademoiselle (Dancer)
  *9.-20.3.1835; *20.-23.5.1836.

German Minstrels
  *?18.-21.1.1831 (Michel and Madame Boai [*q.v.*], Engels, &c).

Gill, Mrs. Charles—*see* Vining, Miss Fanny.

Giroux (Dancer)
  *3.-29.11.1809; *9.12.1811-1.1.1812; *26.12.1814-23.2.1815; *12.4.1822.

Giroux, Miss Caroline F. (Dancer)
  *3.-29.11.1809; *9.12.1811-1.1.1812; (sc) 26.9.-28.10.1814; (sc) 9.12.1816-
  5.5.1817; *8.9.-15.10.1817; *3.4.-5.5., 22.5., 7. & 12.6.1820; *21.2. & 28.2.-
  12.4.1822; *22.9.1824.

Giroux, Miss Cecilia (Dancer)   -1856
  *3.-29.11.1809; *9.12.1811-1.1.1812; (sc) 26.9.1814-16.6.1815; (sc) 25.9.-
  27.12.1815; (sc) 12.2.-27.5.1816; (sc) 13.11.1816-6.1.1817; (sc) 17.2.-5.5.1817;
  *8.-12.12.1817; *5.5.1820; *12.4.1822.

Giroux, Miss F. (Dancer)
  *2.-29.11.1809; *9.12.1811-1.1.1812; (sc) 26.9.-28.10.1814; (sc) 25.9.-27.12.1815;
  (sc) 12.2.-3.6.1816; (sc) 15.11.1816-5.5.1817.

Giroux, Miss Louisa (Dancer)
  (sc) 17.2.-5.5.1817; *8.9.-15.10.1817; *3.4.-5.5., 22.5., 7. & 12.6.1820; *21.2. &
  14.3.-12.4.1822; *22.9.1824.

Giubelei, Madame Augustine Proche (Dancer)   1813-1848
  *1.-16.1.1846.

Glover, Mrs.—*see* Betterton, Miss Julia.

Goldsmid, Lionel (Actor)
  *4.-15.1.1836; *20.9.1836; *4.4.1842; *2.-9.5.1842.

Goll (Harlequin)
  *23.1.-1.2.1822; *2.-10.2.1824; *26.-30.12.1825; *16.-20.1.1826.

Gomersal, Alexander Edward (Actor)   1788-1862
  *3.11.1826; *17.-28.11.1851.

Gordon, Miss Harriet (Singer)   ?1835-1869
  *2.-6.2.1857.

Gouffee (Animal impersonator)
  *26.-30.12.1826.

Gough, Miss Catherine (Actress)
  *3.12.1798 & 7.1.1799.

Grammani (Clown)
*14.1.-7.2.1851.
Grand English Opera Co.—*see* Grand National English Opera Co.
Grand National English Opera Company (including Grand National Opera Co.
and National English Opera Co.)
*2.-13.3.1857 (Grand National English Opera Co.) (Aynsley Cook, Charles
Durand [*q.v.*], Grosvenor, Grundy, Henry Haigh [*q.v.*], Manvers, Muller, Newman, Temple; Miss Cronin, Miss Dyer [*q.v.*], Miss Lucy Escott, Miss Hammond,
Miss Lanza [*q.v.*]).
*12. & 15.5.1857 (Grand National Opera Co.) (Aynsley Cook, Charles Durand
[*q.v.*], Grosvenor, Grundy, Henry Haigh [*q.v.*], Manvers, Muller, Newman, J.
Temple, Ward; Miss Cronin, Miss Dyer [*q.v.*], Miss Lucy Escott, Miss Hammond, Miss Lanza [*q.v.*], Miss Leng).
*2.-12.2.1858 (National English Opera Co.) (Aynsley Cook, Charles Durand
[*q.v.*], Grosvenor, Grundy, Henry Haigh [*q.v.*], Manvers, Mulley, Newman, J.
R. W. Temple; Miss Lucy Escott, Miss Emma Heywood, Miss E. Hodson,
Miss Annie Leng, Miss Mortimer, Miss Harriet Payne).
*12.-23.2.1866 (Grand English Opera Co.) (F. Burgess, C. Durand [*q.v.*], Gros-
venor, R. de Lancy, J. Manley, W. Parkinson, A. Shaw. J. or T. Tempest; Miss
A. Alessandri, Miss Jenny Baur, Miss Hodson, Miss Emma Willing).
*13.-24.5.1867 (Grand English Opera Co.) (Baildon, Bentley, Burgess, Charles
Durand [*q.v.*], Goodwin, de Lancy, H. Lewens, W. Parkinson, T. Tempest, W.
M. Terrott; Mrs. Berry, Miss Helen Clayton, Miss Blanche Cole, Miss Collins,
Miss Glover, Miss Hodson, Madame Florence Lancia, Miss Tempest, Miss
Walker).
Grand National Opera Co.—*see* Grand National English Opera Co.
Grand Opera Co.—*see* Italian Opera Co.
Grattan, Henry Plunkett (Actor)   1808-1889
Grattan, Mrs. Emily, née Byron (Actress/Singer)   1812-1849
*11.-15.2.1839.
Gray's Fantoccini
*13.-18.9.1824.
Green, J. (Clown)
*26.12.1867-10.1.1868.
Grey, Douglas (Actor)
(sc) 21.9.-21.12.1857; (sc) 26.12.1857-28.5.1858; (sc) 6.9. & 13.9.-17.12.1858;
(sc) 27.12.1858-20.5.1859, 15.6.1859; (sc) 26.9.-16.12.1859; (sc) 26.12.1859-
30.5.1860; *13.-17. & 29.8.1860 (Melville's Co.); (sc) 17.9.-14.12.1860; (sc)
24.12.1860-24.5.1861; (sc) 16.9.-18.12.1861; (sc) 24.12.1861-16.5.1862; (sc)
15.9.-20.12.1862; (sc) 24.12.1862-27.5.1863; *24.-28.8.1863 (Melville-Rouse
Co.); (sc) 21.9.-15.12.1863; (sc) 24.12.1863-18.5.1864.
Grimaldi, Joseph (Clown)   1778-1837
*3.11.-5.12.1814; *6.-27.11.1815.
Grimaldi, Master Joseph Samuel William (Juvenile Clown)   1802-1832
*27.11.1815.
Grisi, Carlotta (Dancer)   1819-1899
*30.1.-4.2.1850.
Grisi, Giulia (Singer)   1811-1869
*31.8.1835 (Concert); *19.8.1840 (Concert); *21.9.1843 (Concert); *23.9.1846
(Concert); *13.-17.10.1856 (Italian Opera Co.); *15. & 18.10.1861 (Italian
Opera Co.).
Grossmith, Master William Robert (Child prodigy)   1818-1880
*14.-17.3.1826.
Haigh, Henry (Singer)
*5.-23. & 30.3., 9.-20.4.1855; *2.-13.3.1857 (Grand National English Opera
Co.); *12. & 15.5.1857 (National English Opera Co.); *22.-26.3.1857.

Haigh, Mrs. Henry—*see* Dyer, Miss.
Haigh-Dyer, Madame—*see* Dyer, Miss.
Hammersley (Actor)
  *3.-18.3.1842.
Hammersley, Miss (Singer)
  *20.5.1825; *19.-23.9.1825; *1.-5.1.1827.
Hammond, W. J. (Actor)   ?1799-1848
  (SC) 16.1.-31.5.1822; (SC) 18.11.1822-23.5.1823; *8.-15.1.1838.
Harrison, William (Singer)   1813-1868
  *22. & 24.9.1845; *1.-12.4.1861 (Pyne & Harrison Opera Co.).
Hartland, Frederick (Clown)   1783-1852
  *22.1.-17.3.1817.
Harwood, James (Equestrian)   1816-1900
  *29.1.-2.2.1849 (with his mare, Black Bess).
Haymarket Company
  *23.-27.9.1850 (Bellingham, Braid [*q.v.*], William Clark, Coe, Ellis, Howe,
  Rogers, Charles Selby [*q.v.*], Tilbury; Mrs. Buckingham, Miss Coe, Mrs. Laura
  Seymour [*q.v.*], Mrs. Stanley, Mrs. Sturley, Miss Villars, Mrs. Villars).
  *5.-7.11.1850 (Braid [*q.v.*], William Clark, Clifford, Coe, Ellis, Howe, Lambert,
  Parselle; Mrs. Buckingham, Mrs. Coe, Mrs. L. Seymour [*q.v.*], Mrs. Stanley,
  Miss Vining).
Hays, Miss M. M. (Actress)
  *16.10.1848.
Henderson, Miss Marie (Actress)   1843-1902
  *26.5.1865; *31.5.1865 (Melville's Co.); *5.-9., 14.-16., 22. & 23.6.1865 (Mel-
  ville-Rouse Co.); *21.5.-1.6.1866 (Melville's Co.).
Hengler, "Young" (Acrobat)
  *8.-11.4.1851.
Henry, Miss (Singer)
Henry, Miss Maria (Singer)
  *30.6. & 1.7.1859.
Herbert, Miss Louisa (Actress)   ?1831-1921
  *15.11.1854; *7.-18.9.1863 (St. James's Theatre Co.); *16.-27.9.1867 (St.
  James's Theatre Co.).
Her Majesty's Theatre Opera Company—*see* Italian Opera
Heron, Miss Matilda (Child prodigy)   ?1835-1877
  *17.-27.2.1845 (with sister, Miss Fanny Heron [27.2.1845 only]).
Herrmann (Conjuror)
  *31.5.-7.6.1848.
Hervio Nano (Freak)
  *22.-26.10.1838.
Hill, Miss (Singer)
  *27.-30.4., 10.-18.5.1819; *22.6. & 12.7.1819; (SC) 30.8.-14.9.1819.
Hill, Mrs. (T.)—*see* Kelly, Miss H.
Hine, M. or E. L. (Singer)
  *27.2.-?16.3.1848.
Hogg (Clown)
  *26.12.1828-16.1.1829.
Holman, Joseph George (Actor)   1764-1817
  *19. & 26.11.1804; *27.9.-20.10.1806.
Honey, George (Actor)   1822-1880
  *17.-28.9.1855 (English Opera Co.); *1.-12.4.1861 (Pyne & Harrison Opera Co.).
Honey, Mrs. Laura (Actress/Singer)   ?1816-1843
  *21.-25.1.1839; *7.-11.10.1839; 10.-14.1.1842.
Hooper, Edward (Actor)   1774-1865
  (SC) 11.2.-?24.5.1833; *15.-29.10.1838 (with Mrs. Hooper).

Horn, Charles Edward (Singer)   1786-1849
  *7.-9.3.1831.
Horncastle, G. (Singer)
  *6.-10.4.1840; *4.-8.2.1850.
Howell (Harlequin)
  *11.-15., 24.-28.9.1827; *20.4.-1.5.1840.
Huddart, Miss Mary Amelia (later Mrs. Warner) (Actress) 1804-1854
  *5.-23.9.1836; (as Mrs. Warner:) *11.1.-5.2.1847; *10.5.1848.
Hudson, James (Actor)   1811-
  *27.-31.12.1847; *21.-25.2.1848.
Hughes, Master (Harpist)   ?1827-
  *17.9.1834.
Hughes, Miss Elizabeth (Singer)
  *18.3.-5.4.1816; *17.-21.9.1827; *23.-27.9.1828
Hughes, Miss Frances (Actress)   1822-1888
  (SC) ?13.1.-?31.5.1852; *25.6.-6.7.1855 (Lyceum Theatre Co.); *1.-9.9.1856
  (London Dramatic Co.); *28.8.-8.9.1865 (Prince of Wales Theatre Co.).
Huguet, M.—see The Elephant of Siam
Huline, James (Pantomimist)   1815-1890
  *21.8.-1.9.1854 (Princess's Theatre Co.); *24.12.1866-8.2.1867 (with sons, Mas-
  ters H. and J. Huline).
Hunt (Singer)
  *18.4.-4.5.1827; *14.-29.1.1828.
Hutchings (Actor)
Hutchings, Master (Singer)   1834-
  *19.-22.3.1839.
Idalie, Mademoiselle Ida (Dancer)
  *30.10.-10.11.1865.
Incledon, Charles Benjamin (Singer)   1763-1826
  (SC) 9.5.-25.7.1785; (SC) 3.10.1785-15.5.1786; (SC) 9.10.1786-14.5.1787; (SC)
  10.10.1787-12.5.1788; (SC) 26.9.1788-11.5.1789; (SC) 21.9.1789-?10.5.1790;
  *25.3.1793 (Concert); *12.1.1798; *22.12.1800-16.1.1801; *21. & 28.2.1803;
  *2.-9.4.1804; *15.8.1804; *31.12.1804; *4.-18.3.1805; *6.-20.1.1806; *16.-
  23.7.1810; *15. & 22.4.1811; *25.11.1811; *18.5.1812; *12.-19.5.1813; *21.10.-
  11.11.1816.
Irvine (Tight-rope performer)
  *14. & 15.2.1842.
Isaacs, Miss Rebecca (Singer)   ?1828-1877
  *10.-14.3.1856; *15.-26.9.1856 (London Grand Opera Co.); *9.-13.2.1857 (Lon-
  don Grand Opera Co.).
Italian Opera Company
  *20. & 27.2.1809 (managed by Madame Catalani [q.v.]. Bennett [Stock Com-
  pany], Miarteni; Mrs. Ashe, Madame Catalani [q.v.], Madame Miarteni;
  Madame O'Moran).
  *14.12.1853 (Attard, Chierini, Coleman, Formes, Gabusi, Gregario, Kuchler,
  Marinietti, Moelder, Reichardt; Mademoiselle Caradori, Mademoiselle Chierini,
  Miss F. Huddart, Mademoiselle Zimmermann).
  *13., 14. & 17.10.1856 (Albicini, Clerici, Gabussi, Galli, Gassier, Lorini, Mario
  [q.v.], Mattoni, Luigi Mei, Rovere; Madame Clerici, Madame Gassier, Madame
  Grisi [q.v.], Mademoiselle Sedlatzek).
  *21. & 24.8.1857 (Aldi, Belart, Beletti, Beneventano, Biro, Giuglini, Mercuriali,
  Riali, Rossi; Madame Fazio, Madame Piccolomini, Madame Rossi).
  *25.-27.11.1857 (Bartleman, Borchardt, Marianni, Mattoni, Pierini, Sims Reeves
  [q.v.], Tennant; Madame Borchardt, Madame Cherici, Madame Gassier, Mademoiselle Sedlatzek).
  *19. & 20.9.1859 (Badiali, Borchardt, Castelli, Corsi, Giuglini, Mercuriali, Via

letti; Madame Borchardt, Mademoiselle Delanese, Mademoiselle Titiens).
*15. & 18.10.1861 (Aspa, Bellini, Ciampi, Fallar, Galvani; Madame Borsi, Mademoiselle Dario, Madame Grisi [q.v.], Madame Lemoine).

Jackson, Miss (Actress)
  (SC) ?1.11.-14.12.1852; (SC) 27.12.1852-23.5.1853; (SC) 22.9.-25.11.1853; *9.8.1858 (Melville's Co.).

Jams, Mademoiselle Eugenie (?Elizabeth James) (Dancer)
  *30.1.-4.2.1850.

Jarman, Miss Frances Eleanor (later Mrs. Ternan) (Actress)   1803-1873
  (SC) 26.6., 3.7.1815; (SC) 27.12.1815-28.6.1816; (SC) 30.9.1816-23.6.1817; *2.-?11.7.1832; *21.-25.4.1834; (as Mrs. Ternan:) *25.-29.3.1844.

Johnson (Actor/Animal trainer)
  *10.-16.4.1828.

Johnson, Miss (Singer)
  *16.-20.4.1827.

Johnson, Deulin (Pantaloon)
  *24.12.1863-5.2.1864.

Johnston, Henry Erskine (Actor)   1777-1845
  *7.-11.5.1821; *16.-24.4.1822.

Johnstone, Mrs. (H.) (Actress)
  *20.4.-4.5.1807.

Johnstone, John Henry (Actor)   1749-1828
  *16. & 23.12.1805; *1.-12.10.1810.

Jones, Miss Ersser (Actress)
  *22.8.-6.9.1861 (Melville's Co.); (SC) 16.9.-14.10.1861.

Jones, Ersser (Actor)   1805-1877
  (SC) ?11.1.-?11.2.1850; *22.8.-6.9.1861 (Melville's Co.); *24.-28.8.1863 (Melville-Rouse Co.).

Jones, James (Clown)
  *?31.5.-28.6.1819; *2.-10.9.1819.

Jones, Miss Marion (later Mrs. George Gordon) (Actress)
  *24.-28.8.1863 (Melville-Rouse Co.); (SC) 21.9.-18.12.1863; (SC) 24.12.1863-18.5.1864; (as Mrs. Gordon:) (SC) 19.9.-13.10.1865; (SC) 17.9.-19.12.1866; (SC) 24.12.1866-10.5.1867; (SC) 11.11.-13.12.1867; (SC) 6.-14.1.1868.

Jordan, Mrs. Dorothy (Dora), née Bland (Actress)   1761-1816
  *10.4.-1.5.1809; *21.1.-11.2.1811; *11.-25.1.1813; *10.-31.1.1814.

Karl (Pantaloon)
  *14.1.-7.2.1851.

Kean, Charles John (Actor)   1811-1868
  *1.-6.9.1828; *15.-19.3.1830; *15.-19.2.1836; *11.-18.3.1839; *21.-28.9.1840; *25.-29.1.1841; *2.-5.3.1841; *16.-21.2.1842; *16.-23.1.1843; *17.2.1843; *8.-15.1.1844; *20.-30.1.1845; *3.-10.3.1845; *3.3.1848; *9.-20.4.1860; *5.-9.5.1862; *23.-28.1.1867.

Kean, Mrs. (C.)—see Tree, Miss Ellen.

Kean, Edmund (Actor)   ?1787-1833
  *10.-12.7.1815; *1. & 8.-11.7.1816; *2.1.1817; *23.6.1817; *5.-9.7.1819; *20.-22.3.1823; *27.9.-1.10.1830; *28.11.-7.12.1831.

Kean, Moses (Imitator)   -?1794
  *5.-19.1.1789.

Keeley, Robert (Actor)   1793-1869
Keeley, Mrs. Mary Ann, née Goward (Actress)   1806-1899
  *22.5.1840.

Keene—see Aldridge, Ira.

Kellino (Clown)
  *24.12.1862-21.2.1863 (with Young Kellino).

Kelly, Miss Frances Harriet (Actress)   1800-
   *27.1.-3.2.1823.
Kelly, Miss H. (later Mrs. T. Hill) (Actress)
   (sc) 30.10.1811-?20.7.1812; (sc) 2.10.1812-19.5.1813; (as Mrs. Hill:) *10.-
   14.4.1820; *31.12.1827-4.1.1828.
Kemble, Miss Adelaide (Singer)   1814-1879
   *25.8.1842 (Concert).
Kemble, Charles (Actor)   1775-1854
   *8.8.1808; *31.7.1809; *29.1.-5.2.1827; *4.-18.7.1831; *1.-4.9.1835.
Kemble, Miss Frances Anne (later Mrs. Butler) (Actress)   1809-1893
   *4.-18.7.1831; (as Mrs. Butler:) *31.5. & 3.6.1847.
Kemble, John Philip (Actor)   1757-1823
   *11.4.-2.5.1803; *23.11.-28.12.1812; *11.4.-9.5.1814; *16.-20.1.1817.
Kemble, Mrs. Maria Theresa, née de Camp (Actress)   1773-1838
   *8.8.1808; *31.7.1809; *6. & 13.5.1816; *11.-18.5.1818.
Kemble, Stephen George (Actor)   1758-1822
   *15. & 22.11.1802; *5.-15.10.1804; *8.-12.5.1820.
King, Donald W. (Singer)   1812-1886
   *4.10.1839; *5.-12.9.1845; *27.2.-?16.3.1849.
King, Mrs. (D. W.)—see M'Mahon, Miss
King, T. C. (Actor)   1825-1893
   *26.10.-6.11.1857.
King's Theatre Ballet Company
   *20.-25.8.1821 (Albert, Babtiste, Boisgerard; Madame Babtiste, Madame
   Melanie [Aubert], Madame Naniesse, Mademoiselle Noblet, &c.).
Kirby (Clown)
   *13.-18.11. & 16.12.1816.
Knowles, James Sheridan (Actor/Dramatist)   1784-1862
   *21.-25.4.1834; *2.-6.10.1837; *17.-31.1.1840.
Koenig (Brass player)
   *20.3.1841.
Lacy, Miss Maria Anne (later Mrs. Lovell)   1803-1877
   *29.8.-2.9.1826; (as Mrs. Lovell:) *26.1.-6.2., 2.-9.3.1835.
Lalanne (Tight-rope dancer)
   *21.5.1827 (with Miss Poline); *13.-16.5.1828 (with Ching Lau Lauro, posturer;
   Madame Bernardi, dancer; and Mademoiselle Helene, tight-rope artist).
Lanza, Miss (Singer)
   *7.2.1850 ?et al.; *5.-23. & 30.3.1855; *9.-20.4.1855; *2.-13.3.1857 (Grand
   National English Opera Co.); *12. & 15.5.1857 (National English Opera Co.).
Latter, R. (Singer)
   *27.2.-?16.3.1849.
Le Bau (Pantaloon)
   *26.12.1864-3.2.1865.
Leclercq, Madame Carlotta (Dancer)
   *30.8.-7.9.1830; *11.-22.1.1841.
Leclercq, Arthur (Dancer)   -1890
Leclercq, Charles (Dancer)   -1895
   *6.-17.4.1863.
Leclercq, Charles (Dancer)   1797-1861
   *11.-22.1.1841.
Lee, Henry (Compere/Actor)
   *25.8.-1.9.1852; (sc) ?1.11.-14.12.1852.
Leon (Dancer)
Leon, Madame (Dancer)
   *25.9.-6.10.1815.
Leonard (Actor)
   *7.-16.2.1845.

Leonelli, Sga. (Singer)
*8.12.1783.
Levey, Richard Michael (Violinist)   1833-?1904
*11.-15.9.1865.
Lewis, Mme., née St. Amand (Dancer)
*25.11.1805-26.3.1806.
Lind, Jenny (Singer)   1821-1887
*27.9.1847 (Concert).
Liston, John (Actor)   1776-1846
*16.-23.2.1824; *17.-26.1.1825; *24.-30.1.1826; *3.4.1827; *7.-9.4.1828; *4.-
8.1.1830.
Little Devil's Troupe, The
*20.10.-24.11.1783; *15.12.1783-16.1.1784 (Dupuis, Meunie, Paulo Redige [The
Little Devil]; Mrs. Sutton); *12. & 19.12.1784, 18.1.1785 (Mr. and Master
Cassimir, "English Mercury", Fairbrother, Master Mathews, Paulo Redige; La
Belle Espagnole).
London Dramatic Company
*1.-9.9.1856 (Bond, Clarke, Frank Hall, Henry Marston, Edward Murray, Leigh
Murray, James Rogers, Smith, James Worrell, Anthony Younge; Miss Dormer,
Mrs. Laura Honey [q.v.], Miss Frances Hughes [q.v.], Mrs. H. Marston, Miss
Jenny Marston, Mrs. Leigh Murray, Mrs. W. Robertson [q.v.]).
*27.8.-11.9.1857 (J. Adams, George Belmore, Benson, Master J. Bridgeman,
Capper, Clarence, F. Florence, Master D. Francis, Fredericks, Gange or George,
Gregory, Master Keeling, Kendall, George Lee, Edward Murray, Leigh Murray,
John Neville, Master H. Palser, W. C. Parsons, Master F. G. Tomlins, G. Tom-
lins, Webster Vernon, Charles Vincent [q.v.], F. or W. C. Williams; Miss Cleve-
land [q.v.], Miss Cuthbert [q.v.], Miss Decamp, Miss Clara Lee, Mrs. Leigh
Murray, Mrs. W. Robertson [q.v.], Miss Louisa Ross).
London Grand Opera Company
*15.-26.9.1856 (Borrani [q.v.], J. B. Bowler, Eliot Galer [q.v.], Green, Morgan,
Pendygrass, Oliver Summers; Miss Rebecca Isaacs [q.v.], Miss Leng, Miss Mears,
Miss Fanny Reeves [q.v.], Mrs. Sharpe).
*9.-13.2.1857 (Borrani [q.v.], J. B. Bowler, Eliot Galer [q.v.], Hamilton, Hodges,
May, Pendygrass, Price, Ryals, Oliver Summers; Miss Rebecca Isaacs [q.v.],
Miss Annie Leng, Miss Mortimer, Miss Fanny Reeves [q.v.]).
Louise, Mademoiselle (?Louisa Court) (Dancer)
*29. & 30.8.1844; *31.8.-7.9.1846 (Flora Fabbri's Co.).
Love, Miss Emma Sarah (Actress)   1801-
*2.-9.10.1825; *19.-27.2.1827; *3.-10.9.1827; *8.-13.9.1828; *20.-27.4.1829.
Lovell, Mrs. Maria—see Lacy, Miss.
Luccombe, Miss Emma (later Mrs. Sims Reeves) (Singer)   c.1820-1895
*3.-8.2.1850; (as Mrs. Reeves:) *3. & 4.4.1856.
Lyceum Theatre Company
*14.-17.8.1854 (Gladstone, Henry, Frank Matthews [q.v.], Rosiere [q.v.], R.
Roxby, Swan, Templeton, Williams; Mrs. Foote, Mrs. Gladstone, Miss Martin-
dale, Mrs. (F.) Matthews [q.v.], Miss M. Oliver, Miss Wadham).
*25.6.-6.7.1855 (Barnett, Berry, Henry, Frank Matthews [q.v.], Gaston Murray,
Frederic Robinson, Robert Roxby, Swan, Templeton, Williams; Miss Barnett,
Miss Cross, Miss F. Hughes [q.v.], Miss Martindale, Mrs. (F.) Matthews [q.v.],
Miss M. Oliver, Miss Wadham).
Lyon, T. E. (Actor)   ?1812-1869
*12.-15.4.1841.
Macarthy (Actor)
*6. & 20.7., 3.8.1840; *16.10.-9.11.1840.
Macready, William Charles (Actor)   1793-1873
(sc) 1.-27.2.1815; (sc) 11.12.1815-19.2.1816; *29.-31.3.1819; *30.8.-4.9.1819;
*27. & 28.12.1819; *3.-7.4.1820; *30. & 31.1.1821; *9.-13.4.1821; *27.1.-

3.2.1823; *22. & 23.4.1823; *5.-9.1.1824; *31.5.1824; *2.-9. & 19.1.1826; *25.5.1826; *28.8.1826; *11.-15.2.1828; *1.-5.12.1828; *22.1.1829; *11.-15.5.1829; *18.-25.1.1830; *5. & 11.2.1830; *5. & 9.3.1832; *1.-15.9.1834; *26.1.-6.2., 2.-9.3.1835; *18.-25.1.1836; *14.3.1836; *5.-19.9.1836; *28.8.-8.9.1837; *9.-13.3.1840; *19.4.1841; *12.9.1842; *11.-27.1.1847; *3.-7.1.1848; *10.5.1848; *7.-18.1.1850.

M'Donnell (Piper)
  *6.3.1797.

M'Lein (real name McNeil) (Actor)
  (SC) Dec. 1851-?10.5.1852; (SC) 20.9.-14.12.1852; (SC) 27.12.1852-?28.4.1853; *22.8.-6.9.1861 (Melville's Co.).

M'Mahon, Miss A. (later Mrs. D. W. King) (Singer)
  (SC) ?15.4.-?1.6.1836; *12.6.1837 (Concert); (SC) 2.9.-4.10.1839; (as Mrs. King:) *27.2.-?16.3.1849.

Mainzer, Joseph (Singing instructor)   1801-1851
  *1. & 8.6.1842.

Malibran, Madame Felicita (Singer)   1808-1836
  *19.10.1829 (Concert).

Mandlebert, Miss Lizzie (Actress)
  (SC) 30.9.-15.12.1856; (SC) 30.12.1856-27.4.1857; (SC) 21.9.-21.12.1857; (SC) 26.12.1857-28.5.1858; 13.7., 3.8. & 6.9.1858; (SC) 13.9.-16.12.1858; (SC) 3.1.-20.5.1859; 13.-15. & 27.6.1859; (SC) 26.9.-16.12.1859; (SC) 2.1.-14.5.1860; *9.-21.3.1863 (Miss Marriott's Co.).

Mangeon, Miss (Singer)
  *27.1.1817; *23. & 24.9.1817.

Mara, Madame Gertrud Elisabeth, née Schmeling (Singer)   1749-1833
  *21.12.1787 (Concert); *25.3.1793 (Concert); *5. & 12.1.1798.

Marie, Mademoiselle (Dancer)
  *1.-5.6.1857 (Drury Lane Co.); (SC) 20.9.-19.11.1858.

Mario, Giovanni Matteo (Singer)   1810-1883
  *23.9.1846 (Concert); *13.-17.10.1856 (Italian Opera Co.).

Marlowe, Miss—see Chapman, Miss Patty.

Marriott, Miss Alice (Actress)
  *25.-29.4.1859; *18.-23.5.1859; *9.-21.3.1863 (Own Co.).

Miss Marriott's Company
  *9.-21.3.1863 (T. B. Bennett, George Fisher, Howell, Turner, Williamson; Miss Mary Booth, Miss Green, Miss Kate Hodson, Miss Mandlebert [q.v.], Miss Alice Marriott [q.v.]; and various members of the Stock Company).

Martin (Animal trainer)
  *18.-22.6.1832 (with trained lions, &c.).

Mason, Miss (Actress)
  *20.-24.10.1856; *24.-27.3.1857.

Mason, Charles Kemble (Actor)   1805-1875
  (SC) ?3.-25.9.1829; (SC) 26.12.1829-14.5.1830; (SC) 30.8.-1.10.1830; (SC) 27.12.1830-18.7.1831; *31.5. & 3.6.1847.

Mathews, Charles (Entertainer)   1776-1835
  *25.11.1811; *16.-30.5.1814; *7.12.1814; *1.-10.1.1816; *14.12.1818; *21.-30.11.1825; *18.-21.8.1828; *7.-13.1.1831; *10.-16.12.1833.

Mathews, Charles James (Actor)   1803-1878
  *20.-24.10.1845; *22. & 23.10.1846; *22.2.-5.3.1847; *20.-24.10.1856; *23.-27.3.1857; *9.-17.2.1860; *25.-27.3.1863.

Mathews, Mrs. Lizzie, née Davenport (Actress)   -1899
  *9.-17.2.1860.

Matthews, Frank (Actor)   1807-1861
  (SC) 17.5.-3.6.1825; (SC) 17.9.-29.9.1827; (SC) 4.4.-23.5.1834; *28.3.1844; *14.-17.8.1854 (Lyceum Theatre Co.); *25.6.-6.7.1855 (Lyceum Theatre Co.);

*7.-18.9.1863 (St. James's Theatre Co.); *16.-27.9.1867 (St. James's Theatre Co.).

Matthews, Mrs. (Frank) (Actress)　　　　　　　　　　　　　　　1808-1873
    (sc) 4.4.-23.5.1834; *14.-17.8.1854 (Lyceum Theatre Co.); *25.6.-6.7.1855
    (Lyceum Theatre Co.); *7.-18.9.1863 (St. James's Theatre Co.); *16.-27.9.1867
    (St. James's Theatre Co.).

Matthews, Tom (Clown)　　　　　　　　　　　　　　　　　　　?1805-1889
    *20.4.-1.5.1840; *24.4.-4.5.1848.

Matweitsch Family (Singers)
    *28.12.1838-1.1.1839.

Mayhew, Henry (Journalist/Entertainer)　　　　　　　　　　　　　1812-1887
    *10.5.1849.

Meadows, Drinkwater (Actor)　　　　　　　　　　　　　　　　　1799-1869
    *2.-?11.7.1832.

Mears, Miss (later Mrs. G. Norman) (Actress)
    *11.-18.9.1837; (sc) ?18.9.-11.10.1839; (sc) 26.12.1839-29.4.1840 (as Mrs.
    Norman from 7.2.1840); 15.6.1840; (sc) 31.8.-Oct. 1840; (sc) 26.12.1840-
    14.6.1841; (sc) *30.8.-11.10.1841; (sc) ?6.1.-?2.5.1842; (sc) 16.7.1842 et al.

Mejanel (Dancer)

Mejanel, Madame (Dancer)
    *29.6.-1.7.1819.

Melville, George (Actor)　　　　　　　　　　　　　　　　　　　1824-1898
    (sc) 16.1.-14.5.1835 (as child); (sc) 26.12.1851-3.6.1852; (sc) 20.9.-14.12.1852;
    (sc) 27.12.1852-23.5.1853; (sc) 12.9.-16.12.1853; *6.3.-7.4.1854; (sc) 2.10.-
    18.12.1854; *19.11.-3.12.1855; *24.3.-3.4.1856; *12.-19.5.1856; *3.11.-
    16.12.1856; *14.-21.12.1857; *9.8.1858 (Own Co.); *13.9.-26.10.1858; *13.-17.
    & 29.8.1860 (Own Co.); *22.8.-6.9.1861 (Own Co.); *22.-26.6.1863 (Melville-
    Rouse Co.); *24.-28.8.1863 (Melville-Rouse Co.); (sc) 30.9.-7.11.1863;
    *31.5.1865 (Own Co.); *5.-9., 14.-16. & 22.-23.6.1865 (Melville-Rouse Co.);
    *21.5.-1.6.1866 (Own Co.); *10.-12.6.1867.

Melville's Company
    *9.8.1858 (Ash, Ashton, Edwards, Henry, George Melville [q.v.]; Mrs. Ashton,
    Miss Jackson [q.v.], Miss Williams; and various members of the Stock Company).
    *13.-17.8.1860 (Brazier, H. Chester, John Chute [q.v.], Graham, Douglas Grey
    [q.v.], F. Huntley, Frank Hustleby, Leffler, George Melville [q.v.], Henry Mont-
    gomery, Mortimer, Mortlake, Walter; Mrs. Braham, Mrs. Graham, Mrs. John
    Rouse [q.v.], Miss Kate Saville, Mrs. Saville [q.v.], Mademoiselle Carlotta
    Schmidt, Miss S. Vivash; and various members of the Stock Company).
    *29.8.1860 (Douglas Grey [q.v.], George Melville [q.v.], John Rouse [q.v.]; Mrs.
    John Rouse [q.v.]; and various members of the Stock Company).
    *22.8.-6.9.1861 (Rowley Cathcart, J. Clarke, Collett, Ersser Jones [q.v.], M'Lein
    [q.v.], George Melville [q.v.], Basil Potter, Raymond, Rolleston, J. G. Shore,
    Smith; Miss Adelaide Cooke, Miss Caroline Heath, Miss Ersser Jones [q.v.],
    Miss Stoneham, Miss Vivash; and various members of the Stock Company).
    *31.5.1865 (James, Laurence, George Melville [q.v.], Morris, Morton, George
    Rignold [q.v.]; Miss Marie Henderson [q.v.], Mrs. Hollis, Mrs. C. H. Stephen-
    son; and various members of the Stock Company).
    *21.5.-1.6.1866 (Hargraves, James, George Melville [q.v.], George Rignold [q.v.];
    Miss Josephine Fiddes, Miss Marie Henderson [q.v.], Mrs. G. H. Miller, Misses
    Barbara, Clara, Laura and Netty Morgan, Miss Nelly Rollason; and various
    members of the Stock Company).
    *10.-12.6.1867 (Bitson, Chaplin, Hamblin, James, George Melville [q.v.], W.
    Montague, W. Morris, Morton, Ray, Sims, Edward Terry, Thompson, White,
    Wood; Miss Nellie Dietz, Miss Adelaide Ross, Miss Kate Ross; and various
    members of the Stock Company).

Melville-Rouse Company
    *22.-26.6.1863 (Appleby, F. Barsby, J. Graham, Herbert, Frank Huntley, George

255

Melville [*q.v.*], Munro [*q.v.*], Roberts, John Rouse [*q.v.*], J. B. Steele, W. H. Stephens, Sterne, Tomlinson, Westhead or Westland; Miss Claremont, Mrs. Graham, Miss Emma Robberds, Mrs. J. Rouse [*q.v.*]; and various members of the Stock Company).

*24.-28.8.1863 (Bernard, Fitzpatrick, C. V. James, Ersser Jones [*q.v.*], Laurence, George Melville [*q.v.*], Morris, Morton, Riley, John Rouse [*q.v.*], Seymour, Smithson, Thorne, F. White, Wright, Wyborne; Miss Howard, Miss Short; and various members of the Stock Company).

*5.-9., 14.-16., 22. & 23.6.1865 (James, Walter Joyce, George Melville [*q.v.*], Morris, Morton, George Rignold [*q.v.*], John Rouse [*q.v.*], Young; Miss Marie Henderson [*q.v.*], Mrs. Hollis, Mrs. John Rouse [*q.v.*], Miss Florence Smythers [14.6.+], Mrs. C. H. Stephenson; and various members of the Stock Company).

Melvin (Actor)
*16.-30.11.1807.

Melvin, Miss Gertrude (Actress)
*29.8.-9.9.1864 (Addison's Co.); (SC) 19.9.-13.10.1864.

Mercerot, Mademoiselle (Dancer)
*29.6.-1.7.1819.

Messent, Miss (Singer)
*27.2.-?16.3.1849.

Mitchenson (Clown/Sprite)
*26.12.1852-20.1.1853; *14.-25.2.1853.

Molino (Sprite)
*26.12.1853-27.1.1854.

Montessu, Francois (Dancer)
*29. & 30.8.1844.

Montgomery, Walter H. (Actor)   1827-1871
   (SC) 23.11.-9.12.1853; (SC) 26.12.1853-12.6.1854; (SC) 20.-29.9.1854; *28.5.-1.6.1855; *28.8.-8.9.1865 (Prince of Wales Theatre Co.).

Mordaunt, Miss Jane (Actress)
*7.-11.5.1847; *18.-22.9.1848; *19. & 23.2.1849.

Mordaunt, Miss Louisa Cranstoun (later Mrs. Nisbett) (Actress)   1812-1858
   (SC) 3.9.-1.10.1827; (as Mrs. Nisbett:) *7.-11.5.1847; *18.-22.9.1848; *19. & 23.2.1849.

Morelli, C. (Clown)
*24.12.1860-12.1.1861.

Morley (Singer)
*25.2.-1.3.1841.

Morocco Arabians (Acrobats)
*4.-6.9.1843.

Moss, William Henry (Actor)   1751-1817
*20. & 27.11.1783.

Mountain, Mrs. Rosemond, née Wilkinson (Singer)   c.1770-1841
   (SC) 28.1.-29.4.1799; *24.2.-3.3.1800; *9. & 11.9.1805; *23.1-27.2.1815.

Munden, Joseph Shepherd (Actor)   1758-1832
*7. & 12.6.1809; *11.-18.6.1821.

Munro, Louis (Actor)
*13.-17.8.1860 (Melville's Co.); (SC) 20.9.-12.11.1860; *22.-26.6.1863 (Melville-Rouse Co.); (SC) 19.12.1865; (SC) 1.1.-27.4.1866; *21.5.-1.6.1866 (Melville's Co.).

Nathan, Isaac (Singer)   1792-1864
*27.-30.4., 11. & 18.5.1819; *9. & 22.6.1819.

National English Opera Company—*see* Grand National English Opera Company.
National Opera Company—*see* Grand National English Opera Company.
Nelson, Miss Carrie (Singer/Actress)   1836-1916

Nelson, Miss Sara (Singer/Actress)
 *13.-31.3.1865; *17.-28.4.1865.
Nelson, John (Actor)   1830-1879
 *11.-22.2.1867.
Nigri (Singer)
 *10.9.1840.
Nisbett, Mrs.—*see* Mordaunt, Miss Louisa.
Norman (Pantaloon)
 *3. & 10.11.1815.
Norman, Mrs. (G.)—*see* Mears, Miss.
Nunn, Miss (Singer)
 *21.3.1837.
O'Bryan, Miss Adelaide (Dancer)
 *30.8. & 3.9.1847.
O'Hara, Master (Acrobat)
 *27.12.1821-8.1.1822; *21.9.1824.
O'Neill, Eliza (Actress)   1791-1872
 *29.9.-6.10., 13.-15.10.1817; *12. & 23.-25.3.1818.
Opera in English
 *27.8.-7.9.1860 (Bentley, Eliot Galer [*q.v.*], Hodges, Hyatt, Marshall, Patey,
 E. St. Albyn [*q.v.*]; Miss Bronte, Miss Ellen Hodson, Miss Fanny Reeves [*q.v.*],
 Madame Rudersdorff.
O'Reilly, E. (Actor)
 *18.8.-3.9.1862 (Stirling's Co.); (sc) 21.9.-15.12.1863 (as Reilly); (sc) 24.12,1863-
 17.6.1864; *29.8.-9.9.1864 (Addison's Co.); (sc) 16.9.-16.12.1864; (sc)
 29.12.1864-16.5.1865; *31.5.1865 (Melville's Co.); *5.-9., 14.-16., 22. &
 23.6.1865 (Melville-Rouse Co.); (sc) 11.9.-19.12.1865; (sc) 26.12.1865-2.5.1866;
 (sc) 17.9.-19.12.1866; (sc) 24.12.1866-10.5.1867.
Owen, George (Actor)   1825-1882
 *10.-18.2.1851.
Oxberry, William (Actor)   1784-1824
 *14.-18.5.1821.
Ozmond (Harlequin)
 *14.1.-7.2.1851.
Paganini, Nicolò (Violinist)   1784-1840
 12., 14. & 16.12.1831 (Concerts).
Parry, John (Singer)   1810-1879
 *21.9.1843 (Concert); *10.-14.9.1844; *23.9.1846 (Concert).
Parsloe, Charles T. (Posturer)   1804-1870
 *24.-28.9.1827.
Partleton, Master (Dancer/Mime)
 *16.-20.1.1826; *26.10.-3.11.1826 (Ducrow's Troupe).
Pasta, Giuditta (Singer)   1798-1865
 *29.11.1827 (Concert); *21. & 22.9.1837.
Paton, Miss Mary Anne (later Mrs. Wood) (Singer)   1802-1864
 *29.12.1825 (Concert); *14.-18.1.1828; *17. & 18.9.1830; (as Mrs. Wood:)
 *18.-25.4.1831; *9.-20.2.1835; *2.-6.3.1835; *29. & 30.4.1839; *16.3.1840;
 *20.9.-1.10.1841.
Paul, Howard (Entertainer)   1830-1905
 *3.-25.10.1854; *3.-14.8.1857.
Paul, Mrs. (Howard)—*see* Featherstone, Miss.
Paulo (Clown)   1787-1835
 *29.4.-9.5.1823; *30.8.-11.9.1824; *30.8.-7.9.1830.
Paumier (Actor)
 *26.-29.9.1837; (sc) 16.1.-24.4.1838.

Payne, John Howard (Actor)   1791-1852
   *14.4.1817.
Pearman, William (Singer)   1792-
   (SC) 4.10.1816-27.6.1817; *28.5.1825; *29.12.1825 (Concert).
Pemberton, Charles Reece (Actor)   1790-1840
   *28.2.-7.3.1828.
Persiani, Sga. Fanny (Singer)   1812-1867
   *27.5.1839 (Concert); *10.9.1840; *27.8.1844 (Concert).
Persivani (Clown)
   *24.12.1861-7.2.1862; *24.12.1863-5.2.1864.
Petit-Stephan, Mademoiselle Josephine (Dancer)
   *17.10.1845.
Phantasmagoria (Professor J. E. Varey thinks this was probably the show run by
   Philipstal)
   *1.2.-1.3.1802; *13.-20.10.1802.
Phelps, Samuel (Actor)   1804-1878
   *?24.-27.4.1855; *22.2.1856; *14.-18.4.1856.
Phetzo (Animal impersonator)
   *13.-17.1.1826.
Philippe (Conjuror)
   *1.-18.12.1845 (with Les Petites Chiarini [dancers] and the American Family
   [acrobats])
Phillips, Master (Trumpeter)   ?1827-
   *21. & 23.1.1835.
Phillips, Miss (Singer)
   *22.1.1828 (1st app. any stage) -1.2.1828.
Phillips, George (Harlequin)
   *24.12.1862-21.2.1863.
Phillips, Miss Louisa Ann (Actress)
   *28.5.-4.6.1832.
Phillips, Mrs. R., née Barnett (Singer)
   *1.6.-1.7.1801; *11.-27.6.1804; *3.10.-5.11.1804.
Phillips, Thomas (Singer)
   *1.-15.11.1813; *6.-13.12.1819; *26.12.1821; *9. & 23.1. & 20.2.1823 (Concerts);
   *11.12.1823 (Concert); *29.12.1825 (Concert); *6.11.1828 (Concert).
Pietro, Paul (Clown)
   *26.12.1855-25.1.1856; *7.2.1856.
Pitt, Charles (Actor)   ?1818-1866
   *11.-21.2.1856; *16.-20.2.1857; *28.9.-2.10.1857. (On all three visits Mrs. C.
   Pitt played occasionally.)
Plimmeri (Animal impersonator)
   *27.3.-4.4.1837; *27.-31.12.1847; *12.-19.1.1848.
Pope, Alexander (Actor)   1763-1835
   *15.-29.10.1810.
Pope, Mrs. Johanna Coleman (Actress)   1814-1880
   (SC) 26.12.1837-11.5.1838; (SC) 26.12.1838-13.5.1839; *9.-13.3.1840.
Povey, Miss Mary Ann (Singer)   1804-1861
   *28.8.-12.9.1817.
Power (Harlequin)
   *?1.-7.6.1819.
Powrie, Thomas (Actor)
   *29.9.-10.10. & 15.10.1856.
Prince of Wales Theatre Company
   *28.8.-8.9.1865 (Sydney [sic] Bancroft, Bracewell, J. Clarke, Cox, F. Dewar,
   Jones, W. H. Montgomery [q.v], Redmond, Robinson, Stanley; Miss Bedcliffe,
   Miss B. Goodall, Miss Frances Hughes [q.v.], Miss Lavine, Miss Louise Weston,
   Miss Augusta Wilton [q.v.], Miss Blanche Wilton [q.v.], Miss Marie Wilton [q.v.]).

Princess's Theatre Company
*21.8.-1.9.1854 (Addison [q.v.], J. F. Cathcart [q.v.], J. Chester, Collett, Collins, Edmonds, G. Everett [q.v.], Huline [q.v.], Paulo, Raymond, Rolliston; Miss Fanny Clifford, Miss Juliet Desborough [q.v.], Miss Carlotta Leclercq, Miss Murray).

Puzzi, Giovanni (Horn-player)   1792-1876
*20.3.1828; *31.8.1835; *10.9.1840; *27.8.1844 (Concert); *27.8.1845 (Concert).

Pyne & Harrison Opera Company
*1.-12.4.1861 (Henry Corri, Friend, W. Harrison [q.v.], George Honey [q.v.], H. Horncastle, Lennox, Charles Lyall, A. St. Albyn [q.v.], Henry Wharton; Miss Leffler, Miss Louisa Pyne, Miss Thirlwell).

Quick, John (Actor)   1748-1831
(sc) 8.6.-7.9.1768; (sc) ?31.5.-11.9.1769; (sc) 5.6.-?11.9.1775; (sc) 10.6.-16.9.1776; (sc) 6.6.-?15.9.1777; (sc) 1.6.-?12.9.1778; *25.9.-9.10.1797; *22.10.-7.11.1798; *7.-21.10.1799.

Rainer Family (Singers)
*14. & 15.1.1830.

Rainforth, Miss Elizabeth (Singer)   1814-1877
*25.8.1842 (Concert); *10.-17.9.1847; *28.2.-1.3.1848.

Ramo Samee (Juggler)
*4.-7.6.1821; *29.12.1834-2.1.1835.

Ramsden, Miss Marion (Dancer)
*6.-17.4.1863.

Ranger (Actor)
*12.2.1849; *3.-14.3.1851.

Rayner, Lionel Benjamin (Actor)   1786-1855
*9.-13.3.1829.

Reeve, John (Actor)   1799-1838
(sc) 2.1.-13.7.1821; (sc) 8.4.-14.6.1822; (sc) 2.-27.9.1822; (sc) 11.4.-16.5.1825; *14.-18.9.1835.

Reeves, Miss Fanny (Singer)
*15.-26.9.1856 (London Grand Opera Co.); *9.-13.2.1857 (London Grand Opera Co.); *27.8.-7.9.1860 (Opera in English); *31.8.-4.9.1863 (Rosenthal Grand Opera Company); *20.-23.9.1864.

Reeves, John Sims (Singer)   1818-1900
*5.-8.2.1850; *3. & 4.4.1856; *25.-27.11.1857 (Grand Opera Co.).

Reeves, Mrs. (Sims)—see Luccombe, Miss Emma.

Revill Family ("Sixteen Juvenile Artists")
*25.8.-1.9.1852 (with Miss Eliza Farrell, Madame Manley, T. K. Reeves, Walters and J. Warren).

Rice, Charles (Actor)   ?1819-1880
*13.-17.6.1864; *8.-12.10.1866.

Rice, Thomas Dartmouth (Actor)   1806-1860
*8.-12.4.1839.

Richer, Jack (Tight-rope artist)
*7.12.1795-4.1.1796; *13.1.-17.2.1800; *10.-31.1.1803; *3.10.-12.11.1804; *7. & 28.1.1805; *19. & 22.7.1811; *30.12.1811-6.1.1812; *8.-17.11.1813.

Ridgway (Dancer/Harlequin)
*26.11.1804-7.1.1805.

Rignold, George (Actor)   1838-1912
(sc) 26.9.-16.12.1859; (sc) 26.12.1859-30.5.1860; (sc) 17.9.-14.12.1860; (sc) 24.12.1860-24.5.1861; (sc) 16.9.-13.12.1861; (sc) 24.12.1861-16.5.1862; (sc) 15.9.-20.12.1862; (sc) 24.12.1862-11.5.1863; (sc) 21.9.-18.12.1863; *3.4.-16.5. & 31.5.1865 (Melville's Co.); *5.-9., 14.-16. & 22.-23.6.1865 (Melville-Rouse Co.); *21.5.-1.6.1866 (Melville's Co.).

Rignold, William Rignall (Actor)   1836-1904
(sc) 27.9.-16.12.1859; (sc) 26.12.1859-30.5.1860; (sc) 17.9.-12.12.1860; (sc)

24.12.1860-24.5.1861; (SC) 17.9.-18.12.1861; (SC) 24.12.1861-16.5.1862; (SC) 15.9.-20.12.1862; (SC) 24.12.1862-15.5.1863; (SC) 21.9.-18.12.1863; (SC) 24.12.1863-17.6.1864; *26.2.-11.4.1865.

Risley, "Professor" (Conjuror/Acrobat)

Risley, Master John (Acrobat) 1837-
*11.-16.9.1843; *22. & 23.4.1844 (with second son Henry).

Madame Ristori's Company
*22.7.1863 (Borghi, Buti, Giotti, G. Glech, Tessero, Ventura; Mademoiselle Bellina, Mademoiselle Giotti, Mademoiselle Glech, Madame Ristori).

Rivers Family (Acrobats)
*17.-26.3.1840.

Robert, Jean (Juggler)
*27.12.1824-6.1.1825.

Robertson, Mrs. Margheritta Elisabetta, née Marinus (Actress) -1876
*1.-9.9.1856 (London Dramatic Co.); *27.8.-11.9.1857 (London Dramatic Co.); (SC) 21.9.-21.12.1857; (SC) ?7.1.-25.3.1858; (SC) 13.9.-3.12.1858; (SC) 30.12.1858-20.5.1859; (SC) 13., 14. & 27.6.1859; (SC) 26.9.-15.12.1859; (SC) 2.1.-14.5., 28.-30.5.1860; (SC) 18.9.-14.12.1860; (SC) 3.1.-24.5., 10.6.1861; (SC) 16.9.-18.12.1861; (SC) 1.1.-16.5.1862; *18.8.-3.9.1862 (Stirling's Co.); (SC) 15.9.-20.12.1862; (SC) 24.12.1862-11.5.1863; 25.-27.5.1863; *22.-26.6.1863 (Melville-Rouse Co.); (SC) 21.9.-17.12.1863; (SC) 31.12.1863-17.6.1864; (SC) 16.9.-16.12.1864.

Romanine, Sga. Rosolia (Thread-wire performer)

Romanine, Sga. Veronica (do.)
*19.10.-1.11.1826.

Romer, Miss Emma (Singer) 1814-1868
(SC) 28.12.1830-20.6.1831; *3.-14.9.1838; *9.-30.9.1839; *14.-19.9.1842; *2.-9.9.1844; *22. & 24.9.1845.

Rosati, Mademoiselle (Dancer)
*4.-8.9.1848 (with Her Majesty's Theatre Ballet, viz: Georges Martin, Mesdemoiselles Julien and Lamoureux).

Roselle, Master Percy (Infant prodigy)
*8. & 9.9.1859; *28.11.-2.12.1859.

Rosenthal's Grand English Opera Company
*31.8.-4.9.1863 (Bentley, Horton, Lebrun, J. Manley, I. or J. Morgan, H. Parkinson, E. Rosenthal, J. or T. Tempest; Miss Bronti, Madame Haigh-Dyer [q.v.], Miss E. Hodson, Miss Marten, Miss Fanny Reeves [q.v.], Miss Tempest, Miss Annie Wilson).
*30.11.-4.12.1863 (Bentley, Horton, Lebrun, J. Manley, I. or J. Morgan, H. Parkinson, E. Rosenthal, J. or T. Tempest; Miss Adele Alessandri, Miss Bronti, Madame Haigh-Dyer [q.v.], Miss E. Hodson, Miss Marian Taylor).

Rosiere, J. G. (Actor) -1870
*14.-17.8.1854 (Lyceum Theatre Co.); (SC) 16.9.-16.12.1864; (SC) 29.12.1864-6.1.1865; (SC) 24.9.-19.12.1866; (SC) 24.12.1866-2.5.1867; *10.-12.6.1867 (Melville's Co.); (SC) 2.-14.1.1868.

Ros(s)ignol, Signor ?Gaetano (Bird imitator)
*22.6.1778; *19.5.-2.6., & 4.7.1783; *11., 18. & 25.7., 1.8.1791; *31.3.1800.
(There seem to have been two performers using this name.)

Rouse, John (Actor)
(SC) ?27.9.-14.12.1852; (SC) 27.12.1852-23.5.1853; (SC) 12.9.-15.12.1853; (SC) 13.1.-12.6.1854; (SC) 18.9.-18.12.1854; (SC) 28.12.1854-15.6.1855; (SC) 1.10.-14.12.1855; (SC) 26.12.1855-19.5.1856; (SC) 29.9.-16.12.1856; (SC) 30.12.1856-5.5.1857; (SC) 1.-5.6.1857; (SC) 21.9.-21.12.1857; (SC) 26.12.1857-28.5.1858; (SC) 13.9.-17.12.1858; (SC) ?30.12.1858-20.5.1859; (SC) 13.-15.6.1859; *13.-17. & 29.8.1860 (Melville's Co.); *22.-26.6.1863 (Melville-Rouse Co.); *24.-28.8.1863 (Melville-Rouse Co.); *5.-9., 14.-16., & 22.-23.6.1865 (Melville-Rouse Co.).

Rouse, Mrs. (John) (Actress)
  (SC) Aut. 1852, dates unknown; (SC) ?Dec. 1852-23.5.1853; (SC) 12.9.-15.12.1853; (SC) 12.1.-12.6.1854; (SC) 20.9.-18.12.1854; (SC) 6.1.-19.6.1855; (SC) 1.10.-11.12.1855; (SC) ?9.1.-19.5.1856; (SC) 29.9.-12.12.1856; (SC) 26.12.1856-5.5.1857; (SC) 1.-5.6.1857; (SC) 21.9.-21.12.1857; (SC) ?29.12.1857-28.4.1858; (SC) 22.9.-17.12.1858; (SC) ?30.12.1858-20.5.1859; (SC) 13.-15. & 27.6.1859; *13.-17. & 28.6.1860 (Melville's Co.); *22.-26.6.1863 (Melville-Rouse Co.); *5.-9., 14.-16. & 22.-23.6.1865 (Melville-Rouse Co.); (SC) 11.9.-19.12.1865; (SC) 1.1.-2.5.1866; (SC) 17.9.-19.12.1866; (SC) 8.1.-3.5.1867.
Royal Italian Opera—*see* Italian Opera
Royal Strand Theatre Company
  *16.-27.8.1858 (James Bland, Chater, Clarke, Edge, J. W. Hurlstone, J. Irving, Meagreson, J. W. Ray, Arthur Stirling [*q.v.*], W. H. Swanborough, Wilson, Charles Young; Miss Brook, Miss Cooper, Miss Gilbert, Miss Henrade, Miss Hughes, Mrs. Selby [*q.v.*], Miss Swanborough, Miss M. Ternan, Miss Tuttle, Miss M. A. Victor).
Rubini, Giovanni-Battista (Singer)   1795-1854
  *27.5.1839 (Concert); *10.9.1840.
Ruggiero (Singer)
Ruggiero, Madame (Singer)
  *6.10.1842.
Russell, Henry (Singer)   1812-1900
  *12. & 14.8.1846; *26. & 28.4.1847; *10. & 12.4.1848.
Russell, James (Entertainer)
  *21.7.1834.
Russell, Samuel Thomas (Actor)   1765-1845
  *11.-18.5.1818.
Russian Horn Band
  *2. & 6.12.1831.
Ryder, John (Actor)   1814-1885
  *26.2.-9.3.1866.
St. Albin (Dancer)
  *11.-18.1.1826.
St. Albyn, A. or E. (Singer)
  *17.-28.9.1855 (English Opera Co.); *28.1.-5.2.1856 (English Opera Co.), *6. & 7.3.1856 (English Opera Co.); *2.-6.2.1857; *27.8.-7.9.1860 (Opera in English); *1.-12.4.1861 (Pyne & Harrison Opera Co.); *18.8.-3.9.1862 (Stirling's Co.).
St. Casse, Miss Clara (Child prodigy)   1848-
  *28.3.-28.4.1853; *3.-28.10.1853; *6.-9., 16., 21. & 23.3.1854; *21.11.-7.12.1855; *27.4.1857.
St. James's Theatre Company
  *7.-18.9.1863 (J. Allen, Bush, Hooper, S. Johnson, Lacey, Frank Matthews [*q.v.*], Norman, J. G. Shore, Arthur Stirling [*q.v.*], Wilson; Miss Adeline Cottrell, Miss Ada Dyas, Miss Louisa Herbert [*q.v.*], Miss Patti Josephs, Mrs. Frank Matthews [*q.v.*], Miss Nisbett, Miss Wentworth).
  *16.-27.9.1867 (J. H. Allen, Anders, Borfield, A. Brown, T. C. Burleigh, Bush, Carleton, E. Dyas, Gordon, Henry Irving, James, Johnson, Jones, Frank Matthews [*q.v.*], Melvin, Merton, Morton, Gaston Murray, Richards, J. Richards, H. Rivers, Smith, B. de Solla, J. D. Stoyle, W. H. Vernon [*q.v.*], Williams, Wilson; Miss Barry, Miss Ada Cavendish, Miss Louisa Herbert [*q.v.*], Miss Jones, Miss Kate Kearney, Mrs. Frank Matthews [*q.v.*], Miss Wilkinson).
St. Leon, Arthur (Charles Victor Arthur Michel) (Dancer)   1821-1870
  *29. & 30.8.1844; *30.8. & 3.9.1847.
St. Pierre (Dancer)
  *14.10.-7.11.1803.
Sagrini (Guitarist)
  *10.4. & 7.5.1834.

Sala (Singer)
*5.-7.6.1844.
Salmon, Mrs. Eliza, née Munday (Singer)   1787-1849
*8.2.1822; *9., 16. & 17.1.1823; *15.1.1824 (Concert); *20.-29.12.1824; *30.12.
1824 (Concert).
Sapio, Antonio (Singer)
(SC) 4.4.-6.6.1825; *13.2.-6.3.1829 (de Begnis' Co.).
Sapio, Louis Bernard (Singer)   1792-1851
*9.1.1823 (Concert); *5.4. & 3.6.1825; *12.-21.12.1825; *1.-5.1.1827; *17.-
23.12.1828.
Saqui, Mons., Mme. and Mlle. (Rope-dancers)
*6.-17.9.1819; *16.-20.11.1819.
Saunders, Miss Charlotte (Actress)   1826-1899
*23.-27.11.1863.
Saunders, Miss Emily (later Lady Don) (Actress)   -1875
*20.-24.4.1857; *9.-17.11. & 7.12.1857; (as Lady Don:) *15.-19.3.1858; *14.-
18.2.1859; *16.-20.11.1863.
Saville, Mrs. J. Faucit (Actress)   1811-1889
*7.-?15.1.1850; *13.-17.8.1860 (Melville's Co.).
Schmidt (Dancer)
Schmidt, Madame (Dancer)
*2.-?26.9.1839.
Second, Mrs. Sarah, née Mahon (Singer)   ?1766-1805
*28.11. & 12.12.1803.
Sedgwick, Amy (Actress)   1835-1897
*29.11. & 5.12.1853; *28.10.-8.11.1861; *11.-22.2.1867.
Selby, Charles (Actor)   ?1800-1863
(SC) 31.8.-25.9.1829; (SC) 26.12.1829-14.5.1830; (SC) 31.8.-1.10.1830; (SC)
27.12.1830-15.7.1831; *23.-27.9.1850 (Haymarket Theatre Co.).
Selby, Mrs. Clara (Actress)   1796-1873
(SC) 31.8.-25.9.1829; (SC) 26.12.1829-14.5.1830; (SC) 30.8.-?30.9.1830; (SC)
27.12.1830-15.7.1831; *16.-27.8.1858 (Royal Strand Theatre Co.).
Seymour, Mrs. Laura, née Allison (Actress)   1799-1879
*16.-23.9.1844; *23.-27.9.1850 (Haymarket Theatre Co.); *5.-7.11.1851 (Hay-
market Theatre Co.).
Shirreff, Miss Jane (Singer)   1811-1883
*13.5.1833; *10.-17.3.1837.
Siddons, Henry (Actor)   1775-1815
(SC) 16.7.1781 (as child); *15.2.1796.
Siddons, Miss Mary Frances (Actress)   1844-1896
*19.-30.11.1866; *25.2.-1.3.1867.
Siddons, Mrs. Sarah, née Kemble (Actress)   1755-1831
(SC) ?15.-?24.3., 26.4.-31.5.1779; (SC) 4.10.1779-14.7.1780; (SC) 4.9.1780-
27.7.1781; (SC) 4.9.1781-19.6.1782; *1.-25.2.1799; *6.-20.4.1801; *31.8.-
18.9.1801; *30.3.-13.4.1807; *11.1.-15.2.1808.
Silvain (real name Sullivan), James (Dancer/Violinist)   -1856
*9.-20.3.1835; *?30.8.-2.9.1836 (with Miss Foster); *1. & 17.5.1843;
*17.10.1845; *30.1.-4.2.1850.
Silvani (Sprite)
*26.12.1855-25.1.1856.
Silver Miners' Band
*7. & 14.3.1803.
Simeon, Miss Louisa M. M. (later Mrs. Chatterly) (Actress)   1797-1866
(SC) 20.7.1812 (1st app. any stage); (SC) 16.11.1812-?23.7.1813; (as Mrs. Chatterly:) (SC) 1.10.1813-18.7.1814; (SC) 12.9.1814-11.7.1815; (SC) 29.9.1815-
27.5.1816; (SC) 14.10.1816-26.5.1817; *14.-22.6.1820.

Simpson, H. (Animal trainer)
*16.-23.12.1822 (with bear and dogs).
Sinclair, John (Singer)   1791-1857
*3.-19.5.1813; *27.12.1815; *22.1.1824 (Concert); *4.-8.9.1826; *20.5.1828;
*8.-10.4.1835; *19.-26.2.1838.
Sirret (Pantaloon)
*?1.9.-?8.9.1820.
Sloman (Singer)
*28.4.-21.5.1824.
Smith (Singer)
*10.-20.9.1821; *16.-23.9.1822 (with Master Smith [20.9.1822 only]); *15. &
16.1.1823 (with Master Smith).
Smith, Miss (Actress)   ?1785-1850
(SC) 24.9.1804-15.7.1805; *2.-27.10.1809.
Smith, Miss (Singer)
Smith, Miss Julia (Singer)
*11. & ?12.9.1837; *6., 10. & 20.4.1843 (with Miss Maria Smith).
Smith, Richard John ("Obi") (Actor)   1786-1885
*15.-19.4.1841.
Smith, "Yankee" (Actor)
*8.-12.3.1841.
Smithson, Miss Harriet Constance (Actress)   1800-1854
*6.-17.9.1819; *24.-27.5.1831.
Somerville, Miss Margaret Agnes (Actress)   1799-1883
*18.-20.5.1817.
Sothern, Edward Askew (Actor)   1826-1881
*2.-6.11.1863; *25.4.1864; *13. & 14.9.1866.
Southby (Clown)
*22.1.-1.2.1822; *2.-10.2.1824.
Spanish Dancers (from the Haymarket)
*11.-15.6.1855 (Alemany, Marcos Diaz, Estebe, Herrero, Pedro Hidalgo; Sta.
Fani, Sta. Gil, Sta. Le Fuente, Sta. Lopez, Sa. Perea Nena, Sta. Pepe Valles).
Stansbury, George Frederick (Pianist/Singer)   1800-1845
*5.2.1824 (Concert); *29.12.1825 (Concert); *19.5.1826; *27. & 30.4. &
17.5.1827; *5.10.1827; *29.11.1827 (Concert); *12.-16.3.1828; *20.3.1828
(Concert); *7. & 20.5.1828; *13.5.1833; *3.-30.9.1839; *31.8.-7.9.1840.
Steele, J. B. (Actor)
(SC) 26.9.-16.12.1859; (SC) 2.1.-14.5.1860; 28.-30.5.1860; *22.-26.6.1863 (Mel-
ville-Rouse Co.).
Stephens, Miss Catherine (Singer)   1794-1882
*11.-18.9.1820; *10.-20.9.1821; *16.-24.9.1822; *4.-8.4.1825; *27.-31.3.1826;
*16.-20.4.1827.
Stirling, Arthur (Actor)   1807-1893
*16.-27.8.1858 (Royal Strand Theatre Co.); (SC) 26.9.-16.12.1858; (SC) 2.1.-
3.5.1860; (SC) 17.9.-14.12.1860; (SC) 24.12.1860-24.5.1861; *18.8.-3.9.1862
(Own Co.); *7.-18.9.1863 (St. James's Theatre Co.); *31.10.-25.11.1864; *18.9.-
13.10.1865; *26.2.-9.3.1866; *10.11.-6.12.1867.
Stirling's Company
*18.8.-3.9.1862 (Eugene, David Evans [q.v.], Fosbrooke [q.v.], David James,
Oliver, E. O'Reilly [q.v.], Joseph Robins, St. Albyn [q.v.], Sidney, Arthur Stirling [q.v.], Tilbury, Charles Vincent [q.v.]; Miss Ada Dyas, Miss Hemmings, Miss
Sarah Stirling, Miss Kate Terry [q.v.], Mrs. Wharton; and various members of
the Stock Company).
Stirling, Edward (Author/Director/Actor)   1809-1894
*15.-19.4.1844 (advertised and reported as engaged, but not in any cast list
extant); *26.12.1850-13.1.1851.

263

Stonette, Alfred (Clown)
Stonette, T. (Harlequin)
    *26.12.1864-3.2.1865; *26.12.1865-10.2.1866.
Storace, Mrs. Anna Selina (Nancy) (Singer)   1766-1817
    *9.1.-3.2.1797; *24.9.-6.10.1802.
Strauss Band
    *1.10.1839.
Stretton (Singer)
    *5.-12.9.1845; *10.-17.9.1847; *28.2.-1.3.1848; *27.2.-?16.3.1849; *?19.-
27.5.1864 (Swanborough Burlesque Co.).
Strickland, Robert (Actor)   ?1789-1845
    (sc) 3.12.1822-22.5.1823; (sc) 22.12.1823-9.4.1824; *10.3.1842; *27.2.-
10.3.1843.
Stuart (Actor)
    (sc) 15.12.1819-27.6.1820; (sc) ?2.-?14.9.1820; (sc) 20.11.1822-13.5.1823;
*27.5.1831; (sc) 26.10.1831 et al.; (sc) ?30.11.-?5.12.1831; (sc) ?2.1.-
?11.7.1832; (sc) 4.2.-?22.5.1833; *30.1.-3.2.1835; *1.1.1849 (with Miss Stuart).
Swanborough's Burlesque Company
    *19.-27.5.1864 (Archer, Bellair, Brian, Chapman, H. Farrell [q.v.], James
Francis, Hudspeth, Macraken [sic], Parkes, Stretton [q.v.], W. H. Swanborough,
Tillett; Miss Arlington, Miss Amy Conquest, Miss Annie Cushnie [q.v.], Miss
Minnie Davis, Miss Alice Evans, Miss Lupino, Miss Julia St. George, Miss Edith
Stuart, Misses Kate and Julia Summers, Miss Thorley).
Swinbourne, Thomas (Actor)   1823-1895
    *12.-16.4.1858.
Taglioni, Marie (Dancer)   1804-1884
    *17.10.1845.
Talbot, Henry (Actor)   -1894
    *20.-31.3.1865; *27.11.-8.12.1865; *24.9.-5.10.1866.
Tanner's Performing Dogs and Monkeys
    *1.-3.2.1865.
Taylor, Bianchi (Singer)
    *25.5.1831; *12., 14. & 16.12.1831 (Concerts); *1.10.1840.
Templeton, John (Singer)   1802-1886
    *10.-17.3.1837; *3.-14.9.1838; *26.2.-8.3.1839; *9.-30.9.1839; *22.2.1844.
Ternan (Actor)   1799-1846
Ternan, Miss Fanny (Child actress)   1837-
    *25.-29.3.1844.
Ternan, Mrs. F. A.—see Jarman, Miss Frances.
Terry, Daniel (Actor)   1789-1829
    *29.-31.3.1819; *17.-24.4.1826; *7.-14.5.1827.
Terry, Miss Alice Ellen (Actress)   1847-1928
    (sc) 16.9.-28.11.1862; *21.9.-9.10.1863; *11.-22.3.1867.
Terry, Miss Kate (Actress)   1844-1924
    *18.8.-3.9.1862 (Stirling's Co.); (sc) 15.9.-29.11.1862; *21.9.-10.10.1863; *16.9.-
14.10.1864; *11.-22.3.1867.
Theleur (real name Taylor) (Dancer)
    *4.-15.2.1839.
Thillon, Madame Sophie Anna (Actress/Singer)   1819-1903
    *27.-31.3.1848.
Thompson (Actor)
    *30.8.-24.9.1824.
"Tom Thumb"
    *8.2.1845; *11.5.1845.
Travers (Singer)
    *29.12.1835-11.1.1836; *10.-17.9.1847; *28.2.-1.3.1848.

Tree, Miss Ellen (later Mrs. C. Kean) (Actress) 1806-1880
*2.-7.2.1842; (as Mrs. Kean:) *16.-23.1.1843; *17.2.1843; *8.-15.1.1844; *20.-30.1.1845; *3.-10.3.1845; *3.3.1848; *9.-20.4.1860; *5.-9.5.1862; *23.-28.1.1867.
Turpin, Miss Maria (Singer)
(SC) 25.-28.10.1831; (SC) 30.11.-16.12.1831 inc. Concerts; (SC) ?30.1.-?4.7.1832; *4.2.-5.3. & 26.4.1833; *10.3.-10.4.1835.
Usher Family (Pantomimists/Acrobats)
*28.-30.8.1820 (Misses L. and M. Usher); *31.8.-15.9.1820 (Richard Usher, Mrs. Usher, Miss Usher, Misses H., J., L. and M. Usher); *11.-15.9.1829 (Richard Usher); *11.1.-2.2.1830 (Richard Usher [20 Jan.+], Four Misses Usher [Miss, Miss C., Miss H. and "Little Miss"]; Mrs. Usher [1 Feb. only]).
Vandenhoff, Miss Charlotte Elizabeth (Actress) 1818-1860
*12.-16.4.1858.
Vandenhoff, John (Actor) 1790-1861
(SC) 8.10.1813-28.3.1814; *6.-9.3.1837.
Vernon, Joseph (Singer) ?1738-1782
*16.4.1781; *3.-17.9.1781.
Vernon, W. H. (Actor) 1834-1905
*1.5.1862 (as amateur); (SC) 18.9.-19-12.1865; (SC) 1.1.-2.5.1866; *21.5.-1.6.1866 (Melville's Co.); (SC) 17.9.-19.12.1866; (SC) 24.12.1866-10.5.1867; *16.-27.9.1867 (St. James's Theatre Co.); (SC) 11.11.-13.12.1867; (SC) 2.-14.1.1868.
Vestris, Armand (Dancer) 1788-1825
*2.-20.11. & 14.12.1812 (with Charles and Master Charles Didelot, Robert; Madame Didelot, Madame Ducott [2.11. only], Miss Mori, Miss Willis and local dancers).
Vestris, Madame Lucy Elizabeth, née Bartolozzi (Actress/Singer) 1797-1856
*8.3.1827 (Concert); *24.-30.4.1827; *21.-25.4.1828; *6.-11.5.1831; *24.5.1833; *20.-24.10.1845; *22. & 23.10.1846; *22.2.-5.3.1847.
Vezin, Hermann (Actor) 1829-1910
Vezin, Mrs. Jane Elizabeth, née Thompson (Actress) 1827-1902
*4.-15.4.1864.
Vincent, Charles (Actor)
*27.8.-11.9.1857 (London Dramatic Co.); (SC) 21.9.-21.12.1857; (SC) ?29.12.1857-3.5.1858; (SC) 10.-20.5.1858; (SC) 13.9.-17.12.1858; (SC) 30.12.1858-20.5.1859; (SC) 17.9.-14.12.1860; (SC) 24.12.1860-10.5.1861; *18.8.-3.9.1862 (Stirling's Co.).
Vining, Miss Fanny Elizabeth (later Mrs. Charles Gill) (Actress) 1829-1891
*21.2.1842; (as Mrs. Gill:) *11.1.-10.2.1847.
Volange, Madame (Dancer)
*14.10.-7.11.1803.
Waite, W. (Dancer/Harlequin)
(SC) 20.9.-17.12.1858; (SC) 27.12.1858-13.5.1859; *24.12.1860-2.2.1861.
Wallack, James William (Actor) 1791-1864
*28.5.-1.6.1832; *10.-28.2.1834; *4.-8.5.1840; *30.1.-10.2.1843.
Wallis, Miss Tryphosa Jane (later Mrs. Campbell) (Actress) 1774-1848
(SC) 19.10.1789-?17.5.1790; (SC) 4.10.1790-?18.7.1791; (SC) ?19.12.1791-3.8.1792; (SC) 24.9.1792-29.7.1793; (SC) 30.9.1793-4.8.1794; *28.3.-8.4.1796; *12. & 26.12.1796; (as Mrs. Campbell:) *19.-28.4.1813; (SC) 27.9.1813-6.1.1814.
Warde, James (Actor)
(SC) ?27.12.1813-5.8.1814; (SC) 2.10.1814-12.7.1815; (SC) 25.9.1815-20.5.1816; (SC) 30.9.1816-2.6.1817; *11.-20.9.1826; *2.-?11.7.1832.
Warner, Mrs.—see Huddart, Miss M. A.

Watson, Miss (Singer)
*23.-27.9.1828; *27.5.1830 (Concert); *25.5.1831.
Waylett, Mrs.—*see* Cooke, Miss Harriet.
Webb (Actor)
*14.-27.6.1820.
Webb, The Brothers (Actors)
*9.5.1864; *3.-8.4.1865.
Webster, Master (Child actor)
*4. & 19.1.1826; *25.5.1826; *28.8.1826; *11. & 15.2.1828.
Webster, Arthur (Dancer)   1825-
*1.-16.1.1846.
Webster, Benjamin Nottingham (Actor)   ?1798-1882
(sc) 28.3.1814 (as child dancer); (sc) 1.5.1815; (sc) 25.10-?27.12.1815; *17.-
25.2.1839; *10.9.1841; *10.3.1842; *11.-18.7.1842; *27.2.-10.3.1843; *25.-
29.9.1843; *18.-25.5.1846; *22.10.-2.11.1855; *27.-31.10.1856; *15.-26.2.1858;
*5.-9.3.1860; *30.4.-4.5.1860.
Weiss, Josephine—*see* Danseuses Viennoises.
Wells, Miss (Singer)
*23.-27.9.1828.
Wensley, Miss Emma (Actress)
*16.-24.3.1820; *2.-9.5.1822.
West's Equestrian Troupe
*26.7.-9.8.1813 (West, Woolford, Master Woolford and Troupe).
*27.12.1814-6.1.1815 (Jenkins, West, Master West, Woolford, Master Woolford
and Troupe).
Wharton, Madame (Mime)
*5.11.-1.12.1849 (with her Walhalla Establishment of Poses Plastiques).
Whitworth (Singer)
*5.-8.2.1850; (as Herr Helder:) *17.-28.9.1855 (English Opera Co.).
Wieland, George (Clown)   1811-1847
*12.-15.4.1841; *4.4.1842.
Wigan, Alfred Sidney (Actor)   1817-1878
*2.-12.4.1850; *9.-13.11.1863 (with Mrs. Leonora Wigan).
Williams, Barney (Actor)   ?1823-1876
Williams, Mrs. (B.) (Actress)   ?1825-1911
*10.-21.5.1858.
Wilson (Tight-rope performer)
*20. & 21.5.1818; *23.4.-1.5.1821.
Wilton, Miss Augusta (Actress)   -1926,
(sc) 7.-24.11.1853; (sc) 2. & 10.2., 22.3.-4.5.1854; *28.8.-8.9.1865 (Prince of
Wales Theatre Co.).
Wilton, Miss Blanche (Actress)
(sc) 13.3.-12.6.1854; (sc) 26.9.-14.12.1854; (sc) 26.12.1854-16.4.1855; *28.8.-
8.9.1865 (Prince of Wales Theatre Co.).
Wilton, Miss Marie Effie (Actress)   1839-1921
(sc) 26.9.-28.11.1853; (sc) 26.12.1853-12.6.1854; (sc) 19.9.-18.12.1854; (sc)
2.10.-13.12.1855; (sc) 26.12.1855-19.5.1856; *16.12.1856; *31.3.1857; *13.-
24.9.1858; *28.8.-8.9.1865 (Prince of Wales Theatre Co.).
Wolino (Harlequin)
*26.12.1857-1.2.1858; 10.2.1858
Wood (Harlequin)
*27.1.-8.2.1830.
Wood, Miss A. (Actress)
(sc) 17.9.-14.12.1860; (sc) 24.12.1860-24.5.1861; 10.6. & 12.8.1861; *21.4.1863.
Wood, Arthur Augustus (Actor)   1823-1907
(sc) 26.9.-16.12.1859; (sc) 2.1.-14.5.1860; 28.-30.5.1860; (sc) 17.9.-14.12.1860;

(sc) 3.1.-24.5.1861; 10.6.1861; (sc) 16.9.-17.12.1861; (sc) 1.1.-16.5.1862; (sc) 15.9.-19.12.1862; (sc) 24.12.1862-15.5.1863; 25.-27.5.1863; *21.-23.3.1864; *10.-12.6.1867 (Melville's Co.); (sc) 7.11.-17.12.1867; (sc) 6.-14.1.1868.

Wood, Joseph (Singer)   1800-1890
*18.-25.4.1831; *9.-20.2.1835; *2.-6.3.1835; *29. & 30.4.1839; *16.3.1840; *20.9.-1.10.1841.

Wood, Mrs. M.—*see* Paton, Miss Mary Anne

Woolgar, Miss Sarah Jane (Actress)   1824-1909
*5.-9.3.1860; *30.4.-4.5.1860.

Woulds, Mrs. Charlotte (Actress)   1797-1853
(sc) 10.10.1814 (1st app. any stage) -11.7.1815; (sc) 29.9.1815-9.7.1816; (sc) 4.10.1816-30.7.1817; *16.6.1824; *17.5.1827; *1.9.-3.10.1828; *2.-21.9.1829; *25.5.1831; (sc) ?25.-28.10.1831; (sc) ?2.1.1832; (sc) 4.2.-?22.5.1833.

Woulds, James (Actor)
(sc) 20.5.-17.7.1811; (sc) 30.9.1811-?20.7.1812; (sc) 28.9.1812-?2.8.1813; (sc) 27.9.1813-8.8.1814; (sc) 26.9.1814-10.7.1815; (sc) 25.9.1815-9.7.1816; (sc) 30.9.1816-30.7.1817; *16.6.1824; *3.6.1825; *1.9.-24.10.1826; *3. & 17.5.1827; *3.9-5.10.1827; *1.9.-3.10.1828; *2.-21.9.1829; *25.5.1831; (sc) ?25.-28.10.1831; (sc) ?30.11.-7.12.1831; (sc) ?2.1.-?4.7.1832; (sc) 4.2.-?27.5.1833; *27.4.1842; *11.-?13.7.1842; *11.-14. & 22.-29.3.1844; *3.3.1848 *et al.*?

Woulds, Miss Mary (Singer)
*27.4.1842; *11.-?13.7.1842.

Wrench, Benjamin (Actor)   1778-1843
(sc) 11.2.-15.7.1805; (sc) 2.10.1805-14.7.1806; *19.4.-26.5.1819; *5.3.-5.5.1820.

Wright, Edward (Actor)   1813-1859
(sc) 26.12.1836-8.5.1837; *4.-25.9.1837; *27.8.-24.9.1838; *8.4.-6.5.1839; *12.-16.4.1841; *12.-17.9.1841; *9.-13. & 23.10.1848; *29.5.-2.6.1854; *30.4.-4.5.1855; *12.-16.11.1855; *15.-24.2.1858.

Yates, Mrs. Elizabeth, née Brunton (Actress)   1799-1860
*29.-31.3., 12.-23.4.1819; *8.3.1830; *6. & 7.5.1830; *23.4.-14.5.1832; *17.-27.5.1836; *12.-16.4.1841; *15.-19.4.1844.

Yates, Frederick (Entertainer)   1797-1842
*18.-21.8.1828; *5.-7.5.1830; *23.4.-14.5.1832; *17.-27.5.1836; *22.5.1840; *12.-16.4.1841.

Young, Charles Mayne (Actor)   1777-1856
*28.9.-19.10.1807; *3.-31.10.1808; *29.9.-13.10.1813; *15.-29.4.1816; *24.4.-3.5.1820; *29.3.-2.4.1830; *19.-26.3.1832.

"Young American", The (Juggler)
*18.9.1824; *29.11.-17.12.1824.

Zane, Mademoiselle (Dancer)

Zane, Mademoiselle L. (Dancer)
*4.-14.2.1839

Index

Aladdin (1887-8) 170 (1924-5) 196-7
Anderson, James R. 118
Androcles and the Lion 175
Angel, W. H. 127
Animals, Performing 73, 103, 106, 145
Antigone 122-3, 146
Antonio, Il Diavolo 90
Apple Orchards, The 228
Artaud, Stephen 127, 132
Arts Council of Great Britain (former-ly CEMA) 204, 210, 213, 216-7, 219, 222, 223
Assembly Rooms, Bristol—*see* Regency Theatre
Atkins, Catherine 92-3
Atkins, Mr. & Mrs. Michael 92, 129
Atkins, Robert 213

Babes in the Wood, The (1858-9) 141-2 (1911-2) 184 (1939-40) 201
Baddeley, Robert 21
Baines, Cecil Hamilton (W. F. Jackson) 191, 193
Baines, Mrs. (C. H.) 194
Ballet – *see* Dance
Barker, Harley Granville 188
Barker, John 174-5
Barlow, Alan 228
Barrett, Wilson 165
Barry, Mrs. Ann – *see* Crawford, Mrs.
Barry, Mrs. Jane 20
Battle of Agincourt, The 142-3
Battle of the Alma, The 142
Bedini, Jehan 178
Beggar's Opera, The 4
Bellamy, B. P. 101, 106-7
Belphegor the Mountebank 143
Benefits 22, 33, 61-2, 67, 136, 178, 200-1

Benjamin, Christopher 225
Bennett, James 104, 153
Bensley, Richard 37-8
Benson, Frank R. 172, 201
Bernard, John 37-8, 41, 42, 47
Betterton, Julia (Mrs. Glover) 59, 117
Betty, Henry West 74, 75, 80
Biddy 197
Bland, Harcourt 139
Bland, Mrs. J. – *see* Glover, ?Georgina
Blissett, Francis 48, 81
Blue Beard 63, 72
Bode, Milton 197, 201
Booth, John 29, 31
Booth, Junius Brutus 75, 81, 90, 97
Boucicault, Dion (Lee Moreton) 117
Brenner, Nat 223, 225
Brett, William and Hannah 50
Bridges-Adams, W. 189
Bristol, Bishop of (Thomas Newton) 30
Bristol Corporation 179-80, 217-8, 219, 223-4, 229
Bristol Old Vic Company 214 *et passsim*
Bristol Old Vic Theatre Club 215
Bristol Old Vic Theatre School 215, 218, 219-20, 223, 225, 228, 229
Bristol Playgoers' Club 185, 187-8, 189, 208
Bristol Riots 106
Bristol Rotary Club 208
Bristol Theatres Ltd. 191, 193, 194, 209
Bristol University 219, 226, 228
British Broadcasting Corporation 198, 203
Brookes, Doris 193
Browne 51, 79

Brunton, Anne (Mrs. Merry) 58
Brunton, John (jun.) 102
Brunton, John (sen.) 51, 58
Brunton, Richard 101, 102, 105
Bryan, Cornelius 115
Brystowe 51
Buckstone, J. B. 166
Bulkley, Mrs. Mary 24, 28

Campbell, Mrs. – *see* Wallis, Tryphosa
Candida 185
Canning, Mrs. Mary Ann (Mrs. Reddish) 35, 36-7, 42
Captain Carvallo 217
Carey, Clive 188, 190
Carey, Denis 218-9, 225
Caroline (of Brunswick), Princess (later Queen) 68, 98
Carpenter, Mrs. Emma 182, 191
Carpenter, Ernest 175 *et passim*
Carpenter, Frederick (jun.) 184 *et passim*
Carpenter, Frederick (sen.) 180, 182
Carpenter, Mrs. Jessie 184
Carry On! 195
Casson, Ann 213
Casson, Lewis 185, 213
Caste 164
Castle of Andalusia, The 53
Catalani, Angelica 74, 91-2
Cataract of the Ganges, The 95
"Caterpillars, The" 47
Cautherley, Samuel 36
Champion, Richard 6
Chapman, Patty 135
Charlton, Charles 64, 67, 76
Chelsea Players 193
Chew, Mr. – *see* Chute, James Henry
Chippendale, W. H. 103
Christian, The 185
Chute, James Henry 102, 117-8, 124, 128, 131, 135 *et passim*
Chute, Mrs. Mazarina – *see* M'Cready, Mazarina
Cinderella (opera) 104 (pantomime, 1862-3) 152, 158
Clarke, Matthew 6, 21, 37
Cleveland, Louisa 144
Clunes, Alec 213
Coal King, The 177
Coates, Robert ("Romeo") 68
Coghlan, Charles 152, 155
Coleman, John 127
Colleen Bawn, The 141-2
Comedy of Errors, The 222
Connor, Kenneth 215

Constant Couple, The 213-4
Cooper, H. E. 131
Coopers' Hall 29
Così fan Tutte (The School for Lovers) 199
Council for the Encouragement of Music and the Arts – *see* Arts Council of Great Britain
Council for the Preservation of Ancient Bristol 202-3
Courtneidge, Robert 197, 201
Cowlin, Sir Francis 203
Cozens, Charles 86
Crawford, Mrs. Ann (formerly Mrs. Barry) 40
Crosby and Walker 178, 184 (see also Walker, Syd)
Cruise, Maria 165
Crump, Mr. & Mrs. Edward 7
Cumberland, Ernest Augustus, Duke of 69
Cumberland, Henry Frederick, Duke of 23, 56
Cummins, Charles 91-2, 94
Cushman, Charlotte and Susan 126
Cyrano de Bergerac 222

Dance 24, 72-3, 124-5, 143
Danseuses Viennoises 124
Dare, George 200
Daubeny, George (jun.) 76, 88
Daubeny, George (sen.) 24, 76
Davey, C. W. H. 202
Davis, Allan 216, 217
Deserter, The 62
Desert Highway 213
Desmond, Sarah (Mrs. M'Cready) 93-4, 95, 100, 102, 106 *et passim*
Devlin, William 214, 215
Dick Whittington (1910-1) 185 (1923-4) 194
Didier, Mrs. Margaret 48, 83
Dillon, Charles 143, 146
Dimond, William 73
Dimond, William Wyatt 47-8, 58, 63, 65. 66, 69, 73, 79
Dix, Frank 179, 207
Dodd, James W. 24, 28, 30, 31
Don, Sir William 146-7
Donaldson, Walter 95, 129
Donat, Robert 203
Don Carlos 142, 157
Don Juan 62-3
Doughty, James 145
Drury Lane Theatre 8, 10
Dublin Opera Company 146

Ducrow's Equestrian Troupe 95, 106, 119
Duke's Motto, The 169

Earl Goodwin 51-2
East Lynne 155, 165
Economic Development of Bristol 5, 56, 85, 104, 121, 125, 177
Eddison, Robert 215
Edgar, Alexander 40
Edkins, Michael 10, 22, 29, 33, 41, 46, 57
Edkins, William 57, 72, 99, 100, 105
Edwards, J. Ralph 204
Edwin, John (jun.) and Elizabeth 59
Elliston, Robert W. 57-8, 61-2, 65, 66, 67, 78, 79, 81
Elssler, Fanny 112
End of the World, The 189
Espinosa, Judith 184
Exeter Theatre 45, 79

False Dawn 199
Farjeon, Herbert 202, 203, 205
Faucit, Harriet 116
Faust and Marguerite 140
Faustus 95
Fitzwilliam, Mrs. Fanny 125
Follies of a Day, The (Grattan and Eldred) 171 (Holcroft) 52-3
Foote, Josiah 45
Foote, Maria 96
Forbes-Robertson, Frank 198
Ford & Canning 173, 175
Forrest, Edwin 120
Forse, Henry Augustus 367
Fortescue, Frank H. 198, 201
Fosbrooke, William 145, 170
Freischutz, Der 94
French, John 22
French, Thomas (jun.) 63, 71
French, Thomas (sen.) 53, 57, 64, 71

Garrick, David 5, 9, 41, 47
Garrington, Rev. E. T. 213-4
General Strike 198
George IV, King 69
Gilbert, William Schwenk 164
Giroux Family 72
Gloucester, William Frederick, Duke of 69
Glover, Mrs. – *see* Betterton, Julia
Glover, Edmund 116-7
Glover, ?Georgina (Mrs. J. Bland) 93, 117

Godwin, Edward W. 152, 153-4, 158
Gold 142
Gomery, Robert 75
Gordon, George 141, 155, 157
Gordon, William 108, 157
Green, Mrs. Jane 5, 31, 56
Greet, Ben 193-4, 198
Grieve, John Henderson 71, 72
Grieve, Thomas 122, 137, 156
Grimaldi, Giuseppe 32
Grimaldi, Joseph 75, 80
Grimani, Julia, 59, 79-80
Grisi, Carlotta 125
Grisi, Giulia 131
Grosette, H. W. 87, 89
Guenevere 189-90

Haberfield, John Kerle 112
Hale, John 222, 228
Hamlet 48, 172, 194
Harlequin Hobbledy Gobbledy 115
Harlequin Templar 122
Hartley, Mrs. Elizabeth 29
Harvey, John Martin 172-3
Hay Fever 197
Hayman, Fowler & Co. 111
Heath, Caroline 165
Henderson, John 22, 34
Henry 95, 100
Herbert, Louisa 145, 156
Hicks, Seymour 171
Hickson, T. C. P. 200, 204, 223
Hindle Wakes 185
Hippisley, John 4
Hippisley, Mrs. (J.) 5
Hodson, Henrietta 150
Holland, Charles 20, 21, 24, 25
Holloway, George R. 188, 207
Honeymoon, The 71
Hotwells, Bristol 4, 47, 90
Hoy, Robert 89, 120
Huckel 90
Hullabaloo 225
Hunchback, The 106
Hunt, Hugh 214 *et passim*

Icebound 175
Incledon, Charles 54, 75
Inflexible Captive, The 33, 34
Irving, Henry 156
Irwin, Edward 193

Jack Sheppard 114
Jackson, Freda 214
Jackson, Mrs. Hester 35, 36

Jackson, William F. – *see* Baines, Cecil Hamilton
Jacob's Wells Theatre, Bristol 4-5, 9, 41
Jarman, Frances 106
Jealous Wife, The 113
Jeffery, Robert 76
Jenkins, Richard 51
Jenkins, Warren 221
Jenny Villiers 214
Jewess, The 114
Johnson, "Professor" 173
Johnson, Rev. Lewis 190
Jordan, Mrs. Dora 69, 74

Kay, S. 203
Kean, Charles 97, 112, 114, 138-9, 147, 148
Kean, Edmund 75, 81, 97, 103-4, 106, 107
Keasberry, William 65
Kemble, Charles 104, 105
Kemble, Frances Anne 104-5, 126
Kemble, John Philip 81
Kemble, Stephen 74
Kenilworth 94
Kennedy, Laurence 29-30, 31, 37, 41
Killing of Sister George, The 226
King, Mrs. Mary 27
King, Thomas 24, 26, 27, 28, 41
King Arthur 33, 34
King Henry IV i 70, 74, 92
King Henry V 62, 226
King John 139, 144
King Lear 66, 215
King Richard II 94, 95
King Richard III 24, 35, 37, 53, 57, 153

Lacey, George 199, 209
Lady of Lyons, The 155
Laid Up in Port 154
Landstone, Charles 214, 223, 228
Lee, Henry 89
Leighton, Wilfrid 204
Lenox, I. S. 123, 137, 157, 158
Lewes, Lee 27-8
Lewis, Thomas 4
Licensing Act (1737) 5
Licensing Magistrates 182, 190, 193
Lind, Jenny 124, 131
Linley, Thomas 28
Little Bo-Peep 229
Little Devil, The 55
Little Theatre, Bristol 195, 202, 208, 209, 223, 224-5, 229

Little Tom Tucker 163
Livesey, Sam 176
Local Government Act (1948) 117
Lodgings to Let 117
Loraine, Henry 166
Lord Chamberlain 181-2
Lorraine, Paul 200
Lovegrove, William 67
Lovers' Vows 63
Love's Magic 32
Love Spell, The (*L'Elisir d'Amore*) 116
Lundy in the Olden Time 115, 131
Lyne, Ald. R. F. 222

Macbeth 114, 127, 138-9, 194, 214
M'Cready, George William 100, 130
M'Cready, Mazarina Emily (Mrs. J. H. Chute) 100, 118
M'Cready, Mrs. Sarah – *see* Desmond, Sarah
M'Cready, William 65, 89 *et passim*
Macready, William Charles 70, 89, 92, 97, 101, 102-3, 105, 106, 112-3, 118, 126
Macklin, Charles 3, 5
Mademoiselle from Armentieres 200
Mahomet 53
Manxman, The 177
Mara, Mrs. 95
Marina, Princess 226, 227
Married Man, The 51
Marriott, Miss 73-4
Masefield, John 189, 208
Mason, Charles Kemble 102, 104, 126
Mathews, Charles 88
Mathews, Charles James 125-6, 146
Matthews, Mr. & Mrs. Frank 116
May, Val 222-3, 229
Mayhew, Henry 127
Measure for Measure 68
Melodrama 140-1, 154-5, 165, 176-7, 197, 200
Melville, Andrew 296 *et passim*
Melville, George 127-8, 139-40, 155, 158, 167, 169
Merchant of Venice, The 194
Messiah 54
Metal Agencies Co. 202, 204
Meyler, William 51, 52, 95
Midsummer Night's Dream, A 113-4, 140
Miles, Napier 199
Millar, Douglas 196 *et passim*
Milton, Ernest 194, 209

Montgomery, Walter H. 139
Moody, John (actor) 38
Moody, John (director) 221-2
Moral Opposition 3, 14, 23, 30, 155, 213-4, 217
More, Hannah 33, 35, 52
Moreton, Lee – see Boucicault, Dion
Morris, Douglas 225
Morris, Sir Philip 219
Mother Goose 72
Much Ado About Nothing 151, 215
Mude, 118
Music Halls 143, 174, 186, 209

Naughton and Gold 184, 207
Necromancer, The 53
Norma 116
No Room at the Inn 214

Oh! My Papa! 221
Old Vic (London) 214, 215, 219, 223, 227
O'Neil, Eliza 86
One Rake in a Thousand 51
Opera Bouffe 165
Opera Seria 74, 94, 116, 123-4, 147-8, 166, 172, 198-9
Oratorio 54-5
Othello 71-2, 127, 139
O'Toole, Peter 221
Our Boys 164
Our Native Land 122, 163
Owen, George 126, 131

Paganini, Nicolò 106
Palmer, Col. (later Gen.) Charles 101, 107
Palmer, John (actor) 6, 20
Palmer, John (manager) 38-9, 46, 47, 65, 77-8
Pantomime 14, 30, 51, 53, 62, 72, 122, 141-2, 158, 169-70, 178-9, 184, 196-7, 199, 201
Parker family 7-8
Passion's Slave 171
Patent, Royal 14, 30, 38-9, 180, 182
Patriotism 56, 61, 67-8, 98, 142
Patronage 49, 67, 69, 98, 119, 177, 205
Paty, Thomas 8
Percy 40
Perouse, La 72
Phelps, Samuel 146
Phethean, David 225
Philip the King 189, 208
Phipps, C. J. 149, 156, 168

Pink Dominos 166
Pizarro 63-4
Poor Must Live, The 177
Porter, Eric 221, 228
Powell, T. Morton 200
Powell, William 5-6, 9, 19-20, 22, 23-4
Power, John 3
Pratt, Muriel 185 et passim
Preservation Fund 203
Prince Regent – see George IV, King
Prince's Theatre (New Theatre Royal), Bristol 155-6, 159, 170, 200, 201, 209
Promenade Concerts 116
Provok'd Wife, The 217
Prunella 189
Puss in Boots (1897-8) 177 (1926-7) 199

Quick, John 34, 35, 37, 61-2

Rain on the Just 215
Rapier Players – see Little Theatre
Rauzzini, Matteo 54, 56
Raymond and Agnes 64
Reddish, Mrs. – see Canning, Mrs. Mary Ann
Reddish, Samuel 26-7, 32-3, 34-7, 42
Red Riding Hood 201-2
Reeve, John 92
Reeves, Sims 124
Regency Theatre, Bristol 75-6
Rehearsal, The 222
Reid, Beryl 226
Reuben's Wife 187
Revue 201
Reynolds, Dorothy 218, 228
Reynolds, Frederick 51
Rice, Thomas D. 111
Richmond (Surrey) Theatre 8, 10, 13
Riddle, Isaac 137, 157, 167
Ridgeway's Parade 201
Ridley, Arnold 208
Rifle Volunteer Corps 136, 142
Rifle Volunteers, The 142
Rignold, George 144-5, 151
Rignold, William 135, 144-5, 151
Ristori, Adelaide 149, 171, 206
Robertson, Margaret 144, 152, 157
Robertson, Patrick 222
Robertson, T. W. 164
Robin Hood 156
Robinson Crusoe 178
Robson, Flora 194, 208
Rogers, Mrs. Blanche 202, 208

Romeo and Juliet 126, 153
Romer, Emma 104, 116
Rosiere, J. G. 153
Ross, Duncan 219, 223, 228, 229
Rossignol, Sig. 55
Rouse, John 145
Rowell, George 227
Russell, Lord John 142
Russell, Ronald – *see* Little Theatre
Ruy Blas 173

St. Augustine's Back Theatre, Bristol 3
St. Casse, Clara 144
St. James's (September) Fair 19, 90, 96, 120
St. Joan 213
Salad Days 218
Salaries 49, 92, 158
Saunders(on), James 8, 10
Savage, Richard 37
School for Greybeards, The 71
School for Lovers, The – *see* Così fan Tutte
School for Scandal, The 45
Sea-Captain, The 113
Seagull, The 214
Sensation Plays – *see* Melodrama
Severed Head, A 225
Shakespeare Quatercentenary 226
Shakespeare Tercentenary 152, 226
Shearer, Moira 221
Shelley, Walter 139-40
She Stoops to Conquer 166, 205
Shuter, Edward 22, 41
Siddons, Mrs. Sarah 47, 49-50, 60, 81
Siege of Quebec, The 61-2
Silver Box, The 185-6
Silver Tickets 7, 106
Sinbad the Sailor 198
Sixty Thousand Nights 227
Skemp, Professor Arthur 188, 189
Slade, Julian 218, 227
Smith, Richard 65, 98, 106, 110
Smyth, Ethel 198
Soldene, Emily 165
Somerville, J. Baxter 204
Southern Richard 10, 12, 219
Speed the Plough 64
Stanley, Edward 215, 228
Stansbury, George 93, 116
Star System 60, 70, 73-4, 85, 96, 111-2, 125, 146-7, 149
Stirling, Arthur 144, 155, 158
Stoll, Sir Oswald 186, 196
Stranger, The 63

Streets of Bristol, The 154-5, 158
Susan Hopley 123
Sutton, Randolph 201
Symons, Thomas 6, 10

Tate, Harry 201
Taylor, Tom 151
Tearle, Edmund 176
Telbin, William 137, 156
Tempest, The 194
Tenducci, Giusto Ferdinando 54
Terry, Benjamin and Sarah 117
Terry, Daniel 91, 97
Terry, Ellen 150-1, 158
Terry, Florence 165
Terry, Kate 150-1, 158
Tess 215
Theatre Royal, Bath (Orchard Street) 5, 13, 23 (Beaufort Square, 1805-62) 67, 148 (do., 1863-) 149, 155, 164
Theatre Royal, Bristol – Admission Prices 13-4, 34, 39, 45, 74, 77, 106, 107, 119, 120, 125, 138, 147, 174, 177, 187, 189, 192, 197, 201
— Audience 39-40, 55-6, 61, 68, 90, 98, 126-7, 149, 155, 173, 177, 185, 190, 200, 207
— Booking Arrangements 86, 124, 147, 174, 216
— Capacity 13, 66, 205, 208
— Costumes and Scenery 22, 53, 63-4, 71, 94-5, 114, 123, 138-9, 140, 141, 153, 154-5, 158, 175, 189, 222, 228
— Design 8, 10
— Drainage and Sanitation 122, 187
— Fire Precautions 181-2, 216-7
— Frontage 7, 180
— Interior Decoration 10, 12, 33, 46, 57, 66, 77, 86, 99-100, 110, 111, 137, 156, 167, 168-9, 189, 205, 218, 222
— Leases 21, 33, 39, 45, 46, 65, 77, 78, 89, 101, 105, 107, 108, 128, 137, 139, 167, 175, 180, 181, 196, 204, 224
— Lighting 13, 64, 66, 77, 86, 98, 99, 105, 179, 207, 213
— Proscenium Doors 100, 105, 110, 168, 217
— Publicity 26-27, 170, 178
— Sale 175, 192, 196, 197, 203
— Scene-Room 11, 12, 65, 110
— Seasons, Length of 19, 47, 90, 119, 138, 164

Seating 138, 156, 168, 179, 188-9, 196, 198, 205, 222
Site 6, 7, 9, 15, 76, 148, 167, 169, 174, 180, 218
Stage Machinery 11, 12, 105, 110, 168, 187, 201, 206, 207, 213, 227, 228
Structural Alterations 46, 57, 65-6, 77, 98-9, 103, 105-6, 110, 136, 168, 180, 181, 204, 216
Trustees 204, 220, 227, 228
Thorndike, Sybil 205
Three Jacks, The 170-1
Throng o' Scarlet 215
Tinker, The 222, 229
Tony Lumpkin in Town 52
Touring System 138, 143, 150, 171, 185, 197, 213-4
Transparencies 53, 98
Traviata, La 147-8
True as Steel 165
Tutin, Dorothy 217, 226
Two Gentlemen of Verona 218-9

Ugliest Woman on Earth, The 178
Uncle Tom's Cabin 123, 136, 144, 171, 173
Under the Czar 176

Valentine and Orson 141, 145, 157
Vandenhoff, John 70
Venice Preserv'd 40, 104
Verity, Frank T. 181-2
Vernon, W. H. 152
Vestris, Mme. Elizabeth Lucy, 97, 125
Vezin, Hermann 172
Vincent, Charles 144
Virginius 152
Voluntary Contributions 62

Vortex, The 198

Walker, Syd 178 (see also Crosby and Walker)
Wallis, Tryphosa (Mrs. Campbell) 58-9, 60
Walpole, Charlotte 39
War and Peace 223
Watson, John Boles 78, 85 *et passim*
Webster, Ben 117
Wemyss, Francis 92, 99
Werner 102-3
Werter 51-2, 79
West Indian, The 26
Westmacott, Charles 99
Wewitzer, Miss 50
Wharton, Mme. 125
Wickham, G. W. G. 229
Widow and Wife 164
Wild Birds 188
Wild Duck, The 218
Wilkinson, Matt 176, 192
Williams, Charles 3
Williams, Ralph Vaughan 198-9
Wilton, Marie 143
Winged Ship, The 200
Winterset 216
Winter's Tale, The 95, 140
Winwood, T. H. Ricketts 182, 197, 207
Wood, Arthur 145, 156, 163, 165
Wood, Joseph and Mary 116
Wren, Sir Christopher 10
Wright, Edward 117, 125

Yearsley, Mrs. Ann 52
York, Edward Augustus, Duke of 23
York, Frederick, Duke of 62
Young, Charles Mayne 75, 81, 97
Younge, Elizabeth 27, 33, 35
Young England 198

List of Subscribers

John Adrian; Michael Anderson; Michael J. Anderson; Geoffrey G. Andrews; David Anstice; W. W. Appleton; W. A. Armstrong; Janet Arnold; Arts Council of Great Britain; Alexander S. Atchison; Auckland University; Roy and Marjorie Avery; Mrs. S. J. D. Awdry; R. Ayling.

G. C. Baines; Mrs. B. Baldock; Mrs. R. A. Baldwin-Charles; University College of North Wales, Bangor; Harry Barker; Graham Barlow; Mrs. D. M. M. Barrah; K. A. M. Barton; Peter Barwick; Bath High School; R. N. Baum; Deryck R. Bell; J. D. Bennett; University of Birmingham; E. G. Bottle; Frank Bradley; F. B. Brady; William Brasmer; Mrs. J. Breakell; Bretton Hall College of Education; Alison Briggs; Peter Brinson; H.M.S. Bristol; Bristol City Archives Department; Bristol Grammar School; Bristol Public Libraries; University of Bristol; British Council (Bristol); British Council (London); British Drama League; British Institute (Oslo); British Library Lending Division; N. Bennett Britton; Douglas Brown; Eluned M. Brown; Sir Kenneth Brown; Mrs. Edwina J. Bryant; Tina Buckton; Hal Burton; Burton School of Speech & Drama; J. H. Butler; Muriel St. Clare Byrne; J. A. Byrnes.

Adrian Cairns; Colin and Margaret Calcott-James; California State College, Turlock; University of California at Davis; Camden Public Library; Mr. & Mrs. W. J. Campbell-Kease; National Library of Canada; Mrs. J. R. Candish; Mr. & Mrs. Geoffrey Candy; Mrs. Lois Cann; Steven Cann; Mrs. F. M. Cannon; Cape Performing Arts Board; City of Cardiff College of Education; Mrs. Carol J. Carlisle; Mrs. R. Y. Carter; Mrs. F. Carver; Miss H. M. Castle; Frederick W. Caswell; J. C. Causton; Central School of Speech and Drama; Heather M. Charles; D. M. Chaytor; Mrs. Freda M. Chesshire; Brien Chitty; Chorley College of Education; Mr. & Mrs. M. J. Churcher; J. E. C. Clarke; G. E. Clarkson; F. Theodore Cloak; Mrs. J. N. Cochrane; Mrs. Elsie Cockshott; Mr. & Mrs. B. Colico; Colonial Williamsburg Foundation; Mrs. J. Colwell; Connecticut College; Rev. S. R. Connock; L. W. Conolly; Arthur R. Cook; Robert V. Cooke; F. R. Cooper; D. G. Corble; Arthur M. Cordery; A. Cornish; P. M. Cornwell; Mrs. E. E. Cottis; Mr. & Mrs. M. H. Couzins; F. K. Cowley; Edward A. Craig; Mrs. Brenda M. Craig; Leonard Crainford; S. A. & I. Creasey; Anthony R. Cross; Brian G. Crumpler; Mr. & Mrs. Brian H. Cummins.

S. J. Dando; Mr. & Mrs. T. R. Davies; A. R. de Deney; Marjorie de Friez; Philip M. de Grouchy; Antony Denning; Depauw University; Diana Devlin; C. W. Dixon; Joseph Donohue; Gresdna Doty; Mrs. M. E. Dowdeswell; A. A.

275

Dowling; S. L. Down; A. J. M. Draper; Duke University; Miss F. Dummer; University of Durham.

University of East Anglia; Eastern Michigan University; Robert Eddison; Miss M. A. Eden; Edge Hill College of Education; University of Edinburgh; H. G. Edwards; Mr. & Mrs. J. W. Elliott; James Ellis; K. A. Elson; Alfred Emmet; Endsleigh College of Education; Nancy Enggass; P. G. English; University of Essex; Mrs. Mary E. Evans; W. L. Evans; Exeter City Library.

Miss P. C. Farley; B. A. Farr; Andrew Faulds; Rev. J. W. H. Faulkner; Filton Technical College; Richard Findlater; Mr. & Mrs. Walter Finley; Ray and Sue Fisher; Mrs. C. K. Fletcher; Lionel Fletcher; Mr. & Mrs. William Flint; Folkestone Public Library; Mrs. J. J. Foord; Derek Forbes; F. W. Ford; Barbara Fox; Clare Fox; Stuart Fox; F. C. Frank; Mrs. H. A. Frankpitt; Mrs. Deirdre Freke; R. A. French.

Mrs. W. E. Gadd; H. Gaffen; Louis Roland Gaffen; J. D. Gane; Garrick Club; William Gay; W. R. Gell; Kay Gerrett; N. C. Gillett; Victor Glasstone; Gloucester College of Education; Gloucester County Libraries; Julian Glover; Derek Godfrey; Mrs. H. M. Golsworthy; Alastair Goolden; Gordano School; University of Göteborg; Mr. & Mrs. Victor Gott; Alexandra Grajnert; Grange School for Boys; Grange School for Girls; C. J. R. Gray; Harry N. Greatorex; Mrs. E. A. Green; Mrs. Mary Green; Mrs. Ann Greenall; Guelph University; Guildhall Library.

Hamburg University; Rae Hammond; Hampshire Public Libraries; Mrs. D. L. Hampton; Margaret Hancock; Mr. & Mrs. R. W. Hancock; Billy J. Harbin; Miss Hilary Hardiman; Edward Hardwicke; Arnold Hare; Mr. & Mrs. J. B. Harris; Richard A. Harris; H. J. Harrowing; Ald. Marcus Hartnell; B. J. Hatwood; R. L. Haynes; Mrs. Mary I. Hebbes; Hubert C. Heffner; Hengrove School; Ben G. Henneke; Miss I. D. Henson; William J. Herbert; Jillian Highley; Mr. & Mrs. A. H. Stewart Hill; A. Hodgkinson; R. A. Hodgson; C. B. Hogan; William Hogarth; T. R. Holland; Mrs. M. P. Huckle; Alan Hughes; Christopher Hughes; Clair Hughes; Hugh S. Hunt; Mr. & Mrs. D. F. Hurford.

Illinois State University; Indiana University; R. W. Ingram; Col. & Mrs. E. C. Irish; Eric Irvin.

Russell Jackson; S. Jaggard; Michael Jamieson; Mrs. M. B. Jaquet; Richard D. Jefferies; C. S. Jenkins; Ald. Walter W. Jenkins; Warren Jenkins; Frederick S. Jennett; Mrs. C. Johnson; Mrs. Peris Jones; Richard Jones.

Nadia Kempster; E. C. J. Kendall; Kenyon College; King Alfred's College; Mrs. Helene Koon.

Georges Lamoine; University of Lancaster; David B. Latham; Philippa Lawrence; David Lea; Richard Leacroft; A. F. G. Lee; City of Leeds & Carnegie College; Leeds Public Libraries; University of Leeds; Mrs. Evelyn Leeworthy; Charles Lefeaux; Rolf Lefebvre; Leicester College of Education; Mrs. W. Leighton; David Lewis; Miss E. B. Lewis; Licensed Victuallers' School; Victor E. Line; Liverpool Public Libraries; Liverpool University; Mrs. E. Loewenberg; Sir Douglas Logan; London Library; University of London Goldsmiths' Library; W. B. Long; Richard Lorenzen; Miss R. Loxton; Lund University; Miss M. Luscombe.

Mrs. Sylvia Macara; Rosaleen McCoola; Patrick McGrath; V. G. Macgregor; Mrs. Sheila McGuinness; Angus Mackay; Iain Mackintosh; Joseph Macleod; Mrs. G. Mallinson; Dr. B. Malnick; Manchester Public Libraries; Hugh

Manning; Roger Manvell; Frank Marcus; Margate Public Library; F. M. Martin; Mrs. D. K. C. Mason; Masahiko Masumoto; Mather College; Val May; Margaret Meehan; John and Louise Melbourne; Andrew Melville; A. W. Merrison; Metropolitan Toronto Central Library; Michigan University; E. R. Mickleburgh; Miss Elisabeth A. Miller; Mrs. Jean Miller; Ernest Milton; Milwaukee Public Library; Minneapolis Athenaeum Library; University of Missouri at Kansas City; Ronald E. Mitchell; Mrs. A. M. Moffatt; B. Moore; Miss D. M. Moore; Douglas Morris; Sir Philip Morris; Philip G. L. Morris; Sheelah P. Morris; Mrs. Ena Morton; Mrs. Mary Morton; Mount Holyoke College; Robert Mullally; D. A. Murdoch; B. G. Murray; Christopher Murray; Monica Murray; George Muschamp.

Neville's Cross College of Education; Newberry Library; New Brunswick University; Newton Park College of Education; Mrs. S. M. Newton; New York Public Library; National Library of New Zealand; Marie Ney; Allardyce Nicoll; Mrs. Mary A. Nimmo; Northern Counties College; Northwestern University; Notre Dame College of Education, Liverpool; Nottingham University; Mrs. S. A. Nunney.

Brendan O'Brien; University of Oregon; M. A. Ostler; Mr. & Mrs. A. M. O'Sullivan; Oswego State University College; George R. Otter.

Kenneth Parrott; Mr. & Mrs. K. S. Parry; I. Pascoe; Patchway High School; Herbert Payne; Mrs. V. W. Pearce; Christine Perrins; David Phethean; Philbrick Library; John S. Pickup; Mr. & Mrs. F. H. Pierce; Paul Piercy; Robert Pile; Plymouth Central Library; Mrs. P. Poole; Portsmouth City Library; Portsmouth College of Education; Michael W. Powell; Mrs. H. Proudfoot.

Ian Ramsay; Miss Mary J. Randall; Margaret L. Rankin; Michael G. Read; Harry and Leslie Reader; Jack Reading; Reading University; Mr. & Mrs. N. J. Record; Sir Michael Redgrave; Redland College; Mr. & Mrs. P. F. J. Reeve; Lionel R. Reeves; Mrs. S. A. Reid; Miss J. Reilly; A. B. Reynolds; David Reynolds; Neil Rhoden; Rice University; John Richards; Stanley Richards; W. E. Richens; J. W. Robinson; Arnold Rood; Sybil Rosenfeld; Mrs. N. E. Rosse; Donald Roy; P. E. L. Rouyer; Royal Institute of British Architects; Royal Scottish Academy of Music & Drama; Mrs. E. M. R. Rumsey.

Ann Saddlemyer; St. Andrew's University; St. Anne's College; Mrs. Diana St. John-Brooks; St. Mary Redcliffe & Temple Schools; St. Mary's College, Cheltenham; College of St. Matthias; Salford University; Eric Salmon; Mrs. Alma Sanders; Jacqueline B. Sandford; San Diego State College; Leslie Sands; University of Saskatchewan, Regina; George Savage; Roger Savage; John Savident; Graham Sawyer; A. H. Saxon; S. Schoenbaum; R. Le Roy Schulz; D. Seaton-Reid; Shakespeare Centre; Shakespeare Institute; C. H. Shattuck; Sheffield Central Library; Raphael R. Shelly; Shenstone New College; N. D. Shergold; Frances Shirley; J. E. H. Simon; R. Simpkins; Julian Slade; A. E. Smith; Somerset County Libraries; Somervale Comprehensive School; University of South Carolina; Southlands College of Education; G. F. Spaul; George Speaight; Evert Sprinchorn; S. Elton Stacey; Stanford University; R. H. Stanley: Leslie C. Staples; Jane W. Stedman; Peggy Stembridge; Mrs. E. M. T. Stewart; Stockport Borough Library; Geo. Winchester Stone; Peter Stoppard; Miss Lynn Stovell-Smith; Stratford-on-Avon Public Library; University of Strathclyde; Kenneth Sutcliffe; University College of Swansea; S. Symes; A. J. Synge.

Temple University; University of Tennessee; Texas Woman's University; Mrs.

A. Thompson; Edward Thompson; Peter W. Thomson; Miss Jennifer A. Tolley; Mrs. Joan Tolley; Richard Toscan; Linus Travers; Geoffrey Trease; Simon Trefman; Trent Park College of Education; J. C. Trewin; Trinity College, Carmarthen; R. W. Truman; Tufts University; Miss C. E. Turner; Gerald Tyler. University College London.

Victoria & Albert Museum; Vic-Wells Association; Villanova University; Ald. the Rev. F. C. Vyvyan-Jones.

B. K. Wainwright; Donald Walker; Miss Jennie Walton; Mrs. D. Waring; Lou Warwick; Thomas S. Watson; Mrs. E. M. Webb; Miss G. R. A. Wedmore; S. W. Wells; Jane Wenham; Mrs. Evelyn W. Wenner; Rodney West; Timothy West; University of Western Australia; Westminster City Library; George Wewiora; Eric W. White; R. A. White; Mrs. Renee White; Glynne W. G. Wickham; Pearl Wiesen; Helen D. Willard; B. Harding Williams; Clifford John Williams; Mr. and Mrs. D. W. Williams; Miss E. E. Williams; Mrs. Mary E. Williams; Rev. R. J. C. Williams; Jane Williamson; R. J. R. Williamson; Carl Willmott; Don Wilmeth; Rev. and Mrs. Kenneth B. Wilson; M. Glen Wilson; Wiltshire County Library; J. R. Wolcott; Mark Woolgar; Worthing Public Library; Wyvern School.

Yale University; Bernice Yates; William C. Young; Miss Olive E. B. Youngs.